You Don't Know Me, But You Love Me

Copyright © 2018 Caelum Vatnsdal

ARP Books (Arbeiter Ring Publishing)
205-70 Arthur Street
Winnipeg, Manitoba
Treaty 1 Territory and Historic Métis Nation Homeland
Canada R3B 1G7
arpbooks.org

Cover and interior design and layout by Relish New Brand Experience.

COPYRIGHT NOTICE
This book is fully protected under the copyright laws of Canada and all other countries of the Copyright Union and is subject to royalty.

ARP Books acknowledges the generous support of the Manitoba Arts Council and the Canada Council for the Arts for our publishing program. We acknowledge the financial support of the Government of Canada through the Canada Book Fund and the Province of Manitoba through the Book Publishing Tax Credit and the Book Publisher Marketing Assistance Program of Manitoba Culture, Heritage, and Tourism.

LIBRARY AND ARCHIVES CANADA CATALOGUING IN PUBLICATION

Vatnsdal, Caelum, author
    You don't know me, but you love me : the lives of Dick Miller / Caelum Vatnsdal.

Issued in print and electronic formats.
ISBN 978-1-927886-14-4 (hardcover).--ISBN 978-1-927886-18-2 (softcover).--ISBN 978-1-927886-15-1 (ebook)

    1. Miller, Dick, 1928-. 2. Motion picture actors and actresses--United States--Biography. I. Title.

PN2287.M637V38 2018   791.4302'8092   C2018-903876-4
                                                                                        C2018-903877-2

Printed in Canada

YOU DON'T KNOW ME, BUT YOU LOVE ME
The Lives of Dick Miller

Caelum Vatnsdal

*This book is dedicated to Dick and Lainie,
and it was written for Alicia and Leander.*

Acknowledgements

Clearly the first individual to thank when writing a life story is the person who lived it. My permanent and unabashed gratitude goes to Dick Miller for letting me tell his tale, and equally to Lainie Miller, without whom there would hardly be a Dick, never mind a book about him. Their generosity was utter and their support unbounded. On top of that, they were extremely pleasant people to be around.

Joe Dante was of immense and invaluable aid to this project. Not only did he submit to interviews and repeated follow-up questions, he helped make several important connections and provided some vital copyediting.

I am eager to thank the many other people who gave their time to speak or write to me, including Max Apple, Allan Arkush, Belinda Balaski, Ira Behr, Roger Corman, Frank De Palma, Ernest Dickerson, Jon Davison, Mike Finnell, Mike Gingold, Zach Galligan, Jack Nicholson, Bill Levy, Bob Martin, Harry Northup (whose Miller reminiscences came in the form of a posted letter), Tony Randel, Scatman Jack Silverman, Scott Wheeler, and the late Eugene Miller. I'd like also to acknowledge friendly, helpful gatekeepers like Mark Alan at Renfield Productions and Cynthia Brown at New Horizons. The lovely people at the Margaret Herrick Library may simply have been doing their jobs, but they deserve thanks along with their paycheques.

Some may not know how much they helped, like Brad Caslor, who kindly gifted me a stash of movie magazines that turned out to contain many articles germane to my subject; and Tasha Robinson, then of *The Onion AV Club*, who thought publishing an interview with Dick Miller was a good idea, and thus provided the author an extra excuse (if one were needed) to go visit him. I owe a debt, and perhaps must shake a playful fist too, at David Everitt and *Fangoria* magazine, who lit the fuse.

Many thanks also go to Elijah Drenner, who made a dandy movie, *That Guy Dick Miller*, and was nothing less than utterly helpful when I asked something of him in the course of my own project. Dave Barber, Dave DeCoteau, Kier-la Janisse, Joe Ziemba, Gary and Penny Vatnsdal and Bob and Leslie Smith, Todd Scarth and John Samson were all as fulsome in their support as I am in my gratitude to them. I am particularly grateful to Todd Besant and Irene Bindi at ARP, and to Pat Sanders for superlative editing.

The Manitoba Arts Council and the Winnipeg Arts Council provided some of the funding needed to complete this book, and I am grateful not only for their support, but for their existence.

Most of all I thank Alicia Smith and Leander Vatnsdal, both of whom I dearly love.

Contents

    Preface *11*
1. As sure as I'm sitting here, I'm a prince *16*
2. There are certain things you want to put out of your mind *28*
3. Fun Inc. *37*
4. I'll never forget that flying through the air *48*
5. The pigeons are free *60*
6. Big change in my life *74*
7. How do you start this thing? *86*
8. I always liked Roger *99*
9. You're gonna be a star *111*
10. We shook hands and that was it *136*
11. This is what I would do if I was a little nuts *148*
12. No man could have lived through it *159*
13. I got older, but I didn't get any taller *175*
14. Went up, probably coming down *184*
15. You mean I gotta touch those? *203*
16. He had to be a fan *225*
17. I can't do this, I'm an actor! *246*
18. It was all brand new to me *276*
19. I came in, I did the job, I got out *299*
20. Fade in, fade out *327*
    Afterword *352*
    Sources *353*
    Index *360*

Preface

Dick Miller isn't a household name; he's a household face. No controlled experiment or rigorous survey has ever been conducted about this, as far as I'm aware, but, based on purely anecdotal evidence, I assert he's the film actor with the greatest "Who?" to "Oh, *that* guy" ratio on the planet today. He has appeared in more than 200 films and television episodes; has shared the screen and traded lines with Jack Nicholson, Arnold Schwarzenegger, Liza Minnelli, Boris Karloff, Robert De Niro, Leslie Nielsen, Tom Hanks, and Ethan Hawke; has been directed by Martin Scorsese, Steven Spielberg, James Cameron, Quentin Tarantino, Robert Zemeckis, Sam Fuller, Joe Dante, and Roger Corman; has been the subject of a feature-length documentary; and he enjoys a worldwide community of true-blue fans, many more than even he knows. To paraphrase a line of dialogue from *A Bucket of Blood* (one of his greatest films and certainly his greatest role), man, he is *in*!

Perhaps, after all, he is a household name. He certainly was in my house, to which, almost every month during the 1980s, a new issue of the horror movie magazine *Fangoria* was delivered. *Fangoria* was obsessed with Miller for some reason, regularly mustering heavily illustrated multi-page articles on him that surely bewildered many a young gorehound. Why, they must have wondered, was a magazine aimed at blood-crazed teenagers and ostensibly dedicated to "Monsters, Aliens and Bizarre Creatures" devoting so much real estate to a craggy-faced day player of advanced middle age? But some of us knew the answer, and the obsession was contagious.

Deciphering the particulars of Miller's appeal is difficult, but on an Internet message board, a fan of Miller's from Midland, Texas, discussing the actor's appearance at a 2009 horror convention in Dallas and in an apparent effort to pinpoint his most cherished Miller role, settled on this: "It's hard to remember which film your favorite part is in when every film he's in, he's your favorite part."

This is almost inarguable. Miller's performance is often dimensional where the film as a whole is not. He's of a piece with the picture he's in, like any actor of quality, but later, when you think back on the movie you've seen, he typically stands out as a jewel in a lackluster setting. *The Howling* is a good picture, but even there his only real competition is a spectacular, genre-redefining, werewolf transformation; in *The Terminator*, another fine genre film, he's overshadowed only by Arnold Schwarzenegger, who, to be fair, stands almost a foot taller than the 5'5" Miller. In many of his movies there's no contest at all: it's Miller's show all the way, no matter if he's the star or 37th down the cast list playing "Cab Driver."

Miller has played "Cab Driver," or something similar, more often than he has played Walter Paisley, and that is saying a lot. Miller drove a cab in *Ski Party, Fly Me, The Slams,* and *Innerspace*. He has also waited tables (*The Girls on the Beach, Taxi*), sold books (*The Howling*), guarded factories (*Heartbeeps*), grilled burgers (*Starhops, Twilight Zone: The Movie, After Hours*), mopped floors (*Chopping Mall*), sold guns (*The Terminator*), collected garbage (*Dr. Heckyl and Mr. Hype, The 'burbs*), tended bar (*The Trip, Route 666*), run a bowling alley (*Fame*), driven a truck (*White Line Fever, Small Soldiers*), and delivered pizzas (*The Hole*). He's played a cop so many times I'd expect to find a uniform hanging in his closet.

In short, he plays working guys: he's an actor for the 99 percent, a jester whose motley includes a name patch. In Joe Dante's *The 'burbs*, Miller and fellow Dante regular Robert Picardo play trashmen servicing a suburban neighbourhood whose residents—among them, Tom Hanks, Bruce Dern, Carrie Fisher, and Corey Feldman—have gone mad with paranoia over some Munster-like newcomers to the street. Desperate to search the strangers' refuse for incriminating clues, they intercept it just as a bickering Miller and Picardo are about to heave it in the truck. Soon there's garbage all over the street, and an upset Miller demands to know who's going to pick it up. Dern, who always seemed to be abusing Miller in the movies they were in together, sneers at him with unbelievable condescension for a man wearing a housecoat: "*You're* the garbage man, so *you* pick it up!" Miller packs a Woody Guthrie song's worth of angry workingman's dignity into his response: "I pick up garbage from cans, not from the street!" A lesser actor would fold under the pressure of Dern's manic disrespect and higher billing, would roll his eyes, express some kind of mock, weightless bluster, and you'd never feel a thing for him. You'd forget about his predicament as soon as the scene was done; but Miller makes you wonder, even after the picture is over, just who *did* pick that garbage up. Did Miller? He shouldn't have had to, you feel, because here's a blue-collar guy who won't be taken for granted, ill-treated, or made a slave just because of his job or his station; here is a real person with dignity, pride, and basic rights. This handy example of what is known as "acting" is a trick Miller has pulled many times over in bringing his working-class characters to life. And on top of this he can surely deliver a line: the *bon mot* of the scene goes without contest to Miller, who grouses in true Bronx fashion, "I hate cul-de-sacs. There's only one way out and the people are really weird."

Miller's Runyonesque, rough-and-tumble background and series of pre-Hollywood jobs (sailor, salesman, boxer, band boy, psychologist, stock boy, and more) have almost certainly fuelled his ability to communicate sympathy for the proletariat, as has the fact that his station didn't really change when he turned to acting, but his essential talent helps too. All his characters—even his angry resort owner in *Piranha*, his rapist gym coach in *The Student Teachers*, his vicious gangster in *The St. Valentine's Day Massacre*, and his vacuum cleaner salesman in *Not Of This Earth*—earn some empathy from the discerning viewer. "A very good actor, very solid," is how his old beach buddy and co-star Jack Nicholson described him; and Roger Corman, who, after years of prowling acting classes to find the best and hungriest performers for his low-budget productions, well knew what the town had to offer, declared him "the best actor in Hollywood." His performance in *A Bucket of Blood*—funny, touching, scary, and real—alone bears this assessment up, or at least defuses any accusations of hyperbole. Everyone, after all, has their own favourite actor; Dick Miller is mine, Corman's, and a lot of other people's too.

His fifty-five year movie career has an almost perverse equilibrium to it: he had big roles in small pictures at the beginning and small roles in big pictures at the end. It's an arc that would frustrate a more ambitious man, but an essential part of Miller's character, elemental to his screen appeal, is the myopia that prevented any calculation in his professional choices. Having played the lead in *A Bucket of Blood* for Corman in 1959, he turned down the top-lining role in the next year's *Little Shop of Horrors* because it was too similar, and took a supporting part instead. He came to regard that decision as a turning point in his career and life. Had he accepted it, he wondered, and had he continued seeking lead roles thereafter, might he have stayed higher up on the rungs of the Hollywood ladder? Some say he was too short to have ever become a true star, but look at Alan Ladd, Dustin Hoffman, Al Pacino, and Tom Cruise. All short men, all big stars. Miller was the same height as Richard Dreyfuss, Joan Crawford, Woody Allen, and Gandhi, so his stature alone ought not to have been any impediment to his stardom.

My contention is that Miller *is* a star, just not one of the ones you read about in gossip magazines. In a scan of the Internet, it doesn't take long to find expressions of adulation for him of the THIS GUY IS THE GREATEST!!!! variety, and once you've read several dozen such encomiums, it becomes clear that Miller is not just another run-of-the-mill cult figure. He's genuinely beloved by people who see his face, who hear his beguiling Bronx accent, and are reminded of their father, their grandfather, their uncle, themselves. He doesn't *play* a character: he wears one like a pink sports coat.

Dick Miller seemed to me someone much in need of a biography. I knew of his movie work, of course, having been a fan of it for years; knew that he'd spent time in the US Navy, that he'd been in television in the medium's early New York days, where he was involved with the first ever late-night talk show in the Carson and Letterman mode; even knew that he'd had some training in psychiatry and in boxing. I knew there must be a rich life lurking within this sketchy framework, but would it support a biography? Would Miller even want a biography, or a pesky stranger poking into the details of his life? I was not planning a hagiography, despite my admiration: whatever warts there might be would show. Would Miller accept this, and, if not, would an "unauthorized" biography of such a man even be possible? This question quickly became of critical importance, and I steeled myself for the answer.

I met Miller because I flew to California specifically to do so. I'd made contact with his wife, Elaine, or Lainie, who, it turned out, managed both his business affairs and his life, and I persuaded her that her husband's experiences and career needed chronicling. It helped, perhaps, that, like me, she was Canadian-born, and that I'd had books published before, and that I could rave about Miller and his career without, I hoped, sounding like a rabid fan at a convention, or one of the many strange devotees who have telephoned or visited or sent bizarre packages to the Millers over the years, or someone who would fly thousands of miles just to appear at their doorstep. She said she would ask Dick about the biography, and if it was all right with him, it was all right with her.

Lainie Miller sent me a document, the purpose of which was, I suppose, to let me know what I was getting into, or perhaps to underline how much I was asking, or possibly both. The document was of recent vintage and was headed "I can't serve. Please excuse me from jury duty." The text ran as follows:

I am 83 years old and have multiple illnesses. I cannot go anywhere alone because my diabetes and my blood pressure go whacky and I am in trouble at the drop of a hat. I had several major surgeries, among which was losing 2 lobes of my right lung to cancer, a triple coronary bypass, a carotid end-arterectomy, and an aorta bi-femoral bypass.

My blood sugar goes from sky high to a dangerous low that is not compatible with life. As though that is not enough, I have a profound hearing deficit and my legs don't want to carry me anymore. My bladder has a mind of its own and I cannot control the gas escaping from my back door. It is really embarrassing. Please don't make me go through this. You will also be punishing the rest of the jury panel.

It was signed "Dick Miller," though it had pretty clearly been authored by Lainie on her husband's behalf. I hadn't realized just what the man had been through—Lainie called him "my bionic husband"—but now that I'd found out, it was clearer than ever that his story must be told.

It all came together very quickly and easily, and suddenly there I was, walking up to the Millers' Spanish-style bungalow in Burbank, ringing the bell, hearing the crazed shrill of tiny dogs and the slow shuffle of a man inside approaching the door. I could hear his voice, so familiar, patiently admonishing the dogs for their yapping. This was the most unreal moment, the point at which I stepped briefly outside my body and observed the event in mute astonishment: *I'm about to meet Dick Miller in person!*

The door opened and there he was, clear-eyed, dressed comfortably in jeans and an orange shirt, smiling through the goatee he'd settled on half a decade earlier after many clean-shaven years, not seeming the least bit ill or infirm, and extending a firm, dry grip. We shook and the unreality dispelled: he was a real guy after all, a working-class johnny, a Joe Punchclock whose factory floor happened to be a sound stage. Lainie was there too, along with two dogs and a cat, and we all gathered around the dining room table where, with some occasional help, correction, and prodding from his partner, Dick Miller told me the story of his life.

1   *As sure as I'm sitting here, I'm a prince*

The opening shot of any movie is critical to what follows, setting the tone and theme for the rest of the picture, and is rivalled in importance only by the last shot. But our first coherent memories, unless they involve some spectacularly formative event or family legend, are random and meaningless, governed by synapses firing one way or the other, or by outside events, or by choice, and in any case are subject to change as mental acuity fades, sharpens, or disappears altogether.

Dick Miller's first memory is of a cork on a string, fired from a pop gun brandished by his older brother, Eugene, that hit him square in the eye. He was three years old at the time, and remembered thinking, or perhaps being told, that he might lose the eye and have to wear a patch, like a pirate. He kept his eye, as it turned out, and remained gratefully binocular the rest of his days, but much later in life he still vividly recalled the pain and surprise of the cork's impact. Eugene, who was six when he committed this classic boyhood crime, didn't remember the incident at all.

Injuries, firearms, and make-believe all figure heavily into Miller's subsequent life, so this recollection stands as a fair opener. The crack of gunfire, in particular, echoed through Miller's past and future: Dick's father gained his citizenship to the United States by plumping his experience as a machine gunner against the Kaiser in World War I; Dick himself was turned on to the joys of fast-draw six shooting by his New York buddy Sammy Davis Jr., while his own life in the east climaxed in a high-country gunfight; and in *The Terminator*, the 1984 James Cameron movie containing one of Miller's smallest, best-loved, and best-known roles, the actor's pawnshop owner character is professionally impressed by cyborg Arnold Schwarzenegger's computer-bank knowledge of weaponry, until the pitiless robot turns some heavy artillery on him.

Both Miller's parents came to the United States from Russia, though at different times—different eras, in fact, since one of them left before the revolution and the other left after. His mother, Rita Blucher, who had been born around the turn of the century, arrived first, aged about four, in the company of her father, Morris, mother, Miriam, and older sister, Francis, or Fanny. The family's hegira, Miller reported, had been marked by "many harrowing experiences," but in the end they all migrated safely. Four more children—Edward, Florence, Mac, and June—were born to Morris and Miriam in the New World.

The family was part of a wave of Russian Jews fleeing the pogroms that had erupted in the southern part of the country after the assassination of Alexander II in 1881. With trade unionist Abraham Cahan and anarchist Emma Goldman among their number, the new arrivals tilted the political landscape of New York in particular—and the US in general—heavily to the left, at least temporarily. It was an era when socialist candidates like Eugene Debs could collect upwards of a million votes in a presidential election. Morris and Miriam's specific politics are unknown, but the family had a freethinking attitude that would affect young Dick's childhood. Miller's only photograph of the couple depicted them in drably functional Old Country dress, but not scowling or expressionless as in so many such pictures. They were smiling, warm, friendly looking. He remembered them as very nice people.

This was the side of the family with the showbiz bent and the more interesting stories. They were descended, family legend insisted, directly from Gerhard von Blucher, the famed Swedish-born Prussian field marshal who had turned the tide against Napoleon at the Battle of Waterloo. "He came up when Wellington was getting his ass whipped and said, 'Hey, I'll save the day,'" was Miller's précis of the event. For this feat "Marshall Forwards," as the aggressive go-getter had been nicknamed by his men, had the Iron Cross designed in his honour by Frederick the Great and, as a further reward for his service, was made a prince of Wahlstatt, a district in what is now southeastern Poland, before his death in 1819. Miller, as a living relative of this hero, stated it plainly: "I'm a prince. As sure as I'm sitting here, I'm a prince."

He never thought of travelling back to reclaim his realm ("It ain't there any more! It's Prussia!"), but over the years received a handful of post-Treaty of Versailles reparations cheques for tiny sums: $28, $32, numbers like that. He took his peerage with self-amused seriousness (coats-of-arms of the House von Blucher were framed and displayed in both his living room and office, along with likenesses of the good Marshall), and passed his slightly aggressive regality down to his daughter, who, as a schoolgirl, once so energetically insisted she was a princess that her teacher called the Miller household about the distraction she was causing in the classroom. Miller answered the phone, listened to the teacher's complaint, and said, "She *is* a princess. Whaddaya want? Leave the kid alone!" We find it on film too: a key scene in *A Bucket of Blood* has Miller's character Walter Paisley wearing a cardboard crown and seated crookedly on a throne in the grip of drunken self-delusion, a would-be sculptor and a would-be king.

Morris Blucher, though well-educated and agile of mind, was a tailor in the New Country, not because he had any particular talent or love for stitchwork, but because, as Miller himself suggested, if you were a Jewish immigrant of a certain age, you were a tailor. (If you were a little younger and more ambitious, maybe you founded a movie studio.) The performers in the family were Rita and Florence. The younger of the two sisters took the stage name Florence Blue and appeared in the 1924 pre-Broadway production of *No, No, Nanette*, the show that would unapologetically introduce "Tea for Two" to the world (though only after the pre-Broadway iteration had failed, was recast, and had certain songs dropped, added, or rearranged). Family history would naturally put her in the role of Nanette, but in fact she appeared somewhat further down the cast list. Rita, meanwhile, wanted to be a singer of light opera, and to perform on stage and on the radio. "She always loved to sing," Miller said. Her professional career was brief, but she sang with at least two separate opera companies before it was done.

Miller's father, Isidore, born in Lithuania some time in the last few years of the nineteenth century, when the country was still part of the Russian Empire, arrived in America as an adult, at about age twenty-five. His name was in fact Miller (or, at least, мельник) on arrival, indicating the existence of actual millers in the family's ancestry; and the most likely date and circumstance of his landing was March 6, 1919, aboard the *Neuse* out of Genoa, Italy. After changing his first name to Ira, he found work as a typesetter with the Blanchard Press, one of the largest industrial print shops in the city, located in an eight-storey edifice on West Twenty-Fifth Street in Chelsea. A good-looking man with a cleft chin, he began mixing with the New York community of Russian Jews who had mostly settled on the city's Lower East Side, and eventually met Rita Blucher. They married, and then in 1925 she gave birth to a baby boy, Eugene. He might have been named after either playwright Eugene O'Neill (who would be played by Miller pal Jack Nicholson in Warren Beatty's 1981 film *Reds*) or the IWW (Industrial Workers of the World) founder and Socialist Party presidential candidate Eugene Debs—Dick was inclined to think O'Neill, based on his parents' artistic rather than overly political interests—but either option indicated the Millers' leftward leanings and their engagement in culture and politics. The little family took a large apartment in the fast-growing Borough of Industries, the Bronx.

Ira stayed with the Blanchard Press for many years, eventually rising to the position of foreman. "He had a good place in the composing room," remembered Eugene. "We used to get off the elevator and look into this huge, huge room which was dark, all the presses were in there. And I could just see [my father] sitting in his office, which was raised up above it. Everybody else in the place thought he was watching them." Ira was a short man, but wiry and strong, and a hard worker in the fierce Old Country style. He was also a union man, like so many of his fellow immigrants, and organized the Blanchard corps of printers into a labour collective. The Blanchard corporate philosophy was already sympathetic to this: the company's founder, Isaac H. Blanchard, who died unexpectedly of peritonitis in 1931 at age sixty-nine, had chaired the New York Employing Printers' Association's education and apprenticeship committees, and had helped author the first collective bargaining contract made between the city's master printers and the trade union. His nephew J. Cliff Blanchard, also active in the Employing Printers' Association, took over the company and maintained Isaac's labour-friendly policies.

By the end of 1928 the population of the Bronx would climb over the one million mark. Rita was pregnant again, and on Christmas Day, at the Bronx Maternity Hospital, she gave birth to another healthy boy, whom the couple named Richard. (He was not named after anyone in particular; it was, to the best of Miller's knowledge, chosen as "just a good American name.") There was no middle name, though Rita later wished there was: specifically, Noel, to reflect the day of his birth. She would often refer to Dick as "Noel," and in various ways pretend that was her second son's middle name, though it was nowhere made official.

That same Noël night another baby was born at the hospital, a little girl named Gladys Cerney. Twenty-one years later Miller would find himself sitting in Hanson's Drugstore at Fiftieth and Broadway in Manhattan, in the days when drugstores were places in which you passed your leisure hours, where he was introduced by a friend to a young lady, Gladys. They "became friendly," Miller remembered, and stayed friendly for a year or so. They were mutually amazed to discover the synchronicity of their birth. "We were destined for each other!" Miller said with the delighted growl of an old man recalling a long-ago sexual conquest, then gave a sideways glance at Lainie, his wife of many years, and quickly added, "But not for too long."

The Millers lived a middle-class life in their Bronx apartment house, with an easy commute to work for Ira. The Depression hit less than a year after Dick's birth, but printing was a reasonably steady trade and Ira well ensconced within it, and there were no immediate financial repercussions. In fact, the family prospered, and they moved from the city across the Hudson to New Jersey. Miller remembered running away from home during this time, stumping off down the road in response to some imagined outrage, and ending up at the Palisades Amusement Park, which was closed for the season. He whiled away some time in a nearby general store, then, when no one came looking for him, returned home as if nothing had happened. (This would not be the last time Miller staged a rebellion nobody noticed.) When Dick was six or so the family relocated to a large, brand-new house in Baldwin, Long Island, a move possibly inspired by a then-recent Blanchard Press publication called *Unique Long Island: Camera Sketches*. It was a coffee-table book of comely photos, with a special emphasis on pictures of people crabbing on the beaches, and did a good job making the island seem an expansive, picturesque, and peaceful place to live. At the time Baldwin was the outer extreme of the New York suburbs on the island, before the planned community of Levittown and all the rest of the fast-coming city sprawl. Beyond Baldwin, before one came to whatever was left of the louche Fitzgeraldites of the Gilded Age still dotting the easternmost tips of the island with their greenish lights, were forests, and within them, for all Eugene and Dick knew, vampires, mummies or Frankenstein monsters. (Gene joined the Boy Scouts while living in Baldwin, perhaps in a bid to find out.) The house gave the family all the room they needed, plus a basement (a rare luxury), but the new location significantly lengthened Ira's commute. Still, he was making $100 a week, extremely good money, and so he found other things to complain about, usually good-naturedly: his favourite word, barked frequently in his fading Lithuanian accent, was "bum." "Get a haircut, you bum!" he'd tell a teenage Dick later on, or "What are you doing spending time in a pool hall like a bum?"

"He was a nice man," Miller recalled fondly. "Quiet. But when he exploded, he exploded."

"He kicked your dog," Lainie reminded him.

"Oh, yeah. He kicked my little dog." The dog, Miller insisted, had done nothing to deserve such treatment, but Ira, so decent a man in most other respects, apparently just didn't like animals.

Miller showed his artistic inclinations early. He loved movies, had done ever since Rita had taken him to see his first picture, *Frankenstein*, when he was three years old. She later took him to see *King Kong*, which he loved almost as much. After such early exposure to these classics, he figured, "I was destined to end up in horror pictures, I guess." Like his mother he was an enthusiastic singer (though she had evidently put her professional aspirations to bed after having children), and by the time he was six or seven years old, had begun sketching and drawing, a habit he would maintain for life. The family kept moving around to different Long Island locations—to Woodmere, to Hewlitt, to Far Rockaway—exhibiting a tradition of restlessness that both Dick and Eugene would continue. In Far Rockaway the family settled for a while in a large apartment building on Seagirt Boulevard; on the other side of the street was the boardwalk, and beyond that the beach and the piers. It was a rich playscape for a young boy in any season, even in the winter; when the city throngs were absent and the wind whistled across frozen sand, there was a long slope leading down to the boardwalk that was perfect for sliding. You could run around the pilings at low tide, or walk the beach by yourself, listening to the waves and the screech of gulls and the crunch of your boots in the rime.

Summers were spent largely on the beach, of course, where the bantling Miller once won a cursing contest among his neighbourhood buddies, being the only one of them who dared to say "fuck." Another contest involved eating hard-boiled eggs: challenged by his cousins he swallowed more than a dozen of them whole, until stabbing pains in the gut left Cool Hand Dick writhing in the sand. It turned out he had appendicitis on top of egg gut. Vacations took the family upstate, sometimes to a farm near Dansville owned by "strange people" named the Traxlers, whom Rita had befriended, or to the much nearer resorts in the Catskills, where they relaxed right alongside every other middle-class Jewish family from the city. This in particular was a delight for the Miller boys: the freedom, the piney country air, the community of summer friends tearing through the bosky nights as their parents took in music, comedy, and cocktails back at the hotel. When he was at the Traxler farm, Dick, an open-faced boy with a remarkably high forehead and a Garfunkel frizz of curly hair, would don his gumboots and tromp the pastures and forests on the prowl for rural adventure.

Also near Dansville was the Physical Culture Hotel, of which Rita was a devotee. This establishment had been opened in 1883 and run as a health resort by Dr. James Caleb Jackson, a nutritionist, hydrotherapist, and creator of Granula, the first commercially available cold cereal. The PC Hotel, as it was locally known, was a grand edifice indeed, a North American approximation of a castle built halfway up a mountain, high above the town. In 1929 the place had been bought by Bernarr Macfadden, the "Father of Physical

Culture," who by this time in his career was a rich and famous advocate for health, strength, and bodybuilding. He had created his own cold cereal, Strengthfude, and was reputed to be a vitamin-driven philanderer, decreeing stately pleasure domes with different women in locations across the country. Rita tried to get up to the PC Hotel every year, where evenings would often find the hotel's residents mixing with Dansville locals on the rooftop under the stars, dancing to the latest hits still dressed in their athletic togs.

Then came the summer of 1938, an eventful one for the Millers. Following on the pop-gun injury of a few years earlier and the appendicitis, eight-year-old Dick suffered a hernia in a hay wagon incident while vacationing at the Traxlers' farm. A large, heavily laden horse-drawn cart had gone into the ditch, and Dick ran to join the group of farmers trying to push it out. He got under the wagon and lifted along with the others, but kept lifting after the rest had let go. "I was left holding the thing," Miller recalled, "and for an instant, for a half a second, whatever it was, I was holding it myself!" But, of course, it came down right away, bouncing on its springs in the muck of the ditch, and Miller crawled out from beneath it, moaning, "I don't feel so good." He would not get the rupture repaired until his late teens, when he was forced to in preparation for his navy service.

A happier incident for Dick that summer was his first paid gig as a performer. The family was at one of the Catskills resorts they frequented, and something had prevented the arrival of the weekend's entertainment. Young Miller was not shy about busting out a number anywhere in the hotel, in the lobby, the hallways, the dining room, the lounge; and this amateur showmanship had been noticed by the hotel's entertainment director. In desperation he asked the boy if he wanted to perform. "Yeah, sure," Dick told him, "want to pay me?" The manager hemmed and hawed for a while, then offered him five dollars. "Go ahead," Rita said, glad to have another performer in the family. Dick took the stage with a band-aid on each knee and belted out a popular new Gershwin number, "Love Walked Right In." "And I was a hit," reported Miller. "They liked me, they called me back for the second week, but we were gone."

This triumph was soon to be overshadowed by a more serious affair. One day when Miller came home to what he believed was just "one of the usual arguments," he learned that Ira and Rita were getting a divorce. Eugene, with the blinkered view of childhood, can remember no particular strife leading up to the event, and Dick recalled no great trauma in its wake; but this was more than three quarters of a century ago, after all, and unwanted memories fade. Lainie spoke of ferocious arguments between the brothers later in life as they tried to hash out the whys and wherefores of the divorce and reconcile their contradictory memories of whose fault it was, but, later, even the fact of their battles, never mind the substance, was crowded out of both Gene's and Dick's recollections. The reasons for the split, as near as could be figured, were Rita's modern ways and Ira's old-fashioned reaction to them. "He wanted someone to wait on him hand and foot," Elaine Miller said reproachfully.

"Yeah," Miller agreed. "He wanted a homebody, and my mother was still thinking radio, opera."

Rita had held on to her showbiz dreams after all. The boys headed back to the Bronx with Rita, where her wanderlust kept them moving from apartment to apartment and school to school, and where, as time passed, she watched Dick's burgeoning drive to perform. Perhaps, though she never by any stretch became a showbiz mother, she was sublimating her own ambitions into support for her son's; or maybe, like most parents, she was just waiting to see what would happen.

The move to the Bronx brought a change in fortunes. The Depression was continuing to make life particularly tough for lower-income people, and "we went from middle class to poverty," Miller said. They lived in an apartment on the Grand Concourse near Fordham Road, and tried their best to be poor-but-happy. Happiness may have been a challenge for Rita, a single woman of meagre means and frustrated dreams, who was trying to raise two increasingly boisterous boys and who suffered from Type 1 diabetes in a time and situation that did not allow for easy management of the disease. Life wasn't difficult for Dick, however: ever since his thrilling experiences in the dark watching *Frankenstein* and *King Kong*, he had loved movies with a ravening passion, and now, living conveniently near such otherworldly movie palaces as the magnificent Loew's Paradise, he could take his fill. He had no favourite actors: he loved them all, and went with great zeal to see any movie in any genre. (Also in the Bronx, a boy called Stanley Kubrick, the same age as Dick, was attending the same cinemas with an obsessiveness at least the equal of Miller's.)

The Paradise, Miller's local picture house, had opened in September 1929, not very long after Dick's birth, and its premiere presentation, the Warner Oland creepie *The Mysterious Dr. Fu Manchu*, might as well have been programmed in celebration. The building towered over the Grand Concourse like a cliff face; high up in a niche at the top, a figure of St. George slew his dragon on the hour, and below, past a pond in the lobby alive with goldfish and the vast curved staircases to the mezzanine, bronze doors led to a Carlsbad-sized expanse, ceilinged with a triptych depicting "Sound, Story and Film" and a cherubim-ringed mural illustrating the Goddess of Kinema, who soared across the pink sky, an unspooling reel of film in her hands. Projected clouds would move across these wonders, even during the picture. Columns and niches and statuary ranging from boy gods to winged lions crowded the walls; the effect was like watching a movie in a crazed Venetian piazza art film directed by Van Nest Polglase after several hits of acid. "They were like wonderful sets," remembered Miller. Within this dark cathedral and others like it, young Miller and his friends chased each other around the balcony seats, staging duels, slapfights, and wrestling matches, knocking each other into the carpeted wainscoting of the mezzanine until they were inevitably chased away by ushers. Occasionally they might even pay attention to the movies they'd handed over a nickel to see. As Miller matured through the 1930s, he paid more heed, and it seemed to him that movies were getting better.

It was a heady time for a movie lover. Technology was evolving at a lightning pace: sound, colour, special effects, and camerawork were improving in bounding leaps with every new picture. In a sense, after the sophistication of the silents, cinema had begun anew with the advent of sound in the late 1920s, so it and Miller were maturing together at the same accelerated rate. By the end of the decade the medium was regularly pumping out major popular achievements like *Stagecoach*, *Ninotchka*, *Gone With The Wind,* and *The Wizard of Oz*, and every new trip to the cinema was an opportunity to see what new heights of quality Hollywood had attained. He was, at least thrice weekly, an hour-and-a-half late getting home from school: the lure of the movies was just that strong. Still, outside the picture palaces there were other diversions: the 1939 World's Fair provided wonders of the modern age, rides and amusements, and—though Dick had to sneak in, worming beneath stiff canvas and through beer-sodden mud—a look at his first burlesque show.

In school at PS 86, just down the street from the Jerome Park reservoir, Miller was, he said, "a good little boy," but hints of the juvenile delinquent he would briefly become, and sometimes play older versions of onscreen, were showing. He had maintained his sketchbook habit, and like any protean artist worth his salt, he regularly caught heat in school for his "doodles."

For a class drawing assignment he took five minutes to put together a nice picture of a boy and a dog, but the teacher accused Miller of blowing off the assignment. Like the critics who would later make a cruel sport of eviscerating Roger Corman's five-day wonders, the teacher was ignoring the quality of the piece and focusing instead on how little time, and apparent effort, it had taken to make. Miller, demonstrating a ferocious sense of fair play he would never lose, fought this judgment strenuously, taking his case all the way to the principal's office, where he demanded that the teacher be replaced. "Ask the vice-principal," he was told, only to discover the vice-principal was this very same art teacher. His request accordingly went nowhere, but his voice had been heard.

A new activity took hold of the Miller household in the summer of 1940. Rita, using money from who knows where, bought four or five horses and aimed to run them at the nearby Jamaica Race Course. Jamaica had opened in 1903 and was one of New York City's most popular sporting venues, attracting almost two million customers a year in 1959, its final year of operation. Man o' War and Seabiscuit had both run there, and famed trainer Sunny Jim Fitzsimmons had called it his base for a time. All of this caught Miller's imagination, and he decided he wanted to be a jockey, or at least a "bug," racetrack terminology for an apprentice jockey. After all, he was a good size for the sport—he was small even for an eleven-year-old. The horse would barely feel his weight.

Rita's particularly freewheeling style of parenting asserted itself and she arranged Dick's papers, and he was soon a registered bug. He was given a badge he could flash to get into the raceway and felt like a pretty big man whenever he used it; but then, inevitably, came the actual jockeying. After some preliminary training, some running around, some positioning practice, the big day arrived: he was put on a horse and led to the gates, which were then thrown open with a terrifying clang. The horse took off like a rocket, with Miller holding on for his life; a quarter-mile later he was a trembling mess. Next he was set up for a start with one other horse at the gate in the lane beside him, and then again with two other horses, one on either side.

That was enough for Dick. The deafening clang, the lurch of the start, the bone-rattling run were all just too frightening, and he quit the racing game before he ever had a real race. Rita held onto her horses after that, but not for long. One of her brothers took a look at her feed bills and asked how many horses she owned. It must be at least ten, her brother allowed, judging by the amount she was paying. But she had only five, and so she marched down to the stables and confronted the trainer, who admitted he'd been pocketing the difference. The man began to cry, blubbering that he had a daughter in college and needed all the money he could get. The tears had no effect on Rita: she fired the trainer, sold the horses, and got out of the equine business as suddenly as she had entered it.

Miller the sketch artist, meanwhile, had hardly been dissuaded by the trouble he'd faced in school for his doodles. He was honing his creative chops, spending a lot of time with an artistic friend he'd made at PS 86, Billy Levy. Levy had a drafting table in his bedroom at which the two lads would sit elbow to elbow and plan out elaborate comic strips. Miller's drawings were generally of "Spartacus-type gladiators fighting in the arena, with rippling muscles and swinging cat o' nine tails," Levy recalled. But even in the midst of this, he would often talk of his ambition to become an actor. "Great," Levy told him in a flash of innocent but accurate prediction, "you can be the world's shortest cowboy." (The two interests would eventually merge for Miller, briefly at least, when he played a gladiator—presumably the world's shortest—in Roger Corman's 1961 sword-and-sandal spectacular *Atlas*.) This was Levy's recollection; Miller claimed not to have considered acting as a profession until later.

Overriding movies, school, horses, drawing, and everything else were the thunderheads of war. It had been talked about for years and in 1939 had broken out for real in Europe. Newsreels kept Miller and everyone else abreast of developments. Toward the end of 1941, a few weeks before Miller's thirteenth birthday, the Japanese bombed Pearl Harbor, Germany declared war on the United States, and it was finally game on for the USA. Perhaps stirred up by the frenzy of her country's entering a world war, or just ready for a change, Rita's congenital wanderlust took hold of her judgment ("A little Gypsy blood in her or something, I don't know," said Miller), and she packed up Dick and sixteen-year-old Eugene and pointed the family car west, toward Hollywood. She was now in her forties and likely no longer harbouring any serious thoughts of catching a showbiz break of her own; but there was still Dick, the all-singing, all-dancing, cartoon-drawing, movie-loving Dick. Show business was their bond, and Miller would do his best to stay inside that world, that motherhug, his whole life. Eugene had a creative bent too; who knew what would happen with these two? A mother could dream anything.

Everyone else seemed to be leaving California as quickly as they could, fearful of Japanese attacks on the coast to follow up the devastation in Hawaii.

The beaches were strung with barbed wire, innocent Japanese Americans were being harassed and rounded up, and indeed American merchant vessels were being attacked off the coast by Japanese subs. There was damage on the mainland: an oil refinery in Santa Barbara was shelled in February 1942, just as the Millers were relocating, and, later in the war, a Japanese balloon bomb, one of several thousand released to drift over the Pacific, killed a minister's wife and five Sunday school students picnicking in Oregon. Rita was unconcerned by all this, but Dick remembered their being the only travellers on the westbound roads, watching the gridlocked escapees on the eastbound lanes and wondering if they were after all making the wisest move. But when the Millers arrived, Los Angeles, though on a war footing like everywhere else, otherwise appeared disappointingly normal to Dick. Others may have been expecting the buzz of approaching Zeroes at any moment—according to the 1979 Steven Spielberg movie *1941*, in which Miller would appear, *everyone* in California was—but not the Millers, who had arrived just in time for a wartime employment boom. If you had ever wanted to get into shipbuilding, or onto a warplane production line, this was probably the best chance history would ever offer. They stayed for a period with Boris and Tillie Goldblatt, Ira's sister and her husband, who lived in Hollywood on North Beachwood Drive. Soon they settled into a house of their own, also on Beachwood and very near the Goldblatts; and Dick, breathing in hot gulps of movie-star atmosphere, bristling with Bronx-boy attitude, set out to discover where the action was.

2 *There are certain things you want to put out of your mind*

Squinting against the bright California light, thirteen-year-old Miller wandered the Hollywood streets, listened to the dry clack of the palm leaves, and breathed in the pre-smog cocktail of jasmine, woodsmoke, and salt. "What's hot up here?" he asked passers-by, and was told about Schwab's, a drugstore on Sunset Boulevard just west of Fairfax. Schwab's, though not yet as famous as it would be from its 1950 appearance in Billy Wilder's *Sunset Boulevard* or its mention in *Lolita* five years later, was locally popular and hard to miss with its big neon sign, high windows trumpeting the availability of PRESCRIPTIONS and TOILET ARTICLES as well as BREAKFAST, LUNCHEON, and DINNER, pyramidal displays of bottled nostrums and booze, and the penny scale sitting out front. It had opened in 1932. Its side windows opened to a car lot, and it was filled with actors looking to make connections, hear about auditions, or just sit back and get discovered, as Lana Turner had been, or so legend had it. (Legend, as is usually the case in Hollywood, had sprung nearly whole from the pen of a creative studio publicity man.)

Orson Welles, Mickey Rooney, Ida Lupino, and the Marx Brothers were among its regulars. It was also filled with working stiffs, servicemen, matrons, and a whole panoply of Hollywood types, few of whom were there to have prescriptions filled. The main draw was the lunch counter, which was staffed by harried women in white uniforms that made them look like nurses as they pulled sodas and poured Apfel's coffee, while standing all day on a floor made of rough wooden staves. (A pre-fame Ava Gardner logged some time behind the counter.) The restaurant offered its customers hot meals on credit, a helpful and attractive service to the unemployed actors who frequented it. Miller was instantly enchanted with the place, and later, when he moved permanently to Los Angeles, he made it his headquarters, becoming the most regular of its many half-famous regulars. Film producer and historian Alex Gordon (he would executive produce Miller's movie debut, *Apache Woman*) claimed to have once passed Schwab's some time in the late fifties and, on glancing at Miller's regular table and not seeing him there, ran straight to a pay phone and called around to the local hospitals on the assumption that the actor must have become seriously ill or was just plain dead.

The fear of Japanese attacks notwithstanding, to someone of Miller's age wartime seemed more like a lot of boring hard work and needless privation. Victory gardens appeared in many yards, there were air-raid drills regularly, and by March 1942 food, clothing, and fuel were all being rationed. Bossy, white-helmeted air-raid wardens told you what to do all the time, especially during a nighttime drill, when your house had better be completely dark or else. Exercise and so-called fun came from crushing empty cans for aluminum drives. But if wartime was tedious for young Dick, being in Hollywood during it was not: the Millers' Beachwood house was just up the street from Columbia Pictures, at Sunset and Gower, and all around were the low-budget dream factories of Poverty Row, then approaching their days of decline (though you'd hardly notice). Companies like Monogram and Producers Releasing Corporation were the best known of these penny ante sausage factories, but there were also Invincible, Chesterfield, Empire, Mayfair, and more, a dozen of them at least, all cranking out hour-long bottom-of-the-bill programmers on microscopic budgets. Bela Lugosi or Angelo Rossitto (when he was not manning his famous newsstand at the corner of Hollywood and Wilcox) or George Zucco and the East Side Kids might be seen slouching down the street at sundown, on the way to work (studio space was cheaper in the evenings and on weekends) or trying to collect a paycheque. It was real down-home, meat-and-potatoes Hollywood, and Miller sucked it in like sea air.

In the Bronx Miller had graduated from the eighth grade despite his battles with the administration, and, as far as he was concerned, was well prepared for high school. Grade nine was, at that time in New York State, the first year of high school, so when Miller, operating with the freedom of an easily distracted single parent's child, told the administrators he was supposed to be in the first year of high school, they placed him in the tenth grade at Hollywood High. This storied, palm-ringed athenaeum still sits at the corner of Sunset and Highland, and its graduate roll of mid-level thespians looks like the guest star rosters of *The Love Boat* and *Fantasy Island* combined. The school itself has appeared in many films, and had the titular role (though not much screen time) in both *Hollywood High* (1976) and its 1981 follow-up, *Hollywood High Part II*. Miller would often hitchhike from the house on Beachwood to Hollywood High, receiving lifts from Academy Award-winning femme fatale Gale Sondergaard and other familiar B players. It sounds like one of the more lighthearted and wistful *Twilight Zone* episodes: a boy of destiny meeting strange shades of his future self.

Miller's school records were slow in coming from New York; it would be weeks, even months before they'd arrive in LA. So Dick settled into the tenth grade and found himself keeping company with a more mature crowd than he was used to, practising his craft, long before he himself knew what it was, by performing the role of someone several years older than himself. He could hardly hide his Bronx accent, but in all other ways he could be the mystery boy. As well, without knowing it, he was practising one of Robert Mitchum's great film acting precepts: steal, or at least borrow, the reality of the props and sets around you. Simply by being in high school, his portrayal of a high school student became credible; his handling of everything new about high school, from classroom schedules to social dynamics, was expert, for he was a quick study; plus, he tried his best to dress the part. It must have been a little like the sequences in *A Bucket of Blood,* in which Miller's character, Walter Paisley, a simple-minded busboy, impersonates a bohemian *artiste,* sporting a beret and ordering Yugoslavian white wine and papaya cheesecake with a simple wave of his Zen stick.

But, typical of Miller, it was a successful performance. He soon found himself running with a gang of older kids, smoking cigarettes with them in "Nicotine Gulch" or riding in the rumble seats of their jalopies and discovering under their tutelage what Hollywood had to offer an East Coast sophisticate like himself. As in the Bronx, he went to the pictures almost daily. The world's largest bowling alley, the fifty-two-lane Sunset Bowling Center, housed in a repurposed movie studio, was not far away, and, with its stately columns and animated neon signage depicting rolling red balls and crashing yellow pins, was a natural draw for a worldly thirteen-year-old. Yellow neon ran up and down the columns, the horizontal lines were lit up in green, and the name of the place was emblazoned across the geison in bright crimson: it was Times Square all in one building, and how could you resist it? Around the corner from the Bowling Center was the Hollywood Roller Bowl, also a converted movie studio, and the place Miller learned to roller skate; just north of that, at Hollywood and Bronson, was Reginald Denny's Hobby Shop; down on Melrose you could get a hot dog at Pontiac's. Hollywood in that period was, to Dick, something close to a perpetually sunny amusement park, with dissolute winos in place of wandering clowns.

Miller became particularly tight with a pair of high school sweethearts: a tall, flame-haired youth named Rusty, who played football at Hollywood High and also lived on Beachwood, and his friendly girl Maggie. Rusty was a couple of years older than Dick, and owned a car—a useful possession in

Los Angeles, and one in which Miller would catch lifts to school when he wasn't cadging rides from character actors. Rusty, who seems to have been an exceptionally generous and trusting soul, was happy to not just provide Miller with regular transportation, but to take the young New Yorker along when he and Maggie went to the pictures or other dates. He was a good guy, this football star, a solid citizen, and Maggie was warm and open. Dick found he could talk very easily with her in particular, at a mature and heartfelt level of conversation he'd never experienced before.

Another older Hollywood High friend was Tiny, a broad-shouldered and towering lad of nineteen, who had for some reason been declared unfit for military service but eventually found a job in defense. Miller, six years younger and small for his age, looked up to Tiny in every sense; and they *were* an odd pair, but the twosome made the most of their incongruity. "We'd play games to get girls," Miller said. "Everything was about getting girls in those days." They constructed elaborate scenarios in which Miller, acting once again, played Tiny's little brother or some other role; and these skits were intended to somehow razzle-dazzle their (or at least Tiny's) chosen conquests into submission. There isn't a lot of success on record, however. Their base of operations was the Sunset Bowling Center, but they would also frequent the nearby roller rink, where Miller, a natural dancer, became a skilled skater as well, perfecting his closed Mohawks and double flat turns on the Roller Bowl's web-like wooden floor.

Miller's first close-up encounter with celebrity, other than catching the occasional hitchhike with Gale Sondergaard, came at the Roller Bowl. The rink's big cheese was Bobby Jordan, a former Dead End Kid and then-current East Side Kid. Dick, who was five years younger than Jordan but knew a blowhard when he saw one, didn't like him. "A pain in the neck," Dick called him. As an East Side Kid, Jordan's onscreen schtick was mock toughness, so he might have been overcompensating in his off-screen life. He was also a budding alcoholic (he would die at forty-two of cirrhosis of the liver), and had been sliding down the budget, prestige, dialogue, and screen-time scale since his 1937 appearances in *Dead End*, in which he'd co-starred with Humphrey Bogart and Joel McCrea, and *Angels With Dirty Faces*, which featured Bogart and James Cagney. Now he was an East Side Kid, hamming it up on Poverty Row with Bela Lugosi in *Spooks Run Wild* and the like, and being literally crowded off the screen by fellow Kids Leo Gorcey and Huntz Hall.

At the bowling alley, away from Gorcey and Hall and the mainlining Bela, Jordan had the dick-swinging weight of semi-celebrity. He also had a towering buddy who acted as his bodyguard. Dick, of course, had his pal Tiny, and so one day, when Jordan's bodyguard moseyed downstairs to the men's room, Dick saw his chance. He asked Tiny to make sure the bodyguard stayed below decks for a few extra minutes, and then walked over to Bobby Jordan and nailed him right in the chops. Miller's friend Ira Steven Behr remembered his astonishment at hearing this tale: "You beat up a Dead End Kid?" he'd gasped. "Not quite Leo Gorcey maybe, but Jesus!" Behr's admiration was tempered a bit by his conviction that Miller's propensity for physical altercations had been a "detriment to his career." Who knows? It never hurt John Huston's.

All these antics took place mainly on the weekends, of course; the 1941–42 school year was still on, though drawing to a close now that it was May. Dick was looking forward to a summer of frolic, California style: cruising to the beach, sodas at the enormous bowling alley's equally enormous refreshment counter, snowballs and dance contests at the Roller Bowl, movies with Rusty and Maggie, and who knew what else. Miller's school records chose this inopportune time to arrive from New York, and the administration's immediate response was to reassign Miller to Joseph Le Conte Junior High, a brick affair located at the corner of Fountain and North Bronson.

In comparison with Hollywood High, Le Conte was a dour, Dickensian pile filled with children doing childish things, and Miller was devastated as only a thirteen-year-old can be. He responded to this insulting demotion by taking the role of a full-on juvenile delinquent in the classic mid-century style. He filled his hair with goop and took to carrying a knife, and, while becoming proficient at throwing the blade into fences and trees and making it stick—Miller, like any good actor, was adept at picking up physical skills—he never actually threatened anyone with it. Perhaps after all he was more a quasi-JD. But he certainly had the attitude, along with the swagger, the pomade, and the perpetually curled lip. "Just a mean little kid," he called himself.

He maintained his Hollywood High friendships and activities. It was hardly possible, after all, to be running around playing kick the can or over-the-line with a bunch of kids while Rusty and Maggie were driving to the beach, or Tiny was mashing on girls at the Sunset and in need of "Brother Dick's" help. At the same time he tried, in his own juvenile way, to bring some maturity to Le Conte. Touch football was the habit there, but Miller insisted on tackle, and soon the concrete schoolyard was streaked with the knee-blood of fourteen-year-olds trying to keep up with the new boy, who must have seemed impossibly worldly to them. No doubt he was something of a legend at Le Conte before even arriving: the diminutive New York kid who'd fooled the powers that be into letting him go to high school before his time, who'd smoked and drank with the older kids, fooling them too. Miller recalled little or no adulation from his Le Conte schoolmates, but there must have been some.

Time passed in this way. He went to a lot of cowboy movies, mainly because there was a little theatre near Hollywood and Vine, in the shadow of the Pantages, which brought in three new ones a week, and tickets were cheap like borscht. Dick could spend the summer mostly forgetting he'd been cast back into junior high, but once the school year began it was impossible. He continued his movie-going habit, and, among many other pictures, took in *This Gun For Hire*, which had opened on November 2. Like everybody else he was dazzled by Veronica Lake, but he also noticed the movie's male star, Alan Ladd, and thought, "This guy has something. I don't know what it is." At 5'5" Ladd was the same height Miller himself would top out at, but while Dick had no idea Ladd was short, he felt some vague connection to the actor. Miller remained a fan of Ladd's, and years later came into possession of one of the star's jackets, which fit him perfectly.

Miller's acting career might have started during this time if things had broken a little more his way. He vaguely remembered a representative from the Walt Disney Studio coming to his house to chat with his mother about young Dick. "We'd like him to come out to the studio," the man told Rita, and Dick, whose drawing habits had intensified, and who was then considering an artistic career, excitedly assumed they wanted him to work in the animation department. Upon learning they actually wanted him to audition for what became Bobby Driscoll's part in *Song of the South*, then still in the scripting and planning stages, Miller lost interest. "I don't wanna be an *actor*," he told the man. (How they expected the Bronx-accented Miller to pull off the role of a plantation kid in the antebellum South is another question.) Given Driscoll's eventual fate—unemployment, drug addiction, and a pauper's death at age thirty-one in the ruins of a New York tenement, so unknown that he wasn't identified for two full years—it may be just as well Miller shunned this chance at child stardom.

On Christmas Day Dick turned fourteen, but the Millers, non-practising Jews, had long celebrated Christmas in the secular Western style, which meant he never got much of a birthday party, at least in the sense of its being a special day just for him. "That was always my big complaint," Miller said. Rita, who suffered from diabetes, felt poorly much of the time, especially around the holidays, and two celebrations might have been too much for her. Early in 1943 Eugene, who'd found some appropriately Hollywood-style work as a period researcher for 20th Century Fox, enlisted in the service, and after his training would be sent to the Philippines for the duration of the war. Rusty and Maggie and Dick were still all going out together, and often, at the end of the night, Rusty would ask Miller to drive his girlfriend home. Rusty and Miller were practically neighbours; it would be easy to get the car back the next day. It was convenient somehow, or Rusty seemed to think it so.

And on these trips home, Maggie began to talk more freely than ever: it "wasn't happening" with Rusty, and Maggie was unhappy. Maybe she was too young for so serious and dedicated a relationship. Maybe she thought she should have a little fun, poke around a bit, see what else the world had to offer. Rusty was probably feeling all these things too. Finally these conversations reached their logical end point, and, in an act for which the seventeen-year-old Maggie might have been officially chastised even then, had it become public—and for which Miller's hero status at Le Conte would have been replenished three times filled and overflowing—one night, in the car, they, said Miller, "got it on."

Miller stunned himself with his betrayal of Rusty, but was never foolish enough to tell him about it, and Maggie kept her counsel as well. "It wasn't weird, we were little kids," Miller insisted, and Lainie's only comment was, "I'm glad I didn't know any of that when I met you." Of course, young Dick was vibrating like a live wire, filled with confusion, joy, and all manner of conflicting emotions. The playboy of Le Conte Junior High had outpaced even his own self-image, and he spent weeks in a sort of daze, truly now a man among boys. But the school year was ending again, the summer fun would start, and by next September Dick would be back in his rightful place within the seashell walls of Hollywood High, to which once again, no doubt, his reputation would precede him. Nicotine Gulch would be alight with rumour along with Lucky Strikes.

There was riot in the air this summer. Tensions had been rising all spring between young Hispanic Angelinos and the 50,000 or so servicemen who flooded the town each weekend. In the barrios it was rumoured that soldiers were drunkenly hunting down Mexican-American women on the theory they were easy lays; on the bases the word was that Hispanics, and in particular those who self-identified as "pachucos," were going out of their way to make trouble, just as they went out of their way to defy wartime fabric rationing with their big, billowy zoot suits. On May 30 a group of soldiers and a band of pachucos clashed on a downtown street, and in the donnybrook that followed, a sailor named Joe Dacy Coleman was badly injured. It was nobody's fault and it was everybody's fault, and after that it was open season. The servicemen set out en masse taxi patrols, overwhelming anyone in a zoot suit, or anyone who looked like they might be comfortable wearing one. Cops looked the other way as young Hispanic or black men were swarmed, beaten, and often stripped of their clothing. By June 3 the confrontations had bloomed into full-scale riots, which reached a bloody climax on June 7. Order was re-established only once LA had been declared off-limits to servicemen and zoot suits were banned as disruptive to the public peace.

At some point within this roiling cauldron of racial tension, on a sunny mid-afternoon, Miller and Tiny went to their frequent haunt, the Sunset Bowling Center. The place was filled with servicemen, and, behind the fifty-two pindecks, there were legions of Hispanic pin boys watching the sailors carefully as they cleared the deadwood and reset the skittles. At three o'clock it was time for a shift change, and the pinsetters emerged. The atmosphere became charged. Finally, at the coffee counter, there was an incident: a pin monkey was jostled accidentally by a serviceman. The serviceman apparently apologized, but on both sides it was already too late. Punches began to fly, and Tiny, who had been aware of the growing tension, grabbed Dick, who had not, and tossed him over the counter out of harm's way. The fracas spread like a gasoline fire, and Tiny began calling to Dick to pass him things he might use as bludgeons: sugar dispensers, root beer mugs, teapots. "He was busting them over people's heads," Miller said. "It was a scene right out of a picture."

The picture quickly took a nightmarish turn. From his position on the floor, peering out from behind the coffee counter, Miller saw three pachucos holding a sailor down on the floor, pinning him with one arm extended. He was screaming, because they were cutting his arm off with a jackknife, or at least trying to. Elsewhere in the alley groups on one side or the other were dropping bowling balls onto the faces of their prone foes. By the time the Sunset had filled with military police, shore patrol, and regular city cops, and the riot had been quelled, seventeen people had been killed, and the pine floors were slippery with blood.

Miller was astonished to find no mention of this massacre in the next day's papers. Indeed, there seems to be no record of its having occurred at all, aside from his own memories. But those memories are particularly vivid, and while Miller may be an occasional fabulist (he would spend a year and a half writing science-fiction stories later in his life), he's no liar. He pointed out that, by mid-June 1943, the authorities wanted nothing more than to calm the situation and keep a lid on any zoot-related happenings, and this is quite true; and perhaps in wartime, with servicemen involved and a generally combustible atmosphere on the streets, it would be possible to invoke national security concerns as well as public safety and actually keep such a casualty-heavy event secret. At any rate this seems a likelier scenario than Miller's having made it all up from whole cloth.

Tiny, Miller's friend and saviour, overcame whatever his problems of enlistment had been; or perhaps, as the war effort kicked into full gear, the standards that had been keeping him out relaxed. He successfully joined the army before the cessation of hostilities, and was sent overseas to fight. He never made it home. And as the summer wore on, as Miller tried to shake off the shock of his bowling alley experience and the sudden if unmourned end to his childhood, he became aware that Maggie was absent from the scene more and more. Finally he realized that she was pregnant with what could only be his baby. Terrified, he told Rita the whole story, and after some thought she decided it might, after all, be a good time to pack up and head back east.

Rusty, the red-headed cuckold, was never clued in. "He never knew, God, no!" shuddered Miller. The football hero and all-around nice guy had joined the Marines before Maggie started to show, and he, too, was killed in action. ("There's no happy endings to the war stories," Miller murmured.) Dick put the whole thing out of his own mind as quickly and completely as he could; years later when the subject came up, he misidentified even the child's sex, and certainly couldn't remember its name. "There are certain things," he said, "you want to put out of your mind." Rita and Dick packed the car and started for New York, fleeing LA just like the frightened throngs a much younger boy had gaped at through his car window only a year-and-a-half earlier.

3 Fun Inc.

At some point during the long New York summers of his teenage years, as the war was climaxing and then winding down, Dick Miller and some of his pals visited Playland, a legendary amusement park in Far Rockaway ("Playland—Family Fun since 1901"). They did this often—this amusement park, or maybe one on Coney Island or somewhere else—strutting down Rockaway Beach Boulevard, past children selling painted shells on the curb, through the gates and beneath visages of the park's hideous, grimacing Gwynplaine mascot and its disembodied hands, they made a boisterous crew: live-wire showman Dickie Miller; lanky, graceful Bobby Stein; jazzbo Jack Silverman; brainy nerd Shelly Kopp; and quiet, artistic Billy Levy. They might have emerged whole from Woody Allen's *Radio Days*, or just from Central Casting.

On one day in particular, the weather was fine and the midway crowded. Screams came from the gasworks-looking cylindrical roller coaster that was the park's central feature and offered (so it claimed) the World's Greatest Sensation; the clank and grind of machinery and the tootling of calliopes were nearly as loud. The usual fun-fair smells—hot dogs, popcorn, diesel exhaust, and garbage—roiled together into an intoxicating funk. Miller walked past the pitch games, the teacup rides, the Ride Auto Skooter, and the sea-life mural on Davy Jones' Locker until he found something that looked fun: the swing ride.

He paid his ticket and belted himself into a chair. Soon the machinery roared and he was jerked forward and around, rising up, angling sideways with the momentum, holding onto the chains and looking out over the fairground, the beach town neighbourhood that surrounded it: Jamaica Bay was on one side, the crowded beach and shining Atlantic on the other. Hurtling in circles he could catch tilted glimpses of Manhattan skyscrapers, the Empire State and Chrysler buildings towering above all. The sun glinted off the sea, blinding him with its camera flash on each revolution.

Then it happened. The guy in the chair ahead of Dick must have eaten too many knishes, or maybe a whole pack of marshmallow cookies, or he might have put back some fried chicken at the Circus Bar on top of a greasy breakfast at Block's Luncheonette. Whatever was inside the guy, it all came out, all at once, in a single reflexive heave: not a liquid or a mist, but a horrible, solid, wriggling curtain of upchuck. Time slowed for Miller. The vomit hung in the air as a mass, undulating hypnotically, a giant amoeba made of clotted gravy and stomach acid. With soupy pseudopods, it seemed to be waving at him. The helpless Miller could do nothing. Though it seemed he'd been gaping at it for minutes, he hadn't even time to cross his arms over his face. He screamed and bugged his eyes into an expression called the "Skull," just as he would years later playing a doomed vacuum cleaner salesman in *Not Of This Earth*, then ploughed into the bilious mess with a loud *smack*. It was like hitting a warm, sour-wet towel.

He never went on a swing ride again.

A lot of famous people have come out of the Bronx. "Come out of" are the operative words here: from Mark Twain to Al Pacino to Jennifer Lopez, nobody with ambition seemed to stay. Hip hop was born in the Bronx, but the Bronx could not contain that, either. Ira Steven Behr, a Bronxite who would later hire Miller for his most sustained TV gig on *Fame*, wanted nothing more as he was growing up than to make it to Manhattan, which, on a clear day and from the right spot, you could dimly make out in the distance. Maybe this is why everyone leaves with such an energetic finality: you may want to get your shot in the Big Apple pretty badly when you come from a little town in the Midwest, but when you can practically see the place from your doorstep—a shimmering city behind a thick crystal wall, ever-distant like a carrot on a stick or a woman in a dream, as uncrackable as a Mandarin code despite your being technically a New Yorker—the need is that much more insistent.

"It's a borough unto itself," said Behr. "I guess they all are, but the Bronx especially." On the map it hovers above the other four boroughs like a leaking balloon, and is the only part of New York City on the United States mainland. It was established in 1898, the year New York adopted its borough system, and was named for the river that runs through it, which in turn had been named for a Swede named Jonas Bronck, its first European settler. The Bronx alone is twice the size of Manhattan, and as big as Paris, bigger than San Francisco; but fully a quarter of that area is parkland, and it is contradistinctively known as both the Borough of Parks and the Borough of Industries. Why not? It's big enough. It has fourteen institutions of higher learning, so is also tagged as the Borough of Universities; but one epithet it never picked up is the Borough of Showbiz, and that is why Dick Miller and all his friends eventually left it for more brightly lit pastures.

The gang of pals Miller collected in his preteen and teenage years might stand as one of twentieth-century America's most remarkable adolescent social groups. There were five of them, and at least three would become legitimately famous, in certain circles, with the other two having to settle for being merely well known within their own vocations. As kids the quintet could have been the template for any number of fictionalized cliques you find in memoirs by fellow sons of the Bronx such as Neil Simon or Woody Allen, or any of their comic-neurotic brethren. They were close friends for at least half a decade, though the survivors today have seen one another perhaps once in the last fifty years.

"We were talented," said Jack Silverman, understating the case. They weren't just talented; they were multi-talented. They all played music, and collectively their aptitudes ran from performing to comedy to writing, drawing, and song. What they loved most was to dance, and they were lucky to be living in a place and time in which terpsichorean opportunities were almost limitless. Along with the countless other activities it organized—1944's roster included pet shows, skating races, handicraft exhibitions, and barbershop quartet contests—New York's Department of Parks, under the direction of a much-feared administrator named Robert Moses, held "Name Band Dances" at green spaces across the city. Famous band leaders, including Art Paulsen, Frankie Carle, Mitchell Ayres, Lucky Millender, and Glen Gray with his Casa Loma Orchestra, were hired to play the dates, which were sponsored by Consolidated Edison Systems Companies, or Con Ed. Sometimes there were even bigger names: Benny Goodman, Tommy Dorsey, Woody Herman. Crowds as large as 15,000, including many servicemen on furlough, gathered to listen, socialize, and dance.

In the Bronx the Name Band Dances were held Wednesday evenings at Poe Park, halfway up the Grand Concourse at 192nd Street. Other concerts, distinct from the Con Ed series, were put on at the Poe bandshell every few Sundays through the summer, and Rosemary Clooney is reported to have made her debut there. The hot dance in those years was the Lindy—even in New York, it was more popular than the New Yorker. There were Lindy competitions in Poe Park, which drew contestants over from Harlem; the Harlem kids always won. In *Seeing Is Forgetting the Name of the Thing One Sees*, Lawrence Weschler's biography of Robert Irwin (who was born the same year as Miller), the artist provides a good description of the joys of Lindy dancing:

> The key movement was the shoulder twist, where the girl came directly at you and then you spun each other around and she went on out. When you got it going real smooth, you could literally get to the point where you were almost floating off the ground, acting as counterweights for each other. It was absolutely like flying, just a natural high.

This sounds like an excellent way to attain and perfect the grace of movement required of any good actor; once again Miller was training for his life's work without knowing it.

Aside from the Poe Park events and contests, there were dances held at church or temple basements in the neighbourhood; these typically cost two bits at the door, so the gang would send in a single representative to scope out the scene. If the ratio of pretty girls was high enough, the signal would be given and the rest of the guys would follow; if not, only twenty-five cents had been wasted, and they'd move on to the next place.

It always seemed to come back to Poe Park, though, in the summertime at least. The park was named for one of the Bronx's most famous sons, Edgar Allan Poe, and still contains the cottage where the poet lived, wrote, and moped for most of the last few years of his life. It's a small park, very urban, with as much pavement as grass, but was well located for Dick and his friends. (The Miller family bounced around the Bronx a bit, but rarely moved too far from the Grand Concourse or Fordham Road.) In that particular chunk of the Bronx, it was the locus of the Action. It was a place of convergence: the Jewish kids, which included Dick and his pals—"Lovers, not fighters," according to Jack Silverman—would run into the tougher Italian guys, or else the notorious Solomon brothers, and while there might be a fight now and again, rivalries, whether between factions or within them, were generally sorted through dance-offs. When they weren't dancing, they might get up a game of Ringolevio: yell "hide, hide, hide," then run off and go to ground somewhere in the park, or else just go to the pictures and return a couple of hours later to ask the searcher/sucker how he had fared.

Dick met Bobby Stein in Poe Park, of course. Dick was a good dancer and a natural performer (he'd proven as much way back in the Catskills), but for sheer footwork he couldn't begin to match Bobby, who idolized Fred Astaire and Ray Bolger, and who could play the trumpet—could play just about any instrument—and sing too, on top of his hoofer's chops. He'd been born only a few weeks before Miller, in December 1928 (though the obits would claim 1932), and, like Dick's, his first performing experience came in his childhood as a sudden fill-in at a Catskills resort (the stories are so similar you wonder if there wasn't some kind of mnemonic expropriation between the two friends at some stage). Unlike Dick's, Stein's parents were themselves performers, so the showbiz was not just a vocation to be tolerated, but encouraged to the exclusion of anything else. Stein's vaudevillian father had a stage name, King, which Bobby adopted briefly as his own, but, he said, "there were too many Kings in the business." When he spotted a poster of the aw-shucks actor Van Johnson plastered on his little sister's wall, it was settled: from that day on he was Bobby Van. (Jack Silverman, a card among cards, called him Bobby VanKingStein.)

Miller was dazzled by Bobby and by his talent. Everyone was. He had ambition too, which was more transferable than talent, and certainly rubbed off on Dick. Bobby was going to be a star, he was sure, and nobody in the circle doubted it. He and Dick talked about starting a band, or maybe putting together some sort of performing partnership, but they didn't get much further than choreographing a minute-and-a-half-long tap routine, which their disparate heights must have rendered at least a bit comical. Van's father was a dance teacher as well as a performer, so Bobby had a leg up on Dick in that respect as well. He was lean, with an angular head, small mouth, and downsloping, heavy-browed eyes; he didn't have matinee-idol looks, but a sort of intellectual handsomeness that was more memorable.

Van's talent, drive, and myriad other advantages would take him a long way. He legged it first to Broadway, where, in 1950, he debuted in a revue called *Alive and Kicking*, which also featured a young Bronxite named Carl Reiner; four years later he was taking starring roles in the Balanchine-choreographed *On Your Toes*. At the same time he was appearing in films, beginning with a not-insubstantial role in the Mario Lanza vehicle *Because You're Mine*, shot in 1952. He performed a memorable hopping dance that proved the highlight of his next picture, *Small Town Girl* (1953), and, by his third appearance in front of the cameras, later that same year, he was playing the title role in *The Affairs of Dobie Gillis*. The *New York Times* called him "an extraordinarily able dancer and a thoroughly agreeable performer."

Van became a regular sight on television, guesting on Sullivan and Gleason before taking the host's chair on his own shows: forgotten items with names like *The Fun Factory* and *Make Me Laugh*. He staged a Broadway comeback in 1971, starring as Billy Early in a revival of *No, No Nanette*, the same show that had been a career peak for Dick's aunt Florence many years earlier. The revival was a success, as anachronistic as it must have seemed to the longhairs of the day, and proved to be a personal highlight for Van as well. He spent the rest of the 1970s in both films and TV (logging appearances on *Vegas, Battlestar Galactica,* and, of course, *The Love Boat* and *Fantasy Island*). His last public appearance was as the host of the Miss America Pageant in 1980. That summer he would become the first of Miller's old gang to pass on, dying of cancer at age fifty-one.

Billy Levy was, according to Jack Silverman, "a very good looking guy. But he was very quiet. We made a lot of noise, but he just had great looks. That was his forté or whatever." Levy's real talent was drawing, of course, and he and Dick had logged many hours together at the drafting table Levy kept in his room, drawing gladiators and plotting their conquest of the cartoon industry. Levy's mother wasn't happy with her son's choice of a friend. "I don't want you hanging around that Dick Miller," she told Billy. "He smokes." Levy explained to his mother that he himself did not, and wasn't likely to start, since the one time he'd tried it he had nearly coughed his brains out. Still, for whatever reason, Miller was considered an oddball, and not just by Levy's mother. "Our parents thought Dickie was weird," Silverman recalled. "And he *was* a little bit weird, but we loved him, we got along fine."

Miller might well have presented as odd to anyone unacquainted with showfolk. He was a performer, a live wire, a firecracker. At any moment he might throw a zinger, dance a soft-shoe, or let loose with the Durante-esque "Hat-cha-cha-cha!" His ambition was apparent to everyone, yet his goals were obscure even to himself. He was a dynamo without direction, part Andy Hardy, part Duddy Kravitz. He seemed meant for something, but no one knew what.

"We all had music or art in our background, and it developed as it went along," Bill Levy said. Levy's own artistic talents and ambitions, and the music-heavy cauldron in which he'd spent his adolescence, served him well. After he left school he lucked into an entry-level job in the art department of Columbia Records. From there he moved to MCA/Decca and then to Polygram, where he rose to the position of creative vice-president. Along the way he worked with acts from James Brown to Yoko Ono (Levy was the only record exec allowed by the Godfather of Soul to call him "James" rather than "Mr. Brown," apparently), art directed albums like *Jesus Christ Superstar,* and picked up four Grammy nominations for Best Album Cover. In his later years he took up writing, both in prose and screenplay form. Miller is especially fond of one of Levy's unproduced screenplays, a comedy called "Who's Defaming the Walk of Fame," in which criminals pry the cast of *Casablanca* up from the Hollywood and Vine pavements one star at a time. Eventually he retired from the record business, wore a silver goatee, lived in Arizona, and maintained a blog in which he told rock 'n' roll tales from his storied career.

Jack Silverman, or 'Scatman' Jack Silverman as he became known, was another born musician. His father had a music studio in the Bronx, where he gave lessons to Jack and to others, and Silverman became proficient on the tenor sax. He was a good singer too: a perfect front man. He could run a line of patter and keep audiences—that is to say, his friends—laughing. His memory of those years boiled down to simple fun: "We were into having a good time, and music and laughter and all that good stuff." Even as the others made their way out into the world to pursue their dreams, Silverman stayed in the Bronx and kept the party going, making music and having a great time. In 1950 he joined the service and went to Korea; when he came back, he remembered, "it seemed like everybody had kind of disappeared." Dick and Bobby were in California; Billy and Shelley Kopp were in school.

Things didn't break Jack's way at first. Dick recalled getting a letter from Silverman that, he said, "no kidding, was actually tear-stained. And he said, 'I've got to give up my horn. I'm going to work for my uncle so-and-so in the market business'" (Miller, not someone who habitually held on to correspondence, kept the letter for years). For the next while Silverman led the lowest-profile life of the five friends, but in his late 60s he moved down to Florida and took up his music again. The good times came back with it. "I'm alive and well and scattin' and playing the horn and emceeing things," he said, noting that there was no shortage of musicians to play with, as so many big band players had retired to the area. "I'm in the pool every day, the weather is great," he said. "I'm a very lucky guy."

In their late teens, after Miller's navy service, the two friends took a stab at songwriting. Arthur Godfrey's radio show was popular at the time—he was still the warm-hearted chum who spoke directly to you, not yet the peevish control freak who fired people on the air—and his bandleader, Archie Bleyer, was known as a man of limited follicular coverage. With this in mind, Dickie and Jackie got an idea for a satirical song, which they wrote up and sent in to the show. They listened avidly thereafter, but the composition never made the airwaves. Jack Silverman sang all he could recall of this ditty over the phone in a crackly, charming, old-man voice. It went like this:

> I used to say 'I hope my hair will never turn grey'
> But now I like it anyway
> 'Cause I'm getting balder every day ...

Shelley Kopp was in many ways the odd man out in this group. "He was the geek, he was the brain," Silverman recalled. "He wore glasses and he was a little klutzy." Shelley was not a dancer and never joined the Poe Park contests, but he played the guitar. In fact, he tried turning Miller on to the guitar, with near-disastrous results. "That's a good instrument, beautiful instrument," Miller thought, listening to Shelley play. Kopp encouraged him to pick it up so they could play together. Dick signed up for lessons, and after several months Kopp asked to hear what Miller had learned. Dick played the three chords he had been taught and ran a little scale, and Kopp frowned, unimpressed. "That's it?"

Miller, now feeling he was being swindled, returned to the teacher with his fists balled, and demanded to know why he had not yet been taught any proper songs to play. An argument followed, and the hot-tempered young Dick picked up his guitar and clobbered the instructor right over the head. "Like in the movies, I expected this thing to fall apart," Miller said. "But it was a strong guitar. It didn't break, just went BA-A-A-A-NG! And I thought, if I'd been playing the trumpet, I'd have killed him! Never got over that." Police were called, and Miller told them the teacher had struck first, which was completely untrue. The matter ended in court, but the case was tossed out because Miller was both young and, apparently, chagrined by his actions. "The judge," he said, "told me to get another teacher."

Miller gave up the guitar but stuck with the drums, playing in a number of nameless aggregations through his high school years. Kopp was becoming interested in psychiatry, a passion he would also pass on to Miller. Like many of Miller's passions it would flare up, burn brightly for a time, and die out to be quickly replaced by something else. But Kopp would stick with it, brilliantly. He took his schooling in New York City, receiving a master's degree in 1953, married his wife Marjorie the same year, then went to work at various institutions in New Jersey. In the early 1960s the Kopps relocated to Washington DC, and Sheldon soon had a thriving private practice. He also began writing books; eventually he wrote seventeen of them, most of which would have been found in the bookstore's self-help sections. The most famous of these is undoubtedly *If You See the Buddha on the Road, Kill Him!*, published in 1972. It was a bestseller, and though it is often grouped with other New

Agey tomes like *Zen and the Art of Motorcycle Maintenance*, it is ultimately an exhortation to divest oneself of any gurus, or any search for gurus, or any thought of finding a guru to help you through your distress. The book's core, and Kopp's most lasting cultural legacy, is the Eschatological Laundry List, forty-three epigrammatic statements encouraging self-actualization in a sympathetic but no-nonsense tone. Here are some of its points:

1. This is it.
2. There are no hidden meanings.
3. You can't get there from here, and besides there is no place to go.
4. We are already dying, and we'll be dead a long time.
12. It's a random universe to which we bring meaning.
17. There are no great men.
18. If you have a hero, look again; you have diminished yourself in some way.
19. Everyone lies, cheats, pretends (yes, you too, and most certainly myself).
25. Childhood is a nightmare.
27. Each of us is ultimately alone.
31. How strange, that so often, it all seems worth it.

Kopp's list still hits a chord today: it can be found all over the Internet, properly attributed or otherwise. It has at any rate long outlived its author. Kopp was the second of Miller's old pals to shuffle off, contracting pneumonia and passing away on his seventieth birthday, March 29, 1999.

These five friends kept close company for perhaps six or seven years, and even this short time was broken up and diminished by schooling, travels, and Miller's year or so of navy service. But the bonds were strong and lasting. The three surviving men, despite gaps in communication as long as half a century, still spoke of each other as though of their best friends. "Formative" seems a monumentally inadequate word to describe the period in which their bonds were forged. They were the sort of pals you see in the movies or find in sentimental fiction.

But it's not as though they all got together and cured cancer, or went to the moon, or assassinated the Fuhrer. They had fun; that's what they did. In fact, they had cards made to that effect, each guy with his name printed under the official-looking heading "Fun, Inc." These were passed around at the park, at dances, and at parties to any pretty girls who might be expected to fall for such a ploy; and a clever gambit it sounds, on paper at least, though the actual effectiveness of the technique has not been recorded by history.

Pranks and other jollities were a big part of the incorporated fun. Bill Levy told the tale of how he and Miller opened a teabag, rolled the leaves, and passed it off to Shelley Kopp as a "jazz cigarette." They didn't dare smoke it, they told him, but maybe *he'd* be man enough to try. Bill and Dick did their best to keep straight faces as Kopp lit the ersatz joint, took a few exploratory puffs, and proceeded to bliss out, telling his friends between hits and giggles that this was good stuff, man, they really ought to try it. Finally Miller and Levy could take it no longer and burst into laughter, and it dawned on Kopp that he'd been had. It was a classic nerd-burn.

One night, when they were all sitting around someone's apartment, playing cards, they dug a bottle of booze from the liquor cabinet. Jack Silverman "just drank too much, too fast," Bill Levy remembered. Silverman tottered into the shower in a bid to sober up, but, coming out, he was as drunk as ever, and now naked and wet in the bargain. He pleaded for help in getting dressed, and the fellows complied, but put all his clothes on backwards. They helped him home to the apartment he shared with his parents and his sister, and spent the rest of the night laughing at the thought of poor Silverman stumbling around, trying to undress himself.

Another jape: At a party, Bobby Van once filled a large bottle with water, then made his way to the bathroom, hiding the bottle while telling everyone how badly he had to go. He spent the next five minutes trickling the contents of the water into the toilet as loudly as possible, as the rest of the partygoers tried not to listen, while privately wondering how much pee one lanky teenager could possibly contain.

Small potatoes as pranks go, but it was all about fun for these guys—easy, comfortable fun. They were glorying in their youth, in their time and place, in their friendship and in their future. They were confident: they had the talent and they had the time. Romance buoyed them still further. In the summer of his sixteenth year, with a girl named Myrna, Miller had a fling so intense that he had her name tattooed on his arm. Years later it was still there, smudged across Miller's Popeye forearm with all his other navy ink.

Despite all the frolic, harsh realities intruded. One night Miller and a few others were hanging around at a friend's place when the friend got a frantic call from the mother of an East Bronx acquaintance. The boy had taken some kind of drug, had locked himself in the bathroom, and was no longer answering his mother's repeated pounding. Miller's friend decided to go over and see what he could do; Miller and a few others tagged along. By the time they got to the apartment, the bathroom door had been broken down and the boy inside found dead of an overdose. The incident so shook Miller that he kept clear of any drug harder than marijuana for the rest of his life.

It's tempting to overromanticize Miller's teenage gang of friends, who seem to have been hatched with the fog filters and sepia tones of old-time nostalgia already laid over. One can imagine them the stars of a Runyonesque revue, or solving mysteries in their spare time, or fighting ghosts like the Bowery Boys. They went on to have big careers and fascinating lives, but in many ways they never really left the Bronx. Certainly the Bronx never left them.

Miller, in particular, is a walking billboard for the borough, advertising not just its existence but its amiable, homely, occasionally rough-edged qualities. Whether they're from the Old West or outer space, ultimately his characters are always from the Bronx; yet somehow they're still completely convincing. Off-screen, when he tells a story and quotes the other people he's talking about in his laconic, defiantly non-rhotic dialect, those parties are instantly retrofitted as Bronxites themselves. It's a big part of his charm.

As critical to his makeup as the Bronx is, however, the physical break with the place has been complete. A decade or two after leaving it for good, he returned to New York and was in Manhattan visiting with Bill Levy. "I want to go up to the Bronx, I want to go see where we lived," Miller said. Levy told him not to bother: "It'll break your heart what it's become." After thinking on it for a while, Miller decided to take his old friend's advice, and in the end he never did go back.

4   I'll never forget that flying through the air

In the midst of these teenage antics, the war ended. Eugene Miller was discharged, and he returned to live with Dick and Rita in the Bronx for a couple of weeks, during which he announced his intention to move back to California permanently. He had acquired a car, a big DeSoto, and was planning a cross-country drive. Dick, whose memories of the West Coast were mostly pleasant, wasted no time. "I'm goin' with you," he told his brother.

The journey began inauspiciously. The siblings left the city before dawn, and a couple of hours later, somewhere just past Harrisburg, PA, with Eugene probably still at the wheel, the DeSoto skidded out and spun violently into the ditch. Gene and Dick stumbled out. Neither was hurt, but not only was their big, heavy car angled crazily in a ditch, it seemed certain that it was broken somehow as well. The front end had a caved-in, splay-footed look. It was barely six-thirty in the morning and traffic on the road was non-existent; the boys girded themselves for the long walk back to Harrisburg. But suddenly a truck appeared beside them, the window was cranked down, and a huge, friendly moon-face gazed out. "Got trouble?"

"Yeah, we're in the ditch."

"Well," said the man, stepping out, "let's get her on the road."

"I don't think we can move it," Gene started to say, but he went mute as the man emerged fully from his vehicle. He was enormous, easily the biggest man either Gene or Dick had ever seen, a Peterbilt in overalls. His name, he said, was Paul, but neither brother had the stones to prompt "Bunyan?" Another man, strong-looking too but not quite as large, was with him. They got under the bumper and pushed, and the car slid up onto the road as though it was made of balsa wood. The Miller brothers stared in open-mouthed astonishment.

Paul and the other man got back in their truck and told the brothers to follow them up the road. "We're farmers, but we fix cars," they explained. With the DeSoto bucking and grinding the whole way, nose down and ailing, they followed the behemoth and his friend for what seemed miles. Finally, after numerous turns down nameless dirt roads, they stopped in a dusty barnyard. Paul pushed the Millers' broken car into his barn, hooked a chain under the front end, and pulled it up to nearly a forty-five-degree angle. He didn't use some fancy chain lift to do it either, just a simple pulley; and again the Millers marvelled at the man's apparently superhuman strength.

The work took all day and into the evening. Something had been badly bent in the front end, and one of the men had to go into town to get some parts. Paul, of course, did all the heavy labour, handling wheels as if they were hula hoops and axles like bamboo sticks. If a car, a cow, or a wall was in his way, he moved it. Years before this scenario would become the textbook opening to a *Texas Chainsaw Massacre*-type slasher situation, Miller already was attuned to the possibility, and became more convinced with each passing hour that he and Eugene would never leave the farmyard alive. "Gene, they're going to kill us! They're going to kill us!" he whispered, but Gene, who had seen more of the world than his brother, shushed him and told him not to worry. The real concern was how much all this was going to cost. Suppertime came and the men offered the Millers a place at their table. By nine the car was ready, but it was too late to start driving, so the farmer-mechanics offered a spare room for the night. They had an accordion hanging on the wall in their living room, and Gene, who'd taken lessons, squeezed out a couple of numbers before bedtime.

In the morning Gene hurried to settle accounts. The men did a few calculations and named an absurdly low figure for the parts and labour. For supper and the room, they tacked on an extra dollar. Gene paid it happily, and the brothers were on their way once again, not quite able to believe their amazing good fortune in meeting precisely the people they needed to help them out of their jam. "That was one of the few life miracles that I've seen, that I've lived," Miller said, still astonished many decades later.

The long trip west offered the brothers a chance to reconnect after Gene's three years at war, and Dick was much taken with his stories. After finding himself on the scene of some kind of soldierly crime in the Philippines, Gene had been asked to help investigate it, and shortly thereafter had been seconded into the army's Criminal Investigation Division (CID). He'd spent the bulk of the war with the CID and came away with detecting experience he used for the rest of his career. In Los Angeles the brothers stayed with their aunt Tillie and uncle Boris Goldblatt, who had a house on a little street called Glen Green, just off Beachwood, familiar territory for Dick. Tillie was Ira's sister, and Boris was a head carpenter at a movie studio on Melrose called Tec-Art, and was also a big wheel in the union. He was a man of some influence who was able to pull some strings and find Eugene a position at Fox doing historical research for their period pictures. Dick took a job in a warehouse, staying only as long as it took to make enough money to get back to New York on his own.

At the cessation of hostilities, Miller was, he says, "not disappointed exactly, but I figured, 'I'll join anyway.'" He wanted to get in on the action as Eugene had done, to collect some war stories of his own, to salve his adventurous spirit, to serve his country; and he was counting the days until he either turned seventeen or looked seventeen. He probably was a little disappointed when the war ended, but even as a teenager he was a pragmatic sort; joining the navy in peacetime was the next best thing to joining it in war, and certainly safer.

On his return to New York, very soon after his seventeenth birthday, Miller made his way to the hulking post office building at 90 Church Street in Lower Manhattan, where there was a navy recruiting station, and joined up. After years of worrying for Eugene's safety, Rita was understandably unhappy to see her other boy go, her baby. But soon Dick was off to Camp Peary in Virginia for a buzz cut and eight weeks of training. He was issued a sea bag and taught how to pack it. To his surprise he found he was a crack shot on the rifle range, and his chief, evidently a kindly soul and impressed with Miller's marksmanship, somewhere found a cut-down rifle more suited to the young man's diminutive frame. At the end of the training he was given his sailor's apparel—a Dixie cup and crackerjacks—and was assigned to duties on board CV-112, the USS *Siboney*, out of San Diego. It was back to the West Coast for Miller once again.

The *Siboney* was an appropriate vessel for Miller, as she, too, had missed out on the war. She was an escort carrier that could serve as a floating base for as many as thirty planes, and was referred to by her 1,066-strong complement, generally with affection, as the "Sea Bunny." She'd been commissioned on May 14, 1945, with the amiable but protocol-insistent Stanhope Cotton Ring in command, and, after having been loaded up with bombs, aircraft, and personnel, stood out of San Diego for Pearl Harbor. She arrived August 15, the day of Japan's surrender, so drifted around the Pacific conducting supply missions, search-and-rescue operations, and other relatively benign tasks. She arrived back in the US in January 1946, and after a commander switch—the new CO was Rear Admiral William Onahan Gallery—and another short Pacific mission, returned to San Diego in early May, when Miller joined her company.

It was pretty quickly plain this was not going to be a long-term thing for the teenage Dick. There was no war, after all, just an awful lot of float-she-may, shine-she-must; absent another quick global conflict, his tales would never equal Eugene's. He certainly took every opportunity for adventure, even giving the submarine corps a try; but, after a few days below, the claustrophobia overwhelmed him. Miller was constitutionally anti-authoritarian, and though he had no major trouble with his superiors during his stint and never ended up in the brig, obeying orders and following protocols were not in his nature. But, as ever, he acted the part, playing the good sailor as well as he would later play Walter Paisley.

Even with his wiles and natural thespian talent, Miller could not fool California bartenders into believing he was twenty-one. So every weekend, when the other sailors would blow their paycheques on booze, Miller would save his, and he soon had enough to operate a loan outfit for constitutionally light-pocketed swabbies. It must have been regarded by the brass as an essential part of the ship's economy, because Miller didn't have to hide it. He actually had a little scrap-wood booth, like Lucy in the *Peanuts* cartoons, set up beside the official navy pay table, where he waited to accept loan repayments. Like any good navy slusher, he charged a criminal interest—it was twenty-five percent at least—but his business thrived, and he left the service with a lot more than sailor's pay in his pocket. "It's a good thing the statute of limitations is up on usury," Lainie Miller remarked on hearing this story.

As lucrative as the loan business was, it couldn't fully counteract the drudgery of the navy in peacetime. But Miller, being Miller and therefore some kind of living magnet for eventfulness, managed to collect a tour of duty's worth of war stories without his ship's ever leaving port. Trouble first came looking for him in the form of a fellow Bronxite, a hulk named Dutch Cogswell. Cogswell was, says Miller, "a Nazi. A Jew hater and a Jew baiter." So devoted was Cogswell to his anti-Semitism that he roamed the ship actively looking for Jews to beat up—strictly enlisted men, of course. He started with the largest and worked his way down, pummelling each successive "kike" to the deck. To Miller, who'd never in his life experienced any direct anti-Semitism—nothing, at any rate, beyond being called a "Jew bastard" back in the Bronx by Italians whom he was cheerfully calling "Guinea bastards" in return —it was totally baffling. "You're next, Miller," his shipmates all whispered. "Dutch is gonna get you!"

And Dutch surely did. Miller was on deck one day, working out with free weights, when Cogswell made his move. Miller grabbed an iron bar and swung it wildly at the larger man, shouting, "You're not gonna get me! I'm gonna let you have it!" But Cogswell just batted the bar away, picked Miller up over his head, and threw him into the air, past the bulkhead, over the railing and down, down, into San Diego Bay. "I'll never forget that flying through the air," Miller said, still amazed to have been thrown off an aircraft carrier. He landed in the foul, brackish sludge that passed for water in the pre-cleanup days, and, sputtering, managed to glug and slug his way to a pier ladder. He climbed up, "covered in shit and everything from this water," made his way to the *Siboney*'s gangplank, and requested permission to come aboard. "And I just looked at Cogswell and said, 'I'm gonna get this guy.'"

The weekend after his dunking at Cogswell's hands, Miller went on liberty. "*Siboney*—rhymes with 'liberty!'" was the word around the ship. And the first thing anyone stationed in San Diego does when they're on liberty is get out of San Diego, so there Miller was, standing on the highway, trying to thumb his way up to Los Angeles. As he waited for a ride he spotted a familiar, hulking figure approaching from across the road. "Sweet wingalls, what's it gonna be?" thought Miller. "I'm all alone here." But Cogswell, his bigot's rage evidently sated for the moment, merely asked if he could travel with Miller to LA. "We became buddies," Miller says. "Up to a point."

The two made their way up to Los Angeles, where it was easier for Miller to find a drink. He also wanted to look up some of his old Hollywood pals. Tiny and Rusty had both gone overseas and been killed in action, but Miller had other ideas anyway. Steeling his nerve, he knocked on Maggie's door. Whether he did this out of some teenage notion of doing the right thing, or whether he'd persuaded himself the whole pregnancy thing had been a crazy dream or some sort of misunderstanding, is impossible to say now. At any rate the door opened to Maggie's mother, who remembered Dick instantly, even in his navy blues. Maggie was not at home, but she was nearby in Delongpre Park, strolling with the baby. Would Dickie like to join them for dinner later? Dick thanked her and demurred, he had to get back to the base.

He walked to Delongpre Park, a small, treed patch of land with walkways converging on a phallic monument to Rudolph Valentino that had been erected in the centre. Maggie was there, pushing a carriage. The reunion was touching and sincere, but when Miller looked at the baby, any lingering or self-constructed doubts that it was his were dispelled. The little girl looked exactly like Dick. It was uncanny. Despite this, everyone else, including Maggie's mother, had assumed the baby to be Rusty's, and Maggie had never disabused them of the notion. They chatted for another half-hour or so, and then, when Maggie, too, invited him for dinner, Miller mumbled the same excuse about having to get back to base and took his leave. He never saw his daughter again, and today can't remember her name. But Maggie's mother, who perhaps knew more than either Maggie or Miller thought she did, kept in touch. For the next decade, as the little girl grew up believing her father was a red-headed football hero who'd been killed in the war, her grandmother sent Miller progress reports: how she was doing in school, where she was going on holidays, and so forth. Eventually the letters tailed off, and that was it. Where septuagenarian Dickette Jr. is today, nobody can say: not even her, since she doesn't know that's who she is.

Miller found Dutch Cogswell and resumed his weekend. It was a bar crawl mainly, and in a situation like that, with a guy like Dutch—a liberty risk if ever there was one—sooner or later trouble was going to come. It came in the form of some Marines with whom Cogswell promptly got into a shouting match. Punches were thrown, but, improbably enough, the situation calmed and everyone settled down, more or less. But on the way to the San Diego train—nobody on a Cinderella liberty was foolish enough to risk hitchhiking back on a Sunday night, lest rides be scarce—they ran into the same pack of Marines. They were in a salty mood, hungover (Cogswell and Miller, on the other hand, were still drunk), and the conflict heated up again. The Marines followed Cogswell and Miller to the station, jeering, and watched as they got on the train. The two sailors took their seats, and, as the train spat out its first slow chuffs, Cogswell banged on the glass and started making faces at Uncle Sam's Misguided Children, who were not amused. Suddenly a huge Marine fist came crashing through the glass. Cogswell returned the punch, sending his own fist back through the shattered panes, nailing the guy right in the chops. But when Dutch drew his arm back in, he ripped it wide open from elbow to wrist. Sheets of blood poured forth. As the train wheezed and chugged out of the station, Miller wrapped the bleeding arm, "got him all tourniqueted up. Saved his life, basically."

When they arrived back in San Diego, Miller took the pale Cogswell to the navy hospital there, where the doctors patched him up. From then on he had no further trouble with the hulking racist. He even visited him in the hospital and later loaned him money. But Cogswell, evidently an ingrate as well as a bigot, never paid him back, which, to Miller, is one of the greatest crimes you can perpetrate. Cogswell, a short timer, got his discharge before Miller and headed back to the Bronx. "I'll see you up at

St. Anne's Avenue," he told Dick. Miller protested that Cogswell still owed him money, but Cogswell just laughed and waved a meaty fist. "Try and collect!" he challenged.

Miller's Cogswell-related visits to the navy hospital in Coronado were not to be his last. Some time later, on another leave, Miller was travelling on an overcrowded liberty boat full of navy personnel eager for their day or two of freedom. People were hanging off the sides, their legs skipping the wake. A WAVE who'd been clutching a rail fell overboard, and Miller and another sailor jumped in after her. "Naturally I went in," chuckled Miller. "I'm the hero of the picture!" Miller pulled the half-drowned WAVE out and he and the other sailor accompanied her to the hospital. Staff took their sodden clothes, gave them hospital whites to wear, and told them they had half an hour to kill while their clothing dried.

A strange figure then materialized, also in hospital whites. "You gotta picture this guy," Miller said, his powers of description temporarily stymied at the memory of this odd, misshapen, almost phantom character. "He was all freckles, and he had a wild haircut that went up like this"—Miller pushed his hands straight up and then sideways—"and he had this really weird face. A really, really weird face. The guy made Rondo Hatton look like Cary Grant."

This alarming mutant asked Miller and his companion if they were waiting for their clothes. They managed to stammer that, yes, they were. "Come with me," the guy said. "I'll show you something." He led them down through the hospital, and as the smell of chemicals grew Miller realized they were heading into the morgue. Nobody else was there, and the peculiar orderly, or whatever he was, led them to a table with a sheet-covered body on it. He pulled back the sheet to reveal the corpse of a young woman. The dreadful man fixed his hot-needle gaze on the two sailors and grinned terribly. "I like 'em dead," he said. "You want a piece?"

All Miller and his equally horrified companion could do was murmur "No" and back away. Recalling this grotesque incident and the sinister, freckled ghoul almost seventy years later, Miller shivered and shook his head. "It was right out of a picture," he said. "I didn't know it then, but I was starting in the horror field early."

Probably because of his persecution at the hands of Cogswell, and the possibility of other Cogswells making the scene at some point during his service, and also because it came with a host of small perks like better chow and extra free time, Miller took up boxing. He was small, but wiry and strong, and had always been a fighter—just ask Bobby Jordan. On his return from California, still smarting at the forced transfer from Hollywood High to Leconte Junior, he became "just a mean little kid," and found himself scrapping regularly. "One-punch fights," he recalled. "Bang, that's it, it's over. Win some, lose some."

At 112 pounds, Miller was a flyweight, and his opponents were generally the district's Filipino mess boys. "They'd teach 'em to box and they'd get in the ring with me, and I'd belt 'em around for a while," he said. In his weight class there wasn't too much competition, and he ran through the mess boys pretty quickly; after four fights he was the 11th Naval District champ. He didn't keep the title for long. A few fights later a particularly tough *paré* entered the ring with Miller, "and all of a sudden there's blood all over the place. And it's my blood! This guy was killing me, and I couldn't land a punch!" Miller was declared the winner nevertheless, presumably for the racial optics or some such 1940s nonsense, and he quit boxing as soon as they peeled him off the canvas: "That's it. That's what it was like to get beat up in the ring, and I quit." But his reputation as a pugilist had been established, and this was a great help both in dissuading racist bullies and ensuring timely repayments in his loan shark business. It also helped out when liberty weekends threatened to get a little risky.

Dutch Cogswell was not the only bigot on board the *Siboney*, according to Miller. He recalled the ship's executive officer, a man named Keith Elliott Taylor ("I'll never forget *him*," Miller said several times), who apparently just laughed when Miller asked for a leave on the upcoming Jewish holiday of Yom Kippur. "You're not Jewish, are you?" Taylor asked. Miller confirmed that, while he didn't particularly look it, he was, and could the XO please just sign off on the leave? "I'll get around to it," Taylor told him. But in a way he had been right to scoff at Dick's request: Miller's upbringing had been completely secular, and he didn't know much more about these fasting days than any goyim, had never celebrated them, and had played the Jewish card simply to get a day off. The gambit had repercussions. "From then on," Miller said, "it was like hell [on the ship]. It was like a curtain came down. But it was subtle. [Taylor] never mentioned one word of hate, but it was just there." Now there were two anti-Semites aboard the *Siboney* upon whom Seaman Miller wished to wreak his terrible vengeance.

Naturally, along with scars, Miller picked up some ink while he was in the navy. Amidst the usual Popeye specials on his arm—the name of his ship, a skull, an actual anchor—one can find the name Myrna, his pre-navy summer love. "I kind of thought of her as my girl," Miller said, and in this spirit he got the tattoo, just shortly before XO Taylor finally granted his leave. "And when they give you leave, you gotta leave," as the navy saying goes. Back to New York he went, and, after visiting his mother, he made his way to Myrna's apartment building, still wearing his navy blues. He knocked on the door, and an enormous, broad-shouldered young woman answered. "Who are you?" she asked.

"Here to see Myrna, my girl," Miller replied.

"*My* girl," the giantess corrected him, slamming the door.

Confused but undaunted, Miller made his way out onto the fire escape. It was early spring, cold and rainy. Miller spied Myrna and knocked at the window. "Let me in!" he cried, his voice cracking. "Sweet wingalls, what are you doing to me?"

"Go away, would you just go away!" Myrna screamed back. From outside the window Dick pointed out his tattoo, but she just kept shaking her head violently. "I'm sorry about the tattoo, go away!"

"You're playin' mumbletypeg with my heart!" Miller sobbed. He crawled off the fire escape, left the building, paid a nickel, and jumped on the Long Island Railway train. It took him out to Far Rockaway, his old stomping ground. The rain and chill were pervasive, the boardwalk deserted, the sea slate grey and stormy. A dismal beach stretched out before him, wet-sack brown all the way out to the crashing water, and he started walking in that direction. "I wanted to go into the ocean and forget everything," Miller said. "I walked out into the ocean in the cold weather, and a wave hit me and I said, 'What the hell am I doing?'"

He turned around, struggled out, and got back on the train, sopping wet and frozen. By the time they were crossing the bridge, he had the sniffles. By the next morning it was a terrible cold, and he got on the subway to go somewhere. He sneezed, and "it was like a green bedspread." A duvet of snot burst out of his nose, and, like the vomit that had attacked him at the fun fair, formed an eerie, floating slime that seemed to hang in the air, making urgent but arcane gestures, like something out of *Ghostbusters* or the *Necronomicon*. Finally the emerald surprise flopped to the subway floor and oozed back and forth with the movements of the train. The passengers looked on, stepping gingerly as they walked off the car. Miller was aghast, but also strangely cleansed, in both a pulmonary and an emotional sense. "I got over Myrna right after that," he said. The grotesque sneeze had really been a purging.

Just as well: he was back in San Diego before he knew it. The shipboard and liberty shenanigans continued, mostly in the company of the colourful sailor friends he'd collected on the ship. There was another ironically named Tiny, for instance, this one a Mexican kid named Tiny Aguilar. ("When you're my size, everybody's ironically named Tiny," Miller said.) Miller spent some of his liberties with Tiny, visiting his family, who lived somewhere up the coast.

And of course there was a guy named Tex. "I guess every ship in the navy has a guy named Tex," said Miller. Tex had a heavily pregnant girlfriend (though he himself was not the father), and her habit was to take the name of her current boyfriend and use it as her own for the duration, so she also was Tex. Miller and the lady-Tex spent a lot of time together since neither was welcome in the local watering holes. He socialized with lady-Tex and her friends more and more as she advanced through her term. Finally, one evening when she was in her eighth month, Dick was in her apartment along with a number of other young women, and lady-Tex suddenly went into labour. Panic ensued. One of the girls went off to find a doctor; the rest squawked around the apartment, boiling water and wetting towels. The labour was a swift one, and Miller, all of seventeen years old, realized it would be up to him to see it through. "I just figured, okay, I'm going to do it," he said.

Thankfully it was an easy birth, at least from Miller's perspective, though the *Gone With the Wind* line "I don't know nothin' 'bout birthin' no babies!" was running through his head on a loop. There was much screaming and shrieking from the other ladies, but Miller and Tex's girl maintained their cool and managed to extricate the infant; Miller even cut the umbilical cord himself. The doctor arrived, surveyed the scene, and declared that Dick had done a good job. "At that moment," Miller said, "I like to collapsed. I went into shock."

Miller had barely recovered from this when he was put onto a work detail on board the *Siboney*. An ammo locker was to be cleared out: thousands upon thousands of smaller calibre rounds had to be moved from one place to another for some reason that was above a bluejacket's pay grade. Miller was working with five or six others, humping cases of ammunition out of the locker, around a corner, and down the passage to another compartment.

Somebody, not Miller, made the mind-boggling decision to pause in the locker for a smoke. Miller and another sailor were approaching the locker when the ammunition went off. "There was this tremendous explosion," Miller said. "But it was like '*br-r-r-r-r-r-r-tang-tang-tang-tang.*' It went on and on forever. It was individually firing, all these bullets, *pr-r-rang*, like that. And bullets were flying all over the place, my hat was full of them."

Miller was hit in the leg by one of the rogue bullets. The guy just in front of him was shot too, and he fell on top of Miller, involuntarily protecting him. A sailor around the corner was shot multiple times and was killed. The man inside the locker, the genius who had taken the smoke break, was never found. He had simply disintegrated.

And so Miller found himself at the navy hospital once again, but for the last time. The leg wound was not serious and the bullet was removed swiftly and easily; but as Miller limped about the ship it became clear he needed his discharge from the navy, ASAFP. His tour of duty was ending, and scuttlebutt was that the *Siboney* would be sailing soon, making her way to the other side of the continent, to Norfolk, Virginia—or No Fuck, Vagina, in naval parlance. Miller wanted to get to the other side of the continent, sure, but he wanted to take the train there and wear his civvies on the way. He applied for his separation and waited, and in the meantime considered how he might even the score with Lieutenant Commander Taylor, who, he was still convinced, was a bigot who had actively connived to make his tour as unpleasant as possible.

A dirty dicking (you can look that up) might have been apt, but it was risky and not really Miller's style; besides, he wanted something more public. When it became clear that Miller's EAOS (End of Active Obligated Service) would occur on Navy Day, a rough idea presented itself. There would be an admiral's inspection of the *Siboney* that day, and Taylor, the XO, would be on the hook for any less-than-shipshape conditions. October 27, 1946, came along, and Miller packed his duffel. Timing now was critical. The flight deck had been roped off to keep it scuff-free, but soon Miller's sea bag was sitting there, and was noticed by Taylor and the other officers only as they were preparing to receive the visiting admiral. A jeep pulled up near the bottom of the gangplank: Miller's ride to the separation centre, where he would be transformed into the civilian he'd always remained at heart.

As the XO puzzled over the errant sea bag, the admiral's party pulled up on the pier below, unseen by the officers. Miller made his move, leaping into view before the them: "Permission to leave ship, sir!"

"What the fuck are you doing?" Taylor demanded.

"Permission to leave ship, sir! My ride is here, I've got to go!"

"Get off the ship!" Taylor fairly shouted, desperate to have Miller and his gear gone before the admiral's arrival. But it was too late. Miller saluted, grabbed his bag, and headed down the gangplank. The admiral and his party had already started up, and there followed an awkward, Chaplinesque comedy in the middle, with Miller smiling and saluting wildly as the heavy brass were forced to move out of his way while trying mechanically to return the salutes as best they could. Miller made it down to his jeep and asked the driver—a chief petty officer who had taken the driver's seat himself for an opportunity to get a look at the visiting admiral—to wait a few extra moments on the pier. He was not disappointed. The admiral gestured wildly from Taylor to the gangplank, waving his arms in rage, and even from that distance it was clear an epic chewing-out was being delivered to the visibly cowering XO. Miller indicated to the CPO that now would be a good time to screech away, and he spent the next two days at the separation centre, sweating bullets, waiting for the SPs to come and clap him in irons for his insubordination. But nothing happened, and he was soon on civvy street again: Miller the swingin' hepcat, the dancer, the lover, the partycrat. Strangely, his discharge papers listed his middle name as "Noel," when in fact Miller has no official middle name. Rita called him Noel now and again—the name she had wished for her second son because of his Christmas birthday—but how the navy ever got wind of this is a mystery.

What did Miller get out of his year in Uncle Sam's canoe club, aside from a middle name made semi-official and the prolonged exposure to asbestos all navy personnel of the day unknowingly risked? Aspects of human nature previously unknown to him were revealed: he discovered the scourge of anti-Semitism at the very same time the world was learning the true, horrific dimensions of the Holocaust; he suffered his first real heartbreak; he took a journey into the depths of depravity in the basement of the Balboa navy hospital; he delivered a baby; he was shot without assistance from a gun. In that year he accumulated enough fuel for a secondary career as raconteur, and if he was never a professional chatterbox in the manner of Orson Bean or Peter Ustinov, he was surely a top-ranking amateur. He returned to New York bubbling over with sea stories and tales of adventure, but as yet with no plan to become an actor—with no plan at all, in fact.

5   *The pigeons are free*

In late 1946 when Miller returned to New York, Rita was living on Long Island once again. Dick moved in with her, temporarily he hoped, and for the first few weeks spent his time looking up old girlfriends. His navy loansharking had put a lot of money in his pocket: he had almost $7,000, a fortune in those days for a free and easy guy like Miller, and he spent it with gusto.

Some of the money went for a tonsillectomy. He was eighteen years old and somehow still had his tonsils, and he went to the hospital, where he was injected with a local anaesthetic. "It didn't take," Miller said. "Gave me a couple more, and it didn't take. Gave me a couple more, and they figured this is all, we can't give him any more." The surgeon in charge of the operation was new; this was to be his first tonsillectomy. His mentor, an older doctor, would supervise, and he didn't want to hear any nonsense about bum anaesthetic. "We'll get 'em out!" the elder surgeon heartily proclaimed. Miller expected the experienced man to take over, as the young surgeon was not radiating confidence, but this didn't happen. The younger doctor bit his lip and went in to the un-anaesthetized Miller. "I was just, I was in pain," Miller said, blanching a bit in thinking of it.

Some of the money went to education. Miller had always had an odd relationship with schools, schooling, and scholars, and, in all his years of moving around, had racked up an impressive backlist of institutions. He'd missed out on his graduating year of high school, though, so his education felt incomplete. (This feeling would persist through his life, shaping him into a classic autodidact who read everything he could get his hands on.) He looked into college courses on all manner of subjects, hoping to find something that would give him the direction he was still missing. But, stick-to-itiveness not being one of Miller's virtues, a sustained course of study was never in the cards. Nevertheless, he began attending classes at various institutions around the city.

He also bought a car. It was a Crosley, a tiny green auto built by, and looking exactly as though it had been built by, a company better known for manufacturing refrigerators. It was a fine little runabout as far as Miller was concerned—"It makes me look like I'm six feet tall," he told his friends—but it put Dick on the butt-end of his pals' practical jokes. One evening Miller parked the car on the Grand Concourse, just across from the Paradise Theater, and left it; a while later Billy Levy and a few others happened by and spotted it. While waiting for Miller to return they got an idea: positioning themselves around the tiny car, they lifted it and carried it across the sidewalk to the entranceway of a shop that was closed for the night. Miller returned, saw his car, and threw up his hands as his buddies fell over laughing. As Dick was in the driver's seat getting ready to drive off the curb, he looked up and saw a cop's belt buckle outside the window. "These guys, they ..." Miller started to say, motioning at his so-called friends, but he was interrupted by the snap of the citation being pulled from the cop's book. Miller attempted to argue his case in front of a judge; no dice. A few weeks later he tried to improvise a parking space at a crosswalk, got a ticket, and again went to court to fight the good fight. Inspired by his experience on the Grand Concourse, he planned to claim japesters had pushed the car into the illegal zone, but he pulled the very same judge he'd just stood before, who upheld the citation and added a few cranky words of advice on top of it: "Get an anchor for that goddamn car!"

The gang made fun of the little Crosley, but they never turned down a ride. Miller would pick them up in the Bronx and they would motor down to Manhattan. In an effort to fit in with the rest of the downtown swells, they were dressed in the most expensive coats they could afford, and kept them buttoned tightly over the shabby clothes they wore beneath.

Eventually Miller tired of the car's sickly green colour and had it painted, and he once had an accident and found a troupe of itinerant panel beaters to pound out the dents in his bumper. For Miller, the car framed a critical chunk of his life: he remembered this period as the Crosley Years. "God, what a trip it was!" he cried. (Crosleys are not as fondly remembered by history as they are by Miller. Their stamped-tin engines couldn't withstand much heat, and one of the little cars made a crumpled, blood-spattered cameo in the infamously gruesome 1961 drivers' ed. film *Mechanized Death*.)

Hoping to hold on to his savings, Miller took a job washing dishes at a Long Island "candy store"—that is, a pharmacy with a lunch counter in it—for twenty dollars a week. He soon got thrown an unexpected promotion when, one day, the grill man failed to appear. The owner hustled Miller over to the stove, indicated various comestibles, and told him to get cooking: "You make eggs, you make bacon, you make cheese and tomato sandwiches," he said over Miller's protestations. "That's it, it's all right there." Miller, who'd never spent much time in a kitchen outside of peeling potatoes in the navy, figured it out as he went along. He figured out a few other things pretty quickly as well: first, that the owner was paying him a lot less than he'd paid the real, now vanished cook; and, second, that on top of this the owner was pilfering his tips. Miller tossed a small handful of change into the jar as a lure—"Nickels and dimes were the big tips then," he said—and kept watch. The owner's fat fingers soon had the jar emptied.

Miller was by now well practised at plotting revenge. Thanks to the Crosley and the mobility it offered, one of his tasks was fetching cigarettes (rolled gold in those postwar years) from the local wholesaler. Miller waited until cigarette day, made sure to collect his outstanding pay, drove to the warehouse, and picked up a large box packed with ten or twelve cartons of smokes. He stuffed it in the little car, gave a jaunty wave, and took off for home, now well-supplied with cigarettes and never to darken the candy store's doorstep again.

He still hung out in Poe Park, but sometimes there were consequences. One winter's day he was strolling past the park benches, swigging from a bottle of beer he had hidden in a paper bag. (The scientifically baseless scuttlebutt within the gang was that beer drunk in cold weather had twice the kick.) He walked past a bench that held two enormous identical twins—the notorious Solomon brothers. With his performative reflexes briefly overriding his instinct for self-preservation, he held the bag as though it contained not beer but a gun, and put on a nasal, Cagneyesque gangster voice: "Ehhh, ehhh, I'm gonna get drunk and shoot up the town, seeeee?"

One of the brothers motioned him to come over. Miller approached and was saying "What do you want?" when boom, exploding skyrockets, and he was on the ground, knocked out with a cracked jaw from the lightning uppercut one of the Solomons had given him. By the time he woke up the big twins were gone and Bobby, Jackie, and Billy were gathered around him, hoisting him up by the armpits and dragging him over to a group of girls as a conversation piece and object of sympathy. "Make believe you're hurt," they told him as they hustled him along.

"Make believe?" Dick slurred through a broken jaw. The dazed and incoherent Miller was a sufficiently compelling victim to get a conversation going with the ladies, but in the meantime the Solomons had returned and were looking to play Dick a little more chin music. One of the young women saved the day, telling the Solomons Miller hadn't meant anything by his tomfoolery, and was just a harmless neighbourhood buffoon. "He's into dancing, whaddaya want?" the girls said. The Solomons left him alone, and Miller was lucky they did, for they were nasty pieces of work: one of them ended up in the electric chair after reportedly murdering a woman on a rooftop somewhere just above Fordham Road.

Miller packed a lot into the years from 1947 to 1949. He took his first trip abroad, though it was absurdly brief and ultimately pointless. A friend of Miller's, with the Borscht Belt name of Schnozzy Hirsch, who was the son of a Bronx butcher and evidently a committed Zionist, tried to organize a trip to the newly formed and besieged Promised Land. He roped in six or seven Jewish lads from the neighbourhood, promising them high adventure and righteous glory on the order of the Lincoln Brigade's exploits in Spain a dozen years earlier. This sales pitch was good enough for Dick, who figured that if he could survive Cogswell, this would be a cinch.

Israel had been fighting their War of Independence since November 30, 1947; on May 14 of the following year, the State of Israel was officially established and the war was renewed in earnest. Volunteers from across the Jewish diaspora, most of them veterans of the Second World War, flocked to the baby state to lend their fighting skills. These fighters were called "Machal," an acronym for "Volunteers from Abroad" in Hebrew, and they came from at least forty-three countries from around the world. (If they'd formerly been with the Allies, they might well have experienced a bit of battlefield confusion on suddenly finding themselves fighting not just Arab forces but British ones as well.)

For Miller, who had been raised in as secular an environment as could be, and who had no strong opinion on the need for a Jewish state (though he was certainly aware of the ghastliness of the Holocaust, the news of which was motivation for many Machal), much less that particular Jewish state, it was a lark more than anything, another way of possibly gathering some war stories of his own. After a big hustle to organize passports and so forth, with the whole trip almost queered several times, Schnozzy and his squadron hastened to Italy and thence to Tel Aviv to join the rest of the Machalniks. But they found themselves curiously unwelcome. Israeli Defense Force (IDF) intelligence followed them from their hotel every time they left it; eventually they were called into an office and told that, while they were welcome to join the IDF any time they wanted, ragtag weekend warriors barely out of short pants were not what the state currently required. Moreover, American teenagers dying in its defence would not make good clippings for the starter nation's pressbook. Miller, for one, was in no hurry to join any nation's armed forces again so soon, or ever at all. The rest of them felt the same way, and within two days of its glorious arrival the Schnozzy Brigade was winging back stateside.

Miller still had absolutely no idea what he wanted to do with his life. He took different courses at a number of schools, including New York University, New York City College, and Columbia. Shelley Kopp was beginning his psychiatric studies, and Miller, taking inspiration from his friend's enthusiasm, enrolled in some psych courses himself. Eventually he had sufficient credit to be accepted into an orderly-type position at Bellevue, the oldest public hospital in the country, and the last stop for patients who'd hit "the bottom of the barrel," Miller said.

Miller's time at Bellevue was brief, but he used some of the same straight-shooting, emotionally unambiguous strategies he would later call upon as an actor, particularly in his signature role of Walter Paisley. "They had no title for me," he said, "but I took care of the nuts. The trouble was, most of the psychiatrists were terminology-laden. And I had a knack for breaking things down. Like, I could sit there and say, 'You're crazy.'" He lasted three or four months before the old Miller restlessness kicked in. "I just couldn't stand it," he said. "It was pitiful. It wasn't the green couch type of psychiatry. It was Bellevue Hospital, and it was pitiful. I just said, 'This is not for me.'"

At around the same time, Miller tried his hand on the gridiron. Eugene had been a football player in his youth until a broken collarbone ended his career, and Miller saw no reason not to try his own hand at the sport, especially as he could clear ten or twelve bucks a game. The Fordham Rams, the local team, who were going through a period of "good but not great" players, declining crowds, and mounting deficits, accepted him after a tryout. He played scatback, a offensive position calling for speed and cunning on the field. "I could always pick up three or four yards before I got nailed," he said. "I eventually did get nailed, and I quit." It was just like the boxing, Miller admitted, and so many other things: "Everything goes well, and then I get nailed and I stop."

Miller was in a frenzy of trying things out, searching for some traction in his life, some direction. He was entering his twenties, and most of his peers had at least a notion of what they wanted to do. Miller had none. He took wild, unusual jobs: he was a lumberjack, for instance, in Vermont. "They got a thing they called summer logging," he said. He went to see the hiring agent, "and the guy went 'blah-blah-blah,' and it sounded interesting. And I'd seen lumberjacks in the movies." Following his Hollywood idea of what a lumberjack looked like, he kitted himself out with clothes from Abercrombie & Fitch and showed up in the woods wearing pressed khakis, a checkered jacket, and a plaid hat with earflaps. Everybody else was in shorts and t-shirts. "I thought, Jesus Christ, I got the wrong thing here," he lamented. After two weeks of swinging an axe, the logging party went into town for what Miller expected and hoped would be a wild Saturday night, one he felt he'd earned. "Got drunk," he recalled, "and the guys were, 'Nothin's doin' up here, want to play cards?'" It was too much for the high-life-loving Miller. "I just packed it in," he said.

Back in New York—by this time he had left the nest for good and was living in Manhattan—Miller found a job with the Arthur Kudner advertising agency, a large firm whose diverse roster of clients included General Motors, Chesterfield cigarettes, Fruehof trailers, and the Florida Citrus Commission. But Miller was not drinking highballs for lunch, exchanging snappy patter, and chasing secretaries around a desk: he was doing tear sheets. This involved going through newspapers from around the country and tearing out the pages on which the firm's advertisements appeared. It was basement work, as low on the totem pole as you could be at an ad agency, and tedious as hell. Miller's latent instincts for labour organization, culturally acquired and inherited from his father, came to the fore and he suggested a new work routine to his fellow sheet-tearers. "If we skip lunch," he told them, "and if I do all the papers from here, and you do all the papers from here, we'd be going twice as fast." The scheme worked, and by three every afternoon Miller and his co-workers were "just sitting around, shootin' the shit." A manager protested that they were making the other departments look bad, and the work scheme was curtailed. Miller quit.

He tried his hand at sales, going door-to-door in the Bronx, hawking pots and pans; "finest cookware in the world," his patter had it. This job lasted no longer than any other, but it would provide him specific experience to draw on when he played Joe Piper, the doomed vacuum cleaner salesman in Roger Corman's *Not Of This Earth*. Other experience that would be relevant to his future avocation came in the late spring, when a friend invited him up to Hunter, New York, to paint flats for a summer stock theatre company. Though there was no pay as such, the change of scenery, the country air, the free food, and the reportedly abundant girls all sounded good to Miller.

Shortly after he arrived in Hunter, a miniscule part in the company's show (its title lost to history) became available and it was offered to Miller. He would play the role of a butler and have just a handful of lines. Could he handle it, they asked? "Sure," Miller told them. But when he walked out on stage on opening night, his memory deserted him. Fortunately the actor he was playing opposite, the lord of the manor in whatever country-house romance they were enacting, was "an old pro" who immediately recognized what was happening and turned his side of the dialogue into a series of rhetorical requests for clarification:

"You want to see me about something?" the lord brusquely asked his peculiarly young butler.

"Uhh, uhh," replied the faithful, if aphasic, majordomo.

"You say that young imp Johnny is here to call upon my daughter?"

"Uhh, uhh!"

"And he's parked his flivver upon the lawn again?" roared the nobleman, his self-prompted understanding and accompanying rage now fully matured. "Tell the scoundrel to move it elsewhere at once!"

"Uhh, uhh," neighed the slobbering manservant, bowing and scraping his way off the stage.

And that was Dick Miller's acting debut. "All these things I was supposed to say, he just took the lines," said Miller. "But after that it got better, and I played it for a week, and I was brilliant." Nevertheless, blanking out on stage that first night made a decidedly long-term impact, and gave Miller a lifelong horror of going down on his lines.

If the ultimate success of his maiden thespian effort infected Miller with the acting bug, he was still well inoculated against it. The bohemian fun times associated with performing had not escaped his notice, however, and he returned to New York full of showbiz pep. He hung out in Manhattan, mainly with Bobby Van, both of them wearing fancy overcoats fastened tight. They frequented the Brill Building, that famed songwriter haunt at Broadway and Forty-Ninth, standing against the wall at band rehearsals, listening carefully and watching working musicians ply their trade. They did the same at the Brill's nominal rival a couple of blocks uptown, the hipper, more accessible songster's paradise at 1650 Broadway.

Miller and Van themselves played in a small band and gigged at local dances. "Five or six pieces," Miller said. "We'd play a Friday night or a Saturday night, and about four or five or six weeks would go by, we'd get another gig." Miller played drums on a borrowed kit. But they were never going to find fame this way, since the aggregation had no actual name and nobody in it had a showman's zeal. Miller described their promotional technique: "You want the band? It's the B-A-N-D, band!"

A guy they knew from the Bronx, only a couple of months younger than Miller and Van, had caught the showbiz bug too, though with a little more focus than Dick. His name was Vic Morrow, and he wanted to be an actor; it seemed to him that these guys, with their fancy coats and Manhattan manners, might know something about it. "I told him about show business and about how we liked the music world," Miller said, "and he said, 'How do you get into show business?' And I said, 'Well, you look in the green sheet'—that was the local paper at the time for show business—I said, 'Look in the green sheet, and you'll see a director saying, "I'm casting a show," and you go down and you tell him you're an actor.'" Years later, in Hollywood, Miller ran into Morrow again.

"What are you doin' here?" he asked the younger man.

"Well, I took your advice," Morrow told him. "I went down, I told the guy I was an actor, and he gave me a job!" By the time Miller had met him again, he was playing a major role in *The Blackboard Jungle*, and after that Morrow was a busy actor who would become a TV star in the role of tough Sgt. Saunders on *Combat!* But Miller and Morrow would share one last, fatal connection: both would appear in *Twilight Zone: The Movie*, though in different segments of that anthology picture; and for Morrow, who was killed along with two young children in a dreadful helicopter accident, it would be a final curtain.

Nights, for Miller, were a dazzling kaleidoscope of dance, drink, and song in the grand Manhattan style, and went very late. One great hangout, at least when you were flush, was Lindy's, long a legend on Broadway for their smoked tongue sandwiches and crabby waiters, and for the gangs of itinerant songwriters waiting just inside the entrance for famous singers or producers upon whom to pounce. Cheesecake was the popular menu item in the wee hours. Famous newsmen sat by tradition just to the right of the door; schmoozing and table hopping were rampant throughout. From outside, the place looked like a jar full of lightning bugs.

Miller was there, or else, when he was broke, at the drugstore around the corner, Hanson's, where you could nurse a cup of coffee for as long as you wanted, and as you did the world passed through. (It was also, according to reports in the *New York Times*, the easiest place below the park to score heroin.) "Everybody hung out there," Miller said. "I used to run into Tony

Bennett every day; he'd say, 'I'm recording new songs!' and I'm [saying], 'Hope it happens!' Everybody was there. Sinatra's hanging out there, Mel Tormé." Miller and Bennett became friends through their Hanson's encounters: "But I don't see him [for a while], and next time I see him, he's playing Vegas. 'Come up and see me, be my guest.'" Sinatra, too, was a passing acquaintance in those early days, and Miller recalled taking photographs of the young Blue Eyes standing on a street corner, and another in which he's posing with a pair of young proto-groupies. And of course Miller, too, met girls at Hanson's, in particular Gladys Cerney, the young woman who'd been born on the same night and at the same hospital as Dick.

For breakfast and other daytime repasts, or evening coffee or a pre-theatre nosh, there was the Bird-in-Hand restaurant, located at 1659 Broadway, two doors down from Lindy's, and, like Hanson's, a perennial hangout for smack dealers and their customers. This homey eatery knew its clientele well, offering the Bird-in-Hand Hangover Breakfast, which was "For the Morning after the Night Before" and consisted of "Tomato Juice, Two Raw Eggs, Dry Toast, Black Coffee, Aspirin and Our Sympathy." It was crawling with the famous, the used-to-be-famous, the will-one-day-be-famous, and the neither-here-nor-theres. "Earl Barton was the first guy I met in there," Miller recalled. "I went to the men's room in the restaurant one night, and this guy stops me. And I said, 'What is this?' Good lookin' little guy. He says, 'Are you in trouble or something?' I said, 'No, what's the matter?' He says, 'Well, your face! You look worried. I want to be your friend!'"

("Yeah, you get expressions, unbelievable," Lainie Miller said on hearing this story.)

Miller met and befriended Sammy Davis Jr. in the Bird. "We were just bummin' around," Miller said, "come in, come out, and you become friends. Sammy was not a big star then. He was a hell of an entertainer, mostly a dancer, wasn't doing any singing." It was more challenging to hang out with Davis than with his white friends, thanks to the racial realities of the day. "It was quite a thing. We stayed out of certain restaurants, things like that. It was just expected." The friendship with Davis would last beyond their pre-fame New York days, but would come to an unhappy and antipathetic conclusion some years later.

Probably the most important person Miller would meet in the Bird-in-Hand was Jonathan Haze. Back then his name was Jack Schacter, and he was great friends with Earl Barton. Haze, too, was a Bird regular, and soon after Barton's meeting with Miller, the three of them were hanging out and eating there frequently. ("It was like a poor man's Lindy's," said Haze of the Bird-in-Hand. "Famous for its strawberry cheesecake.") Haze was a cousin to Buddy Rich, the famous drummer, which was intriguing enough to Dick, and he had also worked as a stage manager to the great singer Josephine Baker on two of her recent tours. Miller was happy to meet anyone with showbiz connections, and their personalities clicked. He and Haze saw movies together, got drunk, chased girls, and would remain friends, with only a few bumps in the road, from then on.

"Time came, had to get a job," said Miller. He was aware of the trade papers by now, and kept his eyes open for jobs in the entertainment field. He answered an ad for a "band boy," despite having no idea what a band boy was. But he had a friend in that line, who worked as Benny Goodman's band boy and who explained that the job was essentially that of a roadie: setting up the instruments and the music stands, carrying things, acting as general dogsbody. He encouraged Miller to take it up. After three days on the job, right on schedule, Miller's natural instinct for flight kicked in. "I said, 'I've had it. This is too much.' Too much work, running around, getting 'em food, getting 'em marijuana, getting 'em ... I didn't realize the beauty of it. So I quit that."

The beauty of it would be made clear soon enough, but not yet. All through this period Miller was continuing with his schooling—he was an ex-serviceman, and even though, as he had not participated in the war, he was not officially a candidate for the GI Bill, he was still entitled to its 52-20 clause, which would get him a double sawbuck each week for up to a year if he was enrolled in classes—and the search for a vocation was becoming critical as he aged into his twenties. Music was his life, but it somehow didn't seem likely to be his career. He began thinking in terms of security, an unusual frame of reference for Miller, and noticed that upholsterers were making very good money for the time—as much as two dollars an hour, in fact. Some were clearing $100 a week. So, clutching a Veteran's Administration pamphlet listing all the classes offered under the federal aid umbrella, Miller made his way down to New York School of Upholstery and began filling out the forms.

It was a narrow thing, recalling the dark period in which H. G. Wells nearly became a draper. Miller chanced to ask the upholstery school administrator what time in the evening the classes were held. "We don't have evening classes any more," he was told. "Let that drop about a year ago. Mornings only. Classes start at eight a.m."

"I can't take classes at eight," he told the upholstery man. "I don't even go to bed until four." He looked at the pamphlet, and right next to the upholstery school was the notice for the Theatre School of Dramatic Arts. "Can I use your phone?" he asked the man. He dialled the acting school and asked what time the classes were.

"Nine o' clock," said the man on the other end, "or eleven, depending on what you want."

"I want eleven," Miller said instantly, and put down the phone. "Sorry," he told the upholstery teacher, "looks like I'm not going to be an upholsterer after all." He made his way up to Carnegie Hall, the venerable New York auditorium in which the school was housed, and applied. He had to audition with, as the student catalogue advised, "two dramatic selections of opposite style." He was left to choose his audition pieces, and would that Miller could remember what they were.

The Theatre School had been founded in 1926 by an actor named Norman Brace, who rolled around the building in a wheelchair with a plaid blanket across his lap and who retired from teaching the very year Miller joined. The school boasted of its celebrity graduates: luminaries such as Dick Van Patten and his little sister Joyce (then child stars of Broadway), Steve Cochran, Cameron Mitchell, and "Skippy" Homeier. Future *Barney Miller* star Abe Vigoda was another recent graduate, though not at that time a notable one. Miller's teachers included Jason Robards Jr. and Tom Poston, both of whom were six or seven years older than Miller, had served in WWII and seen plenty of action, were athletic, and would go on to big careers on Broadway, in film, and on television. Miller and Robards got along well: "Towards the end," Miller said, "just before graduation, we became pretty tight." Later they would both appear in Roger Corman's studio picture *The St. Valentine's Day Massacre*, though never in the same scene. They ran into one another now and again, at the Academy or other places, and Robards would always point at Miller and crow, "It's Dick Miller! My best student! My *only* student!"

But they lost touch, and more than a decade after Robards's death, Lainie Miller found his phone number in the Rolodex she'd bought for her husband in the 1960s. It was full of dead people, to Lainie's consternation. "I really hate to get rid of 'em," Miller told her.

Lainie scoffed. "What, for a séance you're planning to hold? He died in 2000. Can I at least write 'dead' on here?"

"I guess so," Miller said. "If you like writing 'dead.'"

The workshops at the Theatre School were straightforward, with no Method techniques, no trust exercises, no finding the essential truth in an unpeeled banana. It was about learning how to remember your lines and speak so that people could hear you. There were classes in production, direction, pantomime, improvisation, makeup, costuming, fencing (as taught by "Monsieur Rouget"), eurythmy, and something called "body culture." As part of a radio script-reading class, their words were recorded and played back to them. It was Miller's first time hearing his own voice, and he was amazed. "The school was very thorough," Miller said, "and it opened all kinds of doors in my head." And yet, the whole time he was enrolled, Miller saw the classes more as a way to access the Veteran's Administration payout of twenty dollars a week than as a pathway to a career. "Everybody in there wanted to be an actor but me."

There were diction courses, which aimed to eliminate "careless speech, localisms, foreign accents, vulgarisms and faulty pronunciations" from the student. (One wonders what Miller sounded like *before* these courses.) Action classes helped the pupils rid themselves of "habits that are detrimental to the body; which after a time become both ugly and defective." Life Study classes taught "observation of people in real life," which Miller was already good at and practised further every night after class when he went out drinking with the others in his workshops. There were pretty girls to talk to and he was having a great time, but, he claimed, "I did not know what it was all about. I just knew it wasn't the upholstery school."

After six months in the Junior Course and another six in the Senior Course, Miller matriculated on January 5, 1950, aged twenty-one and, astonishingly, still with little thought of becoming an actor. He took a few stabs at it, though: he recalled answering an ad in the showbiz trades, going up to an apartment, knocking on the door, and finding himself face to face with a bleary-eyed, housecoat-wearing Burgess Meredith, who was putting together some kind of show. Whatever it was, Miller didn't get the part, if there even was a part. ("I don't think he had a project," Miller says. "I think he was just auditioning.")

Answering another ad took him to Astoria Studios in Brooklyn, which had been renamed the Signal Corps Photographic Center (SCPC) because the army was shooting hygiene films there. This would be Miller's grand film debut. He landed the part of the Bad Soldier, the one who fails to heed his sergeant's advice about prophylactics and slatternly women, and winds up getting syphilis; Miller acted in two or three of these ephemeral productions, which have long dropped off both the bottom of his CV and the face of the earth; and the SCPC itself was mothballed in 1970. Miller then briefly joined a Broadway production of Booth Tarkington's *Seventeen*, following his pal Bobby Van, who'd been cast in the lead. But when Van decided he didn't want to be in the show and quit right on stage during a rehearsal, Miller, in a fit of loyalty, did the same thing.

He still needed to eat and pay the bills. He'd supported himself through his schooling with the usual run of part-time jobs to supplement the VA bucks: he was a taxi driver, a cook, a salesman, all of it unwitting research for future roles. He played drums, but wanted to sing, and was always on the lookout for a break. But he needed money, all the more so now that he was out of school, so he took a job as a stockroom boy at Saks Fifth Avenue.

The big department store sat next to St. Patrick's Cathedral—"A magnificent, beautiful edifice," said Miller—and its own upper-crust style was belied, Miller soon found, by the dreary institutionalism of its backstage regions. "Their stockroom is like a prison," Miller said. "It's grey, mesh wire walls and everything, and the only escape we had was going to the men's room and smoking a cigarette. You couldn't smoke in the store." Miller ascended the five floors to the staff convenience as often as he could get away with it, and stood smoking at the window, staring out at the neo-Gothic spires of the cathedral and the pigeons wheeling around them, and stubbing out his butts on the sill. "If you think St. Patrick's is wild from the ground, you ought to see it from five storeys up," said Miller.

Miller was on the job for two weeks when his flight instinct took hold. The mindless, artless drudgery of the position "was driving me crazy," he said, and the penitentiary ambiance reinforced his trapped feeling. But it was not just the job this time: it was his life. He felt like a dreamer, a do-nothing, a bum. He was having fun, but going nowhere. He stood at the window, smoking, pondering, watching the pigeons. Show business had never seemed so far away than it was right now, five storeys down and three streets west. The pigeons flocked around the cathedral towers, landing, then taking off again in a body, their shadows flitting after them. They could go wherever they wanted to, Miller thought jealously. His cigarette burned in his fingers, forgotten.

Slowly Miller became aware of a strange noise, a sort of rhythmic rumble. He puzzled on it for a while, until he suddenly realized it was him, the low chant of his own voice. He was repeating the same phrase over and over again: "The pigeons are free! The pigeons are free! The pigeons are free!" The realization agitated him further, and he panicked. He burst out of the bathroom and ran crazily through the store, shouting now, "The pigeons are free! The pigeons are free!" He clattered down the stairs, straight-armed his way onto 5th, and turned right, running as fast as he could. A policeman stopped traffic for him as he ran gibbering across the street. ("Only in New York," Miller said.) Tears were streaming from his eyes, and still he kept running, dodging the crowds on the sidewalk, heading north. He reached Central Park and ran in, finally throwing himself down on the grass, panting. All his despair welled up and he began to cry in earnest. He was free now, like the pigeons, but he was still speaking aloud. "I don't know what I'm gonna do," he sobbed. "I don't know what I'm gonna do!"

After a while he collected himself and stood up. He trudged back to Saks, quit the job officially, collected his paycheque, and made his way home. That evening the phone rang. It was Miller's friend, the guy who was Benny Goodman's band boy. "You looking for work?" he asked Miller. "I got this job for you."

"What is it?" Miller asked.

"Band boy," the friend replied.

This felt to Miller like some kind of cruel jest, a kick in the ass with a clown shoe when he was as far down as he'd ever been. "I did that once," he told the friend. "I'm not doing it again."

"At least go see him," the friend insisted. "It's Bobby Sherwood, and he doesn't tour, he's in town. Easy job, you carry his instruments around. He's got a trumpet and a piano. You may have to carry the piano, who knows. At least go talk to him, see what it's all about."

Miller finally agreed to meet Sherwood, probably more to get his well-intentioned buddy off the phone than anything. But because he did go see Bobby Sherwood, the stockboy routine at Saks Fifth Avenue was the last straight job Dick Miller would ever have to take. As God was his witness, he would indeed be hungry again, but at least it would be on his own terms.

6   Big change in my life

Bobby Sherwood was in his mid-thirties when Miller met him: tall, lanky, wavy-haired, and handsome, a little like Hoagie Carmichael with the edges knocked off. He was a composer, a bandleader, and a musician who was competent or better on at least ten different instruments. "He was a genius," Miller said. "A musical genius." Sherwood had worked as an arranger and guitarist for Bing Crosby, Artie Shaw, and others, and later played trumpet for Sarah Vaughan and Frank Sinatra. He sang as well, in a mellow, slightly flat voice with just a touch of Bingle's honeyed croon. The Bobby Sherwood Orchestra had enjoyed some hit records of Sherwood's own composition, including their quasi-theme song, "Sherwood's Forest," and a swinging 1942 million-seller called "The Elks' Parade." Miller was a fan of those two numbers in particular. "In all the years I've been listening to music," he said, "they still stand up as the best things I've ever heard." Sherwood had appeared in a few movies, usually playing a bandleader, but his most prominent film appearance would come in the 1957 Sinatra showcase *Pal Joey*. His parents had been vaudevillians, and he was one of many who helped bring the circuit's grab bag culture to the new medium of television.

By some reports Sherwood had been a big band leader only reluctantly, having been pressured into it by Johnny Mercer, and feeling further pressure to continue after "The Elks' Parade" became a hit. Keeping the band together had proved troublesome in the declining days of the swing era, so he was probably quite happy to whittle his orchestra to a quintet when TV came calling; trade papers thereafter took to referring to him as a "reformed" band leader, as though he'd kicked some embarrassing, adolescent peccadillo. By 1950, with rock 'n' roll on the horizon, big band music was considered just that.

Sherwood's first television gig was leading his quintet as the house band on *The Bert Parks Show*. At the same time he was hosting a radio show on WNEW from 5:00 to 5:30 every weekday afternoon; provided music for a CBS weekday evening program recorded at "New York's most New York-iest" night spot, the Stork Club; and hosted his own late night variety show, *Midnight Snack*, from 11:10 to 11:55 each weekday night. To fill in the gaps he made guest appearances on a myriad of other programs, both television and radio. His schedule was compared with that of bandleader Arthur Godfrey, who, when Miller was still a youth, had been one of the first personalities to assume the King of All Media mantle.

Bert Parks was an even busier man than Sherwood, and he, too, was held up in comparison with Godfrey, evidently the barometer against which all showfolk timetables were measured. Parks was a veteran of radio, and had made the transition to television in spectacular style by hosting two game shows at once, *Break the Bank* and *Stop the Music* (Sherwood often showed up as a guest on the latter); he also made plentiful guest appearances elsewhere; sometimes emceed the Macy's parade; and when General Mills, the breakfast cereal company, decided they wanted a new show to sponsor, and that the show ought to be a daytime half-hour hosted by Parks, he agreed without hesitation and didn't even think about giving up his game shows or other activities. He was perfect for the tele-visual medium, "a personable, high-voltage operator with a grin you can read by," according to the famously acerbic TV critic John Crosby. The new show hit the airwaves on November 1, 1950, running thrice weekly, Mondays, Wednesdays, and Fridays, at 3:30 p.m. on NBC. Up to its last broadcast on January 11, 1952, it was an efficient and entertaining method of shilling breakfast cereal. Parks hosted the thing with ebullience, presiding over a group of regulars who included Betty Ann Grove, Bix Brent, Nancy Overton, Jean Swain, Murray Scholman, and the Heathertones. Within that half-hour anything might happen to delight the housewife-viewer: musical numbers, skits, musical numbers that suddenly became skits, or vice versa; special guests, pranks, wisecracks; cereal plugs. Crosby, not an easy critic to please, called it "a very pleasant half-hour, and certainly an ambitious one for afternoon TV. It is awash with gimmicks and elaborate song cues. And it is so strikingly informal that, as a gesture of respect, you ought to remove your shoes while watching it." Crosby's only complaint was that both Parks and his show were "occasionally overwhelmed by [their] own cuteness."

Miller's entrée into this razzle-dazzle world came with his new job as Sherwood's band boy, which mainly consisted of helping the musician carry his instruments from show to show, and for which he earned fifty dollars a week. New York represented the locus—indeed, nearly the entirety—of television production in America at the time, and most of the studios were not even proper TV studios, but repurposed lofts or theatres in Lower Manhattan or Brooklyn. Miller and Sherwood would make their way from one to the other each weekday, beginning with rehearsals for the Parks show at 30 Rockefeller Center, then Sherwood would vanish for a while after the broadcast; on his reappearance they'd head a few streets north to the Stork Club, and then, after a late dinner, to CBS in time for *Midnight Snack.*

They were two easygoing fellows, and the arrangement was congenial and busy, if slightly incongruous. "We looked funny," said Miller. "Bobby was a tall guy, and he used to carry his little trumpet under his arm, and I'd carry his big guitar case. Walking next to him, it looked kind of silly. He told me one day, 'Let's switch instruments!' I said, 'But I'm getting paid to carry it!' He said, 'Never mind that, you're getting paid to keep me company.'"

Miller was happy to leave it there, at first. It was the easiest, most pleasant job he'd ever had. He was mixing it up with musicians and actors, was witnessing the early evolution of an important new medium, and was able to maintain his late-night carousing and sleep in to whatever hour he liked. He was meeting a beguiling new bunch of people too, like Mel Tormé, a Hanson's and Bird-in-Hand acquaintance who was working on a television show in the same studio. The Velvet Fog's show was in colour too, which was unusual and exotic at the time. "They were doing, I guess, experimental things," Miller said of Tormé's program. "We became kinda friends."

He was still keeping company with his old crew, or at least Bobby Van. (Shelley Kopp and Billy Levy were in school, and Jack Silverman had joined the service and would shortly be heading for Korea.) Van was performing, singing and playing the trumpet, and three or four times over the course of a year, Miller backed him up on the drums. Usually they ended up down in the Village at one joint or another, tearing up the place until three or four, but one night the adventurous Van suggested they head up to Harlem, to a jumpin' spot on West 118th known as Minton's. The club's official name was the Play House, and it had been a hot spot since early 1941, when a sizzling quartet made up of Kenny Clarke, Joe Guy, Thelonious Monk, and Nick Fenton had helped turn it from a drab crony club to a Harlem phenomenon and, according to Leonard Feather, the "crucible of bebop." Such was its reputation that a couple of Jewish guys would leave the safety of the Village and venture north of the park at one in the morning just to see what was going on there.

Miller was more than a little nervous—Harlem was no place for a little white fella at that time of night. But there was no trouble on the streets, and certainly none in the club, where people just wanted to dance and have a good time. In fact, there were already a few other white people domino-spotting the crowd. Miller and Van ordered a couple of drinks at the bar near the door and found seats near the bandstand at the back of the room. Bizarre paintings filled the available wall space, smoke clouded the air, and the group on stage was as heavy as you could hope for: Monk, Dizzy Gillespie, and a couple of others, cooking with gas.

But the band took a break, and during it, for reasons of his own, the drummer cut out. "And the guys were saying, 'Anybody here play drums?'" Miller said. "I said, 'Yeah!' They looked at me, and they said, 'Okay, sit in.'" The awestruck Miller settled himself behind the kit and kept the beat as the jazz giants around him did their own thing. "We played one number," said Miller, "must have gone on for ten minutes. In ten minutes, Thelonious Monk played ten notes, and that was it. He was just thinkin' and thinkin' and thinkin'."

As Miller played, he was taking lessons from Monk, who was a great advice giver to his fellow musicians; his pointers were later compiled on a scrap of loose-leaf by saxophonist Steve Lacy. "Don't play everything," Monk instructed. "Let some notes go by. Some music just imagined." Also, Monk counselled, "Make the drummer sound good!" Some of the points were esoteric ("It must be always night, otherwise they wouldn't need the lights."); others, personal ("They tried to get me to hate white people, but someone would always come along and spoil it."); and still others, axiomatic ("Always leave them wanting more."). The advice was intended for musicians, but was applicable on a much broader scope. To an actor, for instance, it could be priceless. "Stay in shape!" Monk exhorted. "Sometimes a musician waits for a gig and when it comes he's out of shape and can't make it. Never sound anybody for a gig. Just be on the scene." It was plain that Miller had absorbed these prescripts, whether he ever heard them spoken aloud or not; and plainer still that he had heard and understood what may have been Monk's most critical lesson: "You've got to dig it to *dig* it, you dig?"

Miller dug. On more than one occasion he, Billy Van, and Sammy Davis Jr. made a fun trio, singing and dancing up one side of Broadway and down the other. "Picture us," said Miller, "three o'clock in the morning, dancing on Broadway to 'New York, New York, it's a helluva town.' Used to do a little turnaround, dah dah dah dah!" (Off Broadway, when he wasn't plotting his takeover of the entertainment world, Davis was deeply into quick-draw shooting, and passed an enthusiasm for gunplay on to Miller.)

Another Broadway pal was a young, blue-eyed actor who rode around on a motorcycle and was perpetually broke. Steve McQueen had been shunted about the country as a child, had worked unhappily at a thousand strange jobs, knowing he was destined for something grander, and had recently done time in the service, chafing under its authority all the while. So he and Miller had a lot in common. McQueen had arrived in New York with the intention of acting, but hadn't even begun the classes that would eventually lead him to Broadway, then television, then gradual movie superstardom. His girlfriend Neile was acting, however, and late one night Miller and a few others were standing on Broadway, in front of the theatre that separated Lindy's from the Bird-in-Hand, when McQueen roared up and told them he had to get to Philadelphia as quickly as possible; his girl had a play opening the next night. But he was busted, flat on his ass, and could they lend him some gas money? Miller dug in his pockets and produced two dollars; the others scrounged too, and all together they were able to stake McQueen's trip. He roared off, waving his hand, and thereafter, whenever Miller would run into the actor out in California—in a Beverly Hills theatre once, for example—he'd point and say, "McQueen! Where's that two bucks you owe me!" McQueen would shout back, "I got it! I got it!" and make a big show of reaching for his wallet, but Miller always waved him off so he could do the joke again the next time. "A running gag," Miller said. "He died, poor guy, and he still owed me the money."

"You never forget a thing if it comes to a buck," Lainie Miller said after this story was told. "There's an actor he doesn't speak to because he welshed on a bet for two bucks."

That actor turned out to be Joe Turkel, who'd appeared in several Stanley Kubrick pictures—most memorably as the malevolent ghost of the previous caretaker in *The Shining*—and played the ill-fated creator of the rebellious replicants in *Blade Runner*. Miller and Turkel had bet on a fight, and then for some reason Turkel failed to pay the tiny wager. "This is forty, fifty years ago," an amused Lainie Miller said.

But Dick stuck stubbornly to his guns, and you could tell that even if the door opened at that moment and Turkel walked in, brandishing two crisp, new, dollar bills and a sincere apology, Miller would remain unimpressed, possibly even surly.

As Miller spent more time on the *Bert Parks Show* set, his acting ambition took on more focus than it ever had before. "I used to sit around and think, 'How can I get on the show? I got a connection here; I must be able to act or something!'" he said. The show's writer-producer team was Paul Harrison and Bernie Gould, known in their press releases as "Genial Paul Harrison" and "Jovial Bernie Gould." Their other productions included the Bert Parks showcase *Stop the Music*, a program that, as John Crosby noted, positively overflowed with both geniality and joviality; and they would later sign a first-look contract with CBS and take the helm of Judy Garland's first TV special. Miller had noticed that Harrison and Gould often performed in the skits they wrote as well; and he figured that he, too, could write a bit for himself to perform. Maybe writing for yourself was the best way to get onscreen. He approached the pair and asked if he might take a crack at submitting some items. "Sure," the jovial producers crowed genially. "If it's good, we'll use it!"

Miller's bits passed muster and began appearing on the show. He wrote skits, introductions, commercial lead-ins, and plain old jokes, and, on a handful of occasions, performed in them as well. For this he made an extra sixty or seventy dollars a week on top of the fifty dollars he got from Sherwood: serious money in a time when the average working guy might pull down half that. The experience reinforced Miller's already strongly held conviction that an average working guy was something he never wanted to be again, unless he was playing one on TV.

Sherwood, no dullard, noticed Miller's talent for writing and invited his band boy to start writing for the late-night show, *Midnight Snack*. Miller accepted without hesitation, and took the opportunity to quiz Sherwood on his daily late-afternoon disappearances. Sherwood told Miller of his WNEW radio show, on which he played a few records and talked for half an hour, and invited him to start writing for that as well. Miller's pay envelope swelled to almost $300 a week. He wrote introductions to ads, mostly things like: "And now, the curtain opens, a hush falls over the crowd, and the magnificent form begins to take shape within the fog ... what is it, they ask ... now the mist clears ... the awe-inspiring object becomes visible ... it's ..." And then a screechy little girl's voice—twelve-year-old future opera star Beverly Sills, known as "The Fastest Voice Alive"—would break in to sing the Rinso White theme: "a hap-py lit-tle wash-day song!"

From his new multimedia vantage point, Miller could see that *Midnight Snack* was merely a televised version of a garden-variety radio show. Many TV shows of the period were just that, the only difference being that, as Steve Allen pointed out, the hosts were now sitting at desks instead of tables. "It was basically a disc jockey show," Miller said. "[Sherwood] would tell little stories, and he was very interesting. Little stories about the recordings that he'd made, and then they'd play 'em. So he'd play about five numbers in the show." Occasionally Sherwood would bring on a guest, usually a musician, who, after a little introductory chat, would sit and listen as his or her song was played. Miller watched this for a while, then told Sherwood, "This is the dullest thing I've ever seen."

"Well, what do you suggest?" Sherwood asked.

"You got all these guests who just come and sit," Miller said. "They could talk."

"What do you mean, just listen to them talk?"

"Yeah," Miller said. "They could tell stories about themselves, not just the songs."

Sherwood liked the idea. He was represented by Dick Gabbe of the firm Gabbe, Lutz and Heller, which had become the first coast-to-coast personal management company when it was formed in 1947 and was also the source of many *Midnight Snack* guests. Sherwood began calling up the agency, asking which of their clients were working in New York and might want to promote their shows on television. It was never difficult to find takers, and less so after Sherwood began inviting them to promote not just their shows, but themselves.

The first guest to enjoy this new format was Gabbe, Lutz and Heller's most illustrious, most bespangled client, Liberace. In 1951 he was famous, but not as famous as he would be a few years later when he'd have a television show of his own, and then essentially play a straight version of himself in a drippy big-budget melodrama. Nevertheless, he was a hit on *Midnight Snack*, particularly among his devoted female fan base, whose hearts beat a little faster as they peered at him through his candelabra, dreading that long-in-coming but surely inevitable day when he would finally meet the right girl. Positive letters and phone calls confirmed the wisdom of the programming shift, and *Midnight Snack* permanently adopted a form that would be familiar to any viewer of David Letterman, Stephen Colbert, Conan O'Brien, or of each iteration of the *Tonight Show* from Steve Allen through Jack Paar, Johnny Carson, Jay Leno, and Jimmy Fallon.

This happened in 1951, and the *Tonight Show* with Steve Allen didn't premiere until September 27, 1954; and yet you don't have to read past the dust jacket of an Allen biography by Ben Alba, *Inventing Late Night: Steve Allen and the Original Tonight Show*, to find the assertion, "It all seems so simple—the desk, the monologue, the announcer/sidekick, the bandleader as comic foil, the breezy chats with celebrities, the wacky stunts, the comedy sketches.... Steve Allen invented this formula." Did he indeed, or did Dick Miller?

If his recollections are correct, Miller appears to at least have helped it along considerably. Guests continued appearing on the show, and topics of conversation ranged more broadly than they ever had before. In the meantime he was writing commercial lead-ins, still coming up with skits and gags, and acting little parts as required, playing a messenger boy bringing Sherwood a telegram at some comically inopportune time, or a studio flunky pulling the wrong lever. (He would often see to it that such roles were required, simply by writing them in himself.) At times he acted as bouncer, as when Sherwood had on a young stage ingénue named Lydia Clarke. Clarke's husband, Charlton Heston, who at that time was a year or so away from his own big break in *The Greatest Show On Earth*, was out in the hallway waiting for her, half in the bag and making a lot of noise, barking to himself about something or other. The studio walls weren't soundproofed, and the stentorian ruckus bled into Clarke's interview. An annoyed Sherwood waited for a commercial break, then hissed, "Get that guy out of here!" to his band boy. "I'd like to say I physically kicked him out," Miller said, "but I just said, 'Go downstairs, please!'"

Sherwood's manager, Dick Gabbe, was as loquacious as his name would suggest; according to trumpeter Max Herman, who'd been in a band managed by Gabbe many years earlier, he was "the first of the great double-talkers." He frequently visited the studio, and during one such pop-by, after observing Miller's multiple talents in action, remarked, "What is it you want to do, Dick? You're doing everything on this show, but you're not establishing yourself in any way." Miller shrugged; he was just doing what he felt like doing. He was still in his early twenties, and he was working in television, making lots of money, living in a "beautiful apartment" on 29th Street, appearing, if briefly, on Broadway (in *Seventeen*), hanging out with absurdly talented people like Sammy Davis Jr. and Steve McQueen, dating pretty girls, dining, dancing, and living it up. No wonder Miller recalled these as "the fun years."

And then there were nuns. Every day while he was working for Bobby Sherwood, Miller's first port of call was Radio City Music Hall, where the *Bert Parks Show* held its rehearsals; he would gather up whichever of Sherwood's instruments he had at home with him, leave his apartment, walk over to 6th, and get a bus up to Radio City. When the weather was foul, or he just didn't feel like lugging the instruments on the bus, he might hail a cab.

He still owned the little Crosley, but parking in Manhattan was impossible even for a car as small as that, and the instruments would barely fit inside.

Across the street from his building was a series of brownstones owned by the local Catholic diocese; these housed nuns. The Sisters often emerged from their residence just as Miller emerged from his, made the same walk up to 6th as he did, and frequently caught the same bus. "And there was this one nun," Miller recalled, "and I'd get on the bus and look at her, we'd ride, staring at each other. And she was rather cute." The nun was as friendly as she was cute, and he noticed that she usually got off at his Radio City stop, where, with black skirts flapping, she would disappear into the midtown crowds. One rainy morning Miller stood on his stoop, laden with instrument cases, and when the pretty nun stepped out of her door, he decided to take a chance. "I'm gonna take a cab," he called across the street. "Can I give you a lift?" Before giving her a chance to answer, he added, "I don't know if this is proper or not—I'm not Catholic."

But the nun didn't care about Miller's religious affiliation, and happily accepted the ride. She explained to Miller that her trips uptown were to solicit funds for the church, and she had to bring back a certain amount each day. Miller grimaced: he didn't want the image of the nun grubbing for money in an unforgiving city to spoil the picture of her pretty, fresh, wimple-framed face. He told her she was welcome to share his cab any time if the weather was bad. The carpooling continued, and after a while the nun asked if she might bring along another, and, later, another. Miller was happy to accommodate them; it was strangely exhilarating to travel uptown in a car full of nuns.

The original nun turned to him one day and in a confessional tone told him, "You're a real light in my life." His laughing and his gags, his casual manner, were refreshing, and were attitudes she had missed since taking her vows. "When you become a nun in a Catholic family," she explained, "you almost become untouchable. They just stare. They don't laugh or joke or talk to you like you're a person. My nephews, they look at me like I'm some golden thing."

Miller, a natural heretic, responded to this by becoming even more casual, almost iconoclastic. He began deliberately leaving his window shades up when he undressed at night. "What colour shorts was I wearing?" he'd ask the nun the next day, and she would correctly answer: "The purple things with the birds on them." It was an exhibitionistic turn-on, and the mild sadism of the tease was amplified by the nun's vow of chastity. The nuns always seemed to keep their own shades drawn, however. "I could never see in there," Miller said, implying that it wasn't for lack of trying.

One morning, instead of the nun or any of her friends, it was the Mother Superior who appeared on the stoop, her brow furrowed in anger. "Mr. Miller!" she called. "Stay away from my girls!" The boss nun fired a few anti-Semitic jibes at Miller's back as he walked up to catch his bus. Miller felt obscurely empty; he was not saddened by the Mother Superior's fading taunts—he had survived Dutch Cogswell, after all—but by the melancholy realization that he would never see his little nun again.

There, he was wrong. One morning, on one of his last days as a New Yorker, she came to him, bearing a package. "We got you a gift," she told him. All the young nuns had thrown together their scarce and hard-earned pennies and bought a present for their dashing gentleman friend. Miller tore at the paper: it was a golf sweater, a knitted cardigan with big, puffy sleeves. He was deeply touched. "I loved that sweater," he said much later on. "Still got it. Never wear it, don't know what condition it's in ..."

"Full of moth holes," Lainie Miller said. "Full of moth holes, but we don't throw it out."

The Bert Parks Show went off the air in early January 1952. Through the rest of that winter and into the spring, Miller saw further signs that his days as a media hyphenate might be numbered. He was told the *Parks* show might not return to the air in the fall. (It never did.) He heard from Sherwood that Gabbe and his partners were trying to get rid of him, preferring to save money. "I'll go," Miller said, but Sherwood didn't want him to, wanted to continue paying him fifty dollars a week to be his band boy and keep him company. *Midnight Snack* and the radio show were still going strong, and Miller was still playing drums for Sherwood at a club in the Village where the bandleader would blow his trumpet now and then. New York was still wild, still vital, still full of women to chase. Miller drank and caroused, smoked grass occasionally, danced, polished the seats at the Bird-in-Hand for hours on end. His old friends had all gone: Shelley Kopp was by now in Washington, DC, and Jack Silverman was in Korea. Billy Levy was still in town, but he was busy in school, and Bobby Van had moved out west to Los Angeles, where he was making movies. He'd already played a small role in a Mario Lanza picture, and would soon enact a show-stopping, all-jumping dance routine in the otherwise-tepid MGM musical *Small Town Girl*.

Even his newer friends were leaving, or thinking of leaving. Sammy Davis Jr. was gone, busy touring and becoming famous, and Jonathan Haze was planning on making the pilgrimage to Hollywood, where he, too, would achieve a species of fame. Haze had been touring with Josephine Baker, stage managing her shows all across the country, and had returned to New York with the intention of acting. Nothing was happening, though, and Haze decided to spend the summer in his hometown of Pittsburgh, where he worked as the stage manager for an opera company. In the fall he joined a friend who was driving to San Francisco, and from there he hitched down to Los Angeles. Miller's brother, Eugene, was in LA too, of course, where he was working as a private investigator.

Miller began to feel that everything he cherished about New York was slipping away. Sherwood decided to take the summer off and spend some time up in the Catskills, near a town called Hunter, so that was it for *Midnight Snack*. But there were benefits as well: the radio show was ending too, and the WMCA executives asked Miller if he would like to take it over. It would be renamed *The Dick Miller Show*, and he could play whatever music he wanted. "Good deal," Miller said. "I was a disc jockey. And I kept the same format, but the music was bluesier." Between numbers he just gabbed, freestyling happily, a hepcat performer running a patter, an actor playing a DJ. This lasted through most of the summer, but after a while he, too, found himself spending time in the Catskills, driving the Crosley up on weekends, hanging out with Sherwood and dating a girl who was singing in one of the hotels. "We went horseback riding," Miller said, "we had a bunkhouse, and we lived like cowboys. We were having fun."

He kept a gun in the Crosley's glove compartment that summer, an automatic pistol he'd bought while under the thrall of Sammy Davis Jr.'s fast-draw enthusiasm. He hung onto it out of youthful affection and a cowboy sensibility, but he also just liked guns. At any rate he had it in the car, and it was there when he and his girl parked at the side of some lonely Catskills road and began "necking, heh heh, that's the only word I can use." It was a scene that would find an uncanny echo in *Night of the Creeps*, a 1986 pulp mini-classic in which Miller would appear: two young lovers, lost in the throes of passion, totally missing the radio announcement describing the violent holdup that had recently taken place in the Catskills region and the mad gunman who was now on the loose, armed and extremely dangerous.

"There's a tap on the window," Miller said. "I rolled down the window, there's a guy, he's got a gun. I said, 'What the hell is this?' He said, 'Get out of the car.'" Miller, immersed in movies his whole life, tended to describe things in movie terms. "I don't remember the dialogue," he said. "It was a lot of screaming, mostly on my part." He screamed at the man, but as he did, he reached for the automatic. He stage-whispered "Bend down" to his girl, "and she bent down, and I fired. I kept firing. I hit him. He went down, he was wounded, and he went to jail. I fired and fired and fired, I emptied this gun, out into the woods."

Of course, he was lucky not to have been shot dead in this encounter: having a gun probably put him in more danger than if he'd been unarmed and had been forced to give up his car to a burglar who most likely only wanted to get away. At any rate, it ended happily for everyone but the gunman, who was left writhing in the dust at the side of the road, ruing the day he tangled with Dick Miller.

Miller's summer romance ended. *The Dick Miller Show* finished its summer fill-in run, and Bobby Sherwood meanwhile traded his bandleader's stool for a host's chair on variety programs like *Stars on Parade*. He didn't need a band boy any more. Bert Parks moved on to game shows and later to the Miss America Pageant, which he would host for years to come, until his birth-of-the-medium cornball avuncularity passed through its retro charm phase and into superannuation, and whichever executives were behind the thing realized Parks had been hosting it since before they were born.

Miller knew it was time for a change, and with a sudden clarity of vision he knew where he had to go. Sherwood tried to dissuade him, or at least to warn him. "It's pretty rough out there," he told Miller. But Miller had seen the blessed vision and would not be turned from his mission. Like anyone in the grip of enlightenment, he divested himself of his goods. The Crosley went first; you couldn't drive a thing like that cross-country. You could hardly drive it across town. Other things he trashed or gave away. He packed up his sharpest clothes, gathered up the books and records he couldn't live without, locked his typewriter case, organized the writing samples he had lying around, then said goodbye to his mother and to the few of his friends who were still left in the city, and turned his gaze westward once again. California, here I come. This time it would stick.

7   *How do you start this thing?*

The last thing Miller did before leaving New York was buy a new car. He had some money saved up and wanted to hit Hollywood in style, so was looking for something especially big and shiny. He went to a Ford dealership and was shown the '53 Crestline V8 Sunliner convertible, the features of which included a "Coachcraft" body, "Deep Breath" manifolding, an "Equa-Flo" cooling system, a Hotchkiss drive, "Hydra-Coil" springs, and "Magic Action" hydraulic brakes. The literature boasted of a "Sleek new 'futuristic' jet plane-shaped hood ornament," and, of particular interest to Miller, an extra large trunk for all his baggage.

He slipped into the driver's seat and discovered yet another feature. "How do you start this thing?" he asked the dealer. It was one of the first models that started with a key instead of a button, certainly the first Miller had encountered, and the dealers informed him he was about to experience the modern pleasure of "Loadomatic" ignition. "Sweet wingalls, this is amazing," Miller said, and bought the car immediately. He loaded it up, said goodbye to his beautiful apartment on 29th Street, guided his unfamiliarly massive automobile through the Holland Tunnel, and, in Jersey now, with the city in his rearview mirror, 110 horses under his saddle and the wind in his wavy blond hair, headed for Hollywood.

It was an enjoyable, carefree, three-day trip. When he was almost there, as he was driving through the California desert, feeling a bit road tired, he gave himself a treat. He stopped the car and pulled out a joint he'd rolled in New York: a little taste of home. He smoked it down to the roach and, before he knew it, was out walking in the sand, where he spent the next several hours celebrating the exotic glory of the desert by pretending to shoot cacti, jackrabbits, and rock formations with his finger. He ducked, turned, aimed, made a child cowboy's gunshot noises: *pshoo, pshoo*! Bad guys rained down off the mesas, their black hats fluttering behind them, and Miller whooped and capered in triumph. "It was a strange day," he said. Eventually he came down, found his way back to the Sunliner and drove the rest of the way into LA.

He moved in with Eugene, who had a place near the beach, and stayed with his brother for a couple of weeks while he got settled. Gene was doing the private investigation work he'd been trained for during the war, and secured some kind of temporary licence for his younger brother so that he could help out. "That didn't last too long," Miller said. "Never went out on any cases." Gene's place was "too far from the Hollywood scene," so Miller found an apartment on Beachwood, returning once again to the old neighbourhood where Aunt Tillie and Uncle Boris still dwelt, and where the Hollywood sign loomed auspiciously at the top of the road. He settled in almost immediately and began hanging out at Schwab's, where he reconnected with Haze and made new friends, while at the same time writing stories and growing a beard. The whiskers helped him stand out the pre-Beat days of LA, when they were worn only by a few proto-hippies like Eden Ahbez, the "Nature Boy" songwriter who lived just up the street beneath the first L in the Hollywood sign. Miller recalled being stopped by a passing movie makeup man, who studied his chin for a few moments, then said, "If you see a beard in any picture I'm on, it'll be yours."

His new pals were generally other recent arrivals, like the painter-turned-screenwriter R. Wright Campbell. Campbell had arrived from the East Coast just a few months earlier, having discovered from his actor brother, William, that Hollywood screenwriters' salaries were frequently huge, at least by the standards of a penniless, unknown artist. He was working on scripts and struggling to make sales, but he still painted; at some point after Miller had fully grown out his beard, Campbell made a small portrait of Miller on cork, then gave it to him. Decades and many moves later, it still hung in Miller's dining room. He hooked up with Jonathan Haze, who was working at a gas station on Sunset, and through him began meeting other strivers, of which Hollywood had no shortage. There were whole communities of them, but this particular gang held Mel Welles, Bruno VeSota, and Charles Griffith. He met Biff Elliott, a jocular tough guy most famous for playing Mike Hammer, and he met John Carradine, who was just re-entering feature films after a long stint in early television. Miller also got to know Forrest J. Ackerman, the literary agent who would found the influential horror magazine *Famous Monsters* and become legendary for his vast collection of movie memorabilia and his coinage of the term "sci-fi." Miller frequently visited Forry's house, the Ackermansion, located, naturally, in the bloody heart of Horrorwood, Karloffornia.

It's hard to say what Miller's ambitions were at this point. Eugene remembered a very specific desire on his brother's part to break into acting, and indeed recalled Uncle Boris wielding his powerful influence again in an attempt to help Dick, but Miller himself only remembered wanting to write. "Acting to me had been twenty dollars a week [from the Veterans' Administration] in school," he said. "And when that was over, it was over." He'd performed on the summer stock stage, in the army films, and on *The Bert Parks Show*, but it was the writing he'd done for the TV and radio programs that had come closest to exciting him. Jokes, skits, and plain old ad copy were fine as far as they had gone, but Miller was also an avid science fiction buff and had been for years, and this was the genre he decided to take a shot at in his new home.

He'd written space fantasy stuff before. A year or two earlier he'd submitted a few tales of wonder to *Amazing Stories* magazine, the original sci-fi periodical, which at that time was edited by Howard Browne. (Browne would later write two hard-boiled, journalistic Roger Corman gangster pictures in which Miller would appear, *The St. Valentine's Day Massacre* and *Capone*.) Dick read fiction almost as voraciously as he consumed movies, and particularly enjoyed speculative works by anyone from Wells and Verne on forward. He was riding the crest of a wave, actually; this was a time when sci-fi fandom and indeed deep nerd-dom were coalescing into a definable movement. Forry Ackerman hooked Miller up with a man named Schwartz, who was planning to produce a science-fiction anthology TV series and was in need of plotlines. Such series were mildly in vogue at the time, with *Tales of Tomorrow, Out There,* and several other now-forgotten proto-*Outer Limits/Twilight Zone* variations on the airwaves.

Ackerman wrote down a Laurel Canyon address and told Miller to pay Schwartz a call. Miller did, but on his first attempt, trying to negotiate the big Sunliner up a snaky canyon road, he nearly backed off a cliff. With one wheel hanging off the edge and panic welling up, he eased his way out of the car, then found an obliging homeowner with a telephone and called a tow truck. Eventually he made it up to Schwartz's house, met the man, and ended up writing a series of outlines and selling them to him one at a time over the course of a year or so for a hundred or a couple of hundred dollars apiece. "I had 'em all in my head," said Miller. "It kept me going." Between these story sales (for a series that was apparently never produced) and his dwindling New York savings, he was able to stay afloat, but barely.

At around this time, Miller's mother, Rita, who had raised her boys as a single mother but lived her life no less intrepidly for it, who had passed on both her love of travel and her unfulfilled show business aspirations to her second son, and who had suffered from diabetes for years without complaint, died at the age of fifty-two. This admirable woman, who was almost totally responsible for the talented and beloved actor Dick would become, never saw him in a single film.

It's worth a few pages of digression to talk about Miller's cousins, the extraordinary Goldblatts, who were his closest family in Los Angeles aside from Eugene, and were described by at least one writer as "a family of Communists." Dick lived just down the hill from Boris and Tillie Goldblatt on Beachwood, and he saw them regularly. He, Eugene, and Rita had stayed with them for a time on arriving in LA a decade earlier. Tillie was Ira's older sister; she and Boris had known each other in their hometown of Kaunas, Lithuania, and had emigrated separately to America, in 1904 and 1905, respectively. In the Bronx they reconnected, married, and became active in left-wing politics. They were already members of the Bund, the Jewish socialist worker's organization that had been formed a few years earlier in Poland, and which often found itself working in opposition to Zionist concerns, or at least in opposition to Zionists. Boris was a cabinetmaker, skilled in woodworking, and "a pretty aggressive atheist," according to his son Lou. The couple had four children, Fay, Louis, Sam, and Saul.

Around 1914, with three children born and Saul still to come, Boris transferred his cabinetry skills to a new industry: movies. He took employment at several New York studios, including Biograph, Crystal Films, and Hearst Cosmopolitan, building sets and props. It was ephemeral work and had to be executed quickly, but he brought his old-world craftsmanship to it nonetheless. "There was nothing he couldn't make of wood," said Lou, "except maybe a wool carpet." Boris soon had a solid reputation in the business and had no trouble finding work.

But the business, not yet two decades old, was already undergoing large-scale change. In 1908 Thomas Edison, Biograph president Jeremiah J. Kennedy, and several other established producers had formed the Motion Picture Patent Company, an entity known colloquially as the "Trust," which was devoted to keeping movie technology, and the resulting profits, concentrated in its own hands by any means necessary. Legal tactics were often sufficient—Edison was able to get a patent on the sprocket hole approved by the Supreme Court, for instance, though the decision was reversed on appeal a few months later—and when they weren't, more street-level gambits were employed. Hoodlums masquerading as extras on New York location shoots would tear off their walrus moustaches, shrug off their topcoats, and beat up the crew, then either knock over and kick, or simply open fire on, the camera, exposing the film and rendering it useless. Studios and laboratories were broken into, film cans tossed around, negatives trampled. There were several major conflagrations also, including the September 11, 1915, destruction of Adolph Zukor and Jesse Lasky's's Twenty-Sixth Street Famous Players studio and the explosion of "Pop" Lubin's negative vault. (These fires, at least, were probably not the work of the Trust—Lubin was a member in good standing—but more likely of bad luck and the flammability of nitrate stock.)

None of this could mute the entrepreneurial spirit of the independent producers, though they recognized the wisdom of relocating their activities to a place they thought would be outside the Trust's influence: California. This would prove not to be the case—there were plenty of cowboys happy to take work as long-distance enforcers—but it didn't matter much, as the waning Trust was facing its own courtroom tribulations; and in any event the producers didn't care, because the California climate and topographical diversity were an ideal place for making pictures. Only the availability of the Broadway actors who deigned to be used as screen talent had kept the industry based in New York for as long as it had been; but now there were actors who specialized in screen work, and were more than happy to live in backwater Los Angeles. Boris Goldblatt, too, had no aversion to a Hollywood life, and decided in 1928 that New York was well and truly washed up as a film production centre, and moved his family to LA.

On his previous trips Boris had worked for a film production outfit called Tec-Art, located across the street from the Paramount studios on Melrose, and he continued to do so as a permanent Hollywood resident. He was the head of their construction department, but, ever the cabinetmaker, logged plenty of hours swinging a hammer in the carp shop himself. He invented a jack to lift and transport the flats used to build sets, and also served as a translator when Leo Tolstoy's son Ilya arrived at Tec-Art to consult on the adaptation of his father's final novel, *Resurrection*. During this time he also bought another property on Beachwood and, with the help of his sons and the odd itinerant carpenter, whom Boris would insist on paying union scale rather than the mere buck a day they were begging for, began building a four-suite apartment building there; this, probably, is where Rita, Gene, and Dick Miller lived on their 1942 arrival in LA.

In 1936 Boris was invited to Russia to help the Soviets modernize—or, more accurately, Westernize—the construction departments of their film industry. Control over the entire Russian industry had been centralized to an office led by an apparatchik named Boris Shumyatsky, who had been charged with the responsibility of making Soviet films more competitive on the world stage—more Hollywood. How better to achieve this than to import sympathetic professionals directly from Hollywood and receive instruction from them on how it was done? Sam had also found employment in the business by then, working in the laboratories of 20th Century Fox under Michael Leshing, where he specialized in Technicolor processing; so he, too, was welcomed into Shumyatsky's program. Boris and Sam stayed in Russia for the better part of a year, consulting, and in return the Party sent monthly cheques back to Tillie and the other children.

Sam's stateside association with Leshing got him notice in other circles. According to Russian spy cables decrypted between 1943 and 1945 through a top-secret military intelligence program known as the Venona project, Leshing, "a serious and unselfish man," the Soviet spies called him, had approached the Soviet vice-consul in Los Angeles, Ivan Ilyich Pilipenko, with an offer to provide formulas for colour film processing. Whether the Russians accepted the offer was not recorded, though it may be that SovColour and Fox Technicolor look similar for a reason. Sam Goldblatt, too, is mentioned in the cables as someone "friendly with and working with" Leshing. (Leshing had been called Mikhail Sergeevich Leshin when he arrived in the US in 1903.) This association no doubt put Sam on a list or two in Washington, where only a few years later the House Un-American Activities Committee (HUAC) would mount its heavily stagecrafted investigations into the "communist influence" in Hollywood.

Hollywood was truly a company town in those days, or at least an industry town, and almost all the Goldblatts were enthusiastic participants. Louis and Saul worked in the studios, and John Vigoreaux, the second of Fay's three husbands, did too. (Each of Fay's husbands had a surname starting with V, so, as the family joke went, she wouldn't have to change the monogram on her towels.) Louis, whose interest was in labour relations, then became an executive with the California Congress of Industrial Organizations and joined a "gaunt CIO organizer" named Jeff Kibre in an effort to rope the craftspeople of Tinseltown into a unified body called the United Studio Technicians Guild (USTG). (Kibre came from a progressive-minded studio family too: their specialty was building miniatures for special-effects sequences.)

There was already a history of organization in Hollywood, of course, though the Depression had fractured it considerably. There were different groups of craft-specific locals (Boris was a member of the Carpenter's Union), and there had been loose coalitions like the Federated Motion Picture Crafts (FMPC), which had initiated a brief strike in 1937; and then there was the venerable but at the time Mob-controlled International Alliance of Theatrical Stage Employees (IATSE). The IATSE had been taken over by shady Chicago figure Willie Bioff and sad-sack alcoholic George Browne in a 1934 election, and Bioff had since put the Hollywood studios under his thumb, extorting hundreds of thousands of dollars a year for himself and the Chicago concerns he ultimately represented. Studio accountants calculated that the Bioff buy-offs, which were characterized as extortions or bribes, depending on who you asked, would cost them a lot less than straight union representation. Windy City strongmen had been imported to help put down the FMPC strike, and when it came down to an election in which the craftspeople of Hollywood were to decide whether they would be represented by Bioff and Browne's wormy IATSE or Kibre and Goldblatt's as-yet uncorrupted USTG, there was more violence. Sam Goldblatt was among those who suffered a beating from IATSE goons, even though he was an IATSE member. Bioff had assured the studio bosses that the IATSE would win the election by whatever means were necessary, and so they did. Bioff and Browne would not be around to enjoy their victory for long, however. By the end of 1941 they were in prison, indicted on racketeering and conspiracy charges; and Bioff would ultimately come to a very Martin Scorsese ending, blown to bits while starting his car in the driveway of his Phoenix, Arizona, home, where he'd been living as "Bill Nelson," retired businessman.

Lou Goldblatt moved on to a position as the secretary-treasurer of the International Longshoremen's and Warehousemen's Union (ILWU), becoming, ultimately, "one of the country's foremost labour leaders," by one description. Lou was an honest dealer and a genuine progressive, and the ILWU was accordingly "one of the most progressive, democratic, powerful, influential and corruption-free of unions." After a falling out with the powerhouse ILWU president Harry Bridges, Goldblatt was forced to retire from the union in 1977, filling his time thereafter by working for peace between Israel and Palestine and organizing exchange programs between labour groups in China and the US. He died in 1983, as ardent a socialist and humanist as ever.

Two of the other Goldblatt children had equally distinguished, sometimes controversial, careers. Fay took her doctorate at the Sorbonne in Paris, one of the first American women to do so. She learned a number of languages and wrote her doctoral thesis on what Lou recalled only as "an obscure French poet." Her third and last V husband was named Vinock, and under the name Dr. Fay V. Vinock she became the Dean of Women at Pasadena City College. She passed away in 1999.

After his stay in Russia, his labour activism, and his mention in the Venona decryptions, Sam found himself *persona non grata* in Hollywood as the HUAC witch hunts heated up through 1947. He abandoned film work and evidently his politics too, changed his surname to Gilbert, and started a construction company, Sam Gilbert and Associates, becoming wealthy and powerful within a few years. By 1970 his worth was estimated at $25 million. In the late 1960s he began a relationship with the University of California Los Angeles (UCLA) basketball team, the Bruins, at first merely dispensing fresh fruit to the players in the locker room after games, but quickly becoming a patron and father figure to them, providing advice on everything from how to negotiate their contracts to, so it was alleged, how to arrange abortions for their girlfriends. He became known to the athletes as "Papa G" or "Papa Sam"—"Papa" in any case—and had them over for dinner or to lounge around the pool with him and his second wife, Rose, a renowned Los Angeles schoolteacher. Miller, who never felt shorter than when he visited his wealthy cousin, recalled that "their place was always overrun by basketball players." He met Kareem-Abdul Jabbar (then still called Lew Alcindor) at Sam and Rose's place, and was amused at the admixture of young black giants and stubby old Jews.

To the frequent chagrin of the coaches, Gilbert was an incredibly profligate sugar daddy to many of the top UCLA hoopsmen, providing them with "clothes, cash and whatever else they needed." He sold them season tickets at discount prices and bought them back for much more. He offered cars to prospective UCLA players. Sam didn't appear to get anything in return but their friendship, the joy of seeing them play, and the satisfaction of helping out his former alma mater; but still the relationship seemed decidedly unsportsmanlike. John Wooden, a coach who retired in 1975, claimed Gilbert's largesse really had no effect on the team; others energetically begged to differ; and it was in any case an egregious flaunting of National Collegiate Athletic Association (NCAA) rules. Coaches who complained reported later of feeling "threatened" by Gilbert, believing he had Mafia ties; others were merely wary of him; but nothing changed except by getting worse. But in 1981 the bough broke when Gilbert co-signed a loan on a car for one of the players. The NCAA ordered the UCLA team to cut the cord with Papa Sam, then cited them for nine infractions and suspended them for two years.

Just as restless Lou Goldblatt had needed something to fill the time after his sudden retirement, so brother Sam was not about to rusticate quietly either. According to the US Attorney's Office, Southern District of Florida, Gilbert's new pastime began in 1983, when he hooked up with an old construction business buddy, Jack Kramer, whose son Ben had imported at least half a million pounds of marijuana from Columbia to the Kramers' home state of Florida. Profits from this came to twelve million dollars, and the problem of what to do with it was allegedly solved by Gilbert, with the reported help of his own son Michael. The mountains of cash were sent by a courier, or sometimes transported by Gilbert himself, from Florida to Los Angeles, where a complex laundering scheme involving local businessmen transformed it into cheques, then sent it back to Florida, then to Liechtenstein, then the Virgin Islands, and finally back to LA, where Gilbert used it to finance the construction of a huge casino in Bell Gardens, California, called the Bicycle Club. The scheme went smoothly, with the biggest problem being Sam's inability to lift the heavy file boxes full of cash.

But, of course, the authorities wised up eventually, though not soon enough to nab Sam Gilbert. Federal officials banged on the door of his Pacific Palisades home on November 25, 1987, only to learn that he had died three days earlier. Sam's son Michael still faced charges, however, as did the Kramers and many others who were part of the scheme; and when the Feds seized the Bicycle Club, it stood as "the single largest asset ever forfeited to the US Government," according to the *Los Angeles Times*. But Sam's criminal activities and near-criminal basketball patronage should not be the only things he is remembered for: he was a vocal opponent of the war in Vietnam, and his generosity toward the basketball players was at least in part motivated by a genuine desire to help otherwise marginalized youngsters achieve their hoop dreams. He was a complex figure, almost Shakespearean in the breadth of his ambitions and impulsions.

Even so, the most mysterious and compelling of Dick Miller's LA cousins is Saul, who was also perhaps the most tragic—the last born, the first to pass on. He, too, worked in the studios as a young man, probably in sets or construction. Dick and Lainie Miller remember him only vaguely as, possibly, "the one who was building bridges in Europe," but whether he actually did anything of the sort is hard to determine. Like his brother, Sam, he was mentioned in the Venona cables, though a concordance of the 3,000 decrypted messages assembled by Alexander Vassiliev assumes that Saul and Sam have been mixed up by the spymasters, and that all the references to Saul are really to Sam. This is unlikely, as Saul's age is given as twenty-three in a 1944 cable, and that is just about right, while Sam was over thirty by that time. Saul is referred to in the concordance as an "oil industry engineer," and perhaps he was, but he did also work at Fox, like his brother, and this fact is certainly behind some of the confusion. At any rate the KGB received a "favourable character report" on Saul Goldblatt in 1942, and it was perhaps this report that led to Saul's, like Sam's, changing his last name to Gilbert after the war.

Most mysteriously and most delightfully of all is the final reference to Saul Gilbert I was able to find: his participation as producer, editor, and co-star of Alejandro Jodorowsky's first film, a 1957 short called *La cravate*. The film was shot in Paris through the mid-1950s, was based on a Thomas Mann story, and is a funny little mimed fantasy involving a cute-as-a-button street vendor (Denise Brossot), whose specialty is switching heads for anyone who is sick of their own. Jodorowsky himself plays a Chaplinesque naïf who tangles with a barrel-chested tough played by Gilbert, and all manner of charming, pastel-coloured confusions ensue as both parties romantically pursue the lovely head-vendor. No sooner was the film completed than it was apparently lost forever, while over the next twenty years Jodorowsky became a world-class eccentric and one of the most revered cult filmmakers in cinema for his midnight classics *El Topo*, *The Holy Mountain,* and *Santa Sangre*. But in 2006 a print of *La cravate* was discovered in an attic somewhere in Germany, and it is now easily available to view online.

Was this Saul Gilbert, mime-trained and entangled with an international congregation of neo-surrealists, indeed the former Saul Goldblatt? The obvious person to answer this is Dick Miller, but his recollection of Saul is so blurry that even a close-up photograph of the *La cravate* actor's face was unable to spark any memory one way or another. Dick and Lainie Miller both agreed that the man looked familiar, though, and like he belonged in the family; close comparison with photographs of both Lou Goldblatt and Sam Gilbert confirm that, indeed, based on appearances, this Saul Gilbert could certainly be their brother; and he even looks a bit like Dick in the bargain. Whoever he was, Saul Gilbert, née Goldblatt, died in his forties or early fifties, but not before contributing his share to the mystique of the Goldblatt family.

As Miller was writing his sci-fi stories and trying to drum up any other writing work he could, Jonathan Haze was still working the night shift at the gas station on Santa Monica Boulevard. He had a few regular customers, and one of them was a shaggy, schlubby actor/writer/busboy named Wyott Ordung, who was always talking about the movies he was going to make and promising Haze parts in them. "He told me he was a writer, gonna be a big director, blah blah blah," Haze said, but he didn't really believe anything Ordung was saying, because it was the sort of thing everyone said. But, said Haze, "it was fun to talk to people, so I would talk to him."

As it turned out, Ordung really was going to direct a movie. A couple of scripts he'd written, *Combat Squad* and the notorious *Robot Monster*, had been shot and released, and Ordung had hooked up with a producer who had never made a movie, a young man named Roger Corman. With skeletal funds Ordung and Corman had rented the reception room of somebody else's office, located above the Cock 'n Bull Restaurant on the Sunset Strip, and had pooled together what money they could raise—Ordung mortgaged his house, while Corman borrowed money from his parents and raised funds from old fraternity brothers who'd become professionals of one sort or another—with the intention of making an underwater monster picture. True to his word, once the $12,000 cash budget was raised, Ordung cruised by the gas station and told Haze that if he wanted a part in the movie, he could have one.

He took Haze to meet Corman, where it was determined that the only role Haze could conceivably play was a Mexican deep-sea diver, and Corman didn't think he looked the part. Eager for a job that didn't involve wiping windows, Haze offered to grow a little moustache, fast track his suntan, and work on a Mexican accent. He was given the role, but didn't have to quit the service station because the owner fired him the moment he noticed the incipient moustache. It didn't matter: now that Haze was in with Corman, man, he was *in*. He went out to Catalina with Ordung, Corman, and the rest of the little company for the six-day shoot, did his Mexican scuba-diver bit, and had fun, and when Corman went on to make other movies, he was on most of them too, not just acting but production managing, lugging gear, driving trucks, and staging fights.

As all this was going on, Miller was at extremely loose ends. He was enjoying the California sunshine, the California women; but his sci-fi story writing gig had dried up and he was broke all the time. He'd connected with Sammy Davis Jr., who was now a big Vegas star and living in an LA mansion, and ended up selling Davis a story idea for $5,000. Except, he never got the $5,000, the friendship was soured as a result, and Miller was still busted flat. As ever, he went to movies whenever he could afford it, and visited his first Hollywood movie set in early 1955, when one evening Mel Welles said,

"You wanna meet Clark Gable?" Who doesn't, Miller thought, and went with Welles to the Fox lot where Gable was making an action picture called *Soldier of Fortune*. Welles had a part in the picture—he'd been known to play smaller roles in bigger productions. "He got good parts, but they were bits," Miller said of his friend's career. Still, he was playing in the majors, and when Miller got there he was dazzled. "We hung around for a couple of hours, and then Gable showed up," he said. "And he was the nicest, just the nicest guy I've ever met." The star chatted amiably with Miller and Welles, and even invited them to his dressing room, where he uncorked a bottle of wine and continued his friendly discourse. Miller was amazed that "a man of his stature" could be so down-to-earth.

Mostly, Miller spent his days in Schwab's, nursing coffees, eating 85-cent meals, and reading the magazines for free, or palavering with Bobby Campbell, Chuck Griffith, Welles, and all his other new friends. He was aware of the drugstore's reputation as a place of star-making discoveries, but was equally aware that, as gossip hound-memoirist John Gilmore wrote, "No one was ever 'discovered' at Schwab's. None of the hopefuls nursing coffee at the counter, like Sally Kellerman or Warren Oates or Harry Dean Stanton, expected to be discovered, because no one came into Schwab's looking for talent—only to mooch money or try to get laid."

There was plenty going on at Schwab's without discovery; the drugstores were intensely social. "Drugstores were the centre of things," Miller said.

> Because you had to meet your friends. You don't come over to my house; this is California, you gotta go someplace. So I'll meet you down at the drugstore. And we'd spend hours, just literally, eat breakfast, have lunch, have dinner. And if there was nothing else happening, you spent the whole day there. They had that huge, huge, fifteen-foot sidewalk in front, and everything happened out there. Schwab's was wild. Everybody hung out there. This is why it, and Hansen's in New York, were important. They had bookies, they had gangsters, they had hookers, they had actors.

Eric Morris, an acting teacher of some renown and infamy, declared Schwab's "a haven away from the boredom and depression" of being an unemployed actor. "It seemed that all of us bonded and shared what we felt, even if we didn't talk about it." In 1953 *Time* magazine called it "the best-known corner drug store in America," and Miller was on his way to becoming its figurehead and most passionate advocate.

Occasionally he could be pried away. He'd been listening with interest to Haze's accounts of working on movies, and at the same time was acutely aware of his own career, which largely involved sitting in Schwab's and listening to others talk about their careers. It was the summer of 1955; he was twenty-six years old and considered himself a writer, but was doing no writing, or none he was able to sell. It was a point at which, if Miller was a movie character (and isn't he?), it would be time for the screenwriter to introduce some kind of twist in his story, a ninety-degree turn that would give him a chance to reinvent himself and forge the identity for which he'd soon become known, if he was ever to become known at all. There was no cosmic screenwriter pulling the strings of Miller's life, of course, but nevertheless there were influences at work. Among them was Jonathan Haze, a supporting character but a pivotal one, who one day, while they were sitting at Schwab's, said to Miller, "Hey, let's get out of here, go to the beach or somewhere. I just gotta make a stop along the way, drop something off with this guy I'm working for. I'll introduce you. His name's Roger Corman."

8   I always liked Roger

"He was Roger's favourite, no doubt about that one," Jack Nicholson insisted. The sentiment is heartfelt; but Corman had a lot of favourites, enough so that it might be better said he had none. He was, by many accounts, and as you'd expect, roughly a father figure to the men and women who worked for him, but a father of a particular sort, like those found in Victorian literature: cordial, proper, distant. He's another complex figure in Miller's tale, with his Ivy League exterior masking a furious subterranean battle between the inclinations of an artist and the instincts of a businessman.

The salient facts about Roger Corman have been told many times—the stories are in their third or fourth generation of being retold, whether they were ever true or not—but it's just possible some younger or more sheltered readers have not heard them. Corman was born in Detroit in 1926, became movie crazed at an early age, moved with his family to Los Angeles in 1940, was educated in the engineering faculty of Stanford, and lasted four days bored stiff as a professional engineer before chucking it for a menial office job with 20th Century Fox. Even in the most basic pressbook biography, we find a few intriguing parallels with Dick Miller. Like Miller, Corman had a brother named Gene; a family that moved to California from the East; a love of movies; and a hesitation in quitting something that disagreed with him measurable in microseconds. Both men also did a stint in the navy, only to find they were not navy men at heart.

At Fox Corman worked his way up to a position as a reader, providing coverage on optioned books and submitted stories and scripts. Because he was the youngest dogsbody in the readers' department, almost everything he was given was dismal, bottom-of-the-barrel crap. Eventually he got a half-decent script, gave some notes and suggestions on it, and was dismayed to see the thing produced with the benefit of his changes, while all the credit (and the associated cash bonus) went to the head of the department, the story editor. He quit Fox soon after, attended Oxford for a while, then, having caught the bug, determined to go into the movie producing business for himself.

He met Wyott Ordung and together they made *Monster from the Ocean Floor*, and with its profits Corman produced a race-car drama, *The Fast and the Furious*, with borrowed autos and non-professional drivers (including Jonathan Haze and Corman himself). Through Ordung he was introduced to Jim Nicholson, who, with his business partner Samuel Arkoff, had started American Releasing Corporation, the distribution company that would soon expand into production and, in March of 1956, become known as American International Pictures (AIP). A deal was made to distribute not just *The Fast and the Furious*, but a whole slate of mini-budgeted films, each financed largely with the sales guarantee of the previous one. This allowed Corman to make pictures in relatively rapid succession, and as long as he kept costs down and schedules short, profits were virtually guaranteed.

Producing, for Corman, was a journey of discovery: specifically of discovering what costs could be shaved from a budget. "Director" was a big one; why not eliminate that? Well, not eliminate exactly, just do it himself. With his next movie, a western called *Five Guns West* written by Miller's pal Bobby Campbell, that's what he did. He was so nervous on the first day, so the story goes, that he stopped his car on the way to the set, opened his door, and threw up. (Howard Hawks did the same thing at the start of almost every movie, so it's told.) But the picture was made and marketed, and something about the ease of shooting in the wide open spaces, not worrying about special effects (which had been a problem on *Monster from the Ocean Floor*), and working with horses instead of cars appealed to Corman, and he decided his next picture would be another oater, *Apache Woman*, from a script by Arkoff's brother-in-law, Lou Rusoff. This was among the projects he was preparing the day Jonathan Haze stopped by the tiny Cock 'n Bull office with a friend in tow.

This is one of Miller's most oft-told stories, and the thumbnail version goes as follows: Miller was introduced to Corman, who asked what he did. "I'm a writer," Miller told him.

"Don't need writers," Corman said. "I need actors."

"I'm an actor!" Miller shouted.

Freed from the strictures of anecdote, the story is more lifelike, but the upshot is the same. On the way to the Cock 'n Bull—a quasi-British Sunset Strip landmark almost as storied as Schwab's—Haze told Miller that this producer was a young, small-time guy, so he was sharing an office. "But when I got there," Miller said, "he wasn't sharing an office, he was sharing a *desk*!" Even if Corman had had the whole desk and the entire office to himself, the operation would have been pretty rinky-dink; some suspected the 10 x 10-foot chamber was simply the restaurant's repurposed cloakroom.

Haze and Miller entered the office, and introductions were made. "I thought [Corman] looked like a high school kid!" Miller recalled. "He was a young guy, he was vibrant, he was always smiling. He was a charming guy." Miller made himself as comfortable as possible on the edge of a desk and looked around, not impressed by the size of the office, but not disdainful either. He was willing to give Corman plenty of credit just for making movies at all. "We sat around and shot the breeze for a while," Miller told *Fangoria* magazine, "then he asked what I did. I gave him my whole background in about ten seconds and then mentioned that I was writing. 'Do you want me to write a screenplay?' I asked. 'I've never done it, but I'm sure I could.'"

"We talked a little bit about writing," Corman recalled, "but I was more interested in him as an actor, because I had two scripts in preparation and I really didn't want to put a third in preparation at that time." Corman was in fact not just developing his own stories, but also having scripts assigned to him by Nicholson and Arkoff; *Apache Woman* was one of these. Corman could see chameleonic possibilities in Miller's look right away, and though he was still just starting his filmmaking career, his instincts were honed enough to know this was a face the camera could love. "I thought he looked like sort of an offbeat character leading man," Corman said. "He was a little bit short, which hurt his eventual career as a leading man, but not as a character actor."

Corman told his visitor he had a Western coming up in just a week or two and still needed a few Indians. There were not many Indigenous actors available in Los Angeles at the time, but in an era when even Asians were generally played by Swedes like Nils Asther or Warner Oland—not to mention Germans like Peter Lorre or Brits like Boris Karloff—it wouldn't have mattered. The Hollywood shortcut for an Indigenous person, when no Armenians could be found, was usually an Italian (Frank de Kova whenever possible) or a Jew; Miller was a Jew who looked vaguely Italian, so he was a shoo-in. At any rate he was as hungry for work as he'd ever been in his life, and was happy to accept the part. "Got any lines?" he asked Corman, who replied that he would probably have one or two. Good enough. Miller ran out and dropped $150 on a membership in the Screen Actor's Guild.

Apache Woman was shot over six days in late August 1955 at Iverson's Ranch in the San Fernando Valley. Rusoff's talky but eventful script was set in a small western town whose residents are preparing to go to war against the Apache tribe down the road, whom they believe to be assassinating their menfolk and rustling their cattle. But actually the culprit is bitter "half-breed"

Armand Lebeau, behind whose pastry-chef name burns a violent hatred of both groups. He's got a small band of renegade followers who take care to leave evidence implicating the innocent Apaches at the site of every outrage. An upright government agent named Rex Moffet tries to dampen the incendiary situation, which is complicated by Armand's sister, Anne, who's aware of her brother's increasing derangement but not of his crimes, and who is resisting a growing attraction to the visiting lawman. A final confrontation sees Armand plunge from a cliff and Rex and Anne united in the standard last-frame clinch. In a demonstration of either Corman's impish humour or his total lack of it, the diminutive Miller was cast as Tall Tree, one of Armand's Apache helpers, who wears long hair and a floppy hat with a big feather in it.

Miller wasn't nervous at all in the days leading up to the shoot; by all accounts he was born to the profession. Film acting is a very specific thing, with a whole set of requirements over and above the actual emoting: the actor needs to perform to the audience but not to the camera; he needs to be at least vaguely aware of how lighting works, of what lenses can and can't see, of the editor's requirements, of motion, of continuity, of hitting marks, and handling props. Miller either sussed out all these things on his own or else simply appeared to, which, in cinema, the kingdom of falsehood, amounts to the same thing. At any rate from day one "he was very natural," Corman said. "He had no problems whatsoever."

Whatever he picked up must have been by some osmosis. "I didn't know where the camera was, I didn't know where the lights were," Miller told me. "Roger said, 'Be natural. Don't notice those things.' And that was it. I never really found out where the camera and lights were." The first piece of movie equipment he really became familiar with was the shovel. He told *Fangoria*, "I remember the horses were running through the street and they all took a shit. Everybody grabbed shovels, and someone said, 'That's your job, every time they—'" This was a twist Miller hadn't foreseen. "Get outta here! I'm not gonna shovel shit!" he told them. But there was a communal feeling to the project that was hard to resist, and he soon got into the *We're puttin' on a show!* spirit Corman tried to foment on all his sets. The experience took Miller back to the wilds of Long Island and the piney nights in upstate New York. "It was just like when I was a kid, playing cowboys and Indians," he told writer Mark Thomas McGee, "only now I was getting paid for it."

He met a number of people he would work with many times over. There was an old Australian makeup man named Curly Batson, an ex-rodeo cowboy who was also working on his first Corman picture; there was key grip Charles Hannawalt, who taught Corman much of the nuts and bolts of moviemaking; there was Floyd Crosby, a cameraman with equal amounts of talent and irascibility, along with a curiously prestigious CV: he'd shot F. W. Murnau and Robert Flaherty's *Tabu* (and had won an Oscar for it), as well as the recent award winner *High Noon*, and he had a musician son named David who would also do well for himself one day; there was production manager Bart Carré and assistant director Lou Place; and there was set decorator Harry Reif, who was older than everyone else by half, but would keep working steadily for the next twenty years. Miller remembered these people later as one might remember any co-worker from sixty years ago—that is, vaguely—but the lessons they taught him were stuck fast. One crucial tip clearly came from Crosby, probably informally, as he wouldn't have had time on a six-day shoot to dispense organized wisdom to the talent. "All I know about cameramen," said Miller, by rote, "is you gotta be friendly with 'em!"

The cast was headed by Lloyd Bridges, the future *Sea Hunt* star who would sire Beau and Jeff, and who here played the stolid Rex; sci-fi queen Joan Taylor as Anne; and Lance Fuller, loaned out from Universal to play the grinning, perpetually sarcastic Armand Lebeau. Haze played a rabble-rousing townsman (he gets an arrow in the back, of course), and Paul Birch, who would work with Corman and Miller again (though for the last time) in *Not Of This Earth*, appeared as a surprisingly realistic sheriff, neither upright nor craven.

Much of Miller's screen time involved either skulking behind Lance Fuller or peering over a rock at Lloyd Bridges, always slathered in Curly Batson's dark makeup. As the shoot progressed his role got both larger and more violent. At one point, when Armand was supposed to snipe an old rummy off his wagon, Miller got the business instead, because Fuller pointed out that Tall Tree was better placed to make the shot according to Corman's hurried blocking. "And then there was another one like that," Miller said. "And it was one of these things where just by chance I wound up the killer. Killed about four people in it, you know, for no reason." He got to do someone in with a throwing knife, an action he was able to sell easily because of his previous blade-tossing experience. Miller got his promised line too, which was "Good chief, you chief now," and he and Fuller both puzzled over its meaning. (This is itself puzzling—the line makes perfect sense in context.) He also got to nod disdainfully toward actor Morgan Jones and say, "White man is afraid."

Tall Tree is finally felled in a gunfight scene, shot down by another tangential character, and after this was filmed Corman approached Miller, wondering if he'd like to play a cowboy. Miller, surprised at this apparent forethought, asked, "You mean in your next picture?"

"No, in this one," Corman replied. There were several scenes of disgruntled townsfolk listening to Haze rabble-rouse, and Corman needed extra bodies to fill them out; ever the pragmatist, he had no hesitation in doubling up his actors. "I've done that kind of thing a few times," Corman told me, "and nobody ever notices it. You always get away with it, providing you change the wardrobe and you put him in the front in one scene and in the back in the other." It was okay with Miller—it meant a few more bucks and two extra lines: the actor's dream, his dialogue instantly doubled! He gets to watch a knife fight between Haze's character and fiery Anne Lebeau, and then, after Moffet stops the fight, he complains, "Tom should have killed the 'breed.'" Upon being told by Moffet to go home, he asks, "Who are you to be givin' us orders anyway, mister?" Though filmed late in the schedule, this is the first scene in the picture, so these latter two lines are the first words movie audiences ever heard from Dick Miller. The rest of the time in his cowboy guise he just stands around, looking surly and filling space. Corman had intended him to be a part of the posse that goes after Armand, Tall Tree, and the other the bad guys, but when Miller, demonstrating the integrity that would get him in trouble down the line, pointed out he might well end up killing himself if this was done, Corman excused him from the scene.

Miller made $300 for his two roles, four lines, and six days on *Apache Woman*, and got a decent billing—he's the tenth name on the cast list, not bad for a guy hired largely because he was upright, breathing, and could talk. The picture itself is the very definition of a "programmer": a product, a movie made to complete a double bill, to provide something for the patrons to look at while munching popcorn, or not to look at while necking. It was shot in widescreen and vibrant Pathécolor, though, when it was released on video, the cropped, monochrome TV transfer was used; at least the level of industry respect accorded it was consistent through the years. Clearly the weather was fine while it was being made, for at one point the crew is visible in a window reflection and they all appear to be wearing white t-shirts. It's heavy on chat and light on action, and the same scenes seem to recur three or four times each, just as the same bushes, trees, and rocks rush by over and over again like Hanna-Barbara backgrounds; but it's a brisk little oater for all that, and, if nothing else, a great showcase for Miller's versatility. Here he is, a kid from the Bronx, playing both a cowboy and an Indian in the same picture, and taking it all just as seriously as Corman did. And he's good: as the renegade Apache, he glares with intensity, handles his guns with absolute plausibility, and delivers his lines such that even the immortal "Good chief, you chief now" is a little bit touching; and in its heartfelt delivery it provides a concentrated burst of background otherwise missing from the Armand–Tall Tree relationship. Even in death, as poor felled Tall Tree lies in the dust of a California rancher's gully, Miller is delivering a performance: one hand is open, fingers splayed, reaching upward as though for a last precious grasp at life. Tall Tree, we hardly knew ye. Corman, who was never an actor's director and was certainly anything but in those early days, couldn't have had anything to do with this post-mortem gesture, but he knew enough to put it in the centre of his frame.

Just a month after *Apache Woman* wrapped and Miller had finally been minted as a professional actor, James Dean, age twenty-four, crashed his Porsche Spyder into Donald Turnupseed's Ford coupé. It would be hard to overstate the impact this had on the community of young male actors in Hollywood. Dean had been a regular at Schwab's and especially Googie's, the late-night diner next door, and was well-known and liked, disliked, mooned over, or envied by the clientele of both spots. Most of those thought they could be him, or should be him, and when he died only three films into what would have been an extraordinary career, beneath the assertions of grief there was the drumbeat of *my turn now, my turn now, my turn now.* Miller's old pal Steve McQueen was supposed to have said, "I'm glad Dean's dead—it makes more room for me." Miller was possibly unique, certainly uncommon, in that he had no ambition to become a movie star; probably it hadn't yet occurred to him as a possibility. It would have been hard, though, not to get caught up in the rush to fill the Dean-sized hole in the Hollywood firmament, and if Dean could come to stardom from apparently nowhere (he had actually come out of theatre and television, which is to say, New York), then why couldn't a tiny, barely reviewed Corman picture serve as a launching pad? (Time, and Jack Nicholson, would prove that indeed it could.)

Miller was only a couple of years older than Dean, so he might have entertained some of the same thoughts all his peers were having, even if despite themselves. But as *Rebel Without a Cause* showed, Dean could play teenagers if he had to, and Miller couldn't have even when he was one—he'd spent his entire adolescence acting older than his age. He never was able to play young, and *Sorority Girl*, a couple of years down the line, gives us an idea of how it would have turned out if he'd tried. So Dick likely had no illusions about shouldering the Dean mantle—he seems barely to have acknowledged he was an actor at all, just at a moment in American history when, thanks to the Actors Studio and Brando and Clift and the rest, the profession had as much currency as it ever would. There was no hustling from Miller, no auditioning, just the vague promise of another Corman quickie down the line now that he'd done well in one. "I never thought seriously about being an *ac*-tor," Miller said. "I was acting 'cause it was easy. I was having fun in Hollywood. This to me was … it was the land of lands, the place to be when you're a young guy."

Writing was on the far back burner, and after Saks he'd sworn he would never take another straight job. How did he survive? Rent, food, everything was cheap then, and there was the unemployment line, where Miller could pick up a few bucks and palaver with all the other starving actors he was getting to know at Schwab's, and now on Corman sets. There were surprise special guest appearances on the unemployment line too: "Rudy Vallee would come in," Miller said, "with his butler. Swear to god! Stand in line, get his cheque, thank you, thank you. He'd thank everybody in line and walk out."

Pretty soon there was indeed another Corman picture, a Western again, and another woman, an *Oklahoma Woman*. But there was no juicy dual role for Miller this time, only a lowly bartender, the kind who glowers, perpetually wipes down shot glasses, and wears one of those elastic straps on his sleeve. (The type is lampooned perfectly in *Blazing Saddles*, alongside every other Western cliché.) It's a perfectly reasonable part for a young actor to take on in his second picture, but in retrospect, considering all the bartenders and varied nameless menials Miller would play later, it was a rather grim foreshadowing; certainly it was no kind of role for someone looking to step into Dean's shoes. At the time, it was work: a few bucks, a couple of lines, and a step closer to semi-regular employment with the still-coalescing Corman company.

The Oklahoma Woman was another Lou Rusoff script, and another demonstration of his (budget-dictated) preference for argument over action. It was a tale of good guys and gals fighting bad guys and gals in the Old West; having reduced itself to its most critical elements by the end, it climaxed in a catfight. It might as well have been a low-budget, straight-arrow adaptation of some recent studio Western or other, maybe Fritz Lang's *Rancho Notorious* or Nicholas Ray's *Johnny Guitar*. For Miller, film acting was still a lark, not yet a job, certainly not a calling; and this was a chance for him to hang out once more on a set with Haze, and to make the acquaintance of B-movie subalterns like Richard Denning, the picture's male lead, who had fought *The Creature from The Black Lagoon* only two years earlier; 'Touch' Connors, who would become better known as Mike Connors in the role of TV detective Joe Mannix; and Bruno VeSota, a heavyset fellow, frequently sweaty, who would play many roles in Miller's professional life, and whom he liked (everybody liked Bruno), but would never get to know very well. "Just a chubby guy who liked acting," Miller called him.

In the midst of this, in early October 1955, *Apache Woman* was released as the bottom half of a double bill, beneath the comparatively big-budget Audie Murphy war picture *To Hell and Back*. (After this, Arkoff and Nicholson would pair their films with one another rather than with big studio releases, an arrangement that had been making them no money.) It got some decent notices, and *Variety* even noted the movie's "excellent performances." The *Hollywood Reporter* called it an "okay programmer." *The Oklahoma Woman* looked to be more of the same—"OK" was even in the title.

One of the reasons Corman hadn't been interested in Miller as a writer was probably because one of Dick's new Schwab's pals had moved in first. Jonathan Haze, the lynchpin to so much of the early Corman cohort, had carried a stack of Chuck Griffith's unproduced spec scripts to the tiny office over the Cock 'n Bull. Corman read through them quickly and decided Griffith had talent (he did) and should write for him. This led to a Confederate war story called "Three Bright Banners," the scale of which was beyond Corman's reach. Griffith then wrote a Western called "Hang Town," but it, too, demanded resources Corman couldn't provide. The director gave Griffith a few pointers on how to write to a budget, then took him to the movies, to a Randolph Scott Western, not as a social outing but as further instruction. He told Griffith to write a budget version of the story they'd just seen and match it as closely as he dared, but to make Scott's sheriff character a girl. "It's Randolph Scott," Griffith pointed out. "He's already a girl." But he went ahead and fulfilled Corman's request, and in short order had a script called "The Yellow Rose of Texas."

Griffith had been one of the first people Miller met on his arrival in Los Angeles, and they stayed close for a long time. He was "a character," Miller says, "a weird, strange man." He was in fact a standout oddball in a town full of oddballs, and a writer who turned out quality work so quickly that people assumed he could be brilliant if he was given more time, but who was probably at his best in the straitjacketing environment of American International. He called himself "lazy," telling interviewer Aaron Graham that he'd always planned to write for the big studios and the big bucks, but it was simply easier to go back and do another one for Corman.

Griffith was born in Chicago in 1930 and had gained some early, practical writing experience while attending a military school, where he impressed his fellow students by writing romantic poems in which any girl's name could easily and euphoniously be inserted. Why he was in a military school at all is a mystery: his people were thoroughgoing show folk. His grandfather had been a tightrope walker; his father, a vaudevillian; his grandmother and mother, both actors. His grandmother's name was Myrtle Vail, and she had created a radio soap opera in the 1930s called *Myrt and Marge*. She played Myrt; her daughter—Chuck Griffith's mother—played Marge; and the show was popular enough to run through almost two decades. In 1933 it was turned into a feature film complete with guest appearances from the Three Stooges. In 1951 Myrtle decided her creation should be adapted for television and that Los Angeles was the place to try it, and Griffith tagged along to help write the scripts. *Myrt and Marge* never made it as a television program, but Griffith wrote six or seven feature films on his own while his grandmother was trying to sell the thing, and this was the stack of scenarios Haze had trucked over to Corman's office.

"The Yellow Rose of Texas" was retitled *Gunslinger*, and would be Griffith's first work to actually go before a camera. The picture was shot in January 1956 at a ranch in Topanga Canyon, quickly put together on a five-day schedule to beat an upcoming IATSE regulation that would see crews paid six days' worth for five days' work. This was anathema to Corman, of course, but he counted it a victory to get a last five-days'-pay-for-five-days'-work picture in under the wire. It was not a reprise of the balmy experience of *Apache Woman*, however; it rained every one of the five days, which turned it into a six-day shoot anyway. On the sixth day the charcoal clouds parted and the sun shone brightly, and it would be speculation to suggest Corman might have found a lesson in this. But Griffith correctly pointed out that the heavy skies ultimately worked in the picture's favour: because the company could not afford the big lights that might have given it the bright look favoured at the time, or the hours and manpower needed to set them up, cinematographer Fred West was left with just his box of flags and reflectors, and the result was a movie with an attractively, appropriately, and uniquely leaden look.

It was a dangerous picture, on which the "pain is temporary, film is forever" approach Corman had taken on his pictures thus far finally caught up with him, or, at any rate, with his actors. Beverly Garland, Corman's girlfriend at the time, was playing the lady sheriff, and twisted her ankle trying to jump on a horse. Allison Hayes, the villain, broke her arm falling off a different horse. A love scene beneath a tree between Garland and male lead John Ireland was interrupted by a nightmarish invasion of marching red ants. Of course it didn't suit Corman or his schedule or his basic sense of human compassion to have his actors hurt. He showed some pity towards Miller, who was playing a Pony Express rider. "I asked him if he could ride a horse," Corman said, "and he said something like, 'Can *I* ride a horse?' Well, of course he couldn't ride a horse, but I think he took one or two lessons." There was a particularly challenging scene in which Miller had to race up, riding one horse, jump off, run over to another, jump on, and ride away. "I could see that he was out of control, and this horse had to really be racing," Corman continued. "So I printed the first or second take. I thought, 'I don't want to put him on that horse any more than is absolutely necessary! I might have a very injured actor here.'" It has been told elsewhere, however, that Miller's precariousness during one part of the scene became the subject of an on-set betting pool: Would he fall? The story is that extra takes were called for just to keep the game going. But Miller was one of the few to walk off *Gunslinger* uninjured, though at the same time *Gunslinger* seems to have been one of the few sets Miller walked off uninjured.

Miller's character was the subject of a slightly pedantic but perfectly interesting note on the generally unreadable and now discontinued Internet Movie Database message boards. A man named George Gauthier, evidently a student of the Old West, wrote,

> Several scenes show a Pony Express rider. This movie is set in 1878. The Pony Express was in business only for only 18 months from the spring of 1860 till the fall of 1861 when the telegraph line reached the West coast. It lost its investors a lot of money, but it provided a faster mail link than the Overland stage coach line. It operated during a critical phase of American history, strengthening the links between California and the East during the days leading up to the Civil War. Also, Pony Express riders went unarmed to save weight. They relied on speed for safety. The actor in the movie was

too old and too large to be a rider. Those who rode for the Pony Express could weigh no more than 125 pounds. They were all young, wiry lads with a spirit of adventure and can-do attitude.

"Too old and too large," lacking a spirit of adventure and can-do attitude—it's a good thing this notice didn't appear until almost sixty years later, or the sensitive Miller might have hung it up after only three pictures, and we'd never have gotten *A Bucket of Blood*.

After the release of *Apache Woman*, Miller found there was another Dick Miller listed in the Screen Actors Guild rolls. "That's my name and I want it!" Miller raged. He went to the guild office and was told, "Ah, we'll straighten it out." For a few films, however, he had to call himself Richard Miller, or even Richard "Dick" Miller. He's Richard in the *Gunslinger* credits, and appears ninth on the cast list, his highest placement yet. He'd barely had billing at all on *The Oklahoma Woman*.

For Corman, the movie was the last straw bale. Whatever practical advantages he'd seen in Westerns had faded, eclipsed by the constant hassles. People fell off horses, trucks got stuck, locations were limited, there were always weather concerns. He'd been warned by his brother Gene not to do this one, in fact, but had ignored the advice. He was listening now. Corman didn't try another Western until years later, and Miller was in that one too. But it didn't end happily for Corman, and Miller finally got the horse-riding injury one would have thought the fates had in store for him on *Gunslinger*.

That was in the future. The relevant thing now, as far as Miller's career was concerned, was Chuck Griffith's approaching Roger Corman and suggesting that maybe they try a science-fiction picture next.

9 You're gonna be a star

On a nice day when he had no work, which was many more days than not, one could find Miller out in front of Schwab's, shooting the breeze with his pals, watching the Sunset traffic go by. It sounds sedate, and largely was, but occasionally there was excitement. Just a few doors down there was a store called Thrifty's, and on one occasion, when Miller was still a relative newcomer in LA, the front door opened and a well-dressed man came running out. He was followed closely by another man, who shouted, "Stop that guy! He robbed the place!"

"Why I went after him," Miller said, "I will never, ever be able to explain." But he leapt up reflexively, took off after the bandit, and chased him south down Laurel Street. Frank de Kova, sitting outside Googie's, watched them go. They ran downhill, Miller only feet behind the bandit, and momentum overtook them: they hurtled along the pavements pell-mell and out of control. The robber managed to stop and turned back to Miller, making as if to speak, but Miller barrelled into him and knocked the man down. Miller, too, hit the pavement, and in a second they were both up again and running down the street. The thief got to Fountain, ran into the road, and hit a slow-moving car; he bounced off and fell to the ground, and Miller sat on him until the other pursuers caught up.

"I look up," Miller said, "and these guys are comin' around from the parking lot, saying, 'You got him? You got him?' I said, 'Yeah,' huff-puff." The men dragged the exhausted robber back up the street, leaving Miller on the pavement. He staggered to his feet and followed, still gasping for breath. When they got back up to Sunset, Miller tried to follow the men into the store that had been hit, but was denied entry. "You can't go in there," a burly cop told him. "Place was just robbed." The guys in front of Schwab's snickered.

"I know, I just caught the guy," Miller said to the cop, but the officer wasn't convinced. There was a shout from somewhere within the crowd: "Ah, ya fink, why didn't you let him go? He was just a junkie, needed the money for drugs!" Miller didn't get a reward for his heroics, or even any thanks, just the crowd's mild abuse and a local reputation as an unpredictable man of action. At least four years later, when Lainie Halpern got to town and found herself at Schwab's, he was still known as "the guy who chases bank robbers."

Corman, meanwhile, was way ahead of Griffith's fantasy film suggestion; he already had a science-fiction script, a thing Lou Rusoff had written. It needed some work, but when Corman talked to Rusoff about a rewrite, he found the scribe on his way to his hometown of Winnipeg, Canada, to be with his brother, who was dying. (Rusoff himself would succumb to an early death from brain cancer less than a decade later.) So Corman gave it to Griffith, who read the script but couldn't make head nor tail of it. He put it down and, he claimed, started utterly from scratch, writing something new on the same theme in three days. (Rusoff still got a solo screen credit, though, at Griffith's urgent request.)

The story involved an extraterrestrial invasion, not from Mars for once, but from Venus. The invader was bestial, like *The Thing from Another World*, but was also an intellectual, like Klaatu from *The Day the Earth Stood Still*: a silver-tongued devil who could flatter the greatest brains on Earth to his will. As in all tightly budgeted invasions, this alien was merely a point man or scout, paving the way for a presumably more epic incursion to follow. Griffith, as budget-conscious a writer as ever worked in Hollywood, had the alien hiding in a cave for most of the picture, issuing orders by shortwave radio and sending rubber bats out to do the dirty work. He appeared only briefly at the end of the story, still lurking in the shadows of his cave.

Griffith's script combined two established 1950s sci-fi movie traditions: scientist-as-hero and scientist-as-patsy. The story opens as a NASA-like organization is frustrated by their repeated failure to launch a satellite—every attempt ends in an explosion. By his ham radio transmissions, a recently arrived Venusian convinces astronomer Tom Anderson that his greatest wish is to help Earthlings overcome their penchant for violence. Really his goal is complete planetary takeover. An upright, do-gooding scientist, Paul Nelson, a friend of Anderson's, suspects first that his pal is crazy, then a dupe. Meanwhile the alien is hexing local authority figures through mind-control darts fired by the rubber bats in his employ.

Corman was good at finding actors, and he cast Peter Graves as Nelson and Lee Van Cleef in an early role as Anderson. Beverly Garland took on the role of Anderson's worried wife, and did good, persuasive work with the part. Russ Bender played the Morris Ankrum part of the general in charge of the local army base. Miller and Haze shouldered the comedy relief, playing two bickering soldiers sent out on pointless manoeuvres by the possessed general, sort of a proto-C3-PO/R2-D2 pair. Haze dusted off the Mexican accent and little moustache he'd adopted for *Monster from the Ocean Floor*, while Miller got to do comic frustration and an Edgar Kennedy slow burn, along with an action scene at the end. "That was the first film that Dick Miller and I kind of did a comedy duo together, and it was effective and everybody loved it," Haze rather wishfully told an interviewer. "If we had done it later on, after television had gotten really hot, we could have been a really good comedy team."

The actors on the picture were all professionals, keeping up the better-than-you'd-expect level of talent Corman was fast making one of his trademarks; but the key role in this picture, everybody knew, was the Venusian. Paul Blaisdell, an illustrator and science-fiction fan whose transition into head creature creator for Corman had been midwifed by Forry Ackerman, was enlisted to design and build the thing, and from the beginning Blaisdell insisted this wouldn't be just another man in a suit. (Though there would indeed be a man in the suit, at least it wouldn't be a man-shaped suit.) Blaisdell looked into the conditions on Venus, which were supposed to be hot and misty, and concluded that some sort of plant or fungus would be the planet's most likely inhabitant. In Blaisdell's imagining the thing was a tall, vertically corrugated cone with a heavy brow, rubbery lips, a vicious toothy underbite, and long arms terminating in crab claws. Instead of legs it had a series of finger-like protuberances around its broad base, though any locomotion provided by these would have to be heavily faked, or, as indeed was the case, merely imagined. The artist made a small sculpture of his idea and showed it to AIP president Jim Nicholson. "Paul, you've done it again!" Nicholson enthused.

Everyone had a different name for the creature. Blaisdell called it "Beulah," but other, less respectful observers declared it the "Carrot Creature," or the "Mushroom Monster." Chuck Griffith called it "Denny Dimwit," but "he called everything Denny Dimwit," said Miller, whose own nickname for it was the "Ice Cream Cone." (Frank Zappa, introducing a song called "Cheepnis," his sung tribute to *It Conquered the World*, described it in his stage banter as "an inverted ice cream cone with teeth around the bottom, or like a teepee or a rounded-off pup tent affair.") When the thing arrived on the set, it was sitting on a five-foot-tall base so that it would tower imposingly over the actors. This it certainly did, but it wouldn't fit into the cave. "The thing just wouldn't work with the base," Miller said. "That's how we got a four-foot-tall monster." Even with Beulah truncated, Corman himself was well satisfied with it, but a nonplussed Beverly Garland is supposed to have exclaimed, "*That* conquered the world?" and kicked it over. As the carrot creature was five feet wide at its base and took three stout men to upend when it finally was supposed to fall over at the climax of the movie, this seems unlikely. Garland herself claims only that she told Corman she herself could easily counter-conquer the alien by "bopping it with [her] handbag."

The picture was shot in early April of 1956. Miller had fun at first, doing routines with Haze and tromping around Griffith Park in baggy pants and army boots and one of those milk-bag hats. He was delighted with Beverly Garland ("A doll!") and charmed by the Ice Cream Cone. When it came time to shoot the climax of the film, Corman, against Blaisdell's wishes and in defiance of the script, brought the monster out of its dimly lit cave and into the unforgiving California sunlight, "'sneaking a shot on the road,' as Roger used to say," laughed Miller. "Everything was 'shoot fast and we gotta get out of here.'" At first it all went as scripted: Miller's character, Sergeant Neil, orders his little squad to fix their bayonets, and they troop into the famous Bronson Caves to check things out. The monster appears (it's Miller's historic first cinematic encounter with a creature), shots are fired, and a soldier is killed by the frantically waving crab claws. The rest spill out of the cave, Miller firing his snubnose over his shoulder as he goes, the monster in hot but unseen pursuit. Soon it emerges, and though Miller orders salvo after salvo from his men, nothing harms the carrot. At this point, Miller told David Everitt of *Fangoria*, he felt the tip of a bayonet poking under the edge of his helmet. "There was some extra behind me ... and every time I took a step back he hit me with that bayonet," Miller complained. While ducking the bayonet, he "took a funny step" and hurt his ankle.

Paul Blaisdell, trundling along in his monster costume, was dodging bayonets too, and would have taken one through the head had his wife not advised him to don one of the spare army helmets before the shot. He heard a clang, felt an impact, and found a dent on the helmet later, once he'd crawled out the hatch in Beulah's backside. It was a bad day for Blaisdell all around: in his Topanga workshop, he'd given the creature claws nimble enough to pluck handkerchiefs from breast pockets, but on the day, before Beulah had even had a chance to show her stuff, clumsy crew members trod on the arms, dislocating them so that all they could manage was a sort of drunken wave.

Blaisdell was out of the cone for the final dust-up between Van Cleef and the alien, and a good thing too, for it required Van Cleef to fire a blowtorch into the monster's face. The beady-eyed actor waved his torch at the carrot, then stuck it directly into the monster's equally beady eye. When the close-up of the blowtorch was taken, Corman called "Cut" as soon as the implement left the frame, and turned his attention immediately to the next shot, as was his habit. He failed to notice that smoke was spewing from every orifice in the monster's head, a weird and spectacular display, and one that would have provided a fitting end to the invading tuber. Miller saw it, though, and yelled, "Don't cut!" But it was too late. Corman had missed the moment and didn't order the camera to roll, which was too bad as far as Miller was concerned. "It was a fantastic effect," he lamented.

He was pleased with the film when he saw it, and thinks kindly on it still. "I remember it fondly as being kind of like my breakout film," he said. In a way it was: he had a character name, some dialogue, a little action, and a fair bit of business; and it was his entrée into what would become thought of, accurately or not, as his signature genre. He worked a few days and made a few hundred bucks, hung out with pals like Haze, and stayed on Corman's radar and in his good graces. He liked Blaisdell immensely: "A funny little guy, great little fella," he said. It was a salutary experience all around. When it was done he paid his rent (thirty or thirty-five dollars a month at the time) and his Schwab's tab (significantly more), and went back to his true vocation: lazing around and having fun.

By late June the movie was finished, and it was released in August to reviews that concentrated more on Beulah than on any of her co-stars. To the *LA Examiner* the creature was "a garish scarecrow"; to *Variety* it was "awesome looking," but a "mechanically clumsy rubberized horror" that "inspired more titters than terrors." (The showbiz bible praised Haze, complimenting his Mexican accent, but ignored the seventh-billed Miller.) And yet the monster has survived both the ages and the movie of which it is the star, retaining its personal fame through endless reproduction in books and magazine articles, on t-shirts, and as a plastic scale model. The fearsome cone may never have conquered the world, but through its sheer weirdness and audacity of design, it conquered nonetheless.

Alien invaders had by this time eclipsed cowboys and Indians completely on the Corman cine-scape. After *It Conquered the World*, Chuck Griffith went to Corman's tiny office and declared it was time to do another science-fiction picture. "He said, 'Okay, go ahead,' and that was that," Griffith shrugged.

He came up with a space vampire story called *Not Of This Earth*, involving a grumpy space vampire investigating Earth's human plasma resources in advance of a full bloodsucking invasion. (The "alien point man" scenario, in which many aliens are implied but only one is ever seen, was a great low-budget trope, as *It Conquered the World* had proven.) The intergalactic hemogobbler, suffering from low platelets and limpsy, enlists a nurse to give him transfusions, and sets himself up in a mansion with a manservant close at hand. Griffith, who knew the ins and outs of low-budget screenwriting very well by now, kept the locations simple and sparse and the cast list short, but he made sure to write in a small part for himself: a pesky door-to-door salesman who bothers the alien at just the wrong time.

Paul Birch, who'd played the sheriff in *Apache Woman*, was hired as Mr. Johnson of the planet Davanna. Beverly Garland played the nurse and Jonathan Haze took the manservant role. The picture went to camera at the end of the first week in June 1956, and somehow in the process, maybe as a sign of Corman's growing confidence in Miller as an actor, Miller was cast as the salesman. The switcheroo doesn't seem to have bothered Griffith. The part had been written as a nerd selling brushes, and after Miller was cast it was reconfigured to be, well, Miller; and now he was selling vacuum cleaners. In concert with Corman's confidence in the inexperienced young actor came an awareness of his limitations. He was just not ready to play a nerd—yet.

After a couple of days' shooting on the streets of Los Angeles, the production moved to a mansion off Hollywood Boulevard, and Miller's bits were the first things filmed at this location. Miller's costume, a tight shirt with a pocketfull of pencils and a little bowtie, was left over from the character's conception as a nerd, and when Miller saw it he knew it was time to make a stand. He went to Corman and said, "Look, Roger, I sold up in the Bronx, and when I did, I dressed the way I dressed anyway. Let me wear a black shirt, a jacket, let me just come to the door." Corman, who was having actor troubles enough with his lead, Paul Birch, said fine, okay. "I think it was the first time I argued about wardrobe," Miller said.

Miller's hepcat salesman, Joe Piper, peppers his spiel with exclamations of "Crazy!" and arches his eyebrow slightly when the alien suddenly responds to his line of hard-sell patter and unexpectedly invites him in. The performance was largely aleatoric: Miller's extemporizations included things he must have said back in his days of selling in the Bronx: "If you want to purchase, purchase! If you don't want to purchase, don't purchase!" It's a strangely understated interpretation for all that, though there's nothing understated about Miller's death scene, for which, after both a triple-take and a "Can you believe this?" stare into the camera lens, he adopts a bug-eyed, rictal expression he referred to later as the "Skull." (This may have been in reference to his character's later Yorick-like reappearance as an actual skull.) Before this, as he's preparing to demonstrate his wondrous sucking device to Mr. Johnson (just before Johnson demonstrates his own to Piper), Miller's salesman throat-warbles a little tune to himself. "What are you doing?" Corman asked him after the rehearsal.

"Doing a little Jackie Gleason," Miller explained.

"Oh," said Corman, "that's interesting."

Miller took this as consent and went ahead with it for the take.

"That about sums up my relationship with Roger," Miller told interviewer Sharon Williams. "Everything I did, he would say, 'That's interesting.'"

It's an unashamedly hambone performance: clearly Miller having a bit of fun, at least until the alien feeds him into a furnace. The fun is contagious, and it was cameos precisely like this one that led to Joe Dante's, and many others', reporting a good feeling, a feeling of rightness and harmony and balance, on seeing Miller suddenly walk onscreen in whatever film they were watching, at a hardtop theatre, a drive-in, or on *Million Dollar Movie*. Miller remembered his *Not Of This Earth* bit as "the first time Roger saw me do comedy," and believed it led to an expansion of the roles Corman was offering him. Strangely, at this point in his career, Miller seems not to have been aware that he was allowed to work for people other than Corman: he wasn't auditioning very energetically, he wasn't looking for representation, he wasn't doing much of anything except little parts in little films. He occasionally felt he should treat it more like a career, but that feeling passed.

The especial tininess of the Joe Piper role meant he wasn't around at the end of the week when the tension between Birch and Corman finally boiled over and the two men squared off for a fist fight. Birch, whose frustrations came from the crude and painful contact lenses he'd been asked to wear and the hurried chintziness of the production in general, cast off his sunglasses and Panama hat and stalked off the set before any punches were actually thrown, and Corman had to finish the Mr. Johnson scenes with a double. The picture was released in February 1957 on a double bill with Corman's *Attack of the Crab Monsters*.

Chuck Griffith had another script ready, and it was one of the strangest scripts he would ever write, which is saying a lot. Corman had asked him to come up with a story that would riff on the reincarnation craze sparked earlier in the year by the publication of a bestseller called *The Quest for Bridey Murphy*. Several movies on the subject, including a direct adaptation titled *The Search for Bridey Murphy*, were in the works; there were also pop songs and dances devoted to the phenomenon, and amateur hypnotists sprang up on every block. Griffith, having heard that the Bridey Murphy picture was a turkey, predicted the fad would be over and done with even by the time the super-fast Griffith/Corman team could get it into the marketplace; but he nevertheless gave the project his all, writing its past-life scenes in iambic pentameter and inserting interstitial passages that would feature Richard Devon as a laughing devil. Griffith was pleased with the results: "It was the best piece of writing I'd done up until that time, or maybe since, I don't know," he said. Corman liked it too, but after showing it to a few people and fielding their perplexed questions afterward, he developed cold feet and had Griffith rewrite the script in standard prose. The entire cast was disappointed, in particular Mel Welles, even though his role as a singing oaf would probably have been the least affected.

For Miller, there was further disappointment waiting in the wings. He had another small role, as a leper who signs a pact with the devil and is cured even as an ominous brand indicating Satanic ownership appears on his hand. Somewhere, maybe from Paul Blaisdell, Miller had picked up a homestyle makeup technique he wanted to try out, a way of using wet Kleenex to create the illusion of skin wrinkling and sloughing off. He approached Curly Batson, the old Australian makeup man, and together they created what Miller later called "some fantastic makeup things."

The picture was shot in a repurposed supermarket on Sunset Boulevard in late July 1956. Potted palms provided the forests, and atmosphere came courtesy of bumblebee smokers, whose fumes had the cast coughing and choking between takes. Corman filmed Miller's entrance in a wide master, with Devon's devil in the foreground and the tissue-deformed Miller well away from the lens, and then, in the same breath as his call of "Cut!" he asked for the makeup to be removed so he could get a close-up of the leper's now-flawless skin. "You missed this fantastic makeup," Miller pointed out, but the unstoppable Corman momentum demanded they move ever forward, and the opportunity was lost. All Corman had to do was pop on a longer lens and take the shot again, but, to him, this would have been, to quote *Patton*, "paying for the same real estate twice," and there was no way Roger was doing *that*. Miller's extravagantly raised eyebrow and lip curled in anger as seen in the close-up may well have had some motivation beyond that demanded by the script. "Me with my be-bop haircut trying to play a medieval leper," a bitter Miller spat in an interview years later. "It was unbelievable."

When the Bridey Murphy picture tanked that October and it became clear the hypno-regression kick had waned, *The Trance of Diana Love* was retitled *The Undead* when it went into general release the following March. Despite Corman's retreat on the poetry and the typical corner-cutting haste in which he shot the picture, it remains one of the best examples of his ability to create something weird and unique even as he believed he was being ruthlessly commercial.

Miller was on the dole again, left to his long, happy days of polishing the chairs at Schwab's. It didn't trouble him much, because in those years Corman always had another picture prepared before too long and usually there was a part for Miller. This time he had only a couple of weeks to wait. Bob Campbell, the actor/artist who was one of Miller's closest pals, had written a script, or part of a script at any rate: a crime story with a tropical setting. Corman passed the unfinished fragment to Chuck Griffith, just as he had done with Rusoff's *It Conquered the World,* and asked him to make something shootable out of it. "I don't know what stopped [Campbell], but it was incomplete," Griffith told Mark Thomas McGee, "and I really used Bob's story and wrote a script on top of it." Griffith's take was modelled roughly on *Key Largo*, and so featured a small gang of crooks fleeing a heist, an unhappy moll, a square-jawed hero, and other assorted innocents, all of them trapped and bound fractiously together by foul weather. At Corman's request, Griffith would recycle the same premise for at least another three pictures, sometimes adding a monster (*Beast from Haunted Cave, Creature from the Haunted Sea*), sometimes not (*Atlas*).

Griffith's script, titled *Naked Paradise*, was, according to the credits, written in conjunction with Mark Hanna, just as was the case with *Not Of This Earth, The Undead,* and a number of other pictures; but, Miller told McGee, "his only contribution was to wake [Griffith] up in the morning to write them." Hanna had assured Griffith that he had contacts who would help get any script they "collaborated" on produced, and Griffith's typically grumpy, quite possibly apocryphal implication was that this was the extent of it, and the ideas and actual composition were strictly Griffith's work. Hanna did have credits of his own, including *Attack of the 50 Foot Woman*, but Griffith simply pointed to these as further proof that Hanna couldn't actually write.

Corman, meanwhile, wanted the script in shape as quickly as possible, because another producer, a Brooklyn-born lawyer named Ludwig Gerber, who counted Howard Hughes, Peggy Lee, and Troy Donahue among his clients, had brought him a separate tropical script called *Shark Reef*. In a typically canny Corman move, he plotted to shoot the two projects back to back, and quickly persuaded the two sets of producers, AIP and Gerber, that the scenario was win–win. Theoretically, it was, and the money men bit, with Arkoff and Nicholson even deciding they would come along for the trip. Miller also admired the stratagem. "It was a good idea," he said.

Miller's easy comic interaction with Haze on *It Conquered the World* had not gone unnoticed by Corman. *Naked Paradise* also featured a semi-comic pair of young men, hoodlums this time instead of soldiers, and Corman, who never resisted a clear-cut casting choice, stuck them in. *Shark Reef* was to be shot first, but Corman told them, "You can come out and sit around for three weeks while we do [*Shark Reef*], and then we'll do your picture." They wouldn't get paid for those three weeks, of course, Corman added emphatically, but they'd get accommodations. Miller and Haze jumped at the opportunity. Griffith pleaded with Corman to let him go along too, but had no luck.

The company travelled to Kauai in August of 1956 and settled in at the Coco Palms Resort, then only a couple of dozen small thatched cottages on the edge of a sleepy lagoon. (These would stand in for the native village depicted in *Shark Reef*.) Haze and Miller shared one of the cabanas and began, Miller said, "trying to tear up the island with the little Hawaiian girls." They also acted informally as stunt coordinators on *Shark Reef*, helping stage fist fights and water gags. They pulled other kinds of gags as well, playing practical jokes on Corman, short-sheeting and the like, whenever they felt they could get away with it. All in all, it was a glorious time, a high point of Miller's career in pictures. Corman, too, remembers it fondly. "It was really a wonderful time," he said. "I truly enjoyed the shooting of these two films, probably more than any other films I had made." The recently divorced Beverly Garland, whom Corman was still dating, may not have been so sanguine, as she'd been looking forward to the trip as an opportunity to spend time with her new boyfriend. For Corman, though, it was anything but a vacation.

After two weeks of shooting, *Shark Reef* was done, and after a day's rest—during which, one hopes, Corman and Garland were able to spend some time together—the company turned their attention toward *Naked Paradise*.

Miller played Mitch, and Haze was Stony, the two henchmen of ringleader Zac, played by Leslie Bradley. Garland was the moll and Richard Denning was the boat captain hero. Lisa Montell, an exotic-looking beauty who'd been one of the leads in *Shark Reef*, was the island girl who becomes Mitch's love interest. Sam Arkoff even had a part in the picture, reluctantly playing a plantation owner with a single line of dialogue. It took Arkoff four takes to get it right, which must have been close to a record for Corman at that time, and surely anathema to a man who, as Miller has often claimed, never made a second take unless the camera fell over on the first. But Arkoff had at least come *gratis*, and Corman was able to wring further savings from him, since Arkoff and Jim Nicholson had both brought their families along on the trip and Corman could employ their wives and children as unpaid extras.

Miller and Haze had learned a few things in their three weeks of island loafing and tropical romance, and they were able to put this knowledge into action once *Naked Paradise* began rolling. "You should never run on coral," Miller was told by the islanders, and so when Corman asked him to run down a coral spit, Miller told him it was inadvisable. A disbelieving Corman made the run himself and tore his tennis shoes into strips of rubber and canvas.

Next it was Haze's turn. "Run off through that sugar cane field," Corman instructed him. But Haze had learned that the sugar cane was full of tiny needles, and that brushing against the stalks was unwise. Again, Corman undertook the action himself, and again received a painful lesson. Author Mark Thomas McGee, in his book *Roger Corman*, claimed the production had to shut down while the needles were extracted from Corman's flesh, and if that's so, it was surely the lost time that caused him the most pain that day.

Miller derived no satisfaction from this, or from the scene in which his character, Mitch, gunned down a hapless plantation accountant played by Corman himself. He and the director were getting on famously despite the makeup and costume differences they'd had earlier in the summer; the shoot was going well; everyone was having the time of their lives. The only cloud on the horizon was the title, *Naked Paradise*, which Miller mumbled inaudibly whenever he was asked what movie he was working on. "I was ashamed of that title," he told McGee. "I thought they'd think it was a porno film or something." But both *Naked Paradise* and *Shark Reef* suffered title changes some time after their completion. *Naked Paradise* became *Thunder Over Hawaii*, "an action title," Miller said; and *Shark Reef*'s title was expanded to *She Gods of Shark Reef* when it was eventually sold to AIP two years after it was made. It was a dull, tropical, turkey of a picture, and Gerber had been unable to sell it to anyone else; though when it was finally released, on the bottom half of a bill with *Night of the Blood Beast*, a young Martin Scorsese, who went to see anything with Corman's name on it, caught the movie and inexplicably loved it.

Naked Paradise was a felicitous experience for Miller beyond the pleasures of the actual shoot. It instilled a love of the islands; he and his future wife, Lainie, would travel there more than thirty times over their long marriage. ("We stay a lot on Oahu because it's got everything," Lainie Miller said. "But Kauai is really our favourite.") It solidified his status as "a regular member of our stock company," as far as Corman was concerned. More immediately, it helped boost Miller to a new level in his career. Corman's practice was to preview his pictures in the smallest, most out-of-the-way burgs he could find, and after *Naked Paradise* had been cut and scored in the fall of 1956, he organized just such a premiere. Miller, who liked seeing himself onscreen, attended, and when the picture was over Beverly Garland cornered him in the lobby. "You walked away with that movie," she told him enthusiastically. "You really came out looking great!"

Miller, pleased, said something like "Aw, shucks" and thanked her. He liked Garland immensely and respected her opinions even when they were not about how good an actor he was. Better than the compliment itself was the fact that Corman was standing within earshot of it, and evidently it made an impression. A year earlier Corman had seen and enjoyed a half-hour drama called *The Little Guy*, which had aired in September 1955 as part of *The Jane Wyman Show*. It was the story of Shorty, a stubby misanthrope whose attempt to sit and brood at a local watering hole is interrupted by a pair of lanky holdup men on the lam. Shorty uses his scorn for tall people as his best weapon against the gun-toting beanpoles, and ends up disarming them first psychologically and then physically. Corman bought the rights to the story and, as he had done before with unfinished or undersized screenplays, hired Chuck Griffith to expand it to feature length, or at least to the barely-cracked-an-hour format that passed for feature length at the time in the low-budget realm. Griffith had to work even faster than usual: "Roger threw me that and said, 'We're shooting Monday,'" he told interviewer Aaron Graham. "This was a Friday, you know!" Corman had seen that it could fairly easily be turned into a rock 'n' roll performance movie, so Griffith's modifications included a framework for the performances (which mainly involved writing "musical number here" and calling it done); an opening scene at another club, "Ye Olde Rocke," where Miller comes into conflict with an obnoxious drunk played by Bruno VeSota, then is tossed out the door by a doorman fully a foot taller than himself; and the inclusion of a beatnik impresario character called Sir Bop, a role written for Griffith's pal, the eccentric poet and performer Lord Buckley, a clear precursor to *A Bucket of Blood's* Maxwell Brock. Griffith later claimed the whole thing had taken him only twenty-four hours to write.

The order of events has been lost to the mists of time: it's unclear whether Corman purchased the piece as a part for Miller, or whether he bought *The Little Guy* on its own merits and exploitative possibilities, and realized later it was a perfect role for one of his stock performers. The upshot in either case was that, after a year-and-a-half in the business, Miller had his first leading role. He had to find that out for himself, however. Corman gave him the script, saying only that there was a part for him in it; then they made the standard handshake deal. "He'll beat you to death in the office," Miller said later, "but if you shake hands on it, you've got it." As Miller read the scenario and saw the name "Shorty" appearing over and again, he slowly realized that he was indeed the hero of the piece. "Afterwards I found out that Chuck had been told to write it, stretch it out, make a feature out of it, and that it was for me," Miller said. "And Roger wouldn't tell me those things, because that meant money!"

But the deal had been made. Miller didn't care. He didn't mind fighting cucumbers and falling off horses, or fast-talking aliens into a vacuum cleaner purchase, or hiding money in pineapples, but he was glad to play a contemporary character with recognizably human problems; and though he wasn't a Dean wannabe or cultist, Miller was nevertheless pleased to have something with some emotional meat to it, something closer to the roles Dean had played. On top of that, it had clearly been written, or adapted anyway, with him in mind, and for a small-time character actor who had only ever worked with one director, this was extraordinary. *This is perfect for me!* Miller thought.

Corman felt the same. It seemed natural to him that Dick should be taking on leading parts, and his reasoning was basic. "It was simply that he was a good actor," Corman said, "and as I do with all good actors, I try to give them bigger roles and build up their roles. Because, as you know, Hollywood is filled with a lot of bad actors, so when you find a good actor, not only do you use him again, you use him in bigger roles."

It was mid-December 1956. Sets were repurposed, cast were hired, musical acts—the Platters and the Blockbusters—were booked. (Miller renamed the latter group the "Ballbusters" during the shoot.) Corman, meanwhile, was going crazy. "I produced and directed, I think, seven or eight films [that] year," he said. "I remember one time I was shooting during the day, casting the next picture during the lunch and cutting the previous picture during the evening, and I went to bed and I said to myself, 'I have to sleep fast.' And I thought, 'I am clearly out of control!'"

But everything was ready for the first day's call. The cast included Abby Dalton, a tall and lithe actress who would later find television fame playing a nurse, the female lead, on a proto-M*A*S*H navy doctor show called *Hennesey*, set at the very same San Diego naval hospital Miller had visited so many times during his service. Dalton was a dancer, had never acted in a film before, and it was thanks to Miller that she was appearing in one now. "I was seeing some young lady at the time," he said, "and [Dalton] was a friend of hers. And she kept talking about the picture, when it first started. And I said, 'Why don't you come up there, you're right for the part. You make me look short.' And she went up, and Roger bought it." Dalton played Julie, a nervous would-be singer managed by the blustery Sir Bop.

The supporting cast was dotted with oddballs, many of whom were Miller's bosom chums. Lord Buckley couldn't make the scene, so Mel Welles played Sir Bop, and got so into the part that he wrote and published a dictionary of hipster slang, *The Hiptionary*. Russell Johnson, another future TV star, who had just appeared in *Attack of the Crab Monsters*, played Jigger, the tall criminal, and Jonathan Haze played his jittery comrade, Joey. Bruno VeSota was in there as a boorish souse; Beach Dickerson, who'd been playing small parts and acting as a general dogsbody on some recent Corman productions, had a good-sized part as The Kid, a meek boxer; and Barboura Morris made her first appearance in a Corman picture as the Kid's straight-talking girlfriend. Reminiscing about his pre-fame days in the Corman company, Jack Nicholson said, "I'm sure [Miller] talked about Clegg Hoyt"; and indeed he had. Hoyt was a Schwab's regular, almost twenty years older than Miller, who acted with reasonable consistency in movies and television, and who sported a glass eye with an American flag imprinted on it. He was an inveterate gambler who lost money as quickly as he came up with it, and it was said he'd come from a wealthy and powerful family in the East, which had shipped their problem child to Hollywood just to be rid of him. "A real character," Jonathan Haze told an interviewer. Hoyt appeared in *Rock All Night* as The Kid's supportive but ineffectual manager.

Miller's character, carrying a chip the size of a dinner plate on his shoulder, treats the bar's patrons with scorn, and quiets down only when Johnson sticks a gun in his face. But Miller skilfully shows the decent guy beneath the crusty exterior, and there's never any doubt he's the hero of the piece. Once the criminals have been vanquished and the loose ends more or less tied up, the picture comes to a sweet conclusion when Shorty and Julie head off to a revival screening of *King Kong*, which, according to the hangdog bartender, Shorty has seen at least twenty times. A barfly asks what's so special about the picture. "Remember the size of that beast?" the bartender asks. "Remember the size of the guy that knocked him over?" The two characters share a laugh, and the picture comes not to an end, but to "The Livin' End."

King Kong was the second movie Miller ever saw and a personal favourite of his as much as of Shorty's, and its mention in *Rock All Night* is surely a little tip of the hat from Chuck Griffith to his pal Miller. But aside from their taste in monster movies and their startling physical resemblance, there is little else to connect Miller and Shorty. Miller, always a confident man, never suffered from "short man's syndrome" or had any discernable beef with taller people. He might have preferred to be taller, and would certainly have appreciated whatever career boost an extra six or seven inches might have given him, but it was something he rarely thought about. At any rate he had no hesitation or regret in taking the role of a man defined mainly by his shortness—whatever aerie of stardom Miller might achieve in his life, he would never be one of those celebrities who refuse to step up on an apple box, but instead demand a trench be dug for everybody else.

Late in 1956 Miller saw up close that diminutive stature and stardom were far from incompatible. Bobby Campbell, his writer friend, had worked on the script of the Lon Chaney biopic, *Man of a Thousand Faces*, which was shooting over on the Universal lot. "Want to meet Cagney?" Campbell asked, to which the only possible answer was "Of course!" Miller and Campbell found James Cagney sitting on a chair on the soundstage, a little off to one side of the set, waiting patiently until he was needed. Miller was introduced, and they chatted about the business. "I'm in it—I'm an actor," Miller told him. "Good luck," Cagney said. All the while Miller was marvelling at the man: at 5'5" each, they were the same height, and here Cagney was, a superstar and Oscar winner only in the middle of what would prove to be (with one two-decade break) a fifty-year career. For Dick, it was a little like the time he'd purchased Alan Ladd's jacket and found it fit him perfectly.

When the shot was ready and Cagney was called to the set, to Miller's delight the actor didn't just walk the fifteen feet from his chair to his mark: he danced, shrugging off his fifty-seven years, suddenly helium-light in his movements, a celestial talent performing for no special reason, which, for an artist, is the best reason of all. It made Miller, who'd danced on Broadway with Sammy Davis Jr., practically giddy. "Did a little tap dance all the way up there," Miller said, dreamily replaying the moment in the screening room of his mind. "I never forgot it."

Shortly after *Rock All Night* wrapped, Miller was in Schwab's when he spotted Dane Clark, the actor who'd played Shorty in *The Little Guy*. Clark, a tough little Brooklynite born under the name Bernard Zanville, had gained fame in wartime pictures playing good buddies and hard sergeants, but moved largely to television in the early '50s. Miller, still high on his first starring role, his first role of any real substance, approached the actor. "Excuse me, Mr. Clark," Miller said to him. "I just did a picture called *Rock All Night*, and I believe you did the same thing, and ..." Clark was looking up at him but not responding, and Miller found himself rambling. "I went on and on and on," Miller remembered. "And he finally said, 'Yeah, kiddo.' That was it. So I said thank you, fuck you. And I walked away."

But Clark, evidently realizing he'd sounded curt, made his way over to Miller's table. "I didn't mean anything," he said to Miller. "Everybody's 'kiddo' to me." He sat down and the two men began chatting about Shorty, about acting, about Hollywood. "And we became friends," Miller said. Moreover, he soon picked up the very mannerism that had initially so irritated him. "That's where I got it—I say 'kiddo' too. I call lots of guys 'kiddo.'"

Looking back on 1956, Miller felt comfortable calling it a banner year. He'd acted in five different pictures and had, in *Variety*-speak, 'toplined' one of them; he had worked and played in Hawaii; and he had earned a total of $1,500 for his trouble. Big parts, he'd discovered, were fine, but so were little ones—there wasn't much difference in pay because an actor was generally paid by the week, and when it came to time spent on set, the difference was measurable in hours. As well, Miller simply didn't possess the sort of ego that might be bruised by few lines or scanty screen time. At first this may have been as much a matter of cluelessness as humility, and it both helped and hindered his career.

But as 1957 began he was still stuck on Corman, either fearful of auditioning for others or unsure how to; and for almost the first half of the year, Corman had nothing to offer Miller. But when two young filmmakers, director Irvin Kershner and producer Andrew Fenady, pitched Corman a project called "Stakeout on Dope Street," he agreed to help finance it on the condition that they hire Jonathan Haze and Miller as two of the three (nominally teenage) main characters. (The third was played by Yale Wexler, brother of the film's cinematographer, Haskell Wexler.) Miller read the script, but when he saw the schedule he balked. The picture was shooting on weekends, and even though nearly every day was a holiday for Miller, he didn't want to work on Saturdays and Sundays. "I have no idea why," he said more recently. It almost certainly cost him work, as Fenady and Kershner both went on to big careers in TV and film. Nick, the part intended for Miller, was taken by a tall muscleman called Morris Miller, who later gave himself the stage name Steven Marlo.

So it was Schwab's most days, or the beach, and once a week there was the unemployment office. Miller was also drawing a lot in this period, producing pen-and-ink artwork inspired by his nightmares: disembodied hands, torsos open and spilling viscera, uprooted flowers, half-built brick walls, and a long road to a distant, shining city. There were also pictures of superheroes and of monsters, of Lilliputians dissecting a screaming head, and at least one drawing of a topless, solemn-looking woman called "Danielle," whom he was seeing steadily around this time. "I started noticing that, whenever I got into a bind or something, I'd wind up grabbing a pencil and starting to draw, very intensely." His Schwab's pals were more professionally active than he was: Mel Welles, one of the few able to travel between Corman productions and more legit gigs without friction, had gotten into TV and was doing larger-scale features; and even Haze had done an episode of *Dragnet* and some other small-screen stuff. It was time, Miller realized, to spread his wings and leave the Corman nest, if only temporarily and sporadically. His first step was to get new representation, since the agency he'd been with thus far hadn't done a thing for him. All his work had come by way of direct phone calls from Corman; maybe a new agent would invite calls from someone else too.

Largely on the strength of his *Rock All Night* performance, Miller was able to sign with Meyer Mishkin, a classic cigar-chomper of the old school. Mishkin was "about five foot five," said one of his clients, "and he had all these alpha males as clients." Mishkin had discovered Gregory Peck, Kirk Douglas, Tyrone Power, and Jeff Chandler, and his list later included Charles Bronson, Tom Skerritt, Robert Carradine, and Gary Busey. Lee Marvin was a client and close friend. But he did not represent only tall people. Prefiguring his later discovery of Richard Dreyfuss, whose career he would champion despite warnings that Dreyfuss was "too short, too Jewish," Mishkin took on Dick Miller. The only trouble was that he didn't bother telling anyone at his agency.

"I signed with him, and I went to the office, and they didn't even know who I was," said Miller. "And I said, 'Well, ask Meyer,' and they said he wasn't in town. He's up in San Francisco." Miller was unsure whether Mishkin had actually signed him or not, so, using skills he'd learned from his brother Gene, Miller "played detective," calling Frisco hotels until he got the one the agent was staying at. "Am I signed or what?" Miller asked him. Mishkin confirmed that of course he was, ya schlemiel.

There were further hints that it was time to step out and sell himself a little. When *Rock All Night* opened in April, double-billed with another AIP youth picture called *Dragstrip Girl*, Miller saw to his amazement that he was being not just mentioned in the reviews but praised. *Variety* called the movie "extremely mediocre," but went on to insist, "Only the performance (very good, especially considering the so-so production and direction) of Dick Miller in the lead keeps the audience's interest in the film from disintegrating." A British film journal called *To-Day's Cinema* remarked that "Dick Miller as Shorty has real appeal." "Miller is excellent and cracks his good lines with effect," enthused the *Hollywood Reporter* in the midst of a generally positive notice.

Miller was delighted with these, his first trade-paper reviews, and wondered how best to capitalize on them. A full-page promotional ad in the daily *Variety* seemed the ticket. After glancing at and approving the copy, Sam Arkoff and Jim Nicholson of AIP agreed to pay for half the cost of the ad, and it appeared in early May. It was a minimalist affair, displaying a still of Miller in his striped *Rock All Night* bomber jacket in the top left quarter, and, in the bottom right, beneath his name, it read "Currently starring in ROCK ALL NIGHT," which, we are assured, was "Another … American International Hit!" The *Variety* and *Hollywood Reporter* reviews were briefly quoted beneath that, and a couple of small stars filled out the vast swaths of blank space left over.

Chuck Griffith remembered the advert, but told interviewer Aaron Graham that "it didn't do him any good." Miller himself can't remember any direct effect from it either, except that the *Variety* quote Miller had reproduced—"Only the performance of Dick Miller keeps the audience's interest in the film"—made Arkoff and Nicholson angry. Apparently they hadn't read it over closely enough, and now, apoplectic at the idea of paying for an ad that suggested their movie wasn't very good, they threatened to take back their half of the cost. "Gimme a break on this thing!" Miller pleaded, and they relented.

Even if Miller can't remember the ad's paying specific dividends, and even if 1957 had been completely employment free thus far, the year would eventually further his career. It first picked up a bit in May. After Corman's Miller-free *Teenage Doll* in March, on May 15 another weird melodrama-sploitation concoction, along the line of *Rock All Night*, went to camera. *Carnival Rock* came from a script by Leo Lieberman, who wrote a couple of pictures for Corman, but was never in his writers' stable alongside Griffith, Bobby Campbell, and, later, Richard Matheson and Charles Beaumont. There were musical numbers in it: the Platters and the Ballbusters were back, which took care of the teenagers as far as Corman was concerned; and the rest would be gut-wrenching drama or an approximation thereof. It was *Rock All Night* with the gunmen removed and more elaborate sets, as though Corman wanted a do-over that would be taken more seriously.

Reinforcing this theory is Corman's choice of star. He was just beginning a phase of his career in which he paid more attention to the actor's craft, and to directors like Elia Kazan for whom it was paramount. Abby Dalton had introduced him to Jeff Corey, a blacklisted, Group Theatre-trained actor who'd begun giving classes out of his renovated garage, and many of the young, serious-minded actors in town were taking them. Who, Corman might have asked himself after plunging into this environment, would Kazan hire? Naturally he would go with someone he had worked with himself on stage, someone who had won the 1953 Clarence Derwent Award for Most Promising Male. David J. Stewart of Manhattan, formerly Abe J. Siegel of Omaha, fit the bill. Stewart had won his award for playing The Baron in Tennessee Williams's poorly received fantasia *Camino Real*. "What Roger didn't know about David Stewart," Miller said, "was that he'd won the award for playing a homosexual. It had nothing to do with great acting ability." Miller's theory, that playing a gay character was considered in itself so daring as to be award-worthy, is questionable, but his assessment of Stewart's performance is not. "David Stewart was terrible in the part," he said. "He was atrocious." Still, Corman was excited to get him, a serious, award-winning actor straight from Broadway. It was an early example of Corman's occasional impulse to class up the joint a little.

The story, as cribbed from *The Blue Angel*: at a carnival perched on a pier, there is a nightclub, Christy's, with all the atmosphere of a shipping container.

The owner, Christy Christakos, fifty years old and sporting an unplaceable accent (only his name tells you he's meant to be Greek), is in the thrall of love, mooning over his new singer, Natalie, instead of paying attention to his mounting bills and falling custom. This frustrates his inexplicably loyal factotum, Benny, and angers the decaying orbit of bill collectors, bookies, and stiffed employees whirling around him. Christy gets progressively more stressed and irrational until, having lost the club to Natalie's boyfriend, Stanley, and taken a position as the world's saddest baggy-pants clown just to stay close to his unattainable lady love, he starts a fire on the dance floor and nearly kills himself and Natalie. In the end a totally defeated Christy, leaning on Benny's shoulder, hobbles away from the smoking ruins and off the pier, the two of them leaving town to start new lives running a television station back east.

Corman asked Miller to play Stanley, the boyfriend, but when Miller read the scenario he said, "This is no part." He thought he could do something with Benny, the mysteriously devoted friend. There was no explanation in the script for why Benny, almost twenty-five years younger than Christy and no blood relation, hangs out with the lumpy "Greek," who neither gives nor is supplied with any indication that he was ever a fun guy despite all Benny's mooning about "the old Christy, the Christy I used to know." Miller's writing instincts took hold and he crafted a background for the pair, something about Benny's having been found by Christy on the streets as a boy, being raised by him like a son, and as a result feeling bound to him by a debt greater than any man could pay. Stewart and Corman accepted this interpretation, but on the very first day of shooting it led to trouble. "If he is like my son," Stewart said during the rehearsal of an argument scene, "I feel I want to hit him." Stewart naturally considered himself a Method actor, but what he knew of the Method seemed to have come seventh hand and garbled, as in a game of Telephone. He clouted Miller on the side of the head, and the impact sent the smaller actor reeling off to slam against the rickety flats.

"It's a movie," Miller pointed out, rubbing his head. "You can miss by a mile and it'll still look good." Corman, cowed by his star, gingerly suggested a no-contact rehearsal, but after they tried it Stewart complained that he was just not feeling the scene. Corman asked if they could try it Stewart's way, just once. "Okay," Miller said dubiously and was clobbered again, this time over the ear. "I tell ya, I had a ringing in my ear for six months after that," he complained. It was one time at least that he was thankful for Corman's practice of shooting a single take and moving on.

Stewart's Method madness continued throughout the shoot. A scene in which he tries to pull open the locked door of Natalie's dressing room had to be shot over and over again, as Stewart kept pulling the handle right off and could not come to terms with the idea that he had to fake the action. "The whole game of acting is make believe—they try to strive for reality, they're full of shit," Miller said. This was his philosophy of the craft in a nutshell, and might have been formed on the set of *Carnival Rock* while exchanging wry smiles with Haze as Stewart played havoc with the sets. Several times in the picture Benny has to pull Christy away from a door or a window or a person, and each time Stewart would resist the pull with everything he had. Since he outweighed Miller by at least fifty pounds, Dick had to clutch and yank as hard as he could, and after a couple of days of this Stewart rolled up his sleeve to show Miller the black and green bruises his grip was leaving behind. "Gee, I'm sorry," a genuinely chagrined Miller said, but Stewart assured him that it was fine, he was using the pain in his performance.

Of course, that's a valid technique, but Stewart took it further than most and without any discernable performance dividends. Corman was still keeping an awed distance from the actor, even though his tactics were costing the production time, but the rest of the cast and crew were fed up. A grip pounded a finishing nail halfway into the exact part of the wall Stewart's head would most likely hit in yet another scene of struggle, and when his head did indeed glance off the nail, and the blood was running down his neck, Stewart again claimed it was a pain he could use. For a scene in which Christy learns that Natalie has a boyfriend, Stewart asked Haze, who would be standing behind him in the shot, to jab him in the leg with a dart at the moment of realization. Haze sidled up to Miller and showed him the dart. "What the hell do I do? Guy wants me to stick him with this thing," he said.

"So stick him," said Miller.

Haze did, and Stewart once again used the pain. For all this, though, his performance, though committed, was as hammy as any ever seen in a Corman picture. Years later, after Stewart's untimely death at fifty-one, Miller was playing a green-hatted assassin on an episode of *McCloud*. It was call time on a night shoot, and Miller was chatting with his fellow guest star, Joseph Wiseman, a Canadian actor most famous for playing the first Bond villain, Dr. No. The subject of Stewart somehow came up, and Miller told all the *Carnival Rock* stories with great gusto, emphasizing the time on set that had been pointlessly wasted by Stewart and the terrible performance that resulted. "This idiot, this moron, this asshole, this imbecile," Miller called him. When Miller had finished, Wiseman looked at him gravely and said, "David Stewart was my dearest friend."

Miller was gutted, and the whole night could not stop thinking about his terrible blunder, all the worse because he revered Wiseman as an actor. "I felt awful all night long," he said. "It affected my performance." At the end of the day, wrung out and abashed, Miller approached the actor and began a stammering apology. Wiseman cut him off with a chuckle. "Actually, *I* have to apologize to *you*, Dick," he said. "I've never even heard of David Stewart."

A month after *Carnival Rock*, in mid-July, Corman had another Leo Lieberman story ready to shoot. *Sorority Girl* was the story of Sabra, a nasty rich girl who spews venom on her sorority sisters and anyone else who stumbles into her orbit. She bullies, insults, and even spanks Ellie, a meek gooney-bird student; attempts to blackmail the secretive but more prepossessing Rita; and tries first to steal then to frame Rita's boyfriend, Mort. After she nearly drives a Girl-in-Trouble to take a high dive off a seaside cliff, her peers finally rise up to give her the shunning she has so ably, but somehow sympathetically, earned, and a dejected Sabra turns and walks into the waves one last time as THE END bursts forth on the screen.

Susan Cabot, who had played Natalie in *Carnival Rock* and was dating Roger, got the role of the nasty Sabra, and Barboura Morris, who was married to future director Monte Hellman, but whom Corman would later date, was sensible Rita. (One ought to point out that Morris, Cabot, and Beverly Garland, strong actors all, did not get their roles because they were Corman's girlfriends; they were Corman's girlfriends because they were in the movies—and as such were the only women the workaholic director ever had a chance to meet.) Corman called up Miller and asked him to play Mort, the boyfriend, "a fresh-out-of-college type guy who ran a coffeehouse or something," Miller recalled. It was the male lead, but Corman made sure to tell him he wasn't getting top billing. "'Dick Miller in *Sorority Girl*'—it doesn't sound right!" Corman said. "You'll have to split it with Susan." Miller was happy for the role nonetheless; it was a serious part in another of Corman's weird dramas, and there was no rock 'n' roll this time. Mort, like Miller, was a part-time artist, so there was an easy and immediate point of entry to the character. As a bonus it provided Miller with another career milestone: his first movie kiss. There are two in the picture, actually: a peck from Barboura Morris and a smooch from Susan Cabot.

Corman, who was auditing Jeff Corey's acting classes when he wasn't shooting, was still reaching toward a greater communication with his actors, and for once he had some specific character direction to impart. "Play it like Mort Sahl," he told Miller. Sahl was one of the new brand of comics, maybe the first of the new brand, in fact: not a Catskills collar-puller demanding someone take his wife, but a sweater-wearing quasi-intellectual prefiguring Lenny Bruce and Woody Allen; and his name was Mort, just like the character. Miller got the cadence right in Mort's first big scene, when he gives his mission statement "Beer and laughs," but by the end, when he has to get tough and enact an heroic rescue on the cliffs, he's got no time for patter or sloganeering.

Cabot, whom Corman called "a very dedicated Method actress from New York," gave a strong performance, and reinforced Corman's determination to become more of an actor's director. Miller liked her, but found her odd. "She was an interesting little girl," he remembered. "A nice girl, a little confused. Too weird for me. But she was a good actress." Cabot, for her part, was fond of Miller too, telling interviewer Tom Weaver that he was "a nice guy, very cooperative." Cabot did a run of Corman films in this period, playing another villainess in his next movie, *The Saga of the Viking Women and Their Voyage to the Waters of the Great Sea Serpent*, a lady scientist in *War of the Satellites*, a gun moll in *Machine Gun Kelly*, and a wasp woman in *The Wasp Woman*, her last picture. The end of her life, in December 1986, was tragically cinematic: she was bludgeoned to death with an iron weight bar by her drug-addled son, Tim, in the Encino Hills house they shared as semi-recluses.

Sorority Girl marked the end of Corman's weird *sui generis* cycle, at least for the nonce; the title of his next picture, *The Saga of the Viking Women and Their Voyage to the Waters of the Great Sea Serpent*, might as well have been a full-page *Variety* announcement that he was moving back into more or less identifiable genres. *Sorority Girl* also marked the last work of the "extremely friendly" Curly Batson, who died of lung cancer late in September. Miller had enjoyed working with the makeup man on the leper cosmetics for *The Undead*, even if they hadn't been properly showcased by Corman's camera, and was fond of him because Miller, who disliked wearing makeup, could generally persuade the old jackaroo that he didn't need any. "I kept up my tan—still do—because you can't shoot white guys," Miller said. "It used to work. A little liner on my eyes, but that's it."

"He always refused makeup, if he could avoid it," Joe Dante said. "But sometimes people insisted."

In the fall of '57 Miller started working on projects outside the Corman bubble. It was TV, which was made on budgets and schedules not much greater than Corman's, so there was little or no difference as far as he was concerned; just a few different names to learn, and it was tougher to avoid wearing makeup. The first TV part he shot was probably an appearance on *The Gale Storm Show*, a sitcom in which Storm played Susanna, a cruise director from the days when cruising was a much more exotic and rarefied pursuit, dealing with the nutty crew of her ship and a new set of nutty passengers each week: a proto-*Love Boat*, more or less. Everyone was on this show at one time or another, from Corman stalwarts Richard Garland and Touch Connors to future Miller co-stars Boris Karloff and Robby the Robot. Miller played Sparks, a goofy radioman.

He was in an episode of *Whirlybirds*, another forgotten show that every jobbing actor of the day seems to have done at least once. This was a half-hour program about adventuring helicopter pilots, and Miller appeared in several of them; his first episode, titled "The Killer," aired on St. Patrick's Day, 1958. He also guested in the Lee Marvin cop show *M Squad*, playing essentially the Jonathan Haze role in *Rock All Night*: a crazed gunman's nervous pal. This role in particular was a sizable one, and very good exposure when it was broadcast at the end of March, a couple of weeks after *Whirlybirds*. He also did an episode of *Dragnet* called "The Big Perfume Bottle," where he played a thief who stole only perfume, jewellery, and other womanly things.

There was finally a little money in Miller's pocket, enough at least that he could think of acting as his profession, something he wasn't going to walk away from. He bought a car, a Triumph TR3, a beautiful little two-seater with long teardrop fenders. He went to movies, including his own (*Sorority Girl* came out on October 21), and the beach, to Schwab's of course, squired ladies about, and tried his hand at racing cars in an unorganized fashion, as had been seen in Corman's *The Fast and the Furious*. Street racing was something Jonathan Haze was into as well, and more than once, apparently, Steve McQueen took part in the competitions; and Miller called out for the two bucks McQueen still owed him as the movie star roared by. And though he generally paid little mind to movies Corman was shooting that he himself wasn't in, Miller found himself in the orbit of a picture Roger was producing (but not directing), *The Cry Baby Killer*. The actor playing the cry-baby killer was a young man Corman had seen in Jeff Corey's class, Jack Nicholson, in his first sizable role. Popular legend has Corman himself spotting Nicholson's nascent genius in the class, pointing at him and bellowing, "*You*! shall star in my new picture!" In fact it's more likely that Nicholson heard about the role through Corey's class, probably from Roger; auditioned on Corey's recommendation for director Jus Addiss and screenwriter Leo Gordon while Corman was off in Asia on a trip around the world (where he was hypnotized by "a Sikh in a white turban" and warned not to associate professionally with anyone bearing the initials DK, which meant bad news for Corman's assistant David Kramarsky); and had the part by the time Roger returned. "Yes, he seems very talented," Corman said when told who'd been chosen. Still, the Corey connection was the essential and primary link. If one accepts, as Nicholson does, that *The Cry Baby Killer* and subsequent Corman work were the critical first steps in the superstar's career, then we must trace the line back and give credit where it's due: Nicholson hooked up with Corman through Corey's class; Corman was in Corey's class because of Abby Dalton; Abby Dalton met Corman originally because Dick Miller dragged her in for an audition; therefore, Miller deserves at least a nod for helping to start Nicholson's career. Of course, it may all have happened anyway, but it has been said Miller possesses some strange, star-making aura that has rubbed off on more than one colleague, even if it never did much for him. Miller himself has pointed it out. "I notice that if you work in a Dick Miller picture, you become a star," he said once, much later in his career. "Every one of these pictures, there's somebody in it, worked on it, got a scene with me.... You're gonna be a star."

10 We shook hands and that was it

Neither Dick Miller nor Jack Nicholson can remember exactly when they first crossed paths, but research and triangulation indicate it was sometime near the end of the *Cry Baby Killer* shoot. Whenever it was, they soon became pals. "[We] were buddies off-screen, I think, from the day we met," Miller told *Fangoria* magazine. "Beach buddies, party buddies, everything." It helped that their social circles already overlapped: Nicholson, too, was a Schwab's regular, taking his breakfast there every morning. He had, in fact, met his new agent there, so the old Schwab's magic had done its bit for the arch-eyebrowed striver. It was Corman who introduced them, and he told Miller, "This is my new leading man. This guy's going to be something." Miller wasn't so sure. "The truth was, I just didn't see it," he said. "But he was a good-looking kid."

"We hung out together, we went to the beach together almost every day, for a long time," Nicholson recalled. "We used to have a good time at the beach. Dick was a bit of a sun worshipper."

"Spent all day on the beach," Miller confirmed. "Sun-up 'til sundown. State beach. We did some surfing, body surfing mostly. It just seemed like we were just there all day long. Nobody was working."

Nicholson didn't work for a year after *The Cry Baby Killer*, but Miller, despite his best efforts to make no effort, snagged the occasional part. "Once I found out that you could get by in [Los Angeles] for very little money, I never looked for work," he told interviewer Anthony Petkovich. "The phone would ring and somebody would say, 'Roger's got a part for you next week.'"

In December just such a phone call came. Corman, the caller said, had a fresh and remarkably timely project ready to go, with a plum role for Dick. On October 4, 1957, the Russians moved ahead in the space race by launching their satellite, Sputnik 1; on October 5 Jack Rabin, who had provided Corman productions with their opticals (titles, wipes, dissolves) and special effects, and would continue to do so for many years, came to the producer with the idea for a satellite-themed picture. Corman, who enjoyed a challenge, saw the opportunity to make a picture truly ripped from today's headlines, and promised an executive at Allied Artists (for whom he had made *Not Of This Earth* and *Attack of the Crab Monsters*) that he could provide a finished satellite picture in eight weeks. A script was written from Rabin's story, which he'd conceived with his special-effects partner, Irving Block, and the picture went to camera a couple of weeks before Christmas.

The story concerned the efforts of the United Nations Rocket Operations, headed by Dr. Van Ponder, to send a series of manned satellites into orbit, only to see each of them atomized by a mysterious glowing barrier. Van Ponder, along with romantically linked rocket scientists Dave Boyer and Sybil, and the UN council that governs their operations, finally realize the meaning and general provenance of the barrier when a message from space is discovered: stop the experiments, the message warns, or else face the wrath of the universe. On his way to address the UN, Van Ponder is killed in a wreck, but shows up to deliver his speech anyway. It turns out the aliens have assumed his form in order to disable the satellite program from within, and it's up to the heroic team of Dave and Sybil to defeat the alien menace and carry on Van Ponder's work.

Miller was to play the hero, Boyer, and his casting was notable enough to be reported in a small article in the November 15 issue of *Variety*. It was the sort of role Peter Graves or Richard Garland had played in previous Corman pictures: the upright, square-jawed young scientist who solves problems through an admixture of impassioned speeches and punch-ups. "Jesus Christ, I gotta beat *him* up?" Miller said on hearing the six-foot-plus Richard Devon had been cast as Van Ponder. Later Miller expressed amazement he'd been cast at all, saying, "It was a real quote/unquote leading-man type, and I was a foot too short for the part." In his opinion the role "should have been given to William Lundigan or Richard Carlson," each of whom were a good deal taller than Miller, but also a decade too old for the role. In fact, his height works well for the part: he's meant to be an intellectual, not an adventurer, and his incongruence with Devon gives him an appealing underdog quality in the physical confrontations. As well, he was the perfect size for a romantic clutch with petite Susan Cabot, playing Sybil. And certainly Corman knew what he was doing when he asked Miller to play the part. "I've always liked the idea of ... something different than the tall, handsome leading man," he said. "I thought it was much more interesting to do some sort of offbeat casting, so I often used Dick Miller. I felt he was appropriate simply because he was not the obvious choice."

The cameras began rolling on December 9, and there were plenty of familiar faces on set: Bruno VeSota and Beach Dickerson both had small parts, Floyd Crosby was behind the camera, and Chuck Hannawalt was the key grip. Corman not only directed the picture, but took a role as a ground control technician; he even had a few technobabble lines to deliver. There was a new face in the crowd: art director Daniel Haller, who would later spin elaborate-looking sets from paltry resources on the Edgar Allen Poe pictures Corman would turn out through the first half of the 1960s, and who would eventually become a director himself. His budget-enhancing tricks here, as Miller recalled, mainly concerned the hallways of the spacecraft, which were formed from a total of four arches. "You could set them close together to make a short hall or set them further apart and make a long hall," he said. "And at the end of the hall was a flat—you made a turn. So on our spaceship you always ran down to the end of the hall and made a turn. That was the entire ship."

There were also, Miller told interviewer David Everitt, "two of the best lounge chairs money could buy" on the ship's bridge. "The type where you hit the sides and the chair slides down into a lying-down position. At the time they looked pretty good, except they really looked like lounge chairs. We had a lot of fun on those." According to Daniel Haller, it was set decorator Harry Reif, an old-style Hollywood lefty in the mould of Miller's cousinage, and a man who "did everything he could to save a buck for everybody," who brought in the marvellous chairs. "I said, 'Harry, what the hell are you thinking about, this is supposed to be a spaceship!'" Haller recalled. Reif just shrugged and told the art director that these chairs were the very latest thing in office furniture.

"We had space recliners with anti-gravity features," Corman pointed out.

It's easy to laugh at this bargain-bin set dressing, like the "satellite launcher" that was really a sound transfer machine, but somehow Corman pulled it off. The scripts, the acting, and the direction were a little bit better, or executed with a little more conviction, than what Roger's contemporaries, working on similar budgets, had to offer. A solid script, compelling performances, intelligent direction—these things lend the credibility they buy to the lounge chairs and flimsyboard archways. Miller knew it, telling David Everitt that

> it had to do with Roger's knack for making pictures. His competition at the time were people like Sam Katzman, and I think what made Katzman's pictures what they were was that he did a ten-day low-budget film and it looked like a ten-day low-budget film. Roger would shoot the same movie and he knew up front that [a good] script wouldn't cost anything—that's

talent, that's on paper. And if you hand-picked the actors and made sure they knew what they were doing, you could save a lot of time by getting everything in one take.

On a Corman set, continued Miller, "You didn't have much time to sit down. 'Don't leave the set' was the standing order. 'You're going to work again in three seconds.' On the last shot on a set, you would hear Roger yell cut, and as you turned he'd be walking, he'd be twenty-five, thirty yards away already, going to the next set-up."

This Speedy Gonzales style of filmmaking allowed Corman to deliver *War of the Satellites* on the schedule he had promised. "We used to joke that the Russians must have stolen the idea from him," Miller said. Corman made the picture so quickly, in fact, that it contains an error: the characters speak of Sputnik as though it were still aloft, when in fact it fell from orbit and burned up on January 4, 1958, three months after its launch and barely two weeks after Corman's film wrapped. The picture is unique in Miller's filmography: it's the only time he really got to step out of the character actor box in which he'd uncomplainingly found himself. He'd played heroes before, in *Rock All Night* and *Sorority Girl*, but these were unconventional leading men whose heroics were mainly verbal. In *War of the Satellites* he gets physical, going *mano a mano* in ways he rarely would again, and even when he did, it would be with grotesque reptilian puppets rather than men.

The role further demonstrated his range, though an actor who'd played both a cowboy and an Indian in his first picture has already shown a good deal of that. Had movie culture stood still for the next decade; had drive-ins maintained their status as passion pits and providers of the best in teen entertainment; had double-features of cheap sixty-five-minute sci-fi pictures remained popular beyond the end of the 1950s and had Corman continued to make them; and had Miller himself taken a more pragmatic approach to his career, he might have been able to coast along on starring roles in small genre pictures for a long while, and might even have taken starring roles in bigger pictures. But none of this happened.

War of the Satellites did make one crucial impression, though. Some months after its initial, headline-riding release, the picture wound up to Toronto, where an eighteen-year-old woman named Elaine Halpern saw it on a date. When Miller first appeared onscreen, "I almost swooned," she said. She turned to her boyfriend and stage-whispered, "He can put his shoes under my bed anytime!" The boyfriend was shocked: "After all, he'd been dating me for a year and could never get to first base with me. I was (believe it or not) a virgin. In those days, that wasn't unusual."

A few months later, Elaine Halpern, known as Lainie to her friends, would make her way to Los Angeles, and eventually she, like everyone else who ventured there, discovered Schwab's drugstore, along with its most devoted patron.

On December 21, three days after *War of the Satellites* wrapped, Miller's *Gale Storm Show* episode was broadcast. Then Christmas came, Miller turned twenty-nine, and all of a sudden it was 1958. The year began inauspiciously: Corman was, as ever, prepping a new movie, and he wanted Miller for the lead. It was a gangster movie, *Machine Gun Kelly*, and the script had been written by Miller's good Schwab's pal, Bobby Campbell. Susan Cabot was to play the role of the gangster's moll, the powerful woman behind the gun-toting nebbish.

The trouble was, Bobby Campbell had written the part for his brother William, and, for Campbell, blood was thicker than Apfel's coffee. He wasn't shy about petitioning both Corman and AIP on Billy's behalf. "[Bobby] sent a telegram from New York to Roger, and he said something about 'No one should play this part except Billy Campbell,'" Miller maintained. He wouldn't have minded this, or at least would have understood, except that, he says, Campbell had been instructed from the start to tailor the part for Dick, and had gone off-piste at his own discretion. This had the ring of betrayal.

It may also have been Miller's receiving a little karmic payback for doing a runner on *Stakeout on Dope Street*. In any case Arkoff and Nicholson at AIP wanted no part of any internecine battle between actors. The minute the conflict erupted, they instructed Corman to pay Miller off and find a third actor to play the part; he picked Charles Bronson, who was then still more coal miner than actor (though maybe he always was), and put the squinty bohunk on the road to tough-guy immortality. Miller was despondent, later telling an interviewer, "I walked away from a lot of parts, but this one walked away from me, and I really wanted it." It took some time before he forgave Bobby Campbell his minor treachery. It wasn't so minor as far as Miller was concerned, either: "I think the role would have done for me the same thing it did for Charlie," he said. Well, possibly. Miller was certainly the better actor, but not of a type that would have followed the same route as Bronson.

Corman recalled the events a little differently, or else his memory simply elided the Campbell/Miller conflict. "[Dick] was my first choice for *Machine Gun Kelly*," he said, "but the heads of AIP, for whom I made it, felt he didn't have the look, he was short, he didn't have the toughness. And probably they were right." Miller's "toughness" was not in question some years later when Corman drew from the gangster well again with *The St. Valentine's Day Massacre*: his grim visage wreathed in Thompson smoke as he mows down rival goons is a frightening sight indeed. And, in fact, given that the real Machine Gun Kelly never actually killed anyone, had screamed at the cops not to shoot him as he surrendered, and was renamed Pop Gun Kelly for his meek compliance in the jug, it's Bronson who seems ill-suited to the part. With Miller in the role, Kelly might have come off as an angrier though less homicidal Walter Paisley, but that's what he was.

In March two more Miller TV appearances were broadcast, *Whirlybirds* and *M Squad*. In May came his *Dragnet* episode, "The Big Perfume Bottle." You can't eat television appearances though, not until they go into syndication, and the summer stretched out devoid of employment opportunities. He didn't waste time in a depression, or in auditions; there was, after all, the beach. He raced cars and fell in love regularly. He got to know a dancer, Helena Kallianiotes, who lived on Laurel Canyon Boulevard, a street away from Miller's place, and was also a friend of Jack Nicholson's, and together they sped in the Triumph up to where the races were, north of the city. "I got myself in about three races," he said. "Didn't win. That was before Elaine." Helena, he insisted, was "just a friend. And she was a little … exciting."

"Did you date her?" Lainie Miller asked.

"No, I didn't," Miller said firmly. "God, I'm getting a divorce already!"

"I just wondered. Somebody said you dated her."

Miller shook his head. "To tell you the truth, I have not talked to her in 30 years. There's just nothing there."

But she was fun, and gorgeous too, and decades later Miller still had a sketch of her in his book, all raven hair and cheekbones. She had famously been a biker (she'd straddled a bronze Triumph back in Boston, where she grew up and everybody knew her by sight), and then a belly dancer; then she got into acting, and later lived on Nicholson's property and managed it in some fashion; and, between roles in films like *Five Easy Pieces* and *Shanks*, engaged in such curious enterprises as co-hosting (with Cher) celebrity roller-skating parties, appearing on an Art Garfunkle album cover, and opening a club in Silver Lake, called Helena's, of course, that accepted only the most exclusive of mid-'80s Hollywood royalty. She was, in short, an excellent person to go road racing with.

Another Miller pal was Biff Elliot, a tough actor best known for playing Mike Hammer in a 1953 3-D version of *I, the Jury*. Elliot was a jocular tough guy, an ex-boxer and a veteran, and he did a lot of small parts in big naval-battle pictures like *The Enemy Below* and *PT-109*. He was for many years a close golfing buddy of Jack Lemmon's, and naturally was a diehard Schwabbie. He and Miller expressed their affection for one another in the manner of any tough, mid-century man's man: "I love Dick," Elliot said to an interviewer, "but you tell him I can take him any day of the week."

War of the Satellites had a preview screening on May 6, double-billed with *Attack of the 50 Foot Woman*, and opened to the general public two days later. Helpfully providing the sort of publicity money couldn't buy, the Soviets launched Sputnik 3 a week later. Satellites were popping up all over; the subject could hardly be timelier. But reviews were mixed, and skewed negative, with *Variety* complaining about the "over-talkative script." (The same journal, in an article published while the film was still shooting, had praised Corman for taking "an editorial stand almost without precedent in filmmaking. ... Corman is revising the screenplay ... to include a criticism of U.S. officials who have let the Russians forge ahead in the missile and space projects race. Pix rarely take a stand on contemporary domestic issues involving federal administrations' failures or policies.") What critical praise there was focused on the actors: *Film Daily* lauded the acting in general, while Jack Moffitt of the *Hollywood Reporter* declared Miller in particular to have "a very pleasant screen personality." Bill Warren, the author of the comprehensive genre film survey *Keep Watching the Skies*, wrote that Miller had been miscast in the role, but was nevertheless "quite good." Warren accurately pointed out that Miller was "much more comfortable when he can be a crabby smartmouth, at which few actors are better."

There was more TV work that summer: another episode of *The Gale Storm Show*, this one called "The Sweepstakes Ticket," which aired in October, and a small role as a knife-waving thug in a detective show pilot clumsily titled *The Fat Man: The 32 Friends of Gina Lardelli*. Miller's bit in this latter program is measurable only in seconds: he plays one of three goons hired to terrorize the show's portly, epicurean hero, and was given some nonsensical hoodlum poetry to spout. "You're square. You're so square you're gonna wind up in a square box," he threatens with a Richard Widmark giggle just before the tables are turned by the arrival of the fat man's friend. It was based on a Dashiell Hammett character and spiced with hints of Nero Wolfe, but the show never went to series—in fact, never aired.

Little was happening that was not leisurely, and 1958 strolled on. Coffeehouses were popping up here and there, and men walked around looking like Miller had five years earlier, in beards and black workshirts. Miller was aware of the Beat movement, watched it all happening, but stayed aloof from it. "It wasn't *my* thing," he said. He read voraciously. He went to the movies, saw *South Pacific*, *Vertigo*, *Touch of Evil*, *The Vikings*; was tickled to see his old pal Steve McQueen fight off a crimson mass of jelly in *The Blob*; saw Jack in *The Cry Baby Killer*. Elvis was in the army, but he was also on the radio, and so were the Everly Brothers, Andy Williams, and Frank Sinatra. The Silhouettes' "Get a Job" blared up and down the Strip through the early part of the year, but Miller, a die-hard jazzbo, ignored it. Corman, meanwhile, shot *Teenage Caveman* in May; *I, Mobster* in July; and *The Wasp Woman*—Susan Cabot's last film—in December; and executive produced *Attack of the Giant Leeches*, featuring Bruno VeSota at his sweatiest, in October. There were no parts for Miller in any of them.

Despite Miller's love of jazz, Chuck Griffith was the one more attuned to Beat culture and more particularly to beatniks. "Everybody went to coffeehouses in those days," Griffith said. Even Corman, who always asserted he was the squarest member of a reasonably hip crowd, could now and again be found in the smoky embrace of the Strip's bars and coffeehouses. The culture had been rumbling beneath the macadam of America since the late 1940s and was brought to national attention in 1957 with the obscenity trial of Allan Ginsberg's *Howl*. A year later, in early April 1958, *San Francisco Chronicle* columnist Herb Caen, a man fond of wordplay whether or not it made sense, combined 'Beat' and 'Sputnik' and got 'beatnik.' This coincided with a commercialization and homogenization of Beat appurtenances, and, however playfully Caen had intended his neologism, went along with the ongoing Establishment backlash and a suspicion that the counterculture was a hotbed of communism. Felt berets and rub-on goatees were available in plenty at the doo-dad shops: the clownification of the movement was well underway.

To Corman, it looked every bit as fertile a source of commercial film stories as Sputnik. By Corman's recollection, the light bulb alit while he and Griffith were in San Francisco, sitting in the famed Bagel Shop at the corner of Grant and Green, in the heart of North Beach. If the culture had a locus, this was it, though by early 1959 it was losing any cohesion it might ever have had. Corman and Griffith and some others in the crew—they'd been making a picture up there—ordered drinks and were taking in the atmosphere when Corman noticed they themselves were part of the atmosphere, as far as the tourists who crowded the place were concerned. If he, the button-down Stanfordite, could be taken for a beatnik, there surely must be a hunger to see beatniks and a lot of latitude in how to portray them, and accordingly his Give The People What They Want instincts came instantly to the fore.

AIP had asked Corman for a horror movie, but didn't have much money to offer. Corman figured the clapboard, bare-light bulb world of the beatniks would be simple enough to recreate on a budget, and so, when the company had returned to LA, he and Griffith toured the Sunset Strip coffeehouses and brainstormed plots. According to Corman, while on this jaunt they roped in an acquaintance, an aspiring actress named Sally Kellerman, who was working as a waitress and who would eventually play Hot Lips Houlihan in Robert Altman's film M*A*S*H. "She sat down and helped us work out the final details of the story," Corman asserted. The story soon had a name, "The Yellow Door," though this was eventually changed, by AIP head Jim Nicholson, first to "The Living Dead" and finally to *A Bucket of Blood*.

For about three years, Beatsploitation pictures were a real thing, a profitable little sub-genre; and nearly all of them were just lowbrow crime films in Maynard Krebs drag: *The Beatniks, High School Confidential, The Cool and the Crazy, The Bloody Brood, The Fat Black Pussycat, The Beat Generation*. Beatniks were on television and in comics, in magazines and on postcards; they were paid to sit in café windows to attract square custom. Mel Welles, whose Sir Bop persona was a genuine part of him, kept the flame burning whenever he was around, and Griffith marinated in the hempy surroundings all through the early weeks of 1959.

Then, in April, after AIP made the request for a quickie horror movie, Corman found that the Dan Haller-designed sets from a recently wrapped picture called *Diary of a High School Bride* were still erected at the Kling Studios—the former Charlie Chaplin Studios at the corner of La Brea and Sunset—and would stay that way for a week, long enough to make a picture on them, though it would be Corman's shortest schedule yet. Corman brought Griffith down and showed him the sets: "a beatnik coffeehouse, a jail [and] a funky pad with nothing in it," Griffith remembered. Corman told him to tailor the story to these sets, and off you go.

Griffith turned in a thirty-page treatment outlining the story; it was still called "The Yellow Door," after the name of the coffeehouse in the story. This was approved, and Griffith wrote the script in about five days. The story told of a coffeehouse busboy, Walter Paisley, who, even as he cringingly removes the cups and saucers of his clientele, aspires to be as great an artist as he assumes each of them are; and at the same time he pines for the hand of the lovely Carla. Leonard, the owner of the Yellow Door, alternately mocks and slave-drives poor, lonely Walter, while in the background a bearded poet, Maxwell Brock, barks his majestically silly verse. Back in his dingy room Walter attempts a clay sculpture of his own, but he's completely talentless. However, an accident involving his landlady's pet offers him the opportunity to create something after all: a clay-covered cat with a knife stuck in it. The piece, *Dead Cat*, proves a hit with the coffeehouse denizens, and Maxwell extemporizes a poem in Walter's honour. Leonard quickly discovers that the sculpture contains a real cat, but says nothing after a wealthy art collector offers to buy Walter's work. As the beatniks' adulation fades, Walter realizes more works are required, and when he accidentally kills a policeman who is attempting to arrest him on spurious drug charges, he understands he's got more raw material to work with; the result is called *Murdered Man*. Now Walter turns a corner and begins killing purposefully; his first victim is a snarky beat-groupie who models for him on the promise of money. But she gets a rebozo around the neck instead. Walter next decapitates a buzz saw operator working after hours, and produces his first bust. Now he's got enough work for a show. However, his technique is discovered by the horrified crowd even as Walter, driven berserk by Carla's final rejection of him, warms up his strangling hands and chases her through the streets. But the voices of his victims sound in his frazzled head, and they order him home to make one last piece, *Hanging Man*, a self-portrait.

Griffith always insisted that when he turned his script in, and Corman saw that it had become a comedy, the director blanched and cried something like "But I don't know how to direct comedy!" whereupon Griffith sagely counselled him to simply direct it straight, as he would a drama. But Corman's memory is different, unsurprisingly, and he told the story as many times as Griffith did his own. "I'd been making a series of horror films," he said,

> and I noticed that, at the sneak preview of one film, the audience really screamed at the exact moment I wanted them to. I thought, 'I really got that horror sequence right.' And right after they screamed, some people

laughed. And I thought, 'Is that a bad laugh?' And I thought, 'No, it's actually a laugh of appreciation. It's a winding-down and letting-go of the horror, and sort of a recognition of what had happened.' So as a result, I began to think about horror and comedy together, and I came up with a theory that—I don't know if it has any real meaning or not, but I was studying Freud at the time, and I felt there were similar arcs to horror, sex, and humour. In all of them you start with a rising level of tension, you build the tension up to the breaking point, and then you snap it. With horror they scream, with comedy they laugh, and with sex you come. And because at that time there were the MPAA regulations, there was no sex particularly in pictures, but I decided to use the theory in *Bucket of Blood*.

Wherever the idea and will to attempt a comedy had come from, *A Bucket of Blood* was a comedy. But, as the synopsis indicates, it was not slapstick, it was not Borscht Belt; it was of the new style of comedy, the Mort Sahl, the Lenny Bruce, the Jules Feiffer—this last from whose recent book *Sick, Sick, Sick!* the AIP promotional department would lift the picture's tagline. It was dark comedy pitched to a hip crowd, and in the suddenly crowded field of beatnik pictures it would prove by far the best of the bunch.

Near the end of 1958, in Toronto, Elaine Halpern was planning a trip to sunny California, travelling with her grandmother on the Acheson, Topeka, and Santa Fe. "We went to visit my crazy aunt who married an American," she said. Before she left another aunt, Becky, read her Tarot cards. "You will marry a man from New York," Becky said, peering at the rods, queens, and cups. Elaine allowed as how that was unlikely. "How on earth would I meet a New Yorker when I wasn't going to be anywhere near New York?" she asked. "I shrugged it off, thinking that in spite of her reputation for accuracy in tarot card readings, surely she'd made a mistake this time."

In Los Angeles Lainie stayed with her aunt and made new acquaintances. It was wintertime; she was in no hurry to get back to Toronto. The warm air and sea breezes of southern California were as intoxicating to her as they had been to Miller on his first visit eighteen years earlier. Winter turned to spring, but nothing changed much; the scent on the breeze, perhaps, as the prevailing winds shifted with the season. It was enchanting. So was Schwab's, where one of Lainie's acquaintances took her one fateful day in early May 1959.

It was May 8, to be exact, a Friday. Schwab's itself had recently changed: it had been expanded from a simple lunch counter to a dining room with tables and booths, and there was Dick, as usual, sitting at one of them, shooting the shit with some showbiz pal or another. Lainie was with a group of people, and one of them was a friend of Miller's. The friend introduced them, and Miller stared straight ahead into Elaine's water-gypsy face. "We shook hands," he said, "and that was it. I never let go."

11   *This is what I would do if I was a little nuts*

Dick Miller and Elaine Halpern met on Friday, May 8, 1959, and on the following Monday *A Bucket of Blood*—still referred to by everyone as "The Living Dead," though it contained no ghouls or zombies or living dead—began its five-day shoot. Miller had been hired to play Walter (though Griffith pictured someone weenier in the role, like Elisha Cook Jr.), and Barboura Morris, who was divorced from Monte Hellman and whom Corman was now dating, played Carla, the object of his affection. Strangely, Mel Welles had not been cast as Maxwell Brock, though it was a role that could have been, and probably was, written expressly for him. But Welles was busy in TV Westerns that summer, and in any case had never been quite as devoted as some to his membership in the Corman company. The role was competently, in fact expertly, filled by Julian Burton.

Antony Carbone was the café owner, Leonard Di Santis; Julian Burton's sister Jhean was heroin-slinging, good-time girl Maolia; Chuck Griffith's grandmother Myrtle Vail played the landlady, Mrs. Swickert; other parts were filled out by people such as Bruno VeSota and John Shaner; and the role of Lou, the vice cop whom a panicked Walter brains with a frying pan, was an early appearance by future game show king Bert Convy. Lou's partner, the other undercover man, was Ed Nelson, who had begun his acting career beneath one of Corman's giant Styrofoam crabs on *Attack of the Crab Monsters*, and would attain a species of stardom on the soapy TV show *Peyton Place*. Daniel Haller had redressed and rejigged his sets, transforming the jail into a beatnik crash pad, and Corman, who regarded the tiny schedule as a challenge, came prepared. He was pleased to see his actors taking it seriously too. "Dick worked very well with Barboura," Corman said. "On five days you do not have much time for rehearsals. You run it through once or twice in a reading before the shooting, you give it a one or two time rehearsal on the set, and you shoot. And he and Barboura worked together on and off the set to develop their relationship." Corman was pleased with the results. "I think one of the good things about the picture is that within the comedy there's a very human and touching relationship between Dick and Barboura."

He was even more pleased when, after Julian Burton's performance of the film's opening poem, the crew spontaneously applauded. It was a first, according to Chuck Griffith. "Nobody ever liked anything before," he said. An excited Corman told Griffith to start thinking about another movie just like it. "Not just a similar sort of thing," Corman instructed. "I want the same exact movie again."

While Griffith began considering ideas for a xerograph of *Bucket of Blood*, the shoot proceeded at as rapid a pace as Corman and his people had ever worked. Like Corman, Miller had come prepared, though developing the Walter Paisley character had been pretty simple. "I'd like to go on and on and say how I extrapolated on the character and found his inner being and all this, but no," he said. "He's a little nuts, so I play him down a little bit. I say, 'This is what I would do,' but then I say, 'This is what I would do if I was a little nuts.'" In earlier interviews Miller indecorously described Paisley as a "mental retard," which, if accurate, would at least indicate that for all his greed and venality, Leonard Di Santis is an equal-opportunity employer.

Though he played down the commitment of his portrayal later on, while still allowing that it wasn't an "accidental performance," Miller evidently took it very seriously at the time. Antony Carbone even detected a whiff of Method in Miller's madness. "[Dick] had the kind of attitude that he had in the film, even *off* stage, even *off* those films," Carbone told writer Tom Weaver. "I don't know if he was like that all the time—maybe Roger got somebody who would fit with those characters, a little retarded, a little this and that! Not that Dick is retarded, but he had that kind of attitude and he just carried it off-stage." Carbone's impressions were similar to those of the parents of Miller's long-ago Bronx pals. "I often thought, 'Gee, he's kinda weird, this guy, isn't he?'" Carbone said. "But he was very nice to work with, very giving."

Everybody on the shoot thought someone else was weird. To Miller, Barboura Morris was "another weirdo! She was a very intense actress, but I never understood her motivation for the things she did. In acting, she'd go into these deep, deep things. Stare off into the wilderness." But he liked her, and they spent a lot of time working together on their scenes. "We were friendly too," Miller said. "Nothing uptight about her, just this intense thing. I think she does it in the movies too. She does a lot of staring."

Both Carbone and Miller remembered the set as harmonious and suffused with a sense of fun and experimentation. Some Corman veterans, actor Richard Devon in particular, have complained about Roger the martinet, but he was quite able to strike a pleasant tone when he wanted to. The atmosphere was friendly, relaxed, collegial. "The beatniks in the coffeehouse scenes were all my friends," Chuck Griffith said. Miller in particular was on cloud nine: he had just met the love of his life and was acting in the role that would define him, all of it in the same week. He was having fun with it, ad-libbing bits: for example, lines like "Be a nose!" shouted by Walter as he's trying desperately to sculpt a face, or his whooping and capering in response to some positive feedback about his work. "It just felt right," Miller said. "The sculpture, the joy of his statue finally. You know. Extreme, hysterical." There were subtler performative devices too, small things that were equally insightful, as when Walter "cleans" his crepe pan by wiping it on his leg.

The "Be a nose!" scene stood out to a lot of viewers—whatever your level of artistic skill, it's easy to empathize with Walter's frustration. Art Spiegelman, the venerated graphic novelist who created the famous *Maus* books and the even more famous Garbage Pail Kids, was transfixed when he saw the movie, declaring the "Be a nose" moment as "the most accurate evocation I've ever seen of my own creative process." In 2009 Spiegelman grouped three of his sketchbooks into one small book he called *Be a Nose!* On the cover of at least one edition was a still from *A Bucket of Blood* showing Walter Paisley working at his clay, and below that a small drawing underlining just how easily Dick Miller could be drawn to resemble Dick Tracy.

At the time Miller probably had no idea that this was the best movie he or Corman or anybody else on the set had yet been involved in, but there were certainly hints. "It's the best script Chuck ever wrote," Miller said later, with complete accuracy. Griffith was especially pleased because in writing the picture he believed he had stumbled across "a new structure. That's the most precious thing you can find, a new structure." The structure was sturdy enough to reuse, just as he recycled *Naked Paradise*; and the *Bucket of Blood* script itself was strong enough that it would be remade in 1995 with Anthony Michael Hall in the Walter Paisley role, adapted for the stage the same year for a Winnipeg, Canada, fringe theatre festival, and transformed into two separate musical versions in Chicago alone, one in 1993 and another in 2009.

"I believe *A Bucket of Blood* is truly the cult film of all cult films," Miller told an interviewer. "Of course, every picture made they say is a cult film. If it's a year old and it didn't do any business, it's a cult film." Indeed, the picture didn't do spectacular business, despite a go-for-broke ad campaign that played up the "sickness" of the picture's comedy and invited people to bring down an actual bucket of blood to receive free admission. It wasn't a flop, though; according to Corman, "it wasn't a breakout success or anything like that, but it was a solid success." It proved to him not only that humour could go hand in hand with horror, as he had theorized, but that he had talent enough to make the combination work. Credit for the film is spread across three different people: Corman, Griffith, and Miller, and there's enough of it to go around.

Griffith was initially pleased with the picture, but later on, when he realized how popular its follow-up, *The Little Shop of Horrors,* had become, his allegiance shifted. Corman "always thought *Bucket of Blood* was funnier than *Little Shop of Horrors,*" though he preferred the latter film's title, saying that "*A Bucket of Blood* was a pretty standard type of horror title, whereas *Little Shop of Horrors* was a tongue-in-cheek title that led you to believe it was something different." Miller himself thought it was "a classic picture in every way except the money.... If only they'd had some money. Everybody's good. The story's good ... but then they would show a mannequin and say it was a statue." He was especially disappointed with the ending, in which Walter Paisley is meant to have covered himself up with clay before his suicide by hanging, but there had not been enough time to create a hanging, clay-covered Paisley effigy. "It would have been a more startling effect than some grey make-up," Miller said. "They didn't have any money in it for production values, and it suffered." Even so, of all the pictures he made, it stands as Miller's personal favourite, and no wonder: it's all Miller, no filler.

When the shoot ended, as Corman swung into preparations for his next picture, *The Last Woman on Earth,* Miller returned to the cocoon of new love and stayed in it nearly the entire summer. It wasn't that he was being lazy or that he didn't want to work: he managed, for example, to squeeze in a few days on an episode of *The Untouchables,* playing a taciturn, sleeve-gartered accountant in the employ of gangster Dutch Schultz. The show was produced by one of the execs who'd created *The Bert Parks Show,* Miller's old New York boss Genial Paul Harrison; and though Miller had the talent, the right face, and certainly the time to play the part, it seems unlikely this reunion was entirely a coincidence. With his multitasking back in New York, Dick had certainly proved himself to the amiable producer. Harrison would hire Miller for another of his shows, the soufflé-light sitcom *Our Man Higgins,* a few years later. Miller auditioned for other jobs, and came close, he believed, to nabbing the role of Little Joe on *Bonanza.* But this opportunity, Miller said, "kinda fell through," and Michael Landon got the part. Had Miller prevailed, he'd have been set for the next fourteen years at least.

By summer's end, Lainie Halpern was living with some girlfriends and was no longer entertaining thoughts of returning to Toronto. She was in love, and the twelve-year difference between her age and Dick's didn't make the slightest difference to either of them. On October 6, "on the spur of the moment," Lainie says, "we got quickie blood tests, ran down to the courthouse in LA, both of us wearing jeans and bush jackets, and got married. Two complete strangers at the courthouse were our witnesses. We told our families after the fact." Lainie moved into Dick's small apartment on Laurel Avenue, and their married life—one of the most durable unions in Hollywood history—commenced in earnest. It was a quiet beginning, virtually uncelebrated. "We did not have a party or a honeymoon," Lainie said. "We couldn't afford anything like that."

But Lainie, the young bride, had no regrets. "If it's right, it's right," she later said. "If it's not right, it's not right. I'm not saying every single day was wonderful …"

In this she was quickly contradicted by a smiling Miller. "Oh yes," he said, "it was wonderful."

Roger Corman, daring to believe he had something of real comedic value, held a few preview screenings of his weird new picture. "It got huge laughs," he told the French cineaste journal *Positif 59*. "I previewed the film at the same time as a Jerry Lewis film because I wanted the opinion of comedy lovers. However, the theatre owner told me that I had gotten more laughs than the Lewis film and that it was the funniest film he had ever seen. I felt like I'd taken a huge step forward."

A Bucket of Blood appeared in theatres on October 21, a few weeks after Dick and Lainie's quickie wedding, but, like many now-beloved classics, it wasn't thought much of on its original release. *Hollywood Reporter* critic Jack Moffitt reported that he'd seen the picture "in a theaterful of teenagers, and their laughs were whole-hearted and continuous.… They laughed at it and not with it. At the break, many were saying, 'This is better than a monster picture.'" He liked the picture's lead player, writing, "Miller as the shuffling, sniffling busboy exudes false humility every minute and delivers quite an offbeat comedy performance." Miller was, in fact, getting some of the best and most verbose notices of his career. "Dick Miller's ability to sustain a sense of poignancy while acting conceited and committing atrocities is responsible in large part for the picture's appeal," *Variety* said, and it's easy to see Miller sharing the review with his pals at Schwab's, then tearing it out as carefully as he'd once torn out Fruehof Trailer ads in the basement of the Kudner ad agency. When the movie made its way to England in 1960, he got admiring notices there too, with the British Film Institute's *Monthly Film Bulletin* saying, "Dick Miller gives a performance of sustained poignancy as the half-wit hero." And this was the period in which Corman reportedly bestowed Miller with the title "the best actor in Hollywood." ("He probably took it back afterwards!" a chuckling Miller told Corman historian Beverly Gray.)

If Miller had been waiting for his moment, the time when he might hoist himself from the B-picture mire, this was probably it. But he hardly noticed: he didn't feel he was in a mire, for starters, and he was a newly married man: careerism would, for the moment, take a seat even further back than it had occupied before, at just the time a little strategy might have done him some good. In fact, from an outsider's perspective, he seemed to be actively working to sabotage himself. He cared less than ever for auditions, and though he was unhappy with his agency, he made no move to change it. He'd just begun to think of himself as an actor; how could he be expected to think of himself as a star? He'd been playing lead roles for Corman, but had no sense of the value such roles could have to his career, even if they were in penny-ante, seemingly ephemeral movies. Nobody, certainly not Miller, expected any of these pictures to last longer than a few months in the public consciousness. After that, they may as well never have existed at all. "You made [the movie]," Miller said, "you got as much money as you could out of it, and then it became, you know, mandolin picks."

A Bucket of Blood did well enough to justify a follow-up, which Corman would produce for his own recently founded distribution company, Filmgroup. After being instructed to write a *Bucket* simulacrum, Chuck Griffith came up with "Gluttony," about a salad chef turning to cannibalism, but even cannibalism presented in a black-humour context was bound to run up against the Production Code, the industry-set standards by which all publicly exhibited films must abide. According to Mel Welles, the writer also tried something called "Cardula," about a vampire who doubled as a music critic, but Roger didn't like it. As they'd done while brainstorming *A Bucket of Blood*, Griffith and Corman went on a Sunset Strip pub crawl. A soused Griffith got into a fight with Lawrence Tierney, and, after he somehow survived that, Griffith and Corman once again ended up at the place Sally Kellerman was working. Corman later wrote, "As Chuck and I vied with each other, trying to top each other's sardonic or subversive ideas, appealing to Sally as a referee, she sat down at the table with us, and the three of us worked out the rest of the story together." The story involved a monstrous, man-eating flower and the hapless schlemiel who provides his meals; Griffith wrote it up and gave it the title "The Passionate People Eater." Later Corman would come up with a new title: *The Little Shop of Horrors*.

Corman had moved his office from the Cock 'n Bull restaurant and was now renting space at the Kling studio at the corner of Sunset and La Brea, which had been the Chaplin studio until the Little Tramp sold it in 1953. One day late in 1959 Roger had lunch with the studio manager, "and he mentioned that they had a rather nice set built for some picture that was finished, and nobody was coming in and it was just sitting there," Corman said. "And I just had the idea: I could go in and shoot for the fun of it." The studio manager laughed at Corman and promised him a special deal on the space if he was serious, and this, of course, was an offer Roger couldn't resist.

The new iteration of *Bucket*—which itself had been shot on borrowed sets in not much more than two days—seemed a perfect project for this arrangement, and when Griffith finished his work Corman sent the script to his presumed star, Dick Miller. Miller was amazed to read what might as well have been a more fanciful version of the *Bucket* script, with maybe a few details changed and some crazy new character names stamped over the old ones. He thought about it for a few moments, then, in a decision he would feel low-level regret over for the rest of his career, called Corman back and turned down the lead role of flower-shop dogsbody Seymour Krelboyne. "Like an idiot, I said, 'This is just like *A Bucket of Blood*,'" Miller told Chris Nashawaty. "I didn't think of it as a step up furthering my career. Now, I could kick myself!" Instead, almost at random, he took the part of Burson Fouch, a flower-eating cosmopolitan who happens into the little shop where most of the action takes place.

Indeed, despite their different tones—"I wrote *Bucket* as a satire and *Little Shop* as a farce," Griffith said—the two stories were exceedingly similar, especially when considered with the lead character in the foreground. Walter Paisley and Seymour Krelboyne are both put-upon employees at a small business, none too good at their jobs, berated constantly by a tyrannical boss, increasingly desperate to find something that will set them apart and bring them some measure of respect. In both cases they succeed, but at a price paid by other people, until finally they pay the ultimate toll themselves. Seymour had a mother rather than a landlady, though they perform the same story function (and were played by the same actress, Griffith's grandmother

Myrtle Vail); he had a less complicated romantic life than Walter; and the rich character arc afforded Walter was graded down to a dull hump for Seymour. Really, Seymour was just a goofier, less interesting Walter Paisley, and little wonder Miller could find no acting challenge there. On top of this, because Corman was paying his principals for a full week, there was no difference in remuneration between the lead role and the secondary role Miller ultimately took. Nevertheless, Miller's later misgivings were profound. "I think, at that moment, I stopped being a star in pictures, and I went back to being a character actor," he lamented.

When he turned down the role, Miller advised Corman to "give it to Jonathan," and although Corman and Haze had experienced something of an estrangement over the previous couple of years, Corman couldn't think of anyone better. He called the actor in mid-December, a week before the shoot, and offered him the role. Haze accepted with something of a shrug: "I needed the money, so I took it," he said. "It was a job." The character of the flower-shop boss, Gravis Mushnick, had been in large part inspired by the Yiddisher shtick Miller and Mel Welles engaged in almost constantly at Schwab's, at parties, and wherever else they were hanging out, and which Griffith had consequently heard plenty of; so Welles was the perfect candidate for the part, and was given it. Jackie Joseph, a newcomer to the Corman stable, whom Corman had seen and admired in a stage revue, was cast as Audrey, the goofy love interest; and Griffith himself took a couple of small parts, as well as providing the voracious plant's hectoring voice. John Shaner was the sadistic Skid Row dentist, Dr. Phoebus Farb, and Jack Nicholson came in for an hour or so to play his masochistic patient, Wilbur Force. (Griffith's bizarre character names—his trademark, really—usually invite either pleasurable bafflement or a pained wince.)

Cameras—there were two shooting simultaneously, as on a TV sitcom—began rolling at 7:45 a.m. on Monday, December 21. The cast had rehearsed for a few days, and now in just over twelve hours they set about delivering fifty pages of the most malaprop-ridden script ever written. They went at it until 9:30 at night, then came back the next day and did it again, another fifty pages, all shot more or less in sequence. (Welles, Griffith, Haze, and a very small crew—but not Corman—went out into the streets for a few subsequent nights to get location material and several full scenes involving Seymour collecting victims.) The two-camera method sped things up, but meant Corman was more miserly than ever with the number of takes he was willing to do. "One take was it," Miller told *Cinefantastique* magazine. "You were either clear on one camera or the other. When you're shooting with two cameras, you're never really clear. You're always behind somebody on one camera or the other, so there's a lot of strange shots in there."

"Everyone took it as kind of a joke," Corman said. "Everybody was laughing and making up lines." Haze, doing a broad Jerry Lewis thing that Miller would never have attempted, had more screen time, but Welles had a lot more dialogue, all in the broad Jewish caricature that nearly had the movie strangled aborning. It was declared anti-Semitic by a number of exhibitors, and there was a delay of several months in its release. Neither Corman nor Griffith was Jewish, and all the Semitic material had come from Welles and Miller, who had done their best to school the goyim in Catskills humour and intra-culture stereotypes. The provenance of all this hardly mattered to the offended parties, but eventually the heat wore off, and in early 1961 *Little Shop of Horrors* ("The funniest picture this year!" per the ad copy) hit screens on a bill with *Black Sunday*, a violent, velvet-black Italian creepie AIP had acquired ("The most frightening motion picture you've ever seen!"). It was a decidedly odd bill, but the picture also did some time on a pairing with Corman's own *The Last Woman on Earth*.

With Haze in the lead instead of Miller, *Little Shop* was a different animal, or vegetable, than it might have been had Miller's scruples not prevailed. "I played things more outrageously than he did," Haze said. Griffith and Corman had assumed Fouch would be an outrageous character; after all, here was a guy who chomped on flowers. But Miller saw it another way. "Chuck had written kind of a weirdo character," he said, "a weirdo who comes in and eats flowers. I said no, this is a very straight man who comes in and eats flowers."

Miller had fun with Fouch, though, and seemed to enjoy not carrying the film and working in every scene, as he had on *Bucket*. "He had less pressure [than Haze] in the film and could chat between takes," Jackie Joseph remembered. Miller brought some little touches to his "Mr. Yellow Vest," like a laid-back hipster attitude and the little salt shaker he keeps in a fob on his belt for seasoning flowers at a moment's notice. "Eat the flowers," Corman told Dick on the set, and Miller replied, "Eat 'em? Well, at least get some fresh flowers, Roger, not two days old from a funeral!" But when Miller tucked into the blooms, he found them to his liking. "The prettier they smell, the prettier they taste," he discovered. Corman invited the actor to spit them out once the cameras had cut, but Miller, perhaps unaccustomed to getting nourishment of any kind on a Corman set, swallowed them happily.

"I didn't believe him, so he ate flowers in our apartment," Lainie Miller said. "I had a great big thing of carnations, and he just dug into them to prove to me that he did that on the set." ("I've got to go home, my wife's making gardenias for dinner," Burson Fouch says at one point in the picture, and this was closer to the truth than we ever knew.)

When *The Little Shop of Horrors* was adapted into a musical and then into a big-budget Frank Oz film, the Fouch character didn't make the transition. Nevertheless, as pointed out by author Geoffrey Hill, he's important, even critical to a mythology-based reading of the movie. First, as a man who eats plants, he alone stands in diametrical opposition to the plant who eats men; furthermore, wrote Hill in his essay "*Little Shop of Horrors*: The Battle Between Heaven and Earth,"

> just as the sun is symbolically connected to the supreme male god, so the sun color of Burson's vest is symbolic of his role as Zeus.... While death and destruction happen all around him and hysteria progressively abounds, Burson Fouch stands proud and poised.... It is actually he that encourages Mr. Mushnick to put the plant on display in the first place, as if he knows something of which the rest of the characters are unaware.... While the combatants of the war consistently cudgel and digest one another, Burson stands alone, like Zeus, watching, yet lending encouragement to Seymour, the chief victim on both sides of the conflict.

Whether or not you buy into this interpretation, it properly underlines the importance of Miller's character. "Mr. Yellow Vest" unsurprisingly became a fan favourite when the movie achieved its cult status in the years after its initial release, and even inspired a specific haircut, the Fouch, modelled after Miller's own December 1959 coif. And in a strange coincidence, in 1980 a poet also named Dick Miller published a collection called *Yellow Jersey*, featuring poems like "A Two Minute Juke Box Hot for Old Billy" and "Too Many Flicks." What to make of this is uncertain.

It's nevertheless interesting to speculate on what might have been had Miller played Seymour, the lead in *Little Shop*: the picture is among the most famous Corman ever made, not just because of Nicholson's wacky turn, but because of the legendary two-day shooting schedule (plus three or four nights, of course), the public-domain status that assured it repeated TV broadcasts and college film society screenings, and the cult reputation it eventually acquired as a result of all this, and for being a funny, clever little picture. But even had Miller headlined such a high-profile item, he'd not likely have benefited much from it; after all, it didn't make Jonathan Haze a household name. Still, Miller retrospectively felt it broke his stride, and in the years after, as the film's popularity grew, he spent a lot of time kicking himself for his youthful integrity. "Ahh," he said, "what a dope I was."

12 *No man could have lived through it*

Near the end of 1959 Ronald Reagan was elected for a second time as president of the Screen Actors Guild (SAG), which many people, including Dick Miller, found odd, since he was also the host and producer of the CBS anthology program *General Electric Theater*. He was also very tight with Lou Wasserman of MCA (Music Corporation of America), who represented him; and MCA had not so long ago been granted the waiver they needed from SAG in order to get into production; and this waiver, unique in the industry, had been granted during Reagan's previous tenure, by Reagan. It was all very buddy-buddy, replete with conflicts of interest, oily as Reagan's own pompadour. But the SAG membership evidently saw something of potential value in the actor-producer's hyphenate status and his mutually beneficial relationship with the entertainment titan MCA. A strike vote was in the air, and the principal issue was the payment of residuals for television and other ancillary sales. Actors had watched their movies lucratively sold to the newer medium, and while they had been paid only once for their work, studios were making bank over and again from new sources. It didn't seem fair, and it wasn't. Maybe Reagan could get Wasserman onside, persuade him that some kind of residual payment scheme was in order, maybe a pension plan and a couple of other things as well.

So the Gipper was made president again, and through the late winter of 1960, as pressure to strike increased, Reagan, unexpectedly, encouraged it. The actors walked on March 7. Reagan negotiated with studio heads, some of whom actually cried real tears while describing the depths of abject penury to which either a strike or a residual scheme would send their companies. But in the end, he announced triumphantly to the membership, he had prevailed. The studios, he said, also triumphantly, had caved. They would fund the beginnings of a health insurance plan! And a pension plan! And best of all, residual payments for all! There was just one catch: this applied only to films shot beginning January 1, 1960, or just over three months earlier. To a guy like Miller, who hadn't yet worked a day in 1960, this was bullshit.

He thought it was bullshit not just because it was of no immediate advantage to himself—he was still young enough not to be much concerned about a pension—but also because of Reagan's clear management bias and the fact of MCA's recent purchase of the entire Paramount Pictures catalogue from 1948 and earlier: movies they could sell to TV as many times as they wanted and never pay a penny in residuals. The money MCA saved vastly outweighed whatever they'd be paying toward a pension plan. Reagan and Wasserman had washed each other's hands beneath the boardroom table, and no matter how beneficial the residual deal would prove to future generations of Hollywood performers, there was, aptly enough, an unmistakable residue covering the whole manoeuvre. (Reagan would resign the SAG presidency only a few weeks later, on the grounds that, as an active producer, he should never have been president in the first place.)

So at the SAG meeting in April at which Reagan announced his great strategic triumph, Miller held up a sign representing not just his opinion, but those of Bob Hope, Mickey Rooney, Gene Kelly, and June Lockhart, who were all equally opposed, and who labelled Reagan's deal "The Great Giveaway." "WE GOT SCREWED," Miller's placard read. He provided verbal accompaniment to his sign: shouts, catcalls, boos, and authentic Bronx cheers. Nearby, he recalled, there were "guys in suits" who were looking at him and listening to everything he was saying. He didn't know who they were, but, Miller said, "they didn't belong there." It happened that Miller did have some work lined up, a TV movie of some kind, but the day after the meeting, he was contacted and told his part had been written out of the script. This was a well-known end run around SAG pay-or-play provisions, "the only way they could cancel you legit," Miller said. It was an unpropitious and dispiriting time to be losing work, because some time in April Lainie realized she was pregnant.

It's not easy being a jobbing actor, and by many accounts it's more difficult still to be a Corman actor. Though it's easy to find actors who were proud of their work with Roger, many others felt there was a stigma attached to it, that it could hurt one's chances to appear in more legitimate cinema. "Making a Roger Corman film, at the time, was the bottom of the barrel," said actress Lori Nelson, who'd appeared in Corman's *Day the World Ended*. "You really felt like you were struggling to get work when you had to make a Roger Corman film.... But you had to make a living." Jonathan Haze felt the same way. "I stayed being a Corman actor," he said, "which was kind of like having a disease as far as anyone wanting to be around you. If you had done a lot of Corman movies and you went on an interview at MGM, they held it against you."

For Bruno VeSota, the Corman Actor label led to a crisis of self-confidence. "Sometimes I think it over, and I say to myself, 'Working for a schlock outfit, you must be a schlock yourself,'" he told interviewer Barry Brown in 1975. "Even if it's the need for money, I think I would have had more respect for myself if I'd worked as a dishwasher." VeSota, too, bemoaned the impact it had on his career. "You give a list of your credits to an agent, they don't even want to represent you because you've been in those movies," he said. "How many crawl out of that? I think that's one of the reasons I'm still crawling."

By the beginning of the 1960s even Corman pictures felt out of reach to many of his regular players. Roger had begun his Edgar Allen Poe cycle, and these were bigger movies, in colour and CinemaScope, and made on unimaginably long schedules of fifteen days; he was now working with bigger actors, or at least Vincent Price. The films had bigger budgets and a new set of pressures, because Corman had persuaded AIP to pony up more than triple their usual budget for these lavish productions, based on his belief that the day of the black and white double shock-show bill was past, as well as his personal conviction that he felt like doing something different. *House of Usher*, the first Poe film, had been shot in January 1960 and had included exactly no one from the so-called Corman stock company, which led to some feelings of abandonment from the actors, as well as from Chuck Griffith, who had not been asked to take a crack at the screenplay. "It was irritating," Griffith told an interviewer, "because I saw Roger was making a value judgment based on how much money people were making and *he* was the one making policy. He said that no screenwriter who gets less than fifty thousand a script is any good."

Who knows if Corman really ever said such a thing, or, if he did, whether this attitude extended to performers? Miller couldn't be sure, but at least he was still getting calls for Roger's smaller pictures. Corman had noticed the popularity of the sword-and-sandal pictures, or peplums, that were arriving from Italy by the month. It was mostly Hercules, labouring, fighting dragons, demonstrating his proficiency in the art of love. Corman and Griffith got together and hammered out a general story involving a hero named Atlas. Griffith always claimed he wanted to call it "Atlas: The Guided Muscle," and would have too if Corman hadn't lost his interest in comedies. So it was written as a straight epic, and after Corman made a deal with some Greek producers, and after that deal completely fell through the moment Corman arrived in Greece, it was rewritten again, frantically by Griffith in an Athens hotel room, into a $1.95 cardboard-helmet Z-picture. The leads, Michael Forest and Frank Wolff, were lying around in the same hotel room, reading the pages as they came out of Griffith's typewriter and laughing at them.

Forest told writer Tom Weaver that Miller had been offered the part of the tyrant, the role Wolff was playing, but no one else can remember this. It might have happened—it was certainly not unknown for Miller to turn down parts. In any case, when the hellish production arrived home Corman needed a lot of battle-scene pickups, and he called Dick. The scenes were shot at UCLA, and involved a lot of sword waving and a lot of killing and dying. Miller did all of that, and, for him, it was the *Apache Woman* days again, fighting on both sides and coming perilously close to killing his other screen self. "Dick Miller was in more fights than you could shake a stick at," Forest said. "In the picture, you see Dick killing somebody and *being* killed every five minutes!"

Corman essentially made the film with his own money, reportedly selling his Jaguar to do so; and, for him, enough was enough of this nonsense. "It was my last attempt to do a big picture on a low budget," he said. Despite the rubber spear tips, the army-soldier extras who couldn't tell left from right, and the slightly wiggy casting of Barboura Morris as a Grecian queen, Filmgroup opened the picture on the drive-in circuit in May 1961 and it did modest but acceptable business before slouching into untraceable oblivion.

When the shoot was done, the Millers went back to their routine: the beach; Schwab's; a lot of time at their little apartment near the corner of Fountain and Gardner, but leaving it almost daily to play penny poker with Jack Nicholson, his roommates, and their constant stream of drop-in guests. John Shaner was there often and Monte Hellman and many others, all talking about acting, the business and its heartbreaks, and drinking from half-gallon bottles of Gallo. Harry Dean Stanton had his guitar out and would play "Cucurrucucu Paloma" for anyone who requested it.

And, despite his vocal opposition to the SAG deal, Dick did get some television work that year. Gangster shows were still big, thanks to the ongoing popularity of *The Untouchables*, and Miller appeared in one called *The Roaring 20s* in an episode titled "The Fifth Pin," which would air the following April. Lainie grew bigger and bigger, and one day, while Dick was off shooting, there was a forceful knock on the door. Before she could answer it, Lainie said, "the door opens, and there's men with guns." They were from the Immigration and Naturalization Service, and were after Lainie, who'd never applied for anything more than a visitor's visa, and must have assumed that marrying Dick would settle her citizenship issue.

She was taken downtown, fingerprinted, and given 30 days to voluntarily leave the country or else be deported. The Millers secured the services of a lawyer, which they could scarce afford; and straightening everything out required, among other hassles, a trip up to Vancouver, from where Lainie had to properly apply for a visa and then re-enter the States; and they could afford none of this any more than they could the lawyer. It was all very stressful, and that anxiety, Elaine Miller reasonably claimed, is what led to their daughter Barbara's making her appearance on October 4 instead of her mid-December due date. She weighed only two pounds, twelve ounces, and was immediately placed in an incubator.

It was a dicey situation, Lainie recalled. "Instead of thirty-six weeks like everybody else, I carried her twenty-eight weeks, and in those days, you were not going to be alive if you were only carried twenty-eight weeks." Tiny little Barbara hung on, but like many preemies, particularly those improperly oxygenated while housed in incubators, she was struck with retrolental fibroplasia, a disease that affects eyesight and commonly leads to complete blindness. Barbara was lucky, and though her vision was impacted, it was correctable with heavy glasses, but she would have to deal with a range of health problems into adulthood. And the whole episode, the stress of it, took its toll on Dick and Lainie too. "We tried to have other kids," Lainie said simply, "and couldn't."

There was more TV work: Miller appeared on yet another gangster show, *The Lawless Years*. This one had come along before *The Untouchables*, but it never became as popular, and never spawned any big-screen Brian De Palma remakes. Miller appeared as the same character on two consecutive episodes, "Blood Brothers" and "The Victor Gorido Story," which detailed the trouble and violence following the attempted takeover of a union by the Mob: a subject Miller had a passing familiarity with from talking with his cousins. The episodes aired in mid-August '61.

But the dry spells kept coming: agonizing to a man newly supporting a family. Casting around for ways to supplement his income, Miller suddenly realized that if pals like Chuck Griffith and Bobby Campbell could sell scripts, there was no reason he couldn't too. Jonathan Haze had roughly the same idea, and, after consulting with Corman, enlisted Miller to help him concoct a story called "The Monsters of Nicholson Mesa." (The "Nicholson" part was a poke at Jim Nicholson, perhaps because, like a mesa, he was sort of distant.) Naturally the two lead roles, a pair of comic bumblers, were intended for themselves; Haze, at least, was still convinced he and Miller could become a classic comedy team if only they were given the right material.

The collaboration quickly went south because the men could not agree on a work method. Haze wanted to write it quickly, then go back through and punch it up; Miller wanted to fuss over every word before moving to the next. "I had several meetings with Dick, and we talked and talked and nothing was put on paper," Haze told an interviewer. "I finally came to the conclusion that neither Dick nor I were good collaborators. We each had our own egos going on and were each in love with our own ideas." Scheduling was a problem too, and Haze decided it would be best if he wrote a first draft and then gave it to Miller so he could "look it over and re-write anything he felt needed to be re-written or [add] jokes he wanted to put in."

Haze finished his draft "and figured I'd give it to Roger and he could sit with Dick and suggest changes…. Roger apparently showed it to Dick, and I don't know what the reason was with Dick, but Dick flat turned it down." According to Haze, "Dick said, 'I'm not going to be in it because I didn't write it.'"

Miller himself remembered the conflict, and indeed the whole episode, only vaguely. "We might have written something," he said. "I mean, we were trying everything. But I don't remember a falling out over it. We probably never finished it, or I never finished it with him." Miller thought further, and more memories came. "We got into an argument and [Haze] finished it," he recalled. "In those days, I figured what the hell. You want it, go ahead and take it. Couldn't have been much more than that."

Haze finished up the script in a week or so, then, after an attempt to peddle it to AIP was mysteriously stymied by parties unknown, he sold it to Mel Welles. Welles had a producing partnership with a financier named Burj Hagopian, but the partnership dissolved and Hagopian was left with a property that was now called *Invasion of the Star Creatures*. Bruno VeSota, of all people, was hired to direct the picture, and a pair of cut-rate comedians named Bob Ball and Frankie Ray took on the comedy-duo duties once meant for Haze and Miller. The picture was shot in six days, but Haze was never even told that it had gone into production, and felt cut out of the process. After that, and after whatever chicanery had torpedoed his attempt to sell the script to American International (who ended up distributing the final product anyway), Haze was disenchanted with his friends and the whole business of show. "I just about decided that I wasn't going to act anymore, wasn't going to write anymore. Didn't want to go back to Schwab's because I didn't want to see any of them." It was no consolation that the resulting movie was almost unwatchably bad; Haze never even saw it.

Miller pushed the unhappy result of the collaboration out of his mind. During this time, he claims, he "didn't much care about acting," and seems not to have thought of himself as an actor at all. But his reaction to the August release of a minor-league spy thriller called *Capture That Capsule*, which featured a beefy, unremarkable actor called Richard Miller in the lead, belied that attitude somewhat. He suddenly seemed to care about acting, and in fact was affronted. He, the real Richard Miller, was standing in the unemployment line while an impostor was taking starring roles! It was intolerable, but late in the year, Corman, who was embarking on the third film in his Poe series, once again called with a job offer at an excellent time. The picture in prep was *The Premature Burial*, which, uniquely in Corman's Poe cycle, featured Ray Milland instead of Vincent Price in the lead role. Miller was cast as Mole, one of a pair of gravediggers described by Milland's character as "filthy and disgusting creatures." It was not a large role, but it was a week's work and a decent billing, and for all Miller knew might mean joining Corman more regularly on his apparent next level.

Miller passed through the costume and makeup departments, where he was given an enormous top hat and dirty mole teeth. The movie contrives to make sinister use of "Cockles and Mussels," and the first appearance of the tune, of many to come, is whistled in the opening moments as Miller and his cohort, Sweeney, dig up a grave to find a corpse twisted from its dying attempts to escape the coffin. Miller cries out fearfully and hops out of the grave like an acrobat. Mole and Sweeney reappear near the end of the picture, when they first bury and then disinter Milland. Milland, however, is less than grateful for his release: he strangles Sweeney, then impales a pleading Miller on the point of a sharpened prybar.

Miller made no attempt to soften his Bronx inflections for the part, even though he was surrounded by mid-Atlantic accents, and, like all of them, was meant to be playing a British character, if a low-class one. There's not a lot of Miller in the picture—the gravediggers appear only at the beginning and again near the end—but the Poe films were getting more widely distributed, so for those brief moments he was at least being seen by more eyeballs. But he spent the winter in the unemployment line, or caring for the baby, or, as ever, lounging and writing and scanning the trades in Schwab's.

It wasn't as though Miller was agonizing about his flatlining career. He wanted to work and he certainly wanted to make money, but he remained sanguine and philosophical, if not quite apathetic. "There's guys that make two pictures and they're stars," he rationalized later. "There's guys that make *one* picture and they're stars. And there's guys that make a dozen pictures and they build up to it. They become stars. And then there are careers that go like mine went. You start early, make a few pictures, you find yourself starring in pictures, and you go along for a couple of years and it starts to drop down. And there's no reason for it.

"I never really cared after that first blush of stardom, whether I made it or not," Miller said. "I was married, having a wonderful time, and settling down from that. So I guess I kind of settled for what I had. Figured it could be better, it could be worse. And I'm a lazy guy. Or maybe I'm too busy doing things to concentrate on my work. So as a lazy guy, I was kind of content with it. You get the job, okay, that's fine. That's great, you know?"

Spring 1962 came, and then summer, and nothing changed. *The Premature Burial* had been released in March and had done good business, but as far as Miller could see nothing in particular came of it. (He little knew that, on the other side of the country, obsessive young filmgoers like Martin Scorsese and Joe Dante were noting his presence in the picture, just as they were noting every aspect of every movie they saw.) He made an appearance in his old boss Genial Paul Harrison's short-lived butler sitcom *Our Man Higgins*, playing a pool shark named "Brandy" in the episode "My First Friend." At the end of the summer he got another call. It was Corman, who'd already directed five movies since *The Premature Burial*. These included a race-car picture, an historical drama, another Poe picture, and his famous, artistically but not financially successful stab at social relevance, *The Intruder*. Now he was wrapping another Poe film, *The Raven*, which featured the combined horror-star power of Karloff, Price, and Peter Lorre, and he was at the same time preparing yet another picture in the same genre. The inchoate new story was called "Lady of the Shadows," but would eventually acquire the aptly generic title *The Terror*.

Miller knew all about *The Raven*, because Jack Nicholson had a part in it, and at parties, or at the beach on his days off, he talked excitedly about the three great horror stars he was working with. In the meantime, on a rainy Sunday two-thirds of the way through the Poe picture's fifteen-day schedule,

Corman, who had planned to play tennis that day, found himself at home, thinking about the Saturday and Sunday at the end of the *Raven* schedule during which the sets would still be standing at the Producers Studio on Melrose. Corman liked the sets; they were some of Daniel Haller's best work to date, he thought, and it would be a shame not to wring the best possible use out of them; and beyond this, Karloff, who was contracted by the week, could work those two days at no extra cost. Corman dreamed up a rough concept that fit the sets and his elderly lead, then telephoned Leo Gordon, the burly actor-screenwriter who'd written *The Cry Baby Killer* and *The Wasp Woman* for him. Over dinner and drinks Corman and Gordon roughed out a plot, and over the next few days Gordon wrote some scenes that revolved around the older character, who was given the name "Baron Von Leppe." By the end of the week, Corman was ready to spring his proposal on Karloff.

Corman convinced a dubious Karloff to throw on some baronial togs and work for the weekend, then seduced Nicholson into the picture by telling him he would be the star. Nicholson thought that sounded great, especially when Corman agreed to cast his new wife, Sandra Knight, in the picture too. Next, Corman called Miller and offered him the part of Stefan, Karloff's manservant. "We're shooting some of the scenes now and some of it a little later," he explained to Dick.

Gordon's script was really just a series of disconnected sequences patched together from stuff he had sitting around, and Miller was baffled when he read it. "This doesn't make any sense!" he moaned, but Corman assured him it would all come together when it was finished. Early on a September Saturday morning Miller climbed into his costume, noteworthy for its extremely slim-fit tights ("Famous Miller legs, heh heh!") and schoolboy bloomers, and an ascot like a turkey wattle. Later he got to wear a top hat similar to the one in *Premature Burial*. He was directed by Corman to look grim and resentful, and, as Stefan, spent the day serving cognac and popping out of shadows, making demands and issuing threats, perpetually grouchy. There was a lot of talk about someone named Eric and a mysterious woman seen in the window, and at the end of the shoot the set was flooded with water and all the actors doused with buckets. (Much of the flood sequence was shot later, however, with Dennis Jakob doubling for Karloff.) The seventy-four-year-old Karloff was in every scene they shot over that weekend, which kept him working steadily from early morning until late at night, fighting, waving his arms, struggling in the water. It was painful for Karloff even to hobble up a few stairs at that point, so these wrestling matches must have had him in agony. "Boris *was* somewhat upset," Corman admitted.

If Karloff was upset with Corman, or at all, Miller didn't notice. He was in awe of the actor, who'd given him frightmares after his mother had taken him to see his first horror movie, *Frankenstein*, at age three. Between shots Karloff was an absolute charmer, telling showbiz anecdotes in his deep North London lisp, or answering Miller's breathless queries about why Karloff had left the balmy climes of California to repatriate in England. Karloff was, bar none, "the most interesting, fascinating person I've met," said Miller, still star-struck five decades later. "Aren't you tired of doing the same role a thousand times?" Miller asked the horror star. Karloff acknowledged that he was, then chuckled and told Miller, "When I get in trouble, I just do Karloff!" The elderly actor graciously signed a photograph of himself as the Monster, writing, remembers Miller, "a bunch of nice things," but the photograph disappeared from the set. (Miller suspected Nicholson might have developed a case of sticky fingers, but, when asked about it many years later by an impudent young rascal, Nicholson denied the charge most vigorously.) But Miller and Karloff remained pals. "I saw him again on two or three of his subsequent visits to the United States," Miller told Sharon Williams. "We'd meet, have a cup of coffee and spend an hour just talking. What a thrill. That was like meeting Superman in person."

Also displeased with the frenzied mystery-movie shoot was Sam Arkoff, who felt Corman was taking advantage of AIP by using its sets to shoot his own personal movie. He made a surprise visit to the studio and found "actors … running in all directions, trying to figure out where they belonged, what they were supposed to wear, what they were supposed to say," and a "noticeably embarrassed" Corman using a slate that still read "American International Pictures: *The Raven*." "If it was anybody but Roger, I might have called the police," Arkoff said. "But Roger is Roger."

On Sunday night, late, Corman finished his marathon shoot and the sets were quickly torn down. Miller returned to his life of low-budget leisure and child-rearing. He saw his friends plenty; Nicholson was living practically next door and reported that "Dick used to come by almost every day." Miller got another gig, playing Sam, a narrow-eyed meanie of a saloon keeper on an episode of *Bonanza*, the show for which he'd auditioned years before, hoping to snag the role of Little Joe. The saloon keeper bit was a walk-on with only a few lines, but Miller projected some of the same desperate intensity he would bring to other struggling small businessmen characters in pictures like *Starhops* and *Twilight Zone: The Movie*, and also got to practise his "nasty dickhead" characterization, which he'd trot out regularly in the 1970s, in pictures like *The Young Nurses*, *The Student Teachers,* and *Summer School Teachers.*

Lainie, meanwhile, was feeling antsy, dissatisfied; and it wasn't Dick exactly, but rather, she realized, the discrepancies in their educations. Dick had gone to a number of different schools, had lived several lives' worth of twentieth-century culture, and was a keen autodidact besides; Lainie, still in her early twenties and already the mother of a three-year-old, felt dull and unformed in some critical aspect. She wanted training, education, experience, and the lack of it bothered her a great deal. "[Dick] was so well-versed in world politics, on everything, and I felt like I knew nothing," she said. "It used to upset me."

She had considered acting—she'd been on the radio for six years as a child in Toronto, performing on the Children's Theatre of the Air, and was "a pretty good dancer" besides—but, after giving it some serious thought, decided against it. She knew about the casting couch, about the harassment that went on in some of these offices, and, she said, "I did not want to have to meet the people he had to meet for a job, and tell somebody, 'Don't bother me, go to hell,' you know." Worried that her refusals might somehow injure Dick's career, and figuring that, after all, *someone* in the family should try bringing home a regular paycheque, she kept out of the business, at least for a while. She decided to enrol in a nursing program. Miller, Lainie reported, became the best study buddy a young wife could want. "Every time I went for another degree, he'd study with me," she said. "I was a *summa cum laude* because of him."

The occasional dark cloud scudded overhead. Danielle, one of Dick's old girlfriends, began pestering the Miller house with phone calls. She was keen to speak with Lainie, and she had a story to tell. "That freak kept calling," Lainie said, "and telling me that Dick came to the hospital when she had a broken leg, and that he took her to bed right there in the hospital, with a broken leg. That's what she was trying to sell me."

"And I *didn't*," said Dick.

"But I was young," Lainie continued. "I thought, 'Why would she tell me this if it wasn't true?'" Discord erupted in the Millers' small apartment. Dick insisted the story was ridiculous, and between his protestations and the increasingly unhinged phone calls from Danielle, Lainie decided her husband was probably innocent after all. "She was just angry because he went off and met me," she said. "Thank God I never met her in person." But Dick had made a sketch of Danielle, and this rendering —of a voluminously bare-breasted woman with a severe, angular face—was still hanging in the Miller dining room when Dick was in his mid-80s.

By that time Lainie was no longer the jealous wife she had been early in the marriage. "I was actually the most jealous, nasty, angry person you could see when people would chase him," she said, cocking her head at an innocent-looking Dick. Danielle, it seemed, was not the only would-be homewrecker in those days. "Oh my god," Lainie moaned. "I mean, they came to the house, they put notes under the door. Fans, but also sort of in the business themselves." She meant "show business," which is always "the business" to those in it. One Miller groupie, Lainie recalled, was the granddaughter of the president of the Academy of Motion Picture Arts and Sciences; she'd been the one who'd shoved mash notes under the door.

Lainie excused herself from the table for a few moments, and, once she was out of earshot, Miller leaned over. "I wasn't gonna talk about these parts," he said in a low voice. "There was a lot of women in my life before Elaine."

In January '63 the phone at the Miller household rang with a job offer. Miller, who had forgotten completely about the harrowing weekend he'd spent working on Corman's nameless spookshow the September before, was initially baffled at this new offer. Corman, it was explained to him, had been unable to make anything out of the footage and had decided to hire a young quasi-protégé, Francis Coppola, to finish the picture. (The only way to finish it cheaply enough was to go non-union, Corman figured, so that let him out of the director's chair.) The Corman footage was mainly a lot of conversation and a great deal of Karloff, Nicholson, Miller, and Sandra Knight walking down hallways and through doors. Nicholson had seen this footage and found it extremely entertaining. "What I remember," he said, "was this series of dailies where you'd see first Boris Karloff coming down the hallway in one jacket, then Dick would come through, and the camera didn't even turn off, you know. Dick would come through, then Sandra would come through, then I'd come through, all in the same shot down the same hallway, and then Boris would come in a second time in a different jacket." Decades later Nicholson was still tickled by the memory. "That was one of the funniest group of dailies I ever watched. Hysterical."

It was funny, but it wasn't a saleable movie. Corman's editor, Mort Tubor, did his best with the material, but after a screening of his assembly made Corman pencil-snapping mad (so Jack Hill claims), he walked away from the project. Coppola looked at the footage and wrote some scenes that added a witch and another manservant to the character roll. The natural candidate for the witch was Dorothy Neumann, who'd played exactly the same role in *The Undead*, and the part of her mute manservant, Gustaf, was given to Jonathan Haze, who had evidently recovered from his *Invasion of the Star Creatures* experience. With Coppola, his future wife Eleanor, and his sister Talia (who would later date Corman) all bundled into the leading car, the production headed north to Big Sur.

They were up there for almost two weeks, shooting mainly exteriors around the cliffs and rocks and crashing waves. Miller tried to be helpful, telling Coppola that Corman liked big close-ups of his actors, but Coppola can't have appreciated this advice very much. Miller didn't let it get him down; he was on location with his buddies Nicholson and Haze, and they sure didn't mind having a few laughs and a little fun. The Coppolas probably felt a little left out of the club, and relations didn't improve when Eleanor chided Miller for telling what he claimed were just "good dirty jokes" on the set. "Well, I don't think they're very funny," she said. Coppola gave Dick a stern lecture, so a frustrated Miller faked up his own prudish mien and counter-barked, "You're up here *living* in *sin* and *you're* talking to *me* about telling *dirty jokes?*"

Miller found Coppola arrogant and pretentious. The director began arguing with one of the actors (Miller didn't say who), and quickly turned the discussion into an intellectual pissing contest. "I've got a degree in cinema!" Coppola apparently shouted by way of justifying his position. Miller muscled in and began shouting about his own certificates and diplomas, further estranging himself from the director. Neither did Miller like it when Coppola sent Nicholson into the sea in his cumbersome Napoleonic costume. "Jack was almost drowned up there," Miller recalled. "He almost drowned because the uniform was so heavy." (You can see it in the footage: Nicholson is supposed to look panicked, but he looks *really* panicked.)

Coppola and Miller at least shared a common opinion about Nicholson: they both thought he was a pretty lousy actor. Coppola, by his own admission, "didn't *get*" Nicholson, and "was very uncomfortable with the assignment." Miller, for all his antipathy toward the future winemaker, recognized what Coppola was up against, and sympathized. "Nobody knew what the picture was about," he told Coppola biographers Michael Goodwin and Naomi Wise. "So there was no advantage to being the director or not being the director. Everybody was in the same boat: *nobody* knew what was happening."

Certainly veteran cameraman John Nickolaus didn't know what was happening, evidently because Coppola had failed to inform him that much of this footage was meant to be day-for-night. The filters that would have provided a quasi-nighttime look hadn't been put over the lens, rendering much of what was shot over the eleven days in Big Sur unusable. Still, Coppola did get some nice material, including an evocative scene in which Miller's character visits the witch's house and finds her enacting an incomprehensible but visually captivating ritual involving coloured lights. All Miller had to do in the scene was look angry and baffled, and on this set he found that remarkably easy.

The company returned from Big Sur and, while Corman reviewed Coppola's footage, Miller watched himself on television. His episode of *Our Man Higgins* aired in mid-February, and his mean *Bonanza* saloon-keeper appeared on St. Patrick's Day. Dick balanced out his life as husband, father, and *bon vivant* as best he could, and tried to keep it all on a budget. Occasionally the Millers managed an outing, though sometimes with mildly harrowing results. Jonathan Haze came by one day and took Dick and Lainie to the stock-car races. They left Barbara with a babysitter, and the busy three-year-old rummaged around and found Miller's Colt revolver, pointing it and yelling "Bang! Bang!" The gun was not loaded, but when the Millers returned home and found Barbara still running around with the gun, Dick shouted, "What are you letting her play with the gun for? Sweet wingalls, what if she fired it?" The babysitter blanched: she'd assumed the large, heavy, obviously metal gun was a toy.

In May Miller learned that he would be facing more *Terror*. Corman, having reviewed Coppola's problematic footage, realized he still could not make a feature film out of it. Jack Hill, who'd worked for Corman in various capacities and recorded the sound on previous *Terror* shoots, was hired to write yet another screenplay, and Monte Hellman would direct it. It was mostly exterior stuff, lots of clifftop antics and creeping through forests and Nicholson riding a horse. No Big Sur this time, though: "We shot a bit in Santa Barbara and a bit in Palos Verdes," Nicholson recalled. "The picture kept moving south." To provide further opportunity to explain the plot, Haze's character was suddenly cured of his muteness.

The shoot lasted five days, and inserts of various kinds—clutching hands, staring eyes, coffins closing—were directed by Jack Hill around the same time. When the footage was put together, it seemed there might be a movie in there somewhere, but if there was, it made absolutely no sense. Corman, who was working on another Poe picture, *The Haunted Palace*, dedicated a further two days of shooting to a last, desperate effort to tie some kind of shabby bow around the mess, and after that further pick-ups and insert shots were filmed by Jack Hill.

An oft-told tale has Nicholson among the directors, but Corman is really the only one who makes this claim. Hill, Hellman, and Miller flatly deny it, and Nicholson himself listed all the directors for me, but did not include himself in the list. Perhaps on the last few days Nicholson suggested a shot or two, and Corman, being a "print the legend" sort of fellow, embellished the rest. Whatever the case, in late May, after nearly a year of intermittent shooting, several writers, and at least four directors, *The Terror* finally wrapped.

Only Miller found any continuity in the successive shoots. "Every time they would write something, I ended up getting beaten," he said. Indeed, Miller's character takes an awful lot of punishment in the picture. "Everyone gets a shot at me," he lamented. "Boris beats me up with a chain, and then I run out the door so Jack Nicholson can beat me up. Then an old witch beats me up. Sandra and Boris beat me up again in the water. It was ridiculous. No man could have lived through it."

Corman's final shoot included the picture's most infamous scene, in which Miller, rendered boneless and tractable from his successive beatings, attempts to explain the entire plot to Nicholson. "That came about on the last day of shooting," Corman told Lawrence French. "I was thinking, 'This picture is really kind of dull.' I was wondering what sort of twist we could put into the picture to make it more interesting." The Karloff character turns out to be someone completely different from who he, Karloff himself, and the first three directors believed him to be: not Baron Von Leppe but the mysterious Eric. Moreover, Miller's character reveals, he himself killed the baron all those years ago, leaving room for Eric to psychologically transpose himself into the baron's place. Miller never got a chance to explain why Sandra Knight's character dissolves into runnels of caramel ooze, but perhaps this is best left a mystery.

"It was hysterical," Miller told writer Mark McGee. "When you see the film, you'll see me walk through a door and I'll gain twenty pounds. And my sideburns kept moving up and down." Even his colour changed from moment to moment, depending on whether the footage had been shot in September or January. "I would leave the castle looking pale, come into the sunlight, and be tan," he said. "It was a wild thing."

The picture opened in the summer of 1963 as part of a double feature and, "weirdly enough," Corman said, did decent business at the box office. For Miller, watching the finished film lent him a perspective on his career he'd never had before. It wasn't just the moving sideburns and the fluctuating weight. "What I could see happening over those nine months, when I watched the film, was that I was changing from a young leading man to something older," he said. "So by the time I finished the picture, I was really a different guy."

Maybe, he reflected for the thousandth fleeting time, it was time to get more serious about acting. He'd been working with Corman for long enough to see what happened to dilettantes. "Most of the guys who starred in those hundreds of films Roger did just disappeared," Miller said. "You look back now and see the Nicholsons, and say, 'All those people who started with Corman and made it big!' But you've got to figure on the hundreds who died by the wayside, never to be heard of again. They came to Hollywood, did a picture or maybe two if they were good or lucky, then disappeared. I guess they went back to Apple Valley and disintegrated. Turned to dust."

13   I got older, but I didn't get any taller

"This was a time for me that happens to most actors," Miller said of the mid-1960s. "It's a time of change, when you either make it or you don't." Miller had never before been so acutely aware of growing older, and *The Terror* was somehow involved with, or even responsible for, this new cognizance. It was as though he had entered one teleportation chamber as someone who could still potentially headline a picture, and clock the bad guy, defeat the alien, and get the girl, and had emerged from the other as a nameless character day player with a spare tire around his middle and a name tag on his chest reading "Joe" or "Ed" or "Mac." (This, even as he'd begun *The Terror* playing a surly but nondescript servant, and ended it having made the opposite transformation, into the principal heavy and only character who knew what was going on.)

Career examples he might follow, both heartening and dire, abounded. On the one hand there were the hundreds of struggling or failed actors he'd seen parading through the Corman lots and nursing coffees at Schwab's: the slobs who'd spent so much time aspiring to stardom that they'd missed out on whatever semi-comfortable niche they might have found in the business. On the other hand there were people like his hero Karloff, who had persevered, had rejected or just failed to recognize ignominy even when he was wallowing in it, and had maintained both his dignity and his marquee value through a long, occasionally prosperous career. So some combination of strategy and nescience was required to achieve longevity, and diversification was a key too. Miller thought of Bela Lugosi, whom he pitied: here was "a one-shot actor," Miller said. "He hung onto this one character, and it probably killed him too. Karloff was magnificent at owning all these characters that he played."

He now felt the first stirrings of regret at having failed to maintain his status as a B-movie star, however marginal, and in particular that he had turned down the lead in *The Little Shop of Horrors*. He was still an expert at having fun and at whiling away the day in Schwab's, but the world was changing and Los Angeles was not as cheap a place to live as it once had been. Lainie was in school, little Barbara still had worrisome and potentially expensive health issues, and Miller was not a kid any more: his face was craggier, his body thicker. The youth culture he had, in his way, helped Roger Corman exploit back in the '50s had grown, gained power, and was becoming pre-eminent; meanwhile, to paraphrase that great '90s youth picture *Dazed and Confused*, Miller had grown older while the kids onscreen, and in the audience, stayed the same age.

As all this hit home he became touchy, insecure, sometimes even violent. "He hit people on the street!" Lainie Miller said. "He was so protective of me, every time somebody would look at me in a strange way, he'd go nuts." Lainie turned to her husband. "Do you remember that? In the street? You gave some guy a shot, and he went around a post and went down?" Miller shrugged and mumbled something about not remembering any such occurrence, and Lainie rolled her eyes. "He just had a hot head when it came to me," she said with a laugh.

It remains a minor astonishment that Corman's Poe pictures, with their ground fog, velvet drapes, and fogey heroes, maintained their popularity for as long as they did. They're engaging and watchable movies, but what did AIP's teenage audiences see in them? Perhaps there was simply not much else to choose from. Youth movies were in any event changing apace with the constituency they served; the AIP boys were keeping their antennae up. In the summer of 1962 Sam Arkoff and Jim Nicholson screened a number of Italian films, as they did every year in Italy, with a view to distributing the most exploitable of them in America. They saw a movie that took place largely at a beach resort; an unremarkable movie, but the setting struck them. They'd also noticed the popularity of domestic movies with sun, fun 'n' sand formulas, like *Gidget* and *Where the Boys Are*, and, to Arkoff, the next move was clear: turn it from a few sporadic successes into a profitable new genre. To that end Lou Rusoff spent several days sitting on the beaches of Malibu, Santa Monica, and Venice, observing and eavesdropping, and, at age fifty, with a sharp nose, heavy eyebrows, and the wavy hair of a boardroom exec, looking much like one of the middle-aged interlopers the beach pictures would frequently include. Immediately on concluding his research he wrote the script for AIP's first stab at the genre, *Beach Party*. Director William Asher later changed it considerably, removing all the drugs, sex, and social problems Rusoff had included; but Rusoff, who was dying of brain cancer and would never write another script, retained a solo screenwriting credit. AIP made the movie (in the winter, with the shivering teens pretending they were perfectly comfortable in the water), released it in August 1963 to the sound of cash registers jingling, and sure enough found they had codified the beach picture into a full-fledged genre. It was the biggest-grossing picture in the company's history so far.

Meanwhile, Miller was still working for Corman. He and Haze reunited as a team for a scene in *X: The Man with the X-Ray Eyes*, which featured Ray Milland as a scientist whose super eyedrops give him the ability to see through clothes, through skin, though brick and steel, through the hypocrisies and manipulations of his colleagues and of society at large, and finally through the very fabric of dimensional time/space itself. Milland becomes a fugitive and takes a position as a fortune teller on Don Rickles's carnival midway. Corman asked Haze and Miller to play a couple of guys heckling Milland, reasoning that Rickles, the abrasive nightclub veteran who was playing the MC of Milland's act, would appreciate some audience bozos to play off of, and might extemporize a few insult-comedy gems in the process. "Roger felt that Don was a terrific comic ad-libber," Haze said, but it turned out the comic just wanted to do the script as written. "The first time Dick and I started to heckle him, Don got mad and said, 'Wait a minute, this isn't in the script,'" Haze remembered. "So Dick and I sat there and did a few lines, and that was it. It wasn't one of our better performances or better roles, to say the least." The performances were perfectly serviceable, and Miller and Haze look great in their tidy casual wear. Milland ends up turning the tables on the hecklers, telling Miller his name (John Trask), address (Phoenix), age (twenty-seven!), and social security number, and about the letter in his pocket from "a girl [he] deserted." Miller clenches his jaw like a coke fiend (a signature move), growls "Shut up!" and flees the tent. The picture opened in September 1963, and marked the beginning of a relationship between AIP and Rickles, who would appear in several of their beach party pictures.

Corman then decamped to England, attracted by a film subsidy to shoot the last two Poe movies there. For Miller, there followed another long dry period, one of the toughest of his career. Money was so scarce that the family was forced to go out picking avocados from the neighbours' yards for sustenance. They went for thirty-cent burgers, which the trio shared; Miller remembers arriving at the stand with only twenty-nine cents in his pocket. "We had to take them the penny the next week," he said.

But they moved around a lot, changing apartments whenever they could afford to, looking for cheaper or better digs. "It used to be that we moved just about every year when the lease was up," said Lainie, "because the only way you could get a freshly painted apartment was to move to another one."

The winter of '63 began badly, with the assassination of President Kennedy, at which Miller, a straight-ticket Democrat, was shocked and saddened. "I liked him," Miller said. "I liked what he stood for. I liked his politics. I liked the fact that he had Marilyn Monroe." The nation endured its Four Dark Days and eventually the season livened up for Dick and Lainie when, one day, Ira arrived for a visit, in the company of a nervous young man of about twenty-one, dressed in a suit jacket, scoop-neck sweater, and necktie. Pointing to Eugene and Dick, Ira said, "Here they are. These are your brothers." Ira's son by his (late) second wife was Bill Miller, a young man in training for a career in law. Father and son had been in the habit of taking a winter vacation in Florida; this winter, Ira had looked at his son and said, "How'd you like we don't go to Florida this year? Let's go to California. We have family out there." On the plane, Ira listed off the people they'd see: "We'll see the Gilberts. And you've heard me talk about Dick and Gene?" Bill nodded; they were, as far as he knew, his father's kid brothers. Ira had a clipping in his drawer, which Bill had found: Dick's *Variety* ad touting his acting in *Rock All Night*. There were pictures of Gene in his navy uniform. "Well, don't be surprised if they meet us at the airport," Ira told Bill. "And don't be surprised if they call me 'daddy.'"

Who knows why Ira had kept his older offspring a secret from his younger, but he had. Dick and Gene knew about Ira's remarriage and his son, and Gene had even met the infant Billy, but otherwise the half-brothers were completely separate from one another. Bill was delighted almost to the point of disbelief, shaking his head and telling himself, "I got two brothers!" the whole rest of the flight west. At the airport everybody was elated to meet one another, and Billy was happily brought into the fraternity. It was a warm reunion, and the balm Miller needed to get through the year.

Miller wrote scripts but couldn't sell them, and avoided job interviews a helpful Gene had set up for him at the Orange County coroner's office. "Dick is the type of person who does not wanna do what he doesn't wanna do," Bill Miller said in an interview. Miller specifically didn't want to work in a coroner's office, especially after reading the frequent newspaper articles describing his brother's work. Gene always seemed quite happy to provide readers with the gruesome details, as in 1962 when his office had to deal with the aftermath of a collision between a train and a gravel truck. "It was a mess," Gene was quoted as saying. Another case that same year was a maritime disaster in which a party of fishermen were attacked by sharks. "They possibly were eaten alive," Gene told the papers. "The sharks kept after the bodies and several even jumped into the stretchers at the victims as they were being pulled aboard." Gene's most famous case came in 1965, when a military jet slammed into the side of Loma Ridge in Irvine, killing 83 people, mostly soldiers on their way to Vietnam. Limbs were stacked like cordwood throughout the Orange County coroner's office, and no wonder Dick didn't care to work there.

Some paying onscreen work finally dribbled in midway through 1964. It was a part on one of the Western series that had held on tenaciously through the space race, *Wagon Train*, and though *Gunsmoke* would outlast it by over a decade, eight years was still a very respectable run. *Wagon Train* had in its earliest years been one of the biggest of the big Western programs, even briefly beating out the mighty *Gunsmoke* in the ratings over the 1960–61 season. For years, through format alterations, network swapping, a musical chairs of times and days, and key cast changes (original wagonmaster Ward Bond had died; others had left), the show had, in the words of one of the kids in *Stand by Me*, "just kept wagon training." But by 1964, in its eighth and last season, the wagon wheels were pretty worn down. The show had been on long enough that guest stars were being reused in new roles, and "The Brian Conlin Story" was Leslie Nielsen's return to the series after having played a rumpot in an episode four years earlier. Here, Nielsen was Brian Conlin, leader of a band of Irish immigrants lost in the boundless West. The Irish accept the wagon train's help, but, unable to trust anyone after many miserable experiences in the new world, they remain surly, distant, and ungrateful. As Michael, one of these Gaelic unfortunates, Miller got to scowl a lot and wear a floppy hat. He took a stab at an accent, but Miller was usually better off not doing them. There's no compelling reason, after all, to disguise a good New York dialect.

"The Brian Conlin Story" aired on October 25, 1964, and three days later Miller was on TV in a cowboy hat again, in an episode of *The Virginian* called "Big Image ... Little Man." From the title it sounds like a replay of *The Little Guy*, but was in fact the tale of a moneyed but intolerable city slicker with a Fauntleroy complex, who is taken on by the Virginian and served a large helping of class consciousness and frontier modesty. Miller again mainly scowled in the background.

The episode was directed by William Witney, a veteran of innumerable Westerns and serials, who by the late 1950s had diversified into *noir* and juvenile delinquency pictures, and then into TV. Television was a comfortable place for the affable journeyman, but he kept a hand in features, turning out movies for AIP and other studios. Roger Corman had signed an exclusive contract with Columbia, which forbade him from making movies for anyone else. To get around this, he enlisted his brother, Gene, to help him ghost-produce some low-budget pictures he thought might turn a profit, and beach movies were high on that list. (Existentialist Westerns written by Jack Nicholson and directed by Monte Hellman were evidently right up there too.)

Corman got hold of a script called "Beach Girls," written by Sam Locke under the pseudonym "David Malcolm." He hired Witney to direct, and whether it was Corman's idea to hire him or Witney's, Miller got a call to play a waiter at the Sip 'n' Surf, the beachside nightclub wherein much of the story's action takes place. Now began nearly the cruellest stage of Miller's career: dressing in a monkey suit and acting out the exact joe-jobs he'd spent most of his life avoiding, playing the square in front of a bunch of wild kids. Miller's character held an inexplicable hatred for the Beatles, and his lines range from "Crickets, Beatles, cockroaches—what's next!" to "Those Beatles should go back to where they came from—under a rock!" to "There's a phone call for you from a … Ringo?" Miller did his best with such dialogue, and thankfully his best is very, very good: he actually makes this stuff funny, and his waiter character feels like a man right on the edge of walking out to start a new life somewhere else. (Miller would capitalize even more effectively on this quality a dozen years later in *Starhops*.)

Miller had often worked as part of a duo, most frequently with Jonathan Haze as his counterpart. Here, he was paired up again, this time with big Leo Gordon, and the height discrepancy was remarkable and obviously intentional. Miller got most of the business, though, as Gordon's character was meant to be both big and dumb. The pair didn't get an awful lot to do, but they were in the background of many scenes and got to hear numbers from the Beach Boys (in the only film appearance they ever made) and the Crickets. However, they also had to suffer through a distaff Beatles knockoff combo warbling something called "I Want to Marry a Beatle." The picture was retitled *The Girls on the Beach* and was picked up by Paramount, who, after several tropical Elvis pictures, were looking to get all in on the box-office excitement associated with sun 'n' surf pictures. They released it in May 1965; it was one of a half-dozen such movies to appear in this, the beach genre's busiest year, but was the only one featuring Bruno VeSota as a telegraph operator named Pops. Unfortunately the picture was registered with SAG under the title *Beach Girls*, which meant that over the next twenty years, until the mistake was discovered, neither Miller nor the rest of the cast received any residuals from its many television broadcasts.

Some time after *The Girls on the Beach,* Miller made another appearance in the genre, this time for AIP itself (though Gene Corman was again the producer). *Ski Party* was actually part of a subset of the beach movies, wherein the action was moved up into the mountains and skiing replaced surfing as the sport of choice. But for the sake of tradition these movies still included a couple of beach scenes, and this is where Miller appeared. The plot required the movie's two protagonists, played by Frankie Avalon and Dwayne Hickman, to flee their ski resort and make the 900-mile trip from the Idaho mountains to Los Angeles by taxi. Miller was the taxi driver, but in the mountains he was only a shadow in the driver's seat, doubled by somebody else. The distinctive taxi cab got to travel to the ski resort location in Idaho's Sawtooth National Forest, but Miller himself did not.

Still, Miller was in the studio for rear-screen driving scenes and at the Malibu beach house location, so he likely got a couple of work days out of it. He hams outrageously in a shot where he's supposed to be sleepy, and generally makes the driver a clown rather than the nonentity, or even the jerk, his minimal dialogue would have allowed him to be. There's a perfectly good reason for this: on arrival at the beach in Los Angeles, the cab fare is $565, and the question of payment is left unresolved at the end. A crabbier or more forthright character would have demanded that loose end be tied, but instead the driver only asks to borrow a blanket so he can go sleep on the beach. Because the character is played by Miller, though, we wonder, even after the movie is over, whether he ever did get his money. We hope he did.

The picture opened a month and a half after *The Girls on the Beach*, at the end of June, and Miller's *annus littus* continued with another Roger-the-ghost production, *Beach Ball.* Lennie Weinrib, a Bronx-born actor and comedian who'd never made a movie before, was hired to direct because Corman thought he was funny. The script was once again by Sam Locke under the David Malcolm pseudonym, and Miller was again cast as part of a working-class comedy duo. This time he was a cop and was paired up with John Hyden, an amiable one-and-done actor/singer who did no other movie work, but sometimes popped up in the choruses of roadshow musicals when they stopped in LA. Like Leo Gordon he was several years older and nearly a foot taller than Miller, so the scenes of the two cops chasing around the movie's dress-clad protagonists at a car show are given more of an odd-couple dynamic than if the men had been of the same height. The car show scenes were filmed guerilla-style a month before the principal shoot, at Corman's instruction, to take advantage of the production value offered by the crowds and vintage autos. Doubles were used for some of the actors, but not for Miller, who duckwalks, pratfalls, and leers around the Long Beach Civic Center in pursuit of the younger characters. A double was used for a car chase scene in some second-unit material directed by Stephanie Rothman, but the hulking simulacrum in the passenger seat looks less like Miller than Dennis Jakob did Boris Karloff.

As in *Ski Party*, Miller took a role that could easily have been played as a conventional hard-ass, but, by appearing to be hugely amused at the goings-on around him even as his dialogue is stern and humourless, he made the cop a legitimate and layered character. He also gives a great fake laugh when he's got to help placate a nitrous oxide victim by chortling along with him. Miller always made the most of his opportunities to do physical comedy.

Beach Ball opened on October 13, 1965, by which time Miller had already dipped his toe into the beach party genre once more, in another of the ski off-shoots, *Wild, Wild Winter*. The script, another Sam Locke-as-David Malcolm creation, was titled "Snow Ball," and yet again Miller was paired up with a much taller actor. ("They're all taller than me," Miller said. "Shirley Temple is taller than me.") This time he was a pocket-square-sporting gangster threatening to foreclose with extreme prejudice on a venerable ski college lagging on its mortgage payments. His heavy-eyebrowed compatriot was played by James Frawley, who would abandon acting for directing and go on to make pictures like *The Big Bus, The Muppet Movie,* and *Fraternity Vacation.*

Miller again leavened his performance in ways not to be found in the shooting script, though he went about it differently here. Instead of radiating secret amusement, he radiated counterfeit menace, creating a character whom nobody but himself really perceives as a threat. Even when he finally draws a gun near the end, it looks like a ten-cent plastic prop, tiny even in Miller's hand. Then he's immediately run over by a bear on skis, and the next time we see Miller and his gangster buddies, they've donned green lettermen sweaters for some reason and are frugging away with the college kids to a boss tune by Jay and the Americans. (Miller's dance looks like a hip-shaking hepcat update of the classic jazz hands, with closed eyes and a wistful smile.) The character even had a name, Rilk, and appeared in both the studio and mountain scenes; so for the first time in a while Miller got to travel for a show, if not very far. *Wild, Wild Winter* was a Universal production, and when they opened it on January 5, 1966, they opened it wide.

That was the end of Miller's beach party boot camp, for the moment at least. It was also near the end of the beach party fad. It was only a few days' work here and there, silly work he'd never have seen himself doing when he was in the navy, but it was fun, and at least he was only *pretending* to be a waiter or a cop or a cab driver. Still, he was cautious, because he had read Kurt Vonnegut's *Mother Night* and agreed with its mission statement: "We are what we pretend to be, so we must be careful what we pretend to be." On the other hand, as Miller knew, a real waiter, or cop, or cab driver, would have made a lot more money than he himself did in the sixties, acting.

14 *Went up, probably coming down*

Around the time his fling with the beach party crowd was finished, Miller got a call from an unlikely source. Andrew Fenady, who had produced *Stakeout on Dope Street*, the movie Miller had walked away from back in 1957, was in the TV racket now, and was producing a Western series called *Branded*. Chuck Connors was the lead, and the show's conceit was that he'd been unjustly branded a coward and drummed out of the army, and was thereafter forced to roam the West repeatedly proving his courage and rectitude. Each show began with Connors' having his hat pulled off and his epaulets torn from his shoulders by a disgusted cavalry officer (and Miller would participate in recreating this sequence nearly shot-for-shot many years later in Joe Dante's *Looney Tunes: Back in Action*, where he plays a head of studio security who cashiers his incompetent junior, Brendan Fraser).

After the *Stakeout on Dope Street* affair, Fenady was the last person Miller expected to hear from. Probably the producer had simply forgotten the whole thing, and didn't in any case bother much with the casting of smaller roles. Miller was hired to play a ghoulish cowpoke who's travelled "a hundred miles just to see this hangin'!" (The episode, called "A Nice Day for a Hanging," is a fiery denunciation of capital punishment, and an extension of the same post-Kennedy era progressivism found in shows like *The Twilight Zone* and *Star Trek*.) Most of Dick's lines were delivered with him facing away from the camera, and the performance is not much different from that he gave for a very similar character in his debut, *Apache Woman*. He's meant to seem bouncy and blithe, if morbidly excited, about watching the hanging, but comes off more like one of the beach party kids waxing enthusiastic over an approaching twist contest. On a good day Miller could ham with the best of them, though he's outdone here by the episode's guest star, a young, wildly emotive Beau Bridges. "Nice Day for a Hanging" aired early in February 1966, and *Branded* had only six or seven more episodes to go before it was cashiered itself.

By the late winter of 1966 Corman had still not made anything under his Columbia Pictures contract. With Sam Arkoff and Jim Nicholson's help, he secured a leave of absence from the studio in order to do another picture for AIP, but in defiance of their entreaties Corman maintained it would not be a Poe film. He was tired of those, bored with the velvet costumes and the low-hanging fog, and itched to do something contemporary: something that had, as he told an interviewer, "relevance to human beings today in our world." The Hell's Angels, a near-constant presence in the headlines at that time, thanks to a lurid rape case and subsequent investigation into their activities by the California District Attorney's office, seemed to offer what Corman needed: the relevance, the action, the sex, and the violence. AIP agreed, so Corman, mounting an investigation of his own, tracked down some Angels and, taking Chuck Griffith along with him, met the bikers down in Hawthorne at a place called the Gunk Shop. Corman made his pitch, and over the next short while (it had to be quick—AIP wanted the finished picture by the summer) he and Griffith were allowed to attend Angel parties, where Griffith scribbled notes for his script as Corman blithely tried to pick up biker mamas. By late March they were ready to go.

Miller got a call and was asked if he could ride a motorcycle. "Can *I* ride a motorcycle?" he answered. He was signed to play one of the bikers, then decided he'd better learn to ride after all. He knew of a guy named Joe who lived in the hills and owned a 500cc Triumph (one wishes to assume this character was legendary cycle film producer Joe Solomon), and one day he and Lainie drove up to get a lesson. "It didn't look like the big hogs we were using in the picture," Miller remembered. "So I figured it was a little bike." Joe asked him if he thought he could handle it, and Miller made noises like an old hand who merely needed a refresher. "So I took off," Miller said, "and that's all I remember."

Miller shot up the road and around a corner, and only luck and momentum carried him even that far. He was never in control of the bike for a second; it was like the terrifying horse races he'd endured in his brief career as a child jockey. Suddenly, he recalled, "I had a choice: I could have made a right and gone out over Hollywood, gone flying a thousand feet up, or I could go straight ahead, right into the mountain. So I chose the mountain." He smashed through a road sign and ploughed into the side of the hill.

Lainie, Joe, and Joe's wife came running up the road: they had all heard the crash and the sudden silence that followed. Miller was lying on the ground, unable to talk, barely able to breathe. At the hospital it was determined that he had broken several ribs and would have to sleep in a chair for the next while. So that was it for Miller's career as an ornery biker: over before it began, like so many of his other careers. He was not the only actor to run afoul of the big hogs: the lead had originally been George Chakiris, but when the *West Side Story* star demanded a double for the riding scenes, he was turfed with little delay, and Peter Fonda, who'd been cast in a secondary part, roared into the top slot. Bruce Dern took Fonda's old part, and there was a general shuffling of the cast list.

Miller was shuffled too. With his ribs taped up under his costume, he appeared very briefly at the beginning of the picture in one of his most blue-collar roles ever: an oily pumpjacker who gets roughed up by Fonda and Dern after he objects to Fonda's Iron Cross. "If you guys had been at Anzio, you'd know what that junk means," he growls, playing the veteran with stories whom Miller himself had once longed to be. After Dern threatens him with a big wrench, Miller shouts, "We used to kill guys who wore that kind of garbage," then works his jaw in what is one of the most frequent and effective of his actorly devices. When Miller does that, you know his character is *really* pissed.

But more pissed than Miller's character or anyone else connected with the movie was Chuck Griffith, ostensibly the screenwriter of *The Wild Angels*. It was bad enough that Peter Fonda had changed his character's name to Heavenly Blues (from, one presumes, Grabson Hufnagel or something similar), but this scene at the pumpjack was the last straw. As scripted, it had been virtually wordless, with Miller demanding to know if the bikers were "those dumb Angels" and Dern merely showing off a tattoo in response. "And that was the end of the scene," Griffith told interviewer Aaron Graham. "But no, Dick had to go into this speech about Anzio. I don't know if Dick wrote that; maybe it was Barboura Morris or [Peter] Bogdanovich. Anyway, it was a whole long bullshit scene. I told Roger, 'Take my name off of it before you make the titles,' but he told me he already had! And he was enraged with me for wanting to."

In *The Wild Angels* Miller was not only again playing an Establishment figure, he was playing one older than himself, old enough to have seen action in the Big One: a particularly grimy Larry Lunchbox who'd stormed the beaches of Italy in the company of Bill Mauldin, Audie Murphy, and James Arness, before returning home and taking a job as a roughneck. This time there was no room for levity or for Miller's occasionally employed Stan Laurel smile. Here, however, was the Dick Miller most people of that era saw, because after its July 20 release in 1966, *The Wild Angels* became a huge hit, returning a massive $10 million on a $360,000 investment; and perhaps this is why Miller was thereafter so frequently cast as a scolding blue-collar grump. If he hadn't crashed that motorcycle, if he'd played an anti-Establishmentarian in such a popular film instead of a scowling hardhat, his career might have taken a different route in the years that followed. He might have been a Harry Dean Stanton or a Warren Oates, talented character actors but no more talented than Miller, who were given the right roles and were thereby allowed a different kind of cult status: cult royalty, where Miller is more an archduke, after many years a bearer.

That spring Dick and Lainie moved out of West Hollywood and took an apartment in Hermosa Beach. They had a nice little place, and the neighbourhood was alive with eccentrics; and with some digging in the sand they were able to add clams to the dinner menu alongside the avocados and occasional hamburger. Barbara joined the Girl Scouts, and so, effectively, did Dick and Lainie: as they had plenty of spare time for it, they became volunteer organizers. Dick in particular was deeply involved with the cookie-hawking youth organization. "There weren't enough parents, and I said, 'Okay, I'll take over,'" he said. "So I'm a girl scout! A legitimate girl scout! I got the card still in my wallet."

The beach was a nice place for a family of girl scouts to live, and a pleasant contrast to Hollywood, but it was far away from their friends and from the work Dick occasionally picked up. It was a long drive to the studios; also an unacceptable distance from Schwab's. There were other, less predictable problems too. "Our landlord, sweet gentleman, we had him arrested," Miller said. The landlord, a high school teacher, projected the image of the classic upstanding 1960s citizen, pipe clenched in his jaw and scotch rocks in hand; but his private life was a little racier. "He and his wife were swappers," Miller said. "He approached us. I said no! He got feisty about it, doubled the rent, got drunk, swore. It was against the law to swear in front of women and children, so we had him arrested. His wife was so mad she left him in there all weekend." Miller had no lingering regrets about refusing the landlord's offer. "Ah, his wife wasn't that good looking," he said.

The phone rang and it was Corman again, calling the hotline like Commissioner Gordon: he had a role for Miller in a new oater, *The Long Ride Home*, based on a 1961 novel called *The Southern Blade*. It was Roger's first Western in a long while. It was being made as part of the Columbia deal, so it was a studio picture; there were therefore no dreary commutes to Iverson's ranch, but location work in both Utah and Arizona. It was a comic part but it had some substance, and the character even had a name, Zolicoffer, one of the best monikers of Miller's career. Again he was part of a bumbling duo, and his counterpart here was an actor named Kay Kuter.

Dick and Lainie decided to make a holiday of it: their first trip together. "It was our honeymoon," Lainie said. The prospect of bringing Lainie along was particularly attractive to Dick, who didn't want to leave her home alone with that creepy landlord around. Besides, he was the jealous type and wanted to keep his young, attractive wife close by his side; so, while Dick would go on ahead, Lainie would join him on the Utah location as soon as possible, once Barbara was set up at the home of a friend who had a daughter the same age.

The Long Ride Home was the first fruit of Corman's association with Columbia Pictures, after eighteen months of contractual bondage to the studio. Over that time, he said, "every idea I submitted was considered too strange, too weird; every idea they had seemed too ordinary to me." Budget was an issue too: Columbia expected Corman to make low-budget pictures, while he wanted to make movies on the studio level. Somehow they agreed on a Civil War story involving a group of Confederate soldiers who've kidnapped the wife of a crusty Union major, which led to shootings and punch-ups and ultimately revenge. It was a slightly bigger picture than Corman was used to, and was budgeted at about half a million dollars; to keep an eye on this investment, Columbia's vice-president in charge of production, M. J. Frankovich, installed his twenty-five-year-old son, Mike, as the film's unit manager.

The picture went to camera in May 1966. Corman had assembled a convivial and interesting bunch for his cast. Glenn Ford was the straight-arrow Major. Harry Dean Stanton brought his guitar and played it every night for anyone who showed up in his hotel room. World-class eccentric Timothy Carey kept things lively and malodorous. George Hamilton, who played his Johnny Reb heavy as a snarling beach boy, was dating Lynda Bird Johnson, the president's daughter, and when she went out to dinner with Hamilton and the rest of the cast, the place was crowded with overcompensating Secret Service men. Hulking Max Baer Jr., playing a maniacal lummox, doomed Inger Stevens as the kidnapped love interest, and a just-out-of-short-pants Harrison J. Ford as a Union soldier, along with stalwarts like Kenneth Tobey and Richard Slattery, rounded out the cast.

It was a tough shoot from the beginning. According to actor Paul Peterson, there was a division, almost an antipathy, between the actors playing the Union soldiers and those playing the Confederates. If that was the case, Miller made an effective double agent, or anyway non-partisan, crossing from side to side with cheerful impunity. It wasn't feudin' Miller had to watch out for, but lazy rehearsing coupled with his own inexperience on horses: though Miller's riding skills had improved since *Apache Woman*, he was still the city boy he always would be.

The scene involved the Union soldiers riding at a gallop past the camera and toward a small river. The actors mounted at the first position and began their ride for the rehearsal, and halfway through, Corman, always looking to save time, called out something like "Okay, that's the idea! Let's do it!" The actors returned to their first positions and, on "Action," began trotting their mounts along the prescribed route. Just past the point they had stopped at on the rehearsal, the ground dipped a foot or two down to a road. "I wasn't expecting it," Miller said. "I heard 'Cra-a-ack!' I said, 'Oh god! Somethin' happened!'" He had cracked his coccyx, and riding a horse was now not just a frightening prospect but an extremely painful one, despite the best efforts of Marvin Hoffner, the unit's first-aid man. "Do you want to be replaced?" they asked him, and Miller said no, absolutely not.

It so happened that one of the drivers was a small guy who looked a little like Dick and could ride, and this fellow was drafted to double for him in the wide shots and galloping scenes. "He was thrilled to death," Miller said.

"Oh yeah," Lainie Miller said. "I came to visit, and he was just puffed out: 'I doubled your husband, you know!'"

Lainie's arrival on the set helped make up for the pain in Miller's tailbone, because here they were, almost seven years into their marriage and finally on something close to a vacation together. They had epic nights out, sometimes just the two of them, sometimes with other members of the company. "On location," said Miller, "you jam. Found a bar and played drums. Played until morning, my hands bled." Trouble, however, was still brewing on the set of *The Long Ride Home*, with the most potent harbingers coming in the form of the suit-wearing studio types who were increasingly visible on the location. Enmity between Corman and the studio had been percolating since the beginning of their association, and had ramped up in the pre-production stage of *The Long Ride Home*. Corman wanted to make something contemporary; Columbia said no. Corman wanted to shoot in a widescreen format; Columbia said no. Corman wanted his regular crew; Columbia allowed him such ringers as art director Daniel Haller and key grip Chuck Hannawalt, but wouldn't let him choose his own cameraman.

(Never mind that Floyd Crosby, the DP Corman likely would have hired, was an Oscar-winner who had shot *High Noon*.)

After the shoot began Mike Frankovich Jr. was alarmed to see Corman leaving as much equipment on the trucks as he took off them. Miller remembered some issue about a crane's not being used as much as the producers thought it should be; Corman story editor Frances Doel recalled, or used as an example, a conflict about ordering an extra generator. The upshot was that Columbia, which had always feared it would get a cheap-looking movie as a result of Corman's anti-profligacy, was certain of it once Junior Frankovich's reports began arriving in Los Angeles. Executives, pitiless as stormtroopers, were immediately deployed.

At the end of the Utah shoot, on May 27, 1966, just before a big unit move to Arizona, the hammer came down. Well-dressed individuals went up with Corman to his hotel room, and when they emerged again, he was no longer directing the picture. Miller heard the scuttlebutt and decided Roger might need some friendly company, a sympathetic ear. "Don't go up there!" the other actors told him, sure that, if he were seen consorting with a fired director, he, too, would be fired, simply by association. But Miller only waved his hand and said, "Faugh," then headed up the stairs to Corman's room. And, indeed, on the way he passed a couple of guys in suits, who asked him, "You on this picture?"

Miller answered carefully: "I *think* so."

And he was, but Corman was off and Phil Karlson was on. (Monte Hellman, who was supposed to be cutting the film, was off soon as well.) Corman hadn't seemed very upset to Miller, was just nodding and packing his bag. Then, suddenly, he was gone. It was great crew gossip, of course, all of it, and though the Corman stalwarts on the crew, guys like Haller, Hannawalt, and assistant director Jack Bohrer, couldn't have been happy about it, the affair seemed to have the effect of uniting the blue and the grey cast members. Détente began during the unit move; and once down in Arizona, on their first day off, they rode down to Mexico in an old yellow school bus to see the bullfights as a group. Glenn Ford, Inger Stevens, George Hamilton, and just about everyone else on the cast list had a good time on the trip, but Miller, an animal lover, was sickened by the killing of the bulls. "Especially when, by now, when they're ready to kill him, he's paralyzed, he can't raise his head," Miller said. "He can't move."

Karlson has a few duds on his resumé but he was no hack, and *The Long Ride Home* emerged as a reasonably seamless picture; though if you can tell Utah from Arizona, you'll have a pretty good idea of who directed what.

And while it's an obviously bigger film than the earlier Corman Westerns, it's still not quite slick, with roughly the production values of a mid-level Spaghetti Western. Still, in the bursting of blood capsules and the crinkled eyes of its elderly hero, one can sense the approach of *The Wild Bunch*, and a new sort of Western, a few years further on.

Back in LA, Miller was feeling pretty good. Corman's dismissal and a cracked coccyx aside, he'd really enjoyed the *Long Ride Home* experience; he had picked up a decent paycheque and hoped it augured bigger things to come. But, as ever, it seemed his agent might as well have been dead, for all the calls Miller got. It wasn't that he was missing them either; as Bill Miller told documentarian Elijah Drenner, "When I first went out to California, Dick never wanted to leave the house. He wouldn't even want to go ten, fifteen minutes away, because he was afraid he'd miss a call." But evidently there were few calls to miss, and Miller turned again to writing.

Where once his head had been filled with science-fiction scenarios, his genre of choice now was comedy. (The failed attempt to partner with Jonathan Haze on "The Monsters of Nicholson Mesa" had apparently served as a sort of bridge between sci-fi and comedy, despite not really qualifying as either.) Spy spoofs were a cottage industry in the mid-'60s, so Miller tried his hand at that, crafting a script called "Help, There's a Spy in My Bed!" A kindly, though explicitly ex-Nazi, German professor has invented "Supergene," a serum that will lead to the birth of an ultra-being if both parties involved in the procreation have been injected with it. Spies from many nations covet the formula, and, by a crazy chain of events, come to believe that a hapless pizza delivery boy called Seymore Peld is the male half of the super-couple. Soon Seymore, in fact merely a schlemiel in the Jerry Lewis tradition, is baffled by the parade of beautiful lady agents from around the world who are trying to seduce him.

The cannabis-scented influence of Chuck Griffith was all over this effort, most apparently in crazy character names like Hinkley Fender and Finsten Durley, and the main character might have been Seymour Krelboyne with a slightly different (and curiously spelled) name. At the pizza parlour where he's employed, Seymore is constantly berated by a crabby boss whose dialogue one cannot read without hearing the voice of Mel Welles. It was as though Miller was writing not just to make a buck for himself, but to craft parts for all his friends.

He couldn't sell "Help, There's a Spy in My Bed" to save his life (though an Italian picture with virtually the same title came along several years later) or the other scripts he wrote, "Rock 'n' Roll Tour" and "Rancho Bikini" either. He jumped into other writing projects anyway, focusing his efforts on another Griffithesque comedy. "Which Way to the Front?" was set in wartime, with a squad of California 4Fs led by a rich patriot, who charter their own boat to go fight the Japanese after being rejected for service by the army. For a war story it was intimately scaled. "I made it small, 'cause I was used to thinking Roger Corman style," Miller said. "So I put a little island, little Japanese force, little American force." He was pleased with the script, and especially with what he reckoned was a pretty good premise, but when it was done he put it away in the drawer with the others.

After his firing from *The Long Ride Home*, Corman didn't spend much time crying in his beer; with Jim Nicholson's help again—Nicholson and Frankovich Sr. were pals—he engineered a more permanent "leave of absence" from Columbia, and very shortly after signed a similar deal with 20th Century Fox, "determined to make it all work this time," he said. In contrast with the Columbia experience, Corman was able to start up a substantial project right away, a gangster picture with a hard-hitting, journalistic script by former *Amazing Stories* magazine editor Howard Browne. At two-and-a-half million dollars, *The St. Valentines Day Massacre*, the story of the war between Al Capone and Bugs Moran and the lead-up to the infamous 1929 massacre, was, and would remain, Corman's most expensive film ever; and though he was beholden to use the studio craftspeople rather than his own, he was able to pepper the supporting cast with his friends and stock company. "Fox dictated that I couldn't give them big roles," Corman said, but people like Miller, Leo Gordon, Jonathan Haze, and even Jack Nicholson were naturals for a gangster movie, and all had experience in the genre. Bruce Dern was there too, playing a doomed mechanic; Joe Turkel—Miller's nemesis ever since he welshed on a bet—was in as a character called Greasy Thumbs; and Barboura Morris would anchor the movie's effective opening sequence. Fox players George Segal and Ralph Meeker sneered and tommygunned their way through the movie, and Al Capone was played by Miller's old acting teacher, Jason Robards. "Dick Miller! My *only* student! My *only* student!" the star boomed again.

Richard Bakalyan, who played a lot of dogfaces, a lot of hoods, appeared as Capone lieutenant John Scalise. Bakalyan was an acquaintance of Miller's,

Miller in baseball regalia for *Fame*. SOURCE: DICK AND LAINIE MILLER

A young Dick Miller (in boots) and brother Eugene with their mother, Rita, c. 1932. SOURCE: DICK AND LAINIE MILLER

TOP: Miller the naval man, c. 1946. SOURCE: DICK AND LAINIE MILLER

BOTTOM: The USS *Siboney* on her maiden voyage. SOURCE: ROBERT HURST

Miller and friends enjoying shore leave in San Diego.
SOURCE: DICK AND LAINIE MILLER

Miller's cousin Saul Gilbert in Alejandro Jodorowsky's *La cravate*.
SOURCE: ALEJANDRO JODOROWSKY

Miller relaxing at home in the late 1950s. SOURCE: DICK AND LAINIE MILLER

Miller's self-promotional advertisement. SOURCE: DICK AND LAINIE MILLER

TOP: A shirtless Miller shows off his ink to Jonathan Haze and an unknown Hawaiian actor in *Naked Paradise*. SOURCE: AMERICAN INTERNATIONAL PICTURES

BOTTOM: Jack Nicholson bullies Miller into telling the entire plot of *The Terror*. SOURCE: FILMGROUP

TOP: Dick and Lainie Miller dressed up for Halloween, 1969.
SOURCE: DICK AND LAINIE MILLER

BOTTOM: Miller in pursuit in *Big Bad Mama*. SOURCE: NEW WORLD PICTURES

SOURCE: NEW WORLD PICTURES

TOP: Miller schmoozes with Robby the Robot in *Hollywood Boulevard*.
SOURCE: NEW WORLD PICTURES

BOTTOM: Tina Hirsch, Joe Dante, and Dick Miller at the New World Pictures headquarters. SOURCE: DICK AND LAINIE MILLER

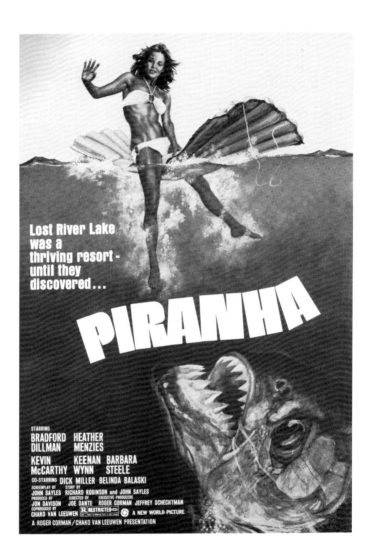

SOURCE: NEW WORLD PICTURES

TOP: Miller faces down an enormous Austrian robot in *The Terminator*. SOURCE: MGM/UA

BOTTOM: A serious Miller around the time of *Explorers*. SOURCE: DICK AND LAINIE MILLER

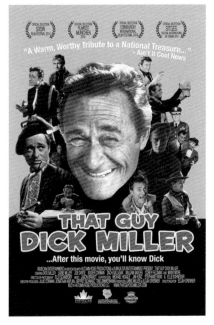

TOP: Miller as a friendly truck driver in *Small Soldiers*. SOURCE: DREAMWORKS PICTURES

BOTTOM: SOURCE: AUTUMN ROSE PRODUCTIONS/ELIJAH DRENNER

Dick and Lainie Miller, 2015. SOURCE: DICK AND LAINIE MILLER

Miller at home in Toluca Lake. SOURCE: AUTHOR PHOTO

and, in concert with a man named Lester Colodny, he was looking for stories or script material that could be adapted and sold. They had a little money to spend, and, after Bakalyan and Miller got to talking one day, Miller brought in his "Which Way to the Front?" scenario. To Miller's great delight, Bakalyan bought it.

Nicholson and Dern both needed money at the time, so Corman made sure they were on at the beginning and towards the end of the forty-five day schedule, which kept them on the payroll throughout. (Joe Dante would later extend this same kindness to Miller on a 1998 picture called *Small Soldiers*.) But other than tricks like that and the supporting cast of Corman players, he played it straight, determined not to make the same moves that had alienated him from Columbia. The very first shot in the picture is an elegant, complicated crane shot showing off an enormous street set and city cyclorama; far from ignoring half the equipment, Corman was using everything the studio had.

Miller was cast as one of the gunmen of that fatal February 14, and though the role was fairly small, the nature of it meant he was present for the key moment in the movie. The most popular still from the film, the gangsters firing, shows Miller in his fake-cop uniform, his jaw clenched, and brandishing a shotgun, so his visibility in the role far outpaced its size. It was nice to be in a big major studio movie, and very odd, but somehow natural, that Roger Corman should still be at the megaphone.

But for the splashes of blood and the brevity of the lingerie on its female stars, *The St. Valentine's Day Massacre* could have been made ten or fifteen years earlier. It was an old-fashioned picture, out of style by 1967 (as would be emphasized by the release of another period gangster picture, the emphatically modern *Bonnie and Clyde*, a month later); but the Miller family would be represented in more *au courant* cinema that year. For his part, Miller showed up as a nameless reporter peppering Kim Novak with questions in Robert Aldrich's loony Hollywood drama *The Legend of Lylah Claire*. (Miller is also reported to have appeared without credit as an MP in Aldrich's earlier hit *The Dirty Dozen*, but he is nowhere in evidence and doesn't remember doing it.) Lainie, meanwhile, had been picking up extra money dancing in shows, all of it fairly conventional dance-troupe stuff. She'd played a "voodoo witch, something with a chicken," in some show or other, and Mike Nichols, the comedian turned director, had seen her. Now, in March of '67, he was in pre-production on his second feature film, *The Graduate*, and in need of a tassel-twirling stripper who could move Katherine Ross to tears with the brazenness of her act. Nichols remembered the sultry voodoo witch and brought Lainie's picture to his production coordinator, saying, "I wish I could find her."

"Oh," said the production coordinator. "She's my neighbour."

The production coordinator knocked on the Millers' door and outlined Nichols's proposal. "A stripper?" Lainie asked, then turned to her husband. "Can I do that?"

"Do it! What's the difference!" Miller encouraged, although as a congenitally jealous husband he must have had some misgivings. (Later on he would only growl "Ahhhh!" and wave his hand when the subject was raised.) Lainie set to practising the signature move required in the scene: the twirling of nipple tassles in opposite directions. It must have been a funny few days in the Miller household. In April shooting began on the picture, and Lainie duly went down to the Sunset Strip club where the cast and crew were at work, and strutted, snarled, and, especially, twirled her breasts, all day long. At the end of it Dustin Hoffman asked her how she was feeling. "My feet are killing me," she told him.

Whatever the particulars of Corman's deal with Fox, they seem not to have included any prohibitions on running out and directing films for other companies. Very soon after wrapping *The St. Valentine's Day Massacre* in the late winter of 1967, Corman was back at AIP, conceiving a new project: something contemporary and relevant, of course, but exploitable too. Drugs and drug culture were making headlines: why not a movie about, say, LSD? This is when Corman went up to Big Sur for his famous acid trip, a gentle, seven-hour freak-out that had him "humping the earth" (according to Chuck Griffith, who was there) and featured a vision of golden ships that were at the same time earthy, sexy, motherly women. While tripping he conceived a way of transferring art directly from the brain and into the earth, where it could be seen instantly by people all around the globe, anyone who was touching bare ground. (This technique, if properly developed, would be a nifty way of bypassing pesky distributors: it was a practical hallucination for a practical man.) Frances Doel took notes the whole time, and the next day it was Griffith's turn to drop a tab. Back in LA Griffith worked up a script no one liked, and Corman had Jack Nicholson, who took his hallucinogens seriously, come in and start afresh. Nicholson's screenplay was conceptually wild, a phone book-thick epic that would have taxed even Stanley Kubrick's special effects and design prowess; so Corman shot only those bits of it he figured could be pulled off on an AIP budget.

Peter Fonda, Bruce Dern, and Dennis Hopper all appeared in principal roles, so Miller was left with the part of Cash, the vest-wearing bartender of a psychedelic club called the Bead Game. He got ninth billing and one or two lines in an exchange with Dern and Fonda, then stood around in the background of further scenes at the club, his arms crossed, clearly meant to be thinking *those crazy hippies*. He is, one supposes, intended to come off as a hip, with-it character from an earlier generation, a guy who's seen it all and has finally had enough. "All the bartenders I know, they don't give a crap what their clientele is," Miller said. But a shaggy paranoiac tripping balls in his establishment is maybe the final straw for Cash—to the viewer it looks very much like he's ready to walk out the door and live out the rest of his days draining *cervezas* on some Baja beach, watching the sun go down.

The Trip was another success for Corman (though not on the scale of *The Wild Angels*), and it cemented his profile as a pop chronicler of alternative cultures. Though the youthful good will it generated paved the way to Corman's later *Gas-s-s-s!*, there's no reason to wish the movie ill: there's plenty to enjoy in the picture, corny as it is. The film's cinematographer, Arch Dalzell, had worked for Corman only once before, for the two days of principal photography on *The Little Shop of Horrors*, and he gave it a colourful and saturated visual quality, if not quite a psychedelic one. The upright Fonda has a rather automatonic presence, but Dern—in real life a teetotaller—is convincing as a gently ursine drugs guru. Dennis Hopper has a nice cameo as a ranting head, and with his whirling camera Corman made good cinema of it. For Miller, the highlight was his costume: a mauve shirt with batwing lapels and a snappy grey vest. "I love the clothes!" said Miller. "Big buckle, they threw at me a great big round buckle."

Miller did some TV that year too. He played, once again, the shorter half of a mismatched duo, this time on *Dragnet 1967*, the Jack Webb series that had been revived, zombie-like, for the paisley and patchouli era. In "The Big Shooting," Webb's Joe Friday and his partner, Bill Gannon (Harry Morgan), are concerned when a police officer is shot by a pair of liquor-store robbers. A police artist produces a composite drawing of the malefactors, and these are shown around repeatedly as Friday and Gannon do their footwork. They finally track the pair to the cell-like hotel room they share: it's Miller, shaving at a mirror, and his taller, meaner counterpart, played by Hal Baylor. (Baylor, a big man a decade older than Miller, had a thirty-year career of playing either cops or thugs before retiring in the late 1970s.) Miller has his shaving cream roughly rubbed off by Morgan, then plays a couple of scenes at the police station, first mocking Friday ("I do hope you'll write my book," he sneers after the Sarge lists his many previous infractions and incarcerations), then, when confronted by the recovered but secretly amnesiac gunshot victim, frantically confessing. Finally, framed as though for mug shots, Miller and Baylor stare into the camera while Friday's voice fills us in on the trial date, sentence, and current whereabouts of the duo.

That was all fine, uncool but fine, and the episode aired on March 30, 1967, at 9:30 p.m. But on the next day, March 31, at approximately 3:30 p.m., inside Schwab's Pharmacy at the corner of Sunset and North Laurel, unemployed actor Richard "Dick" Miller was flipping through magazines when he was approached by two officers of the law. They were plainclothesmen, but "you know right away by the jackets they're wearing that they're cops," said Miller.

"Can I see you outside?" one policeman said. Miller followed him out the door, with the other one close behind, and on the sidewalk the cops sized him up.

"I never forget a face," one of them said.

"Wha-a-at? What'd I do?" Miller squawked.

"You'll find out. Show me some ID."

Miller turned to his car, a blue-green VW bug. "It's in the glove compartment, everything's in the glove compartment." The cops kept a close eye as Miller opened the glovebox, smiling back, leaning out and gesturing to show there was no weapon there.

Miller pulled out his wallet and the cops looked over his driver's licence. "We had a rundown on faces this morning," one of them said, "and I'm sure ..."

"Wait a minute," Miller said. "You watch *Dragnet* last night?" He pulled out his portfolio and showed it to the cops. Inside he had a photo of the very same police composite drawing that had been used in the episode. "This look familiar?" he asked the cops.

Instantly the big tough cops were transformed. "Aw, shucks," one of them said, kicking at the concrete.

"They were so embarrassed," Miller said. "These great big cops, they got like little kids." It was funny but also a little dispiriting, because here was another unwelcome change from the old days: once it had been Miller chasing criminals outside of Schwab's; now it was Miller getting rousted by the cops there. At Schwab's, yet! It was like getting hassled in your own living room.

He also did an episode of *Mannix*, "The Cost of a Vacation," playing a fashion photographer who wears what appears to be a blue *Star Trek* jersey without the insignia. The character is in and out in the first two minutes of the show, but has a few lines and might reasonably be thought a hip kind of guy. Though Miller was still nameless, playing an all-but-in-fact Richard Avedon was a distinct step up from being "Cabbie" one more time. He did another *Mannix* shortly thereafter, "The Falling Star," again playing a fashion photographer, possibly even the same one (though more conservatively dressed this time), and again getting a few lines and two or three minutes of screen time.

Miller was visible, if not copiously, at least at regular intervals through 1967: *St. Valentines* opened in June; *The Trip*, in August; the first *Mannix* episode aired in October; and *The Long Ride Home* appeared in theatres in late November. *The Graduate* opened in December, instantly giving Lainie Miller a great deal more visibility than her husband had that year.

The year 1968 started with Miller on TV doing the photographer bit in the second of his *Mannix* episodes, which aired January 6. Not much happened after that; certainly not much film work. Miller still felt ahead of the game, thanks to the "Which Way to the Front?" script sale, and there was Lainie's *Graduate* money too. He sold another script, a Western called *Four Rode Out*, to his old *Bert Parks Show* boss Genial Paul Harrison. Harrison did his own adaptation of the script, and later that year it was shot in Spain by a TV director, John Peyser, with a cast including Sue Lyon, Pernell Roberts, and Miller's *Wagon Train* co-star Leslie Nielsen. Miller was not in the picture, but contributed some voice work in the post-production ADR process. He did this kind of work whenever possible, just another way of "putting rice in the rice bowl," as Lainie Miller put it. When he was not at his typewriter or behind a microphone, or at the beach or at the movies, Miller played a lot of softball, pitching on an Actors' League team. It was said that James Garner used to come out just to watch Dick pitch. But otherwise the year was not a kind one, or much filled with the blessings of paid work. For what money Miller did earn that year, he often had to fight.

On March 15 a small item appeared in both of the major trade papers, *Variety* and the *Hollywood Reporter*. Warner Bros., it seemed, had acquired a script by authors Lester Colodny and Richard Bakalyan, the very people to whom Miller had sold "Which Way to the Front?" Miller noted the familiar names, but, as the project was untitled as far as the little article was concerned, he didn't think much of it.

By May 30, Memorial Day, he had other things to think about. The day began with Miller's deciding he should prune a tree in his yard. He pulled out a ladder and climbed to the top, balancing precariously, one hand on the tree trunk and the other grasping his saw. The tip of the branch settled onto his garage roof, which held it until Miller had sawed through the whole thing. It fell to the ground, and then Miller started hacking away at another branch on the opposite side of the tree. There was no garage roof there, and once he'd sawed through a good part of it, the heavy branch snapped, swung down past the tree trunk, and knocked the ladder right out from under him. Miller plummeted down and landed on his back across a large root. Lainie ran over and Miller, lying bent over the root with his belly sticking up, croaked, "Get me to a hospital!"

"I took him to the hospital where I was a nursing student at the time," Lainie recalled. "And I knew that his mother had died of diabetes, so I made the mistake of mentioning that to the nurses, that maybe they should check his blood sugar while he was in there. In those days they kept you an extra day to do all the blood glucose, and he heard he had to stay an extra day, and he started yelling and screaming at me."

But the blood tests and his own diabetes were the least of Miller's worries: the fall had injured his back badly. "There followed a series of beautiful operations," he said with grim irony. A few days later Bobby Kennedy was shot in Los Angeles. Though only half over, it was already a hell of a year. Another Kennedy down, war raging in Vietnam, laid up in the hospital, no work on the horizon. It was dire. "Those were the lean years, they really were," Miller recalled. When he got out of the hospital, he tried diversifying a bit, and, taking a cue from his brief position as the in-house fashion photographer of *Mannix*, began taking stills and head shots of other actors. His client roster was never big, and they never became famous (beefy Chesley Noone, aka Chet Norris, an unlikely semi-regular in erotic Westerns, was his biggest name), but Miller remembered it fondly anyway. "I did pretty good with a camera then," he said.

He kept writing too, and managed to sell more scripts. Over the course of the year and into the next decade, in fact, he sold a number of Westerns to a Texas-based company. He can't remember the titles—"'Trail of the Lonesome Pine,' 'Trail of the Friendly Pine,' 'Trail of the Piney Pine,' they were all the same!" he crowed—but the movies were apparently shot and released in a highly regional fashion down Texas way. "I guess Texans are the only ones who'll sit and watch cowboy pictures," Miller mused. He got a few bucks for the scripts but never saw the movies. If he was properly credited for writing them, he neither knew nor cared.

There were mystery projects also, hazy, low-budget things neither Miller nor Lainie could remember the titles of; movies that were never released. In one of them Barbara got a taste of her old man's work when she was cast to play Dick's daughter. Nobody can remember the title of this intriguing (to the biographer) production, or anything else about it.

Otherwise there was no onscreen work, but Miller stayed cool as a cucumber. "In between gigs, you're not doing anything. Just going to the beach, you know. You really don't sweat it. I figured, okay, that's it. Went up, probably coming down." He was hustling, though, in his own way, but was finding his brief time as an AIP star more a liability than a draw. He went to see a director, hoping for a role, and told him, "I've been very active with American International, and I'm looking to movie on to bigger and better things." The director looked at Miller and said, "Yeah, I don't think we can use you." Yet even in the midst of this drought, by August he was visible on movie screens again, though not in any way he'd been expecting. Some months earlier, Roger Corman had offered his former assistant Peter Bogdanovich the chance to make a movie of his own. Typically of Corman, the offer came with a set of absurdly specific requirements, particularly Karloff-centric ones this time. Bogdanovich had to use twenty minutes of Boris footage from *The Terror*, shoot twenty minutes worth of new material with Karloff (who somehow once again owed Roger some shooting days), and make up the balance using other actors in contemporary locations. Bogdanovich and his wife, Polly Platt, later an acclaimed production designer, came up with the sort of idea that seems at once inspired and obvious: have Karloff play himself more or less, an aging horror star planning his retirement from scary pictures because they wither so completely in the face of real-world horrors. One such horror must, of course, intrude: a Charles Whitman-like crazy sniper who, after killing his parents and his wife and committing a spot of freeway mayhem, terrorizes the same drive-in where Karloff is premiering his latest and last movie. This movie is a period spookshow with a strong resemblance to *The Terror*. *Targets* was a timely picture indeed, and, alongside its apposite critique of American gun culture, managed a not especially flattering commentary on Corman and his Poe pictures in the bargain.

When Miller watched it, all he could see was himself, in those tights, acting onscreen without having been paid. *Targets* opens with scenes from *The Terror*, including the bit in which Miller is beaten with a chain, and much more *Terror* footage appears in the drive-in climax. To Miller, it just didn't seem right, especially in the dry and impoverished year he was enduring. Lainie, whose sense of labour justice was as strong or stronger than Dick's, no doubt had an opinion as well. Miller took his complaint to the Screen Actors Guild for arbitration, and, as when the other Dick Miller had appeared on the scene a few years earlier, the SAG panel ultimately found for the Millers. Corman was forced to write a cheque he hadn't seen coming, which was not among his cherished activities. There was no evidence of long-term resentment on his part, though; Corman, it has been theorized (by Diane Ladd), rather respects anyone willing to fight for money owed them.

The cheque was, to Miller, a healthy one, so he was happy. But in February 1969 another cloud of perturbation passed over: a notice, spotted in *Variety* the day before Valentine's Day, announced that Jerry Lewis had signed screenwriters Gerald Gardner and Dee Caruso to prepare a script for *Which Way to the Front?* from a treatment by Lester Colodny and Richard Bakalyan. Miller scanned the item for his own name, but in vain. Bakalyan! It now seemed fitting that the original deal should have gone down on the set of *The St. Valentine's Day Massacre*. This was the whiff of grapeshot, and Miller girded for another fight.

He first called Warner Bros. "Who are you?" they asked. "I'm the writer," he told them and all he got was an "Oh yeah?" and the phone hung up in his ear. He then went to the Writers Guild of America (WGA), with whom he had registered his story, and demanded adjudication. The WGA considered Miller's complaint through the spring and into the summer of 1969. That May Miller's old pal Jack Nicholson went to Cannes for the *Easy Rider* premiere, and Nicholson later had the specific realization, which came as his character made its first appearance in the film, that he was now a movie star and that nothing would be the same for him again. The picture went into general release a month later and confirmed Nicholson's feeling three times filled and spilling over. (Corman had nearly produced the film, and regretted ever after that it had not worked out.)

Miller "kept in touch" with Nicholson for a time after he became famous, but he soon realized "there's a line of demarcation that comes up." In an interview with *Fangoria*'s David Everitt, Miller laid it out: "It's not the difference between an actor who doesn't make money and an actor who makes, say, a hundred or two hundred thousand dollars a year—you can still communicate," he said.

> But when a guy starts making 10 million a year, the money actually separates you, because there's no way I can participate in his level of life, with 'Hey, let's fly to Europe!' and that sort of thing. Perforce, it became necessary for us to stop seeing each other. The only way you can hang around with a person like that is as a subservient, like a coffee boy or something.

"I love Jack," Miller told Everitt in that 1982 interview, "and I think his feelings for me are about the same. The few times we've run into each other the last four or five years we have been very close." Indeed, Nicholson made a point of asking after Miller's health when I spoke with him, and seemed very pleased to hear his old friend was doing well. But after the summer of 1969 their days of lounging at the beach together all the day long were done.

At around this time Dick's father, Ira Miller, died. He and Miller had never quite seen eye to eye on the showbiz thing—that line of work had helped break up his first marriage, after all—but they got along well enough. Dick and Gene would see the old man for lunch when he was in town; otherwise there had been little contact between Ira and his older sons. Still, there was the full-page *Variety* ad Dick had taken out for himself, demonstrating that at one time, to some degree, Dick had been a movie star. Ira had clipped it out and kept in a drawer.

Through that summer Gerald Gardner and Dee Caruso beavered away on their rewrite of "Which Way to the Front?," changing Miller's story from a Pacific to a European setting and adding even more Jerry Lewis-style gags. In October *Variety* announced the film's imminent production, and declared the film "screenplayed by" Gardner and Caruso, and still "from a story by Lew Colodny and Richard Bakalyan." In November they announced it again, unchanged but for correcting Colodny's first name back to Les. The film went to camera on December 1, 1969, and Miller still had no idea whether he'd be credited or not. But the arbitration came down before the credits for the film were shot, and there, the following July, was Miller's name: not large, and shared with two other people he'd never met, but it was there, a story credit on a studio picture. Fine, but Miller never forgot what he considered Bakalyan's perfidy; fifteen years later, when Miller was a regular on *Fame*, writer/producer Ira Behr mentioned that Bakalyan should do a bit on the show, "and [Dick] looked at me, like, 'fuck him!'" said Behr.

When news of the script arbitration came, early in 1970, the Millers celebrated with a road trip. It had been a hard year, in many ways a hard decade, but both of these were over and things were looking up. Who knew what the 1970s would bring? Dick, Lainie, and nine-year-old Barbara jumped in the car and headed north.

They cruised up the Pacific Coast Highway, out of the smog—the federal Clean Air Act would finally be signed this year, and things would improve in LA—and the Pacific gleaming at their left. They stopped after four hours of driving, and there was a park of some kind, with a trail. The family got out to stretch their legs, Miller remembered, "and there were poppy fields up there, and it was the time they were blooming. It was miles of orange flowers." This was Miller recalling, years later, the most beautiful thing he can ever remember seeing. There were California poppies right up to the cliff, with the crashing waves below, the electric blue sky above, and to the east a carpet of blazing tangerine, here sweeping up the shoulders of a small mountain, then essing away in a river down the *barranco*. It was scenery without budget restrictions, in radiant Technicolor. "We were standing there for four hours, it was so amazing," Miller said. "Barbara was running around, up and down these hills and through all these flowers, tired from running."

15 You mean I gotta touch those?

At some point early in 1970 Miller went to an audition, looking for a part as a courtroom sketch artist in the ensemble cast of a Civil War legal drama to be directed by George C. Scott, called *The Andersonville Trial*. *Patton* had not yet been released, so, not thinking of him as a terrifying martinet, Miller was not as nervous to meet Scott as he might otherwise have been; neither did he think to trim his modishly long hair before showing up. Scott was then appearing on Broadway in Mike Nichols's production of *Plaza Suite*, and Scott's co-star, Maureen Stapleton, had confessed to her director that she was frightened of Scott. "*Everyone* is scared of George C. Scott," Nichols told her. But Miller, still the tough Bronx hotshot, was not. As he waited for his turn to audition, he was, in fact, bored, so he began sketching the actors who were waiting along with him.

When Miller was finally called in he sketched Scott too. "This is all I do in the show, right?" he asked the hawk-nosed director, showing him the picture he had made. "Ah, give him the job," Scott barked at the casting director. Miller joined a delightfully eclectic sausage party, including Martin Sheen, Buddy Ebsen, Whit Bissell, Richard Basehart, Cameron Mitchell, and William Shatner. Basehart played Captain Henry Wirz, accused of war crimes in the atrocious running of a Confederate POW camp. Conditions were abominable, and many thousands of Union soldiers died.

A week before the shoot, during the rehearsals, Miller walked into a pole. "One of those thin, narrow iron poles," he said. "Knocked myself cold! Woke up on the sidewalk going, 'What the hell happened?' Had a big welt up there." Though Miller never enjoyed wearing makeup, he accepted it happily this time, because it hid his clumsiness from Scott and his fellow cast members. Otherwise the *Andersonville Trial* shoot was uneventful, with Miller simply sitting in the background through the whole thing, perpetually sketching. He hung onto his drawings and later arranged them in a sort of portfolio, which he occasionally brought out to show off.

Miller returned to the stage that year, playing a hunchbacked Igor in *I'm Sorry, the Bridge Is Out, You'll Have to Spend the Night*. "It's the longest title in the world," Miller said. The show, a proto-*Rocky Horror* musical horror spoof written by Sheldon Allman and "Monster Mash" singer Bob Pickett, opened at the Coronet Theatre on April 28; but two weeks into the run Miller had to quit in order to take another job, probably *The Andersonville Trial*. Miller's hunchback part was taken over by the actor who'd been playing Renfield, Toby Lane, and the part of Renfield was taken over by a young Charles Cyphers, who would later appear with Miller in pictures such as *Truck Turner* and *Vigilante Force*, and thence in a number of John Carpenter films.

For Miller, the stage was always problematic. There was the early incident in which he forgot all his lines; the time he quit a Broadway show in the middle of a rehearsal; and then his premature departure from *The Bridge is Out*.... Later, after *New York, New York* wrapped, he auditioned for a show that his co-star Liza Minnelli was headlining, but he didn't get it.

Miller was ready by then to shrug off whatever love of live performing he might ever have had. "I didn't care too much about losing it," he said. "By then I'd given up on shows. I wanted to work in pictures."

The Millers were still nomads, moving from apartment to apartment, but around the time of *The Andersonville Trial*, Dick and Lainie bought a small house in the Valley, their first property. The fresh new decade, Lainie's graduation from years of schooling into the nursing workforce, and Miller's optimism about his own career lent them both a feeling of confidence and an urge to settle down a bit. The settling down didn't last long, however. On February 9, 1971, there came the drum and shake of a particularly robust early-morning earthquake, a 6.5 on the Richter Scale. Freeways collapsed, hospitals crumbled, dozens of people were killed and thousands injured; the whole valley bounced like sand in a sieve. Shortly after, duly impressed by the physical impermanence of the region in which they lived, and the mortgage looking no more valuable than a rental agreement in the face of such inconstancy, the Millers unloaded their house and moved to an apartment in West Hollywood.

Lainie settled into her hospital career, and Dick flipped through the trades and waited for the phone to ring. It made nary a jingle, but Miller had other things to occupy him—writing, for instance—so for a while he didn't worry. Lainie hoped he would broaden out, find a straight job and a regular paycheque. Whatever the pressures Miller faced to bring some money into the house, he remained steadfast. "He didn't care if he was going through a dry spot, or if he wasn't being called upon in those days," Bill Miller told documentarian Elijah Drenner. "He was just going to wait it out and do what he wanted to do, because he knew what was best for himself." If Dick had known how profound and dispiriting this dry spell would be, he *might* (or might not; it's impossible to say) have been a little more concerned.

In the meantime, forces that would change Miller's life were arraying, but in a slow and slackardly manner befitting the youthful spirit of the times. Through the late 1960s, on the East Coast, a whole new breed of movie-loving filmmakers were milling about, going to screenings and classes at the then-tiny NYU (New York University) film school, smoking a lot of weed, watching endless movies, and embracing the low brow as much as the high. Martin Scorsese was teaching there, and remembered, "Some of my students, like Jon Davison and Jonathan Kaplan, had sort of gotten swept up in the cult of Corman. A lot of the students were walking around with Roger Corman buttons." This love was forged in the crucible of student unrest: one night in 1969, in an attempt to force the administration to create a contemporary American Films course taught by Scorsese, the students staged a sit-in. They occupied the four eighth-floor rooms that made up the entirety of the school at the time, sparked up some doobies, and turned on their projectors. (Billy Crystal was reported to have been the projectionist during this action.) They screened *Rosemary's Baby*, *Help!*, and *My Darling Clementine*, but by 2:00 a.m. they'd run out of movies. Scorsese made a phone call, then sent one of his students, Allan Arkush, out on a mission. Arkush found himself walking up six floors to an apartment on St. Mark's Place, where the door was answered by a mysterious figure who wordlessly ushered him in. The apartment was filled with unlabelled film cans; the occupant and Arkush had to open each one of them and look at the reel to figure out what the movie was. In the oven they found a print of *Stagecoach*, and in the fridge, which was otherwise stocked with nothing but orange juice and mescaline, the man found a movie he declared weird enough to be paired with the John Ford classic. "The perfect film for the occasion," he told Arkush. "I guarantee it."

The movie turned out to be *The Little Shop of Horrors*, and it was indeed the ideal choice. As it unspooled Arkush, Kaplan, and Davison fell about with laughter, giddy from "a night of smoking bad pot," Arkush said. But they were all aware that, stoned or not, they were enjoying this movie as much, or more, than the foreign classics they'd been studying. They all well recalled seeing the Corman films in cinemas as kids; they all remembered the *Million Dollar Movie*, which ran and reran the same cheaply licensed movies over and over again for a week. There was proprietary feeling for these movies, and for the people who'd made and acted in them, and when the opportunity came to champion them, to insist that they were as valid an expression of the cinematic art as any Swedish or Italian import, the NYU student body didn't hesitate. "Embracing Corman was embracing something that was a provocation," Scorsese said. "But it was done with conviction." So out came the Corman buttons and the undergrad defenses of his work, while secretly, or maybe not so secretly, they were all trying to figure out how they could go make movies for him themselves.

At just this time Corman was making some big changes in his business and his life. In the summer of 1970 he made what would be his last film as a director for many years, the WWI dogfight picture *Von Richthofen and Brown*. It was a rough shoot, with a stunt pilot killed and an actor and another pilot injured in a separate crash. Even before this Corman had become equally disenchanted about working for the major studios with their post-production meddling, and for AIP's conservative fraidy-cats, who were getting mighty scissory too. They had re-edited Corman's most recent AIP film, *Gas-s-s-s!*, so severely that a major character—God Himself, in fact—had been nearly elided from the narrative. Corman had already put together his own independent company, New World Pictures; already had an office on the Strip, which, as though to emphasize Corman's Willie Wonka-like capacity for spinning magic and enchantment while aggressively keeping associates at an emotional distance and competitors at a loss, was accessed by a marvellous glass elevator; and already had his first two pictures underway.

Some marketing guru Corman happened across declared that the buying public responded most strongly to the words "new" and "free," so Corman, who wasn't interested in giving anything away for free, had chosen "new" as part of his company name. The inaugural New World picture was *Angels Die Hard*, a biker project brought to Corman by his longtime associate Beach Dickerson. A biker movie sounded good to Roger after the success he'd enjoyed with *The Wild Angels*, and the success he should have enjoyed with *Easy Rider*. Dickerson had drummed up some investment, Corman matched it, and the movie was made; on its June 1970 release *Angels Die Hard* proved a half-decent money-spinner. The second New World picture was a collaboration between Corman's company and the drive-in impresario Lawrence Woolner, with whom he'd partnered before, and was based on Woolner's own brainstorm. Woolner figured that a movie about young professional women, nurses maybe, would afford a profitable opportunity to mix social relevance with T&A. Corman's commercial instinct-o-meter redlined, and when *The Student Nurses* was released in late August, he was proved correct once again. "It really surprised us all how well it did," Corman said. The picture was directed by Stephanie Rothman, who had earlier shot the second-unit chase scenes of *Beach Ball*, using one of cinema's least-convincing doubles to stand in for Dick Miller's cop character. It was successful enough to kick off not just a series of nurse pictures, but, eventually, a whole slew of "three girl" movies, which were generally packaged as sex comedies, but skewed heavily toward drama and the sort of political issue cinema Corman had long treasured.

By the end of 1970 New World was a going concern, and Corman was married to the former Julie Halloran, whom he'd been dating on and off since the mid-sixties. Through 1971 a tsunami of New World product filled the grindhouses and passion pits of America, with every genre represented: a biker picture directed by Barbara Peeters; a vampire movie from Stephanie Rothman; a women-in-prison film courtesy of Jack Hill. There were horror pictures imported from the Philippines, Germany, and Italy; a new biker film and a second nurse picture, this one directed by George Armitage, came along in July. Future superstar directors like Jonathan Demme and Curtis Hanson found themselves in Corman's employ and working with his formulas. All this time Miller was sitting either at home or at Schwab's, unemployed.

Martin Scorsese, who had inspired his NYU students with extravagant pantomime and manic enthusiasm, or threatened them with cap pistols and failing grades when necessary, was the first to head west and actually get work from Corman. By the fall of '71 Scorsese was making *Boxcar Bertha*, and though it was one of the few Corman hayseed pictures in which Miller did not appear, John Carradine was duly present and accounted for. (Carradine's son David was the male lead, and Barbara Hershey the titular Bertha.) Earlier in the year, shortly after Scorsese's arrival, Corman asked him if he knew of any other potential directors he might call upon to helm New World projects, and Scorsese had recommended Jonathan Kaplan. Shortly thereafter, Kaplan, in New York, exhausted after a night of work at the Fillmore, was roused from his bed at 4:00 a.m. by a call from someone purporting to be Roger Corman. "Yeah, fuck you," the sleepy Kaplan said, and hung up. Jon Davison was known for his crackerjack Corman impersonation and Kaplan had no doubt he was on the line, playing some cruel, meaningless joke. The phone rang again almost immediately. "I tell you, this is Roger Corman," the voice insisted, and this time Kaplan recognized that the imperial tone and precise enunciation he was hearing over the long-distance line could be coming only from the legendary producer himself. After letting Kaplan stammer through some apologies, Corman explained that he needed someone to direct a new nurse picture, *Night Call Nurses*. "The third in my Nurses' Trilogy," Corman called it.

The next day Kaplan was on a plane to Los Angeles. Kaplan came from Hollywood stock: his uncle was Van Heflin, and his father was the composer Sol Kaplan. The elder Kaplan was a piano virtuoso who'd scored movies like *The House on Telegraph Hill* and *Niagara* before being inadvertently fingered as a possible communist sympathizer by his friend John Garfield, and compelled to appear before the House Un-American Activities Committee. Sol's sister Rose lived in Los Angeles, and gave young Jonathan a place to live and a lift to Corman's Sunset Strip office. He rode up the glass elevator and met Julie Corman, who'd been given the job of producing *Night Call Nurses*. She had been working in the film industry doing this and that, but this would be her first outing as a producer.

Julie took him in to see Roger, who, Kaplan assumed, would want to talk about the movie they were going to make, or ask to see some of his work: the commercials, or the award-winning short he'd brought with him "in sweaty hands"; Corman did none of this. "I'd like you to show a Jensen automobile and a close-up of a Bulova watch," he instructed. "Waist-up nudity from the front, full nudity from behind. This script will need a rewrite." Corman handed the bewildered youngster a scenario. As Kaplan, realizing he was being dismissed, turned to go, Corman spoke up again. "And find a part for Dick Miller," he said.

In some stories the request to cast Miller came from Julie Corman, and in others it was Jon Davison's idea, but in most tellings Roger was the one who directly spearheaded the 1970s Millerenaissance. Why he made this request at that time has been preserved in no diary, interview, or accessible memory. Miller would have been very glad to hear the words whomever they came from, and for whatever reason. He'd gained weight as the sixties ended and the seventies began; he was not fat, but he was husky, a fireplug. He'd done no acting since *The Andersonville Trial*, except a bit as an assassin in a green hat on an episode of *McCloud*. It aired in February 1972 and was the show on which Miller had told his *Carnival Rock* stories to Joseph Wiseman and been brutally pranked in return. Miller was reunited with one of his *Long Ride Home* co-stars, the legendary *fartiste* Timothy Carey. Neville Brand, Avery Schreiber, and Shelly Fabares were in it too: it was a delightfully odd cast, and Miller's rock-jawed *chapeau vert* came to an appropriately sticky end, of course.

But the job floated by like an island and there were no further shores in sight. He was not sitting idle, though; he was writing, and, improbably enough, getting into an all-new kick: exotic animals. "There's nothing to do in California," he explained. "You get little hobbies." One day he talked to an acquaintance of his, a woman named Pat Barbeau ("She's died now," Miller said. "I don't know how long she lasted."), and the conversation turned to animals. Barbeau told Miller that she had a mountain lion. "Mountain lion? Where do you keep it?" an instantly hooked Miller asked. It turned out the mountain lion lived with Tippi Hedren, her husband Noel Marshall, and Hedren's daughter Melanie Griffith, who had all become enamoured of big cats while in Africa making a picture called *Mister Kingstreet's War*. They began collecting lions, tigers, mountain lions, and other large felines who were homeless. Usually, as in the case of Hollywood diabolist Anton LeVay, the original owners were forced to give up their "pets" by anxious landlords and local authorities. Hedren and Marshall had a home in Beverly Glen, and kept their animals there until they, too, were compelled to find greener, broader pastures. They eventually moved their operation to a ranch 40 miles north of LA and began making a movie about a family and its many lion friends; the picture, called *Roar*, became notorious both for the number of lion-related injuries on its set (at least seventy, including an incident in which cinematographer Jan De Bont was virtually scalped by one of the big kitties) and for its box-office failure when it was released in 1981. Pat Barbeau appeared in it as one of a clutch of committee members who get menaced by the animals.

Miller was fascinated by the idea of a big-cat preserve so near to his home. "Can we visit out there?" he asked Barbeau. It was closed to the public, but somehow she managed to clear it with Marshall and Hedren, and one day Miller found himself driving to the compound. "It was scary," he said. "The first thing I saw were the lions in cages, and I said, 'Oh, this is fine.' And I walked through a gate, and I'm walking around, and all of a sudden I look and there must be 20 lions around me." Most people would find this frightening, and Miller certainly did, but something else happened to him at the same time. "I lit up," he said. "I swear, I just said, 'This is wonderful!' I said, 'This is marvellous!'" It was a natural high, one of the most intoxicating Miller had ever encountered. He'd often experienced the exhilaration of mortal danger, and here it was again, staring at him with almond eyes. "You're with a bunch of wild animals," he explained. "They've never been trained. You can't train them. They're well fed and they're used to people. That's your only hope. Don't mess with them." The effect it had on him never diminished: one visit with the cats, Miller said, "and I'd be high for the rest of the week."

Hedren and Marshall weren't there when he first started going, but he would meet them later. Miller's first encounter with Marshall was memorable, with the producer/wildlife enthusiast as eccentric as one might imagine. "He's laying on the bed, and he's on his back, and when I'm introduced to him, he started moving his legs like a tiger, like a lion. I expected him to growl or something." Miller was a regular at the compound by then, but it was some time before Lainie could be persuaded to join him.

"It took him about six months to convince them it was okay for me to come up, because I'm little," she said. Fear of becoming a lion's canapé was strong, but Lainie overcame it; enchantment quickly followed, and sensual experiences beyond compare were her reward. "We actually gave a Phisohex bath to a full-grown tiger once," she recalled. "I loved it!" She shot Super 8 film of Miller nuzzling the animals. Miller took a couple of other friends up to see the cats, but they didn't care for the experience.

Miller visited the compound regularly for almost two years. On two occasions, while Dick, Lainie, and Barbara were living in Beverly Hills, they actually took animals home for a night: once a tiger cub and once Barbra Streisand's lion cub, Duke. "I always imagined," grinned Miller, "what would have happened if we were burgled that night. And the guy came face to face with this lion. 'Excuse me, I'm in the wrong house.'"

When they weren't chilling with man-eating jungle animals, the Millers spent a lot of time on boats, because for a time they co-owned one with Dick's brother Gene. "First boat we had was a twenty-five-foot cat boat," Lainie reported. "One mast up in the front, full galley, eleven-foot beam." Other, larger boats followed, but, said Dick, "we never owned them." They nevertheless logged a good many hours aboard these vessels and became functionally adept sailors.

And in the meantime, Miller said, "after ten years of just barely making it, some strange things started to happen. I would start running into people who had seen my work when they were kids." It made Miller feel a little old, but he would soon realize these were not just any fans: though they appeared at first blush to be standard-issue gushing nerds, they would soon be making movies of their own, and Miller would have himself an all-new career.

On his way down the glass elevator of the New World Pictures building, Jonathan Kaplan went into a mild panic. He didn't know how to begin rewriting the *Night Call Nurses* script, had no idea how to make the vague but overarching improvements suggested by Corman's weirdly specific instructions; but after some thought he got in touch with his NYU pals Jon Davison and Danny Opatashu and asked them to come out and help. Thrilled, taking this offer as their big break into movies, the two arrived in Los Angeles within days and installed themselves in a motel.

In a subsequent pre–rewrite story meeting, Kaplan had suggested Dick Miller might play the already written elderly flasher who was a barely tolerated fixture of the hospital and a running joke of the script. Corman (rightly, of course) pointed out that the flasher needed to be dapper and elegant, with a British accent if possible; this was, to Corman, obviously not a Dick Miller part. "Make him a masher," Corman suggested.

"Okay, he's not a flasher, he's a masher," Kaplan said to himself, having no idea what a masher was. Later, back in the crowded motel room, Davison listened to Kaplan's story, said, "Masher, got it!" and began to write. Davison, a big Miller fan, was thrilled at the opportunity to write a part for him, and he and Opatashu turned out a new *Night Call Nurses* script in no time. Miller became a character known as Mr. Jensen (he would drive the Jensen automobile called for by the producer), an oily, too-friendly motorist who picks up the most emotionally unstable of the nurses after she has left a creepy '70s self-actualization party. It's not much of a part, but Miller's largely improvised performance is a miniature beauty, running from (apparent) helpful concern to pathetic sexual desperation, to the full-on, slightly threatening masher he was always intended to be, all in the space of a minute or so. Only after considerable pleading does he steer his Jensen to the curb so she can flee.

Kaplan, who, like everyone, recognized Miller as soon as he saw him, was perfectly happy to accept this bit of prescribed casting, though Miller's memory was that "at first he didn't want to use me. I wasn't right or something." If Kaplan suffered such doubts, he got over them quickly. Miller was ready to read for the part, but warned Kaplan that he wasn't very good at auditions. ("And he wasn't," Kaplan recalled.) He wasn't particularly good at getting movie jobs at all, or at least not well practised. His previous work had overwhelmingly come with a simple call from Roger Corman; and now it had again, of course, but for a new director. Miller had only one demand: "I'm not bringing my own wardrobe," he told Kaplan. "Roger always asks you to bring your own wardrobe. He's got to give me some clothes this time."

However shitty his audition, when the time came to perform for the camera, Miller brought his A game. Mr. Jensen genuinely seems helpful at first, and probably intends to be; his mask slips quickly, but not completely; behind it we get glimpses of the self-loathing found in fundamentally decent people acting out their baser nature from what they perceive as sheer need. Miller gives us a real character in that minute of screen time, and enough material to construct a back story for Mr. Jensen should we choose to. Kaplan and the crew loved it too. "I ad-libbed the scene," Miller said, "and I went on and on, and [Kaplan] broke up, and they started going, 'He's great, he's great.'" This was Miller defining himself, consciously or not, as a character actor extraordinaire, and stepping forward to announce himself in this new phase of his career.

By other measures it wasn't the most spectacular of comebacks, but finally the Great Miller Interregnum, as *Fangoria* magazine later designated his late-'60s dry spell, was over. On wrapping the film Jonathan Kaplan, figuring this was the one and only time anyone would ask him to direct a film, packed his bags and returned to New York. *Night Call Nurses* came out in June and did solid business, so Corman immediately began planning a fourth entry in his Nurse Trilogy; he had conceived of similar pictures featuring women in different careers, most notably teaching. Julie Corman called Kaplan to ask if he'd be interested in writing and directing something called *The Student Teachers*, and Kaplan, believing his feature debut had been a career-killing piece of shit, was more shocked to get a second call from New World than he'd been by the first.

Kaplan had enjoyed his earlier experience directing Miller and this time didn't need to be told to find a part for him. The Miller part, in fact, was obvious, and was the right follow-up to *Night Call Nurses*' Mr. Jensen: a bigger role, completely different from anything the actor had done before. Like its predecessors, *The Student Teachers* involved a group of young women embarking on a new career, each finding themselves in a situation with its own unique tone, from sexy and comic to dramatic and political. The story in which Miller is most heavily involved has a touch of horror to it: his character, Coach Harris, is a puritanical, perpetually angry hard-ass who has mystifyingly been put in charge of the school's sex-ed program, and who is eventually revealed as the clown-masked rapist who has been terrorizing the co-eds and young female faculty. The picture went to camera in the spring of 1973, and Miller delighted Kaplan by proving as adept at reading scripted dialogue as he'd been at improvising it in *Night Call Nurses*. Of course, this was no surprise to those who'd worked with Dick before, but he wasted no time before showing off his skills to the new young guard.

It was a whole new cinema in which he was now immersed, a free, easy, and far less censorious Hollywood. As a clown-masked rapist, his character had some unsavoury acts to perform: stalking, chasing, hitting, fondling; but nobody really prepared him for what it would be like. In a deserted school gymnasium, he had to rip the clothes off a comely co-ed and grab maniacally at her breasts. An embarrassed Miller turned to Kaplan and asked, "You mean I gotta touch those things?" Kaplan indicated that indeed he must. "Oh well," Miller said, and turned to his task.

After every take in every assault scene, Miller, an old-school gentleman, would cover up his topless victims and ask if they were all right. This annoyed them: "Will you *stop* that!" they cried. Worse than the gym scene was the shower sequence, in which Miller, in his clown mask, had to grope, fondle, toss around, and tear the clothes off actress Nora Heflin. "It was a brutal scene," he told Beverly Gray. "We were both badly bruised. Bloody knees and elbows and everything.... We were slamming into the wall. They're yelling, 'Rape her! Rape her!' This was ridiculous, but we went at it." Possibly the oddest aspect of it all was that Nora Heflin, whom Miller's character leaves slumped naked and motionless on the shower floor, was Kaplan's sister.

Miller had always been a bit sheepish about such matters, as when he'd found it difficult to admit he was in a movie called *Naked Paradise*. Nevertheless, he remembered Corman's girlie dramas with fondness, if not much detail. "They were nice little pictures, nice parts," he said. After *The Student Teachers* he popped up regularly in the cycle, appearing first in *The Young Nurses* for actor and sometime director Clint Kimbrough. It was a small part: an unsympathetic cop who shrugs off a nurse's concerns at the site of an inner-city drug overdose; but among Miller's co-stars, oddly enough, was director Sam Fuller, who'd been recruited to play a corrupt doctor. This made it a more interesting prospect altogether, and though Miller and Fuller didn't share any scenes, Miller was intrigued enough by the tough-guy director to pursue a part in one of his films some years later.

Miller also appeared in a stewardess variation on the three-girls formula, which was released on November 28, 1973, the same day as *The Young Nurses*. *Fly Me* was shot mostly in the Philippines by director Cirio Santiago, but some additional scenes were filmed in Los Angeles by then-novice filmmaker Curtis Hanson. Miller played a cab driver who runs off and on the road several times as he ferries one of the flight attendants to the airport as she is changing into her uniform. And he appeared in the fifth and last of the Nurse Trilogy, Allan Holleb's *Candy Stripe Nurses*. Holleb was another tyro filmmaker who was glad to have Miller on board, since that meant one less actor he would have to direct. "The beauty of Dick Miller is that you don't have to work with him," Holleb told documentarian Elijah Drenner. "I was probably standing behind the camera greatly relieved that he did exactly what he should have done, and it sounded great and it sounded like Dick Miller, and that's just what you wanted."

It was another tiny part, of course, requiring him to do little more than sit in some bleachers, have popcorn dumped on his head by a Jean Seberg lookalike, and make funny faces. Miller, happily for Holleb and for his movie, was accustomed to making the most of very, very little. "You learn to put a little bit of your personality into each role, no matter how small it might be," he told the *Los Angeles Times* a decade later.

If 1973 was a busy summer for Miller, it was more frantic still for Jonathan Kaplan. From *The Student Teachers* he went almost straight into another movie, a hard-edged prison picture called *The Slams*. It was Kaplan's first step outside the Roger Corman factory, but as the producer was Gene Corman, it was not too far a step. Still, Gene had a deal with MGM, so it would be released by a major studio: a big and appealing deal for a young director. Kaplan quickly found the Miller part in the script: a cab driver who is terrorized by what he believes to be a dangerous escaped convict, though really he's just a pawn in a larger escape plan. In two scenes, one a two-hander with actor Paul E. Harris and the other in a phone booth, Miller got to be frightened rather than brusque, angry, or predatory, and again he was convincing in the part. *The Slams* turned out to be an effectively brutal prison picture, and must have broken some kind of production speed record. Shot in May 1973, mere weeks after *The Student Teachers* wrapped, it was released on September 12, fully a fortnight before the teacher film's September 26 premiere. It was as though Gene Corman had decided, for sport perhaps, to outdo his brother in sheer velocity, just once. In any case the sheer propulsive force of Kaplan's summer of '73 would slingshot him out of both Corman brothers' orbits forever.

After *The Slams* Miller kept right on working. He appeared in *Executive Action*, an adaptation of the Donald Freed and Mark Lane book released in May of that year. The Freed/Lane book was a speculative work purporting to reveal the true circumstances behind the Kennedy assassination: a conspiracy of disgruntled war hawks and hyper-conservative millionaires. Miller, who had always assumed there was something more to it than the Warren Commission ever admitted, was happy to be a part of the project, and was cast as one of the real assassins. As part of a pre-Dallas practise scenario, Miller and the other actors crouched among the Vasquez Rocks, some miles east of Los Angeles, sniping down at a small moving cart with dummies sitting upright inside. While Miller couldn't be sure if this was exactly how things occurred, it seemed to him as likely a scenario as any, and more so than any lone gunman nonsense. "It was pretty well planned, I think," he said of the assassination.

Much of the picture is set in the conspirators' drawing room, with actors Burt Lancaster, Robert Ryan, and Will Geer plotting the president's demise. Lancaster and Ryan had their progressive credentials, but it was Geer, a gay communist who was dedicated to botany and would go on to his greatest fame as Grandpa Walton, who was the most unlikely member of this wealthy, murderous right-wing cabal. It was canny casting indeed, and would not be the last time Geer played a deranged millionaire employing Dick Miller as an assassin.

There was another strange Miller connection to *Executive Action*. Donald Freed, one of the book's authors, was married to Barboura Morris, Miller's co-star in so many pictures. Morris, by then called Barboura Morris Freed, had clearly been involved in the creation of the book: the acknowledgements credit her with invaluable "encouragement and criticism."

Since marrying and divorcing Monte Hellman, Morris had become an activist, and, when she wasn't taking small parts in Corman pictures, was marching, demonstrating, and getting arrested for it. A *Los Angeles Times* photo taken June 29, 1967, showed a relaxed-looking Barboura leaning on her placard, which reads "Fight Police Brutality." Other women, wielding more pointedly anti-war signage, are standing around, smiling and laughing; all of them are in front of the Van Nuys City Hall, having just been arraigned on charges of disturbing the peace in connection with an anti-LBJ march at the Century Plaza that had ended badly several days earlier, with egregious amounts of precisely the brutality Morris and her sign were protesting.

It doesn't come as a great surprise that Morris married the co-author of a Kennedy assassination plot book, but it's a delightful coincidence that her old co-star Miller appeared in the movie version of it. Unfortunately, less than two years after the picture's November 1973 release (timed, of course, to the tenth anniversary of the JFK assassination), Barboura Morris Freed died of a stroke, at the age of forty-three. Her death at that young age remains a tremendous shame. "A very sweet lady and a nice friend," Susan Cabot told writers Tom Weaver and John Brunas, "but she always seemed very sad to me." Barboura Morris had an intelligent presence, as unique as the spelling of her name, and she was one of the best co-stars Miller ever had.

For Miller, the Kennedy movie was interesting, but filming it felt much like doing any of his TV gunman roles: squinting, scowling, scrambling around, and pointing a rifle. Years later, on a road trip, he took Lainie to Vasquez Rocks, the *Executive Action* location that had also provided the alien landscapes for so many episodes of *Star Trek*. Miller climbed the formations to show Lainie where he'd perched and played gunman, and there at his feet were the spent shells from his prop firearm. He put a few in his pocket, brought them down, and displayed them for Lainie, amazed to discover this unexpected bit of proof that he'd once been on that very spot before, pretending to pretend to be shooting at JFK. It was anyway more evidence than the Secret Service ever found on any rooftop or grassy knoll in Dallas.

Like Kaplan, Jon Davison had returned to his East Coast stomping grounds after *Night Call Nurses*, but he'd made a good impression on the New World brass, and before long the company's script and development maven, Frances Doel, rang Davison up and commissioned him to write a script to be called either "India Doll House" or "The Deadly Dolls of Cell 69." (The movie was never made, which Davison regarded as "one of the major blessings of my career.") Davison enlisted Joe Dante to help write it, then used half of the $500 he'd been paid on a one-way ticket back to LA so he could deliver the results to Corman personally. It happened that New World's head of publicity had recently committed suicide, and Davison was offered the position almost as soon as he walked in the door. Davison was a true believer in the Corman style, and it would not merely be his job, or merely his pleasure, but his *privilege* to help sell movies such as New World was making. Corman must have been delighted to find him. Davison was soon scheming to bring out his two movie-mad pals, Joe Dante and Allan Arkush, and find them work in this glorious New World.

Dante, a golfer's son from Morristown, New Jersey, had grown up on a diet of monster movies and just about every other genre he could lay his eyes on. He was catholic in his tastes and insatiable in his hunger to consume cinema, though he nevertheless intended to start a career not in the movies but as a comic artist. The lure of film proved too strong, however, and meeting Jon Davison, possibly an even bigger movie nut than Dante, could only have weakened the lure of anything else. Dante had also been informed by his instructors at the Philadelphia College of Art that there was no honour in a cartooning career and no point for anyone with the soul of an artist in pursuing one, so, with Davison as his producer, Dante was soon spending all his time in an editing room, splicing together seven-and-a-half hours of kitschy footage that would become a thing called *The Movie Orgy*. This entity, an epic mash-up unequalled until Christian Marclay's more disciplined *The Clock* four decades later, was screened on college campuses to audiences who were encouraged to come and go as they liked, and who, while present and basking in the endless clips of B-movie and advertising kitsch that made up *The Movie Orgy*, produced torrents of beer urine and vast drifts of what Dante vaguely remembered as "funny-smelling smoke."

Dante responded to Davison's overtures early in 1973, flying out to Hollywood and taking a job in the New World trailer department; and by October Arkush was there too. Arkush was a slightly different animal from Dante and Davison: he was aware of Corman and his work, but only through the good offices of Davison; Arkush himself had grown up on higher-brow fare. "My parents were film buffs," Arkush said. "So my father would recommend movies for me to go see. That's how I saw *Great Expectations*, the David Lean movie, and *Shane*, and stuff like that. He took me to the Apu Trilogy." But Arkush was no snob; he was, perhaps more than anything, a devoted rock 'n' roller, and he fit perfectly into Corman's cheerfully lowbrow culture factory.

He also fit very well with Davison and Dante, and received a second movie education in the course of hanging out with them. "You cannot be around those guys without watching movies," Arkush said. It was an incidental education in Millerainia too. "We would work all day on Roger's movies," Arkush recalled, "on the New World trailers and TV spots and all that, and then at night we'd screen movies. So inevitably you'd see a movie with Dick in it, and I started to get a pretty full idea of who he was." The crash course in Miller was encouraged further by the wild cheers Dante and Davison made whenever their favourite actor appeared onscreen.

Kaplan was embarking on his third movie of 1973, and his fourth in a row with a part for Miller. Although the picture was originally to have starred Ernest Borgnine, Robert Mitchum, or Lee Marvin, it ended up an Isaac Hayes vehicle; so *Truck Turner* was a natural follow-up to *The Slams*, at least to the executives' nearly antebellum way of thinking. Kaplan had proven that he could direct Black actors, as though it were some special skill on the order of lion taming or bronco busting; studio wisdom therefore dictated he immediately be given another project featuring Black performers. (To add extra star power, the film also featured none other than Morris the Cat as Truck Turner's finicky orange pet, a character clearly added because someone on the production had seen *The Long Goodbye*.)

Miller appears early in the film as a bail bondsman named Fogarty, notable both for the desperation he exudes while talking Truck into a particularly dangerous assignment, and the bright pink sports coat he wears. The jacket was Miller's own, and although *Truck Turner* was the jaunty blazer's first appearance on film, it would not be the last. Miller was fond of the jacket, and while he'd long ago become bored with wearing his own clothes in films, he was proud to show off this little beauty.

The pink sports coat served his character well, and so did Miller's natural quick Bronx clip. Kaplan, hoping for a driving pace that would match the picture's title, instructed all his actors to speak as quickly as they reasonably could. In his first scene, shot in a San Pedro courthouse, Miller took this direction to heart and dazzled his co-stars with his machine-gun diction. "That motherfucker can talk fast," said a duly impressed Hayes.

There was no room for the pink blazer in Miller's next picture, *Big Bad Mama*. This was a period piece, conceived and drafted by Corman's trusty story editor Frances Doel (who found her draft so embarrassing that she didn't own up to having written it), and then polished and finished by another writer, William Norton. Of course, it was based on the Ma Barker story, which Corman had already dramatized four years earlier in *Bloody Mama*, but replaced Barker's four sons with a couple of nubile daughters. More recently Corman had worked with a young director named Steve Carver on an Italian-shot lady-gladiator picture called *The Arena*, and Carver was now hired again to direct the new script. It was the inaugural shot at a new informal series: now that the three-girls cycle was almost at a close, gangster and car-chase movies would take over. It was counterintuitive, and seemed more a product of Corman's own nostalgia than anything going on in the broader youth culture. The cultural lens, inasmuch as it was looking back at all, was casting back only ten or fifteen years, at greased hair and drive-ins and cars with fins. With that in mind a less savvy producer might have called for monster movies and Westerns, but Corman followed his lights and made a healthy profit out of it.

With their budget of $400,000, large for a New World film, Corman and Carver put together a great cast for *Big Bad Mama*. Angie Dickinson, whose *Police Woman* series would debut later that year and prove a hit, played the role of the gun-totin' matriarch. She was by all accounts fearless about nudity and other concerns one might expect a TV star to have; except, of course, she wasn't yet a star when Corman did his negotiating. Tom Skerritt and William Shatner played the men in her life; old ringers like Royal Dano and Noble Willingham popped up here and there; and Miller was a determined but incompetent FBI man named Bonney. Once again he was part of a team, paired up with another agent played by Tom Signorelli, who had appeared in *The Trip* and *The St. Valentine's Day Massacre*.

Like the rest of the company Miller had to get up early every day and drive out from LA to the many rural locations used in the picture, but he didn't mind. He had lots of dialogue and action; got to wear snappy 1930s clothes, drive old cars, and shoot guns, in particular a slightly anachronistic .357 Magnum; spent time in the company of pretty women like Dickinson and the actresses playing her daughters. And the wrap party was a particularly fun one, incorporating the wedding of cameraman Bruce Logan to his girlfriend Kathy. Actor Royal Dano, who'd played a reverend in the picture, performed the ceremony, and everyone celebrated with champagne.

Later, some weeks after the film had wrapped, Miller got a call: Would he narrate the trailer? Rumour had it this was Joe Dante's idea, and it's not a difficult notion to accept. There wasn't much for Miller to say aside from repeating the title, listing the cast (not going deep enough to utter his own name, though), and setting the scene ("Paradise, Texas, 1932"), but it was easy work. He delivered Davison's deathless copy in a firm and resolute manner: "Prosperity was just around the corner—at the nearest bank!" Miller had looped voices before, adding chatter to crowd scenes and so forth, as he had in Robert Aldrich's *The Dirty Dozen*; and he would do a great deal of voice work later. Of course, *The Dick Miller Show* had prepared him for all this: he was no Adolph Caesar, but he was perfectly comfortable behind a microphone. "*Big Bad Mama*! Rated R!"

Another *Big Bad Mama* dividend was his appearance that year on Dickinson's show, *Police Woman*. He appeared in the fourth episode, "Seven Eleven," as a minor bad guy, and during the shoot managed to trip over a wire and break several ribs. He appeared less than a year later in another cop show, *Police Story*, which was an anthology of law-and-order stories; Miller this time was on the right side of the law. Both police stories were directed by Richard Benedict, whom a cinema-going Miller had seen trapped in a cave in the Billy Wilder picture *Ace in the Hole* twenty-five years earlier.

The first phase of the Millerenaissance was done, and Miller returned to his between-work lifestyle. He wasn't seeing his old friends as much any more—Jonathan Haze, Biff Elliott, guys like that. He had a crew, though, as he always had a crew, and saw them practically daily at Schwab's and other places.

His next role was in *Candy Stripe Nurses*, but it took all of a single day to shoot, and he detected little else on the horizon aside from (he feared) another extended dry spell. But soon enough a call came; as ever, it was from Corman, but not for an acting job this time. It was a writing gig, in fact "a rewrite," Miller said. Again, Frances Doel had written the story, or a first draft, and now it was another writer's job to apply some polish and make a shootable script out of it. "I kept the fact that [Miller] was a writer in the back of my mind," Corman said, "but I never really got around to it because I had a series of writers I was working with. I had this regular stable and there wasn't really the opportunity for someone new until this picture came up in the Philippines."

It was tremendously exciting to be offered a writing job, and Miller knew Roger reused screenwriters. "Long, long thing," is how he remembered the job, though the finished film ran only seventy-two minutes. From the beginning he knew the movie was to be shot in the Philippines by *Fly Me* director Cirio Santiago, so Miller, who'd been to Israel and Hawaii and all around the continental US but still hadn't travelled nearly as much as he wanted to or felt he ought, took care to write in a healthy good-guy part for himself, so that he would get to visit the Philippines too. As the date of departure approached, he made the necessary preparations for travel to a tropical location. "Got a thousand and one shots," he said.

TNT Jackson was a standard-issue tale of kung-fu revenge, set in Hong Kong and telling the tale of TNT, an ass-kicking soul sister out to find the motherfuckers who killed her brother. Neither the subject nor the characters were likely Dick Miller material, but he threw himself into it. He took a hand in casting: Corman "was gonna use Pam Grier, and this little girl came into the office and I said, 'Gee, she looks great! I don't know if she can act or anything, but she's a doll!'" Her name was Jeanne Bell, and she seemed to Miller an opportunity to do something unexpected. "Why do we need a big chick like Pam Grier?" he asked. "She could beat *me* up! [Bell] was a delicate little girl." Musing on subsequent action heroes with incongruously slight physiques, Miller said, "I may have started a new trend."

The antagonist in TNT *Jackson* also served initially as the love interest, and one day, while sitting in the New World offices and helping to cast that role, "this kid walked in," Miller recalled, "and he's the real McCoy!" His name was Stan Shaw, and, as with Bell, it was his physical unsuitability for the role that piqued Miller's interest. Shaw was certainly not slight, but, said Miller, "all these guys who'd been kung-fuing, were kind of actors, good-looking guys, and [Shaw] was kind of not too good-looking, but he was well-built." He was adept at embroidery, and he could kung-fu too: Miller was most impressed with his skills. It occurred to Miller that a nice guy like Shaw wouldn't often get a chance to use his fighting prowess in any real sense, and that it might be frustrating for him. "It's like being a doctor and training for surgery, and never operating," Miller figured. He turned to Shaw one day and asked, "Does it ever bother you that you know all these things and never use 'em?"

"Once a year," Shaw told him, "I go downtown wearing my old clothes and I look for trouble."

Miller approved of Shaw's approach. "He turned out to be a fine actor too."

With the principal roles so admirably filled, Miller was more excited than ever as he worked on the script. He turned it in a couple of days early. ("Everything I did was finished early," Miller boasted. "I work that way.") Corman read it, and Miller's recollection was that "when we were about two or three days away from going [to the Philippines], Roger said something about 'Now, I want this …'"

"Wait a second, it's finished," Miller told him.

"No, we got two more days," Corman said, by Miller's account.

"He didn't pay for the job, he paid for the time," Miller asserted. Corman didn't offer any specific notes Miller could remember: "He just wanted me working! It kind of got to him that it was finished and I was finished early."

But Miller felt he was done with the thing, and he didn't want to work on the script any more. There was a meeting about it in Roger's office. "I remember, he had no shoes on," Miller said. "Likes to sit around with his shoes off." But the casual attitude this implied was belied by Corman's intractability. In response a stubborn Miller began acting more or less like his character Shorty from *Rock All Night*, all pissy rebellion and pointless intransigence. Finally, Miller claimed, Corman had enough. "He got up, and I think he broke a lamp or something, and he stormed out of the office. I figured, 'Well, I blew it.'"

"No," Corman later said in a most definite tone, "that's not true. I've never done anything like that. I remember that we had discussions, but no more than normal." The legendary filmmaker thought for a moment, then offered a theory. "You know what it might have been?" he asked. "A first-time writer doesn't recognize that you go through two, three, four drafts. A first-time writer assumes, 'I've written it. That's the first draft, that's it.' A veteran writer knows that you're going to be revising and revising and revising, and I think it was simply that it was [Dick's] first script, and he didn't recognize that."

Maybe Corman broke a lamp and maybe he didn't, but he was evidently peeved enough at Miller to hire another writer to not only rewrite Miller's rewrite, but write Miller's character right out. (Author Beverly Gray reported that Corman was additionally put out by Miller's "padding his own screen role.") In the end Miller suffered his inoculations for nothing: he was not going to the Philippines.

Corman, who by temperament elects to forget unpleasantness after the fact, was pleased enough at the results. "I thought it was a good script," he said. "The picture turned out well." It was released in January 1975, and, reported the producer, "it was a success. Not a great success, but it was a solid success. So for me it was a successful enterprise." He also liked the catch line Jon Davison came up with: "TNT Jackson, she'll put ya in traction!" Corman, sitting in his book- and poster-filled office, called out the line and smiled broadly at the memory.

Miller must have been disappointed, but later displayed no residual animus. "That's the only time Roger ever blew up," he said. "He called me later that night and apologized for his attitude. He didn't have anything to apologize for. It was just one of those things."

It was a rough experience, but Miller was not quite done with writing yet. Spending time on the boat he and Lainie shared with Eugene inspired one idea in particular. He conceived of a character not unlike his brother, "a middle-aged guy who's a coroner and lives on a boat." The character was a hard-headed lone wolf and, despite being "not too good-lookin'," was also something of a swinger. ('A boat with a bed in it goes a long mile with the ladies in 1970s California' was probably the operative theory.) When mysteries of any kind came through his medical examiner's office, the coroner became a crime solver, defying his superiors and running down the culprits, no matter where the trail led.

From this concept Miller wrote a detailed outline, then submitted it to an agency he'd found. He was proud of his effort; it was different from anything else he was seeing in the movies or on television. "There weren't any heroes like that," he said, "who were just kind of bumming it, living on boats and things like that." Once it was in the hands of these dubious agents, he appears to have completely forgotten about it.

But whether it went up into the ether, atomized there, and sprinkled down onto television producer Glen A. Larson's head, or whether it made its way to Larson by some more direct and less ethical means, we will never know. Larson was, after all, known to Harlan Ellison as "Glen A. Larceny" for his habit of pilfering TV show ideas from hit movies, and had once been slugged by Miller's softball pal James Garner for stealing plots from *The Rockford Files*. The actual stickiness of the late Larson's fingers will probably always be in dispute, but in the fall of 1976 a television show called *Quincy* M.E., apparently created and produced by Larson and Lou Shaw, appeared, sporting a concept closely hewing to Miller's. *Quincy* started as a progression of stand-alone TV dramas, part of a series called Mystery Movies on NBC; *McCloud* was one of the other programs that existed beneath the Mystery Movie umbrella and was rotated around with other detective shows. But it proved a genuine hit and before too long became its own distinct show. When Miller got wind of the program, he tried to look up his old agency, but naturally they "had closed their office and disappeared," Miller said. He let it go from there, not believing he had enough evidence to sway the Writers Guild of America this time. Still, he was angry. "It was just such an obvious theft," he said, "because it was so unrelated to what was going down at the time. They took all the little things from it." Not the character's handle, though; whatever Miller had called him, it wasn't "Quincy." "Naw, I didn't give him some funny little name," he sneered.

On top of his experiences with the Jerry Lewis picture and *TNT Jackson*, this was too much. *Quincy* was the last spasm of Miller's professional writing career. "I gave away so many stories," he said. "It sounds funny, but I was busy doing these things, and the idea would occur to me and I'd pass it on to someone else and forget about it." But *Quincy* was the kick in the head that made Dick cry *fuck this*. "I wrote the outline, got everything down, and I got bombed," he said. "So I just figured, what the hell."

16 He had to be a fan

One day in the mid-1970s Miller said, "I was looking at myself. I was thinking, Jesus Christ, I've put on forty pounds! And I'm going to play night watchmen and bartenders. And I figured, okay, that's it." Miller was creeping toward 50 and indeed getting a little tubby; the extra weight sat poorly on his slight frame and gave him a stocky, fireplug look. More than ever before, he felt that he would never be any kind of movie star, and would be very lucky even to continue at the barely sustenance-level living he was managing now. Thank God for Lainie's hospital work.

Miller, the lifelong agnostic, was not literally thanking God, but in his ample spare time he was nevertheless toying around with religion a bit, just for fun. "I joined the Universal Life Church," he said. "Paid twenty dollars, anyone can join up. I'm a minister. I married neighbours." Ministering for someone else's religion was not enough for a free-spirited individualist like Miller, of course, and so, inspired by EST and the other self-actualization movements of the Me Decade, he created IAM: the Institute of Agnostic Meditation. (There was another awareness-training movement with those initials, founded by Pat Grove in 1969 and standing for Individual Achievement and Mastery, but of this Miller neither knew nor would have cared.) Miller's organization had a membership of one, and he practised his IAM devotions almost every weekend when he and Lainie went sailing.

By the last months of 1974 Miller was on the set of Steve Carver's next picture, *Capone*, another verisimilitudinous gangster script by former journalist Howard Browne, who'd written *The St. Valentine's Day Massacre*. The cast was a solid group of old reliables and up-and-comers, including Ben Gazzara, Harry Guardino, and a young Sylvester Stallone. As in his previous Carver film, *Big Bad Mama*, Miller played a cop, but a crooked one this time, shakedown artist Joe Pryor, who tries to strong-arm Gazzara's chipmunk-cheeked Al Capone for five grand. Capone doesn't take kindly to this, and as Pryor is trying to cuff the gangster boss, a moll played by Susan Blakely bashes him over the head with a bottle. (Miller falls down below the frame, but takes care that his legs pop comically back up into it again.) Pryor eventually manages to arrest the bottle-swinging neo-flapper and get his five large, but along with it comes a veiled threat from Capone and the screen fades to red over Pryor's "maybe this wasn't such a good idea after all" expression.

Carver, who liked hiring older, storied actors as much as Joe Dante or anyone else ever would, was delighted to be directing Miller again. Carver was especially a fan of Miller's comedy stylings, and seemed almost to lament that *Capone* was too grim to allow them. But Miller delivered some comedy anyway, like that vaudeville fall and some Stooge-like mugging when he later comes to. "I would play gangsters in movies like *Naked Paradise*, and get laughs," Miller told *Fangoria*. "I always maintain that people have these facets about them anyway. I think when playing tough guys or killers, humor creeps into it, because they're people from the streets and that's how they survive."

At other moments in the picture he's deadly serious: the role offered him several opportunities to set his jaw in anger, a reliable, effectively intimidating Miller trick. Whether it was comedy or drama didn't matter; in either genre, asserted Carver, "he's definitely Dick Miller." But he was just as definitely greedy, corrupt Joe Pryor, and this uncanny concrescence is a critical part of Miller's appeal both to filmmakers and fans.

He was a chauvinist high school football coach in *Summer School Teachers*, a belated entry in Corman's three-girls cycle shot early in 1975 by director Barbara Peeters and released in June. The three girls in this instance were played by Candace Rialson, Pat Anderson, and Rhonda Leigh Hopkins, and it was Rialson, who had previously appeared in *Candy Stripe Nurses* and so knew the drill, whose story brought her into conflict with Miller. Her character, Miss Conklin, is determined to start a girl's football team at the school, a proposal Miller vehemently opposes. Miller is particularly convincing in this role, and one might be forgiven for assuming he shared his character's attitudes, but he did not. He was, in fact, a fairly progressive guy, happy to househusband when the occasion demanded it, pleased to cook when the opportunity arose. "I'm a good cook," he said proudly. Conversely, women taking on traditionally masculine jobs troubled him not a whit. *Summer School Teachers* was Miller's first time being directed by a woman, at least on a movie set; and while this might have bothered some mid-'70s man's man somewhere, it didn't bother him. He was not so much a progressive thinker as a cheerfully broad-minded one.

Sometime after *Capone* came yet another cop role, a thoroughly comic bit this time, in a troubled Gene Corman production called *Darktown Strutters*. It was directed by sixty-year-old William Witney, on the face of it an unlikely candidate to make a surreal musical spoof of the Blaxploitation genre. Witney had directed Miller a decade before in an episode of *The Virginian* and in *The Girls on the Beach*, and *Darktown Strutters*, which had been written in three days by George Armitage and was originally to have been directed by him too, was decidedly outside Witney's wheelhouse.

Miller played yet another incompetent policeman, Officer Hugo, and this time was part of a Keystone Kops gaggle of truncheon-swinging idiots, including one played by 6'4" Milt Kogan. (Height discrepancies must have tickled Witney's funny bone: in *The Girls on the Beach*, Miller's partner had been towering Leo Gordon.) The racist, imbecilic Alert Squad drives around in a cop car adorned with a red bubble light the size of the Cinerama dome on top, repeatedly failing to catch any criminals, though at one point Miller handcuffs a dog. The central characters are motorcycle mamas who drive customized machines and sport brightly coloured jumpsuits adorned with spikes, sunbursts, and three-foot feathers. The picture also features a maniacal Colonel Sanders lookalike, bikers in Klan robes, and a Ghetto Alert Map. And yet the picture achieved some degree of realism one day while Witney was shooting a scene in which a bank robbery took place in the background. A woman named Erlina Ardoin was driving by the corner of Fourth Street and Washington in downtown LA when pink-pimp-suit-wearing hooligans burst out the doors of a bank, brandishing guns and a bazooka issuing rose-coloured smoke. Mrs. Ardoin did the sensible thing and ducked, but failed to take the even more sensible precaution of braking first. Her vehicle ploughed into three other parked cars and put nine people in the hospital. Lawsuits flew, the lax attentions of the police who were supposed to be stopping traffic for the shot were cited, and it was the city of Los Angeles, not Gene Corman's production company, that eventually took the blame and paid out the compensation.

But when the movie was finished, no one would buy it, because it was so terrible. Gene turned to his brother, and *Darktown Strutters* became a New World Pictures release. Allan Arkush cut a trailer for it, the publicity department did all they could to sell the Blaxploitation and musical elements over the nutzoid comedy, and when it was released in August 1975, it tanked. It was released again a year and a half later under the meaninglessly disco-fied title *Get Down and Boogie*, and flopped hard again. To any Dick Miller fans who may have stumbled across this misbegotten artifact, it proved only that the actor was a lot funnier when he wasn't asked to try so hard.

It was only a few days' work, like all the stuff Miller was doing these days, and when he returned to his klatches at Schwab's, or the regular breakfast group he met with almost daily—actors such as Robert Forster, Harry Northup, and Paul Peterson were within these orbits—everyone complained bitterly of the rejection, the humiliation, the never-ending uncertainty of the business. They commiserated daily, but also tried to help each other when they could: Miller and another actor friend signed a form sponsoring Northup for membership in the actors' branch of the Academy of Motion Picture Arts and Sciences, to which a grateful Northup was accepted in 1976.

Miller's despair at his aging, thickening body came as close to a crisis point as it ever would when he was working on his next picture, Jonathan Kaplan's trucker drama *White Line Fever*. "But then," he said, "I lost weight, and I got a little tougher, and things started happening again. By then it was kinda late. But it was good, I was playing character parts, getting a chance to do something."

White Line Fever had been optioned by Columbia Pictures because, Kaplan claimed, someone there had noticed that *Truck Turner* was getting decent box office, and assumed Kaplan was a natural at truck pictures. *Fever* was as much a drama as it was an action picture (Kaplan himself insisted it was a Western, and there he had a point), with a trucker played by Jan-Michael Vincent finding little more than trouble as he embarks on a life astride eighteen wheels and catches the titular ailment, while his wife, played by Kay Lenz, is put through the wringer to a considerably worse degree. In a very pleasant change Miller played an unequivocal good guy, a trucker who, before the prodigal Jan-Michael's return, had been playing the game with the corporate mobsters who were trying to strong-arm the independent truckers, but who now has finally had enough, and helps the hero as best he can. Miller's character was called Birdie, but his full name was R. "Birdie" Corman, a nice little tribute to the old boss. Birdie displays no identifiably Corman-like behaviour, but is warm and avuncular and wears a checkered squirrel-hunting jacket throughout. The movie was shot in Utah and Phoenix, Arizona.

Over at the real Roger Corman's offices, there was mild sedition afoot. Joe Dante and Allan Arkush were tired of the trailer department, ready to bust out and actually make something original themselves. (Well, sort of original.) Jon Davison, in league with his pals, took Corman out to lunch one day and made him a bet: that Davison, Arkush, and Dante could make the cheapest film yet produced at New World Pictures. Corman was reluctant to allow Arkush and Dante to become distracted from their promotional work; they were in the middle of cutting a trailer for Truffaut's *The Story of Adele H*. Finally, perhaps detecting not just a potential for profit but an anecdote he'd be able to drop into conversations and interviews for years to come, Corman found himself unable to resist, and ponied up something close to $60,000 for the picture. (Dante was convinced that Corman never expected any profit; that he was allowing them to make the movie as an act of charity, and, more than that, to just get them off his back.)

The triad's strategy for making a feature film so cheaply was simple: use as much existing footage from previous New World pictures as possible. Arkush and Dante knew what was available; they had been literally wading in the footage for years. Exploding helicopters, screaming Filipino soldiers, cars flipping over or crashing through barriers, all of it was grist for the mill. The structure within which this random footage would be housed was something close to the three-girl movies of New World's recent past, only it would not be nurses, teachers, or stewardesses this time, but starlets, working for a low-budget B-movie company called Miracle Pictures. The groaners wrote themselves: "If it's a good picture, it's a Miracle!"

In fact, the groaners, and such plot as there was, didn't write themselves, but were cobbled together by the brain trust of Dante, Arkush, Davison, and Dan Opatoshu, then written down by Opatoshu under the Fitzgerald-inspired pen name Patrick Hobby. (Some gags were taken from an early short treatment written by Chuck Griffith, titled "Free Popcorn.") Opatoshu appears to have been highly sympatico with the sensibilities of his three co-conspirators, but evidently lacked the urge to become a producer or director himself. He was a writer, and the grandson of a well-known Yiddish novelist, Yosef Opatoshu. He appreciated a Miller performance as much as anyone, and, specifically for the actor, crafted the part of a lowbrow talent agent called, inevitably it seems now, Walter Paisley. "It was a good name for an agent," Joe Dante said.

It also simplified the casting process. "I think it went something like, 'We're writing a character, we're gonna call him Walter Paisley after someone Dick's played, and Dick is gonna play it,'" Arkush said, laughing. "That was the extent of the casting. That was that."

In the meantime Miller was working for Jonathan Demme on a New World production called *Crazy Mama*, the last of the unofficial *Mama* series, though for some reason Corman originally wanted to call it *Crazy Ladies*. It was another period gangster picture, but updated to the '50s, and the gang matriarch was played by Cloris Leachman. Miller played a cop, of course, and not just an angry goofball this time, but an easily panicked officer whose mistakes have real consequences. Near the picture's climax, in a conflict with the most elderly of the gang members, Miller is compelled to fire his gun, blasting the old lady in the chest. Demme included a shot of Miller "recoiling in horror at what he has done," as Demme described it. It was a piece of silent-film acting that transcended and diffused any hamminess simply by having the look of truth, an outrageous theatrical gesture translated by Miller into genuine human behaviour. But Miller's character gets his in return: though he'd been shot many times in past pictures, *Crazy Mama* was the first time Miller experienced the joy of squibs and bursting blood capsules. The first attempt was a bust, however. "They were originally going to squib my forehead and shoot me in the head," Miller told *Fangoria* magazine. "It was a bad make-up job, so they had to pass on that. They squibbed me in the front instead and blood came pouring out." Miller enjoyed the experience and milked it for all he was worth. "I loved it so much, it took me about two whole minutes to die. I fell to my knees, I crawled on my knees a little—I did a James Cagney going up the church steps. And Jonathan Demme is yelling, 'Die already! Die already!'" An amused Harry Northup remembered that "on the second take, Demme had him die a little quicker."

Demme was pleased to have Dick on the show despite this occasional tendency towards ham, considering him "a first-rate actor who makes any scene he's in better." On the *Crazy Mama* DVD commentary track, Demme made the same joke every director makes on their DVD commentary tracks: "It was a New World picture, so of course we *had* to have Dick Miller."

Miller's ubiquity in New World productions was a little strange even to him, and seems to have been almost equally the work of Jon Davison and Julie Corman. Davison was a super-fan intoxicated with the idea that he was in a position to hire his heroes, or anyway suggest that they be hired, while for Julie Corman it seemed mainly to have been a matter of tradition. Miller liked the work, of course, but wasn't so pleased when Julie Corman "used an expression which I didn't like at the time," he complained in a 2009 interview with *Filmfax* magazine. "She said, 'Oh, we gotta give Dick a part for this movie—he's our mascot.'" Miller laughed. "A fuckin' mascot!"

Others appreciated his totemic value too. He made a small, unbilled appearance as a casino piano player in George Armitage's action extravaganza *Vigilante Force*, a Gene Corman production featuring Kris Kristofferson and Miller's *White Line Fever* co-star Jan-Michael Vincent. The picture was shot in the summer of 1975, but wasn't released until the following September, and Miller's appearance in the film—his piano playing accompanies the warbling of Bernadette Peters—seemed to have no better reason than to get him in there somewhere. (This was maybe the first but certainly not the last such role for Miller.) Armitage, like Roger Corman and John Landis, had started his movie career in the mail room at 20th Century Fox, though he quickly made his way up the ladder and became an associate producer on the TV show *Peyton Place*. Corman was on the lot there shooting *The St. Valentine's Day Massacre*, and when Armitage saw how shoddily Corman was being treated by the other filmmakers and even TV people at the studio, how they "snobbed" him because he made B pictures, he made a point of befriending the beleaguered director. This led to a gig writing *Gas-s-s-s!*, one of Corman's last pictures as a director, then to a job directing *Private Duty Nurses*, and further jobs with both Corman brothers. But after a while, directing work seemed to elude Armitage, until, with a little help from fellow Corman alumnus Jonathan Demme, he enjoyed a series of small comebacks, directing pictures like *Miami Blues* and *Grosse Pointe Blank* in the '90s and early 2000s.

Since moving away from the beach back in 1971 and closer to the places Dick had to be to find work, the Millers had settled in a Beverly Hills apartment, and they were there still when one day Miller read a script called "The Starlets." He was amazed to see the name Walter Paisley in there, and more pleasantly surprised still to see how big the role was compared with most of his recent work.

And the directors seemed like nice young guys, enthusiastic, funny, eager to do a good job. Miller was flattered, and a little baffled, by their encyclopedic knowledge of his career and their love of his movies, and he also liked them personally. He still wondered about the Paisley name, though. "Is it supposed to be the same guy?" he asked. No, he was told, just a tribute.

Dante, for whom every Miller cameo was like a hit of some exotic drug, was finally self-medicating. He was pleased and relieved to find that the actor he admired so much was, in fact, a nice guy, but the two didn't become bosom chums right off the hop. "Usually when you make movies, you grow closer to people the more movies you make together," Dante said. "There's always a little bit of 'I don't know you' on the first couple of pictures. But we became very friendly. He and I just hit it off. I really liked him, and he liked me."

Indeed, at Miller's house the temperature seemed to warm a few degrees when Dante's name came up. "Joe is like a son," Lainie Miller said. "We really think of him as family. Anytime Dick has been ill, and he's had some doozies in the health department, Joe is always there. Comes to the hospital, calls every day. He really is a sweetheart."

Miller liked Arkush too. "Allan is just a nice guy," he said. "He's a big, tall lanky, nice guy. A mensch." Camaraderie abounded, so it was with a light heart that Miller reported to work on the first day of shooting, in October 1975, at the Hollywood Gay & Lesbian Center on Highland Avenue, which Dante remembered as the only place they could afford to shoot. The company did a few scenes out on the street, then moved indoors. One small room was plastered with posters, lobby cards, stills, and other B-movie detritus, and became the office of Miller's jolly, lowbrow agent character. When Miller arrived, a glittering dollar-sign brooch was pinned to his lapel and a huge snake draped across his shoulders. ("He was very good with the snake," Dante recalled.) The star of the picture, Candace Rialson, assumed her role as the naïve, would-be starlet fresh off the bus from Ohio. Dante, who was directing the dialogue scenes while Arkush took care of the stuff that didn't require sync sound, was starry-eyed at the prospect of directing Miller. "Dick was the first really professional actor I ever worked with," Dante said. "I mean, all the people in the movie were professional, but he was the one that I knew from the old days." Dante rehearsed his actors and called for action, neophyte cinematographer Jamie Anderson pressed the button on the camera, and the Dante/Miller partnership officially began.

At some point "The Starlets" became *Hollywood Boulevard*. (Corman wanted it to call it *Hollywood Hookers*, but the abject pleading of the two directors, who wanted to retain some modicum of class, or the illusion of it, eventually swayed him from this position.) As a satire of the low-budget movie racket made by employees of New World Pictures, it was, of course, specifically a satire of New World Pictures and of Roger Corman. Paul Bartel, who had directed *Death Race 2000* for Corman, was enlisted to play a fussy, pompous director named Erich Von Leppe (named for Karloff's character in *The Terror*), also apparently the boss of Miracle Pictures. Thus Bartel played Corman's two sides, artist and money man, though both sides were exaggerated, garnished with enough pretension and cluelessness to make the character funny, and to give it sufficient distance from Corman that Bartel, Dante, and Arkush could claim it wasn't meant to be him at all.

Shooting days on the little production were long and onerous, as they must be on any ten-day show. The cast and crew, underfed and underpaid, took to calling it "Day for Nothing," a riff on the great Francois Truffaut movie about moviemaking, *Day for Night*. Special effects were provided by Roger George, a veteran whose specialty was fireballs; Dante and Arkush were a little taken aback to see that their explosives expert had burn scars all over his hands, and soon learned that wherever Roger George told you to stand while he was setting off his mushroom clouds, stand 50 feet further back. With little time to plan or prepare, the pair was grateful for the directors in their cast, particularly Paul Bartel, who offered up mentor-like advice between shots. Jonathan Kaplan was around too, playing a clumsy crew member and discreetly reminding Dante to get a few close-ups and cutaways so he'd be able to put it all together later; and Charles Griffith turned up to play an ex-movie star pool cleaner named Mark Dentine, "kidding Mark Hanna's big white teeth," Griffith said. Chuck and his wife were frequently kind to Dante and Arkush, who had been making very little money working in Corman's trailer department, and less still now that they were directors. "They fed us when no one else would," Dante said.

Miller worked on the picture for a couple of days, doing scenes in four or five different locations. Several scenes took place in the Gay & Lesbian Center, with Dick in different costumes but always with the diamond-encrusted dollar-sign brooch; in a cinema in North Hollywood (playing the role of the Miracle Pictures screening room); at the Gilmore Drive-in on Third Street, where the company beavered away in the back rows as real audiences further up enjoyed the Canadian film *Black Christmas*; and, for a concluding party scene, the penthouse roof of the New World headquarters on Sunset. The party guests included Miller's old acquaintance Forrest Ackerman, future Miller director Lewis Teague, Dante himself playing a waiter, and Robby the Robot, with whom Miller holds a lively conversation. In fact, Miller, wearing his pink jacket and dollar-sign insignia, gets the last words in the picture, pitching Robby the Rhett Butler part in the Miracle Pictures remake of *Gone With The Wind*; this gave him the chance to do a quick impersonation of his old buddy Clark Gable. When it was all said and done, *Hollywood Boulevard* came in at $54,039.43, and Davison won his bet.

Miller had a great time on the show. He was directed mostly by Dante, who had either intuitively sussed out that, with Miller, the best direction was no direction, or else was simply too busy trying to keep it all together to provide any direction at all. "It just seemed like he was never in my hair, he was never bothering me," Miller said. "It was a fun picture, and [Dante's] a fun guy, and I loved it." Altogether the movie functioned as a comic but not inaccurate portrait of life at New World Pictures, and Miller was tickled to be a part of it. Nostalgia was woven into the dialogue, as when Paisley advises Rialson's Candy Wednesday to get in with the Miracle Pictures people, because "they make a picture a week! You do good, you're workin' steady!" It was an opportunity for some good-natured venting too: when Paisley, Candy, and a screenwriter character played by Jeffrey Kramer attend the drive-in to watch Candy's first Miracle Pictures opus, *Machete Maidens of Mora-Tau*, they must first sit through the opening feature, *The Terror*, here renamed *Zombie in the Attic*. For Miller, it was a chance to poke some fun at the movie's earlier drive-in appearance, in *Targets*, and to point out his own performance. "Isn't that kid terrific?" Paisley asks. One review referred to this as "a spooky moment" during which Miller was forced to "reflect on the fortunes which have kept him on the fringe while co-star Jack Nicholson graduated to better things." Admitting that he "used to be an actor," Paisley is asked why he gave it up. "I had a lousy agent," he says. "Walter, shit, you coulda been somebody," Candy Wednesday says, and Miller could not at that moment resist doing his Brando impersonation, raising his palms and mumbling through a broad smile, "I coulda been a contender!"

And then, to top it all off, in the opening sequence Dante and Arkush put his credit (that is, the card he shared with Richard Doran and Tara Strohmeier) over a shot of Schwab's Pharmacy. That was it: Miller was sold on these guys. It would be another few years before Dante and Arkush would each make their first solo projects, but when the time came and he was invited to be in them, Miller had a ready answer: "I'd be delighted!"

Dante and Arkush and Kaplan and Davison were not the only filmmakers to come west, work for Corman, and want to cast Miller because they remembered him from their youth. Martin Scorsese had made his Corman picture in 1972, *Boxcar Bertha*, and Miller, somewhat mysteriously, had not been in the film. (Of course, he couldn't be in everything, but there are certain New World films—*Bertha*, *Death Race 2000*, *Saturday the 14th*—from which his exclusion seems egregious. This general tradition extends back to Allied Artists productions like *Attack of the Crab Monsters*.) Scorsese now wanted to make up for it, perhaps, and called Miller in to talk about taking a role in his upcoming big-budget period musical, *New York, New York*, to be shot entirely in Los Angeles.

Scorsese was hotter than blazes now, with a Palme D'Or and many other awards and nominations under his belt; *Taxi Driver*, released in February, had won some money and much acclaim; and United Artists was willing to gamble something north of ten million dollars on this new picture, a large-scale homage to the old Hollywood musicals, even with its unfinished script and a director who'd newly discovered the ephemeral pleasures of cocaine. On hearing that he was being considered for the part of a New York club owner, Miller went in to his meeting with Scorsese dressed in "this horrible brown and white checked jacket—they called it a horse blanket, but a horse wouldn't be caught dead in it—a dark shirt, a white tie." The outfit was meant to evoke the bad taste of the typical New York club owner as Miller remembered them, but, Miller said, "it turned out [Scorsese] wanted something much more realistic." Robert De Niro, the picture's lead, was there, and Scorsese, who, after *Mean Streets*, had briefly been crowned "The King of Improv," asked the two actors to ad-lib. "So we kidded around for a few minutes," Miller said, "and after a while I asked Scorsese, 'You sure you don't want me to read or something?' And he said, 'Hell, you had the part when you came in. I've been a fan of yours since I was fourteen years old.'" Miller left the interview feeling flattered, but old.

Before *New York, New York* went into production, Miller had another couple of Corman jobs to do. *Moving Violation* was another rural car-crash picture, in a contemporary setting this time, featuring a pair of youngsters who witness a corrupt sheriff murder his blackmailing deputy on the grounds of a mansion owned by equally corrupt millionaire Will Geer. The young couple, played by Kay Lenz (with whom Miller had worked on *White Line Fever*) and a pre-grizzled Stephen McHattie, spend the rest of the picture on the run, a series of crooked cops and hired killers on their trail. Miller played one of the latter, a hard-bitten character named Mack who tries to run the couple off the road but loses control himself, hurtles down a slope, and crashes his AMC Hornet through a haystack, an outhouse, some laundry, and a hillbilly shack. He recovers, catches up to his quarry again, makes another attempt to run them down, and this time crashes through a different car, sets off a skin-searing Roger George explosion, and ends up in the water, thumping the roof of his wrecked car in defeat and frustration. It was a tiny part, and half of it enacted by a stunt man, but after *Executive Action* it marked the second time Miller played a killer working for Grandpa Walton.

Meanwhile, *Hollywood Boulevard* had opened and done very little business, possibly because it was not called *Hollywood Hookers*, and maybe also because, according to Jon Davison, a truck carrying twenty-five prints of the picture was hijacked as it was driving between Jacksonville and Tampa, Florida. Really it was because the New World publicity department never figured out how to market the picture, despite having made it themselves; they finally resorted to plastering the poster with fake quotes from Corman ("The greatest ten-day picture of the decade!") and Coppola ("I directed part of this picture, but they re-cut and ruined it"), and an especially perplexing one from Scorsese ("I haven't clapped so much since basic training films"). In *Cinefantastique* magazine the film was heralded, right in the review's headline, as "A belated but much-deserved tribute to Dick Miller." This somehow failed to help it at the box office. But on a $60,000 budget it could hardly help but make some profit, and Corman was well satisfied with his employees' accomplishment. Dante and Arkush dared to dream that they'd be allowed to make more movies one day in the future, if only so they could have more Dick Miller performances to enjoy.

Spring passed and it was the summer of '76, the big American bicentennial year, so manufacturers of bunting were kept busy. So was Miller. The *New York, New York* shoot began in June; in July came Paul Bartel's *Cannonball*, in which Miller would play a substantial role; and Jonathan Kaplan, who had been shooting his ill-fated *Mr. Billion* in Italy during that time, brought the production to the States in August.

Cannonball was New World's take on the underground cross-country auto race that had been an annual event for several years at that time; the same story was told that very same summer in a more polished picture called *The Gumball Rally*, and would be told again in the *Cannonball Run* films and a late-'80s laggard called *Speed Zone*. As for *Cannonball*, exigencies of budget ensured that it was a race in which very few chose to compete: evidently the $100,000 purse offered in the picture was insufficient to bring out a real crowd. So the competitors include a young couple played by Robert Carradine and Belinda Balaski (it was Balaski's first time co-starring with Miller, but not her last); a self-assured German racer played by James Keach; a van full of women with Mary Woronov at the wheel; Bill McKinney and Gerrit Graham as, respectively, a nasty redneck and a gormless country singer; a two-timing schlub who simply loads his Chevy Blazer onto a plane and flies cross-country; and, the hero of the piece, David Carradine as superstar driver Coy "Cannonball" Buckner.

"*Cannonball* was nice," Miller recalled, this being his recollection of almost any picture in which he had decent screen time, received a reasonable paycheque, and got acceptable billing. *Cannonball* had more to offer Miller, though, and he to it: Miller's character, Bennie, the Carradine character's shady older brother, was a relatively complex part with a varied lot of business. Bennie is friendly and even loving, though not entirely forthright, with his little brother; frightened and desperate in his dealings with Lester, a musically inclined mobster played by Bartel himself; nervously murderous when he sets a speed-controlled bomb in the car of Keach's flamboyant German racer, whom Miller has sussed as Coy's strongest competition; and, finally, as Lester and his henchmen are moving in for the kill at the picture's end, grim and resigned, and reaching for some belated shred of nobility. Miller's oddest scene in the picture comes when Lester's henchmen brutally beat him while the boss sits at his piano and serenades poor Bennie with quasi-Cole Porter tunes of his own amateur composition.

Bartel, who never cared much for crashing cars, wanted to keep the set interesting for himself, and so he made sure the picture was lousy with directors, more so even than *Hollywood Boulevard*. Bartel called in the favour he was owed for playing Eric Von Leppe, and cast Dante and Arkush as a pair of nerdy gearheads. Jonathan Kaplan appeared as a gabby gas station attendant, proving himself better at the wordless slapstick of *Hollywood Boulevard* than at convincingly delivering dialogue. Roger Corman himself played the role of the Los Angeles County DA, a Captain Buzzkill type intent on shutting down the race; and a strange, autonomous little scene has a pair of mobsters played by Martin Scorsese and Sylvester Stallone visiting Bartel and sucking on some Kentucky Fried Chicken as they discuss the waning fortunes of Coy and Bennie. Scorsese was deep into production on *New York, New York*, so how or why he could take the time to make this cameo is perplexing; Stallone, on the other hand, was hanging fire until December, when the release of *Rocky* would make him a star.

Miller's scenes were mainly with Carradine or Bartel, or another future filmmaker, John Herzfeld, who played Bennie's accomplice, Sharpe. (Herzfeld would become a director in 1980 with the After-School Special *Stoned*, featuring Scott Baio as the boy who took one toke and nearly ruined his life.) But it was Carradine who made the biggest impression. He was "a weird guy," Miller told an interviewer. "He ad-libs a lot. He tries things on the spur of the moment and you go along with it, and some of them just turn out wonderfully." Miller was happy for the opportunity to hone his improvisatory skills; he was quick-witted and wordy in the best New York tradition, but had spent most of his working life just saying the words on the page. He rose to the occasion, and the result was one of Miller's more naturalistic performances. There was really no better project to warm him up for Scorsese.

Cannonball was one of Corman's bigger productions, but it was over quickly, because they all were, and then it was on to *New York, New York* for Miller. It was wonderful to go to work on a big studio lot, marvellous to walk on to those big sets, to see the huge, crackerjack crew at work. In the middle of it all was a sort of Tasmanian Devil of direction, Scorsese, jumping around, wired and frantic. Miller remembered Scorsese as "really a marvelous guy. Nice, nervous little guy, talks quickly on the set, just the way he does in interviews." Scorsese was a Corman kid made good, just like Jack, and there was something comforting in that commonality, here in the middle of all this big-budget chaos. It made an impression. Later, when the Millers began a recreational program of ballroom dancing, the movie was never far from Dick's mind. "I hear that song every night!" he said, and with flourishing hand sang "Dah-dah-da-dah-dah," the opening notes of the Kander and Ebb tune.

It was the biggest film he'd ever had any significant part in, and here he was, doing a scene that was just he and Liza Minnelli and Robert De Niro, and a huge crew moving at a pace that seemed glacial to Miller. But the fundamentals were no different as far as Miller was concerned. "I don't care if you're working on a $100,000 picture or one for $20 million," he said. "You sit around and wait. You shoot for twenty seconds and then you sit around and wait some more. It's a long, boring process, but you live for those twenty seconds of shooting time."

Miller's club owner listens to De Niro's sax player character blow for a minute, then complains the horn is too loud for his hangover. De Niro overreacts to some advice from Minnelli, then has a clearly improvised exchange with Miller, who gives as good as he gets. Miller's character never even stands up from his chair, yet manages to project the attitude of perpetual incipient violence so common to Scorsese films. At the same time, as he tries to explain the appeal of Maurice Chevalier to an uncomprehending De Niro, Miller provides a weary resignation that's both touching and funny; and when he barks, "Legs! Show me your legs!" at Minnelli as she dances and sings for him, we're reminded that he's a boorish nightclub owner at heart, though at times almost kindly. It's a performance that hits a lot of bases in a short time: a Miller trademark in serious development since *Night Call Nurses*, his first film for Scorsese's ex-student, Jonathan Kaplan. It might be said he was transitioning from One Take Miller into Three Base Miller, able to move through states of being like colours in a psychedelic wheel, and, if so, the Scorsese picture was an important station on the way. Later, when doing the publicity rounds for the picture, Scorsese would show the Miller scene on talk shows, and would remark not just on his two stars, but on Miller too, whom he referred to as "a star in the 1950s."

Reports from the set of *New York, New York* described a massive, spangled enterprise coming increasingly unmoored as the weeks passed: a kaleidoscope of ego, infidelity, heroic drug taking, and looming disaster. Miller's recollection of the production was simply that he met some nice people on it: De Niro, Minnelli, and Scorsese; and that the result was "a good picture." This is the perspective, and the bane, of the day player or the guest star on a larger film: the dramatic arc of the film shoot, the interplay between the people, the romances and the feuds, the inside jokes, the sustained intensity of the superheated group dynamic, are denied them. They hear the gossip and are welcomed into the fold, but they're nonetheless always the outsiders. There are familiar faces, friends even, on almost every shoot, but the divide is always there. If the shoot is fun, the daily worker is almost an interloper; if hellish, he's an undeserving early parolee of whom everyone else is envious. At the same time, lamented Miller, "you have to establish a relationship with the characters in one day." The day player often has to do extra work to fit in to the picture, to figure out the tone and how he fits in; to hint at what is often meant to be a long-standing relationship between characters with someone he's just met. In the end the effort involved for any serious actor is almost inversely proportionate to the amount of time spent on set.

But on a large, lumbering, troubled production like *New York, New York*, most of that worked in Miller's favour. He could breeze in and do his thing, untroubled by interpersonal politics or the sense of looming crisis felt by those who were on for the duration, and come out of it with nothing but fond memories of the sweet, talented people he'd met on the show. He liked them enough, in fact, that he tried following Scorsese and Minnelli to their next gig, a stage show called *The Act*, which Scorsese called "almost an extension of *New York, New York*." "I auditioned for it," Miller said, "and I don't know. Whatever it was, they didn't like me." He amended this quickly: "They didn't want me, let's put it that way. Everybody likes me."

It was just as well: *The Act* ran on Broadway for almost a year, but it was a troubled show, plagued by the erratic behaviour and frequent absences of its star. With irritating headaches like that, and the notion of spending so much time away from Lainie and Barbara on a crime-plagued Broadway he'd hardly have recognized from the Good Old Days, Miller wouldn't have enjoyed himself very much.

Miller's busy summer continued in August with another troubled production, Jonathan Kaplan's *Mr. Billion*. Kaplan called the picture his "biggest failure," and its poor critical reception, utter lack of box office, and near-complete disappearance from the cultural landscape all bear this out. The concept behind the picture, which Kaplan credited to super-producer Dino De Laurentiis, was introducing Italian comedy-action superstar Terence Hill (born Mario Girotti) to American audiences; the crippling flaw in this plan was not including Hill's frequent screen partner, Bud Spencer. "It was like, 'Let's hire Laurel and Hardy and forget about Hardy,'" Kaplan said. Hill, denied his foil and playing in a language unfamiliar to him, did his best, but failed to become the newest heavily accented darling of American cinema.

For Miller watchers *Mr. Billion* is notable for putting him briefly back in the role of the clown-masked rapist he'd been in Kaplan's *The Student Teachers*. It even appears to be the same mask, although this time it transpires that Miller's character, Bernie, is only pretending to be a rapist, and is in fact working in league with his putative victim, Valerie Perrine. (Perrine, Kaplan claimed, was fond of asking people she'd just met if they would like to watch her smoke a cigarette with her vagina. One wonders how this offer was received by Miller.) Their goal is to bamboozle Hill out of the millions he stands to inherit if he makes it to the West Coast by some arbitrary time; after a brief fist fight with Hill, Miller checks out of the picture for a while, popping back in just frequently enough to give the impression of a larger role.

But, Kaplan asserted, when the film was ready for release, there was virtually no support from the studio and very little advertising, and no courtesy inclusion of him in whatever publicity plan there might have been. The movie died, of course, and what reviews there were panned it thoroughly, though Kaplan believes it "better than its reputation." It could only be.

This was Miller's third job of the summer, which wasn't bad, but wasn't great because the jobs were so short. It left time for other things, though, like moving house. The Millers moved from Beverly Hills to another apartment, in West Hollywood. Miller enjoyed being even nearer to his old Hollywood stomping grounds, where he'd once hitched rides from character actors of varied renown, whom he saw now as ghosts and absent comrades. Barbara was in her senior year of high school, almost ready to think about moving out herself. She had a boyfriend, Blake, whom Lainie remembered as "Blake the Flake."

The Millers were not the only ones moving that summer. Roger Corman, having decided that New World Pictures needed and deserved its own building, had found a location in Brentwood and contracted Beach Dickerson to build it. Dickerson threw himself into the task as readily as he'd thrown himself into the surf on Corman pictures like *Attack of the Crab Monsters*, and by September a nondescript, white, two-storey edifice on San Vicente Boulevard was ready for habitation.

Dick, Lainie, and Barbara settled into their new place. Dick wasn't working much; lately the summers had been much busier than the winters. He did some commercial work—Union 76, Subaru—and a little TV, but no movies. The winter passed, he turned forty-eight, and any sense of momentum from his work with Scorsese and his forays with Dante and Arkush and Kaplan dwindled away. All of it had been so flattering of him, and of his old work, but this year so far it hadn't been paying any bills.

If *Jaws* had impressed Corman as a major-studio incursion into the genre territory of which he was the benevolent, patrician ruler, *Star Wars* confirmed that this was what the future of Hollywood moviemaking looked like, and he would have to get on board or founder. It was a major reorientation for Corman: from innovator to imitator.

For Miller, as it had been the previous few summers, the summer of '77 brought some more feature film work, and for a while it was possible to imagine a renewed feeling of momentum. The pink jacket got its final airing in an obscure little sex comedy/drama called *Game Show Models*, for which Miller portrayed a sleazy game show host exhorting his male contestants to slide their extremities through the Magic Hole Board. It was a one-note role that offered range mainly in terms of vestment: not only did Miller sport the pink jacket, but got to wear an ugly checkered one too.

Miller's bits, and practically the entire game show angle, were reshoots made at the behest of Sam Sherman, the film's distributor, who was, if not quite a cigar-chomping impresario in the tradition of Sam Arkoff, at least a dedicated and sincere purveyor of schlock. Patching up and reworking movies in the editing room, twisting them into genres they were not, was second nature to Sherman, and when he acquired a Hollywood drama called *The Seventh Dwarf*, about the trials of a young writer seeking love and creative fulfillment through his work at a particularly crass PR firm, he had its director shoot some extra sex material and several scenes on a cheap-looking game show set. Miller played the alternately unctuous and angry host of Guessword, and though it was another one-day-and-done gig for Miller, he was at least surrounded by pretty girls the whole time.

Another day's work came in July with *Starhops*, which gave Miller a chance to stage an entertaining but realistic end-of-the-rope moment. The picture was intended as your run-of-the-mill 1970s carhop picture, but when *Star Wars* hit the jackpot, the title was changed from *The Car Hops*, a space theme was given to the drive-in restaurant at the heart of the story, and a spoof of the *Star Wars* opening word-crawl was conceived. The rest of the story, concerning three carhops who purchase a failing drive-in from its creditor-hounded owner—Miller—remained more or less grounded.

Starhops wasn't a New World production, but it seemed like one. The director was originally to have been Stephanie Rothman, who had made *The Student Nurses* and *The Velvet Vampire* for Corman, but she was fired ("creative differences") and replaced by Barbara Peeters, who'd helmed *Summer School Teachers*. She may have left when producer John B. Kelly lowered the budget from $1.2 million to $450,000, and cut the shooting schedule by nearly half: the sort of move Corman himself was not averse to pulling on occasion. As well, it was superficially similar to the three-girls cycle: there were three girls in it, though they were all part of the main story instead of each having their own, and there was little of the social relevance Corman had considered so crucial. And while the *Star Wars* retrofit seemed like something Corman might try, he'd have done a better job of it. He might even have set the whole thing in space.

Miller's scenes were crowded at the head of the picture. He played Jerry, the owner, operator, and cook of Jerry's Drive-In, busy at the deep fryer while fending off an ex-wife, his suppliers, and his employees, all of them hounding him for the cash he owes. He's friendly, even fatherly, with his two carhops, Angel and Cupcake, but when a particularly objectionable customer, played by future director Matthew Bright, causes Jerry to lose his cool, he goes on a destructive rampage in his kitchen, then quits the food services industry for good. Miller packed a lot of comic business into his five minutes of screen time: frustration in dealing with creditors, then getting a basketful of French fries in the face from the psychotically truculent Bright, whom Miller then grabs about the neck and lifts fully out of his convertible. (Off-camera, remembered Bright, "he was very nice.") As Bright drives away, threatening lawsuits, Miller reaches a believable but funny boiling point and tears apart his kitchen. After he's recovered somewhat and agreed to sell his establishment, he gives a final, jaunty wave, walks away like John Wayne, and immediately steps on some gum, which, in a nice example of Miller's physical comedy skills, he has a hell of a time scraping off. He stumps off, swearing, and that's the last we see of Jerry.

"Believable but funny" was a reasonable précis of Miller's most saleable skill at that time. His still-slow but ongoing career reinvigoration was unfolding not just because his fans had come of age to make their own pictures, but because Miller, after years of experience, had honed his craft to the level at which he was able to give his films and their directors exactly what was needed, with a minimum of fuss. His character in *Starhops* suffers the trials of Job, and is not even allowed a dignified exit; humiliations rain upon him the way they usually do to only the most jerkish of characters. Yet, Jerry is consistently likeable, and more than one viewer has wished *Starhops* followed him out the door rather than staying at the drive-in with Angel and Cupcake and their hackneyed adventures. A certain undervaluing of Miller is evident in the end credits, where his character is listed as "Herb."

Miller's third job of the summer was on a slightly more prestigious picture, *Corvette Summer*. The movie, conceived by screenwriting team Matthew Robbins and Hal Barwood, who had written *The Sugarland Express* for Steven Spielberg, and directed by Robbins, featured Mark Hamill as a teenage gearhead who puts together a customized Corvette only to have it stolen by Vegas-bound thieves. Hamill hooks up with an apprentice prostitute played by Annie Potts, and together they travel to the City of Sin, ever on the lookout for the cherry-red 'Vette. At one point, down on his uppers and unable to pay for the hamburger and fries he's just ordered from a very Jerry-like drive-in proprietor, Hamill has the good fortune of running into Miller, who's wearing a powder-blue sports coat and bursting with good will. "Mr. Lucky," as he's called, has had only good luck since arriving in Vegas and has won every game he's played. "Makes you believe in the Almighty," he says. He wins Hamill his food for him, offers some sage advice, and then does what no other winning-streak character in movies ever does: leaves town with his pile of winnings before the streak turns bad.

It was another nice little character part for Miller, well within his areas of specialty. He spoke at the rapid-fire clip that had so impressed Isaac Hayes, but this time it was powered by adrenaline and exaltation, not the usual jaw-grinding desperation. He's as friendly as can be to Hamill, who in return is crusty and suspicious, and ungrateful when Miller presents him with the two-dollar bill with which he began his own winning streak. It's one of Miller's more exuberant performances, and may have reflected the situation of his co-star, who must have felt he'd won the lottery as *Star Wars* became more popular with every summer day that passed.

It was another three-movie summer for Miller, which in real-world terms translated to three days of work. So money was tight, as it always was, but the Millers managed a trip to Hawaii. In the fall an offer came, for another Spielberg-associated production, *Beatles 4 Ever*. This time Spielberg was one of the producers—it was his first outing as a producer—and the director was a young tyro named Robert Zemeckis. Zemeckis and his writing partner, Bob Gale, known in their circle as the Two Bobs, were something like interns for Spielberg; they had, Spielberg wrote, "just barged into my office one day, having just seen *Jaws* and saying, 'It was a terrific picture and we're young filmmakers and we'd sure like a break one day.'" Spielberg liked them and their screenplay well enough to use the leverage he'd gained from his previous hits to help them get the picture made on a budget of about two-and-a-half million dollars.

Beatles 4 Ever, shortly to be rechristened *I Wanna Hold Your Hand*, chronicled the adventures of some New Jersey teens around the Beatles' first appearance in America, on the Ed Sullivan show in February of 1964. Most of the principal cast are in the grip of full-blown Beatlemania, and spend all their time and a tremendous amount of effort trying to get into the Beatles' hotel room; too bad for them that the hallways are protected by the hotel's security chief, tough Sergeant Brenner, played by Dick Miller. As he chases the crazed Beatlemaniacs around, the sergeant expresses no particular opinion about the band itself, but one can imagine Miller drawing from the same well he used to create his Beatles-loathing waiter in *The Girls on the Beach*. In particular, after a scene in which Wendie Jo Sperber's character kicks him hard in both shins, this poor officer might have cause to rue the British Invasion.

Miller's closest interaction with the younger cast members came when he and his squadron of guards discover the characters played by Sperber and Eddie Deezen squatting in a room close to the Fab Four's. Deezen resists this eviction by picking up a lamp and swinging it wildly around. "Careful, he's got a lamp!" shouts Sergeant Brenner. "And it's on!" Zemeckis was delighted by this last bit, a Miller ad-lib; and delighted, too, in a different scene involving a lighting fixture. A service cart from which a hiding Beatlemaniac's foot protrudes passes the sergeant's desk and knocks over his small lamp, and Miller kept right on acting after the light crashed down, making up business and moaning a bitter "he broke my lamp."

Deezen was what might flap gawkily out the telepod door if Arnold Stang and Joe E. Brown teleported together after having Jerry Lewis for supper: a lab-grown gomer, the pinnacle of the form, the Idea of Nerd, the Übergeek. He and Miller would work together again, and on each such occasion Miller suffered a flashback to the climax of the hotel room scene in *I Wanna Hold Your Hand*, for which he had to grab Deezen upside down by the torso and carry him out of the room with his face buried in the outraged nerd's fundament.

The shoot was finished by Christmas and would be released the following summer, to some accolades but small audiences. It's an entertaining picture with much to offer the Miller aficionado. His performance fluctuates between the goofiness of his lamp extemporizations to a few glimpses of Genuinely Threatening Miller, wherein one catches a glimpse of what it would really be like to be on the actor's bad side. Yet, the performance itself is not bifurcated: its poles are well and believably contained within the same person. It counted as classic Miller, and a lot of people were noticing: not only Zemeckis and Gale, but executive producer Steven Spielberg as well. Joe Dante, of course, already knew.

17   I can't do this, I'm an actor!

"I seem to recall," Joe Dante said, "that it was written for Dabney Coleman. But he turned it down." A good thing for Miller, because that meant he was now the number one choice to play what Dante accurately calls "the Murray Hamilton character from *Jaws*" in *Piranha*, his belated rip-off of the 1975 Spielberg hit.

After *Hollywood Boulevard*, Dante and Allan Arkush had requarantined themselves in the New World trailer department, but occasionally they were allowed out. Arkush, for example, was shooting extra material for a Blaxploitation picture called *The Final Comedown*, and directed second-unit car-crash footage on Ron Howard's filmmaking debut, *Grand Theft Auto*. Dante was looking to direct again too, and Corman had something in mind for him. New World had made a television sale of Steve Carver's *Big Bad Mama*, but the copious nudity meant a healthy chunk of the film would have to be cut and it would then be too short for broadcast in a two-hour slot. Corman's solution was to hire Dante to shoot fifteen minutes of new footage featuring Miller's Prohibition Bureau agent and his quixotic quest to nab Mama and her gals. But then, Dante said, "something happened and the project was called off," and this coincided with the appearance of some new opportunities on the New World slate, among them *Piranha*.

The script had come to Corman from an outside source, but had been drifting around Hollywood for a while before lapping up on the shores of the New World; this explained why a quickie *Jaws* knock-off was only getting started three years after the fish story that inspired it. The upcoming release of *Jaws 2* convinced Corman to take the project on; that and the co-financing deal he had with United Artists, who were putting up half the budget, $400,000, in return for the foreign sales.

The way Dante always told it, there were two pictures up for grabs at the time, or at least two projects Corman was willing to allow either Dante or Arkush to direct: *Piranha* and *Rock 'n' Roll High School*. Both men wanted the rock 'n' roll picture, but Arkush, the music-mad former rock-palace stage manager, *really* wanted it, so Dante fell on his sword and took on the killer fish spectacular. Jon Davison, of course, would produce it. But neither of them, they vowed to each other and to Roger, would do a thing until the ludicrous script was rewritten. Among other outrages of logic, there were moronic scenes of a bear, spooked by a forest fire, who chases people into the water so the piranhas would have someone to bite. New World's loyal and elegant story editor Frances Doel was chatting with an agent and was easily persuaded to take a chance on his client, a young novelist called John Sayles. Sayles and Dante got along well from the beginning, finding a particular connection in their like-minded political outlooks. Sayles was a cinephile too, and, growing up, had seen a lot of the same movies as Dante. He knew very well who Dick Miller was, and that counted for a lot.

Early in the process it became clear that Dabney Coleman was not going to play the Murray Hamilton part, and having Miller take the role instead gave Sayles a clear signpost to follow in his newest draft. "Once John Sayles knew it was gonna be Dick, he rewrote the character," Dante said. The film was set, and largely would be shot, in Texas, and Miller's character was a good ol' boy resort operator. This was not on the face of it an ideal role for a man with one of the purest Bronx accents ever recorded, but Miller had beaten those odds countless times before. Either way, conceptually speaking at any rate, "There's something funny about Dick faking a Texas accent," Dante said.

Production of the film started in late February 1978, not in Texas, but in the University of Southern California swimming pool, where the bloody piranha attacks and other underwater material were shot. There were crates full of rubber fish with snapping jaws and piles of fake limbs and torsos, and Dante trying to direct it all from inside a scuba suit. Eric Braeden, the actor Dante had hired to play the lead, looked around at all of this, grudgingly swam a few laps in the pool, and later on "called me up and begged me to get out of it," Dante said. Miller paid a visit, but was charmed rather than horrified by the "rinky-dink" setup, and amused to see the crew pouring milk (for haze), red dye and Karo syrup (for blood), and other substances (urine almost certainly among them) into the water. By the time the production was packing for Texas, strange entities were growing in the pool, and technicians had to come all the way from Sacramento to do battle with them. In the end the pool was ruined, at least for a time, and Miller credited the poor performance of the 1980 American Olympic swim team to the total contamination of their practice pool.

Corman badly frightened Davison and Dante by threatening to call off the picture, then settled for merely clawing back half of his investment, which reduced the total budget by a full quarter. Nevertheless, Dante went to San Marcos, Texas, cheered by the special effects shots, which, in defiance of reason, seemed to have worked out fine. Once on location at a water park called Aquarina Springs, he descended, this time without a scuba suit, into a bog of paranoia and self-doubt. Dante was convinced that his footage was awful and no coherent film could ever be made of it; and he was not encouraged by conversations with Mark Goldblatt, the picture's first-time editor, who was watching and assembling the footage back in LA. But Miller was ready and amiable, cheered to be on location and working a full week, and his cheer was contagious.

He was playing a property developer/waterpark owner who refuses to close his beaches even when told of the approaching piranha menace. In Miller's hands the Lost River Resort seems like an aquatic-themed Catskills resort, relocated for some reason in Texas. He did indeed fake a Lone Star accent, well enough that, after one of his bigger speeches, the local college kids working as extras declared him a phony. "You're not from around here," they told him. "You're from Dallas!"

Miller and Dante decided he should drop the accent at a certain point, to show that the character was a faker by trade. "I thought to myself, 'This guy's a con man,'" Miller told *Filmfax* magazine. "He's down in Texas and he's selling Texas property, so he's a Texan, but when he goes to New England and he sells New England property, he's a New Englander. So in the middle of the phone conversation, I tell the guy on the other end of the phone, 'I give you my word as a Texan,' and then when I hang the phone up, I say, 'Schmuck!' and that was supposed to be the giveaway." It was just as well, since a master of accents was one thing Miller was not. Screenwriter Sayles was in Texas as well, nominally there to play a small role as an army sentry, but really on hand to rewrite his script for just such eventualities as Miller's character mutation, and he peppered the resort owner's dialogue with a few small amplifications on his essential phoniness. "I always like to have the writer on set if possible," Dante said, "because a lot of times things just don't sound right, and then actors are tempted to make up dialogue." Sayles added, "This whole scene was for Dick Miller, explaining about the 'Swimming Swine,'" who was Ralph, a pig who did aquabatics.

When the piranhas turn out to be real and begin eating his guests, Miller's character, like Murray Hamilton's mayor in *Jaws*, is shocked, but instead of lapsing into near-catatonia, Miller becomes defensive and tries to bat away the journalists' Electrolux-sized television cameras. But he's ruined and he knows it, and as he implores them to leave, a particular mannerism in Miller's tone comes to the fore as he's shooing off reporters: a sort of high, desperate quaver that spills down from the hinges of his jaw, a pure tone of pathos. Miller packs enough sincerity and end-of-the-rope edge into this effect, even when the scenes are meant to be comic, to surprise the viewer with a sudden pang of empathy for this character, even if he's a louse in a gaudy sports jacket.

It was another nice role for Miller, and confirmed the pleasure he had felt in working with Dante on *Hollywood Boulevard*. He had fun on the Texas location, a good time with the cast and crew at the San Marcos Holiday Inn, and got a decent billing, coming sixth on the cast list. The picture was released in August, almost two months after *Jaws 2*, to reviews both complimentary and otherwise, and to salutary box office; though there were grumblings from Universal Pictures about its unabashed borrowings from *Jaws*. In fact, a lawsuit was threatened, but Steven Spielberg, preparing his epic *1941* with Universal, saw *Piranha*, enjoyed it, and managed to talk the studio out of its litigation.

Miller returned from Texas to a certain level of domestic discord. Though Miller had been an actor and nothing but an actor since before they'd met and married twenty years earlier, Lainie was at the end of her patience with it. Dick, it was pretty clear, was never going to be a star, or at least not the kind who commands a large paycheque, so she began trying to convince him that hospital administration, not acting, was the career he should be going for. "I can't do this, I'm an actor!" cried Miller whenever the issue came up. He'd play a hospital administrator on TV if anyone asked, he told her, but that was as close as he wanted to get. Lainie eventually dropped her campaign, but it was a fractious time in the relationship.

Barbara wasn't there to witness any of this, having decamped to Japan, where she was stationed in Yokosuka as a navy hospital corpsman. While she was there, she happened to go to a movie, where, said Lainie, "she saw her father talking Japanese, and she called home—that impressed her!" It was the first time Barbara had really noticed Miller's career; before that, Lainie said, she'd been "nonchalant about it, as some of the kids [of actors] are."

"*Most* of the kids are," Miller amended. "Most show business kids who were raised in a show business family just, they shine it on, they're not affected at all." That was Barbara. She stayed in Japan for several years altogether, taking courses in economics at Saito University in Tokyo before returning to Los Angeles in the early 1980s and taking still more business courses at the University of California.

Miller was able to stave off Lainie's career recommendations more easily when bigger, or at least bigger-seeming, jobs came along, and it was easier still when Miller was invited to be a part of a sprawling project with an epic budget and a director who in two blockbuster strides had achieved superstar status. This was *1941*, of course: a script written by the Two Bobs, Zemeckis and Gale, intended as a project for John Milius, but inherited by his pal Steven Spielberg, after Milius found funding for his long dreamed-of surfing project *Big Wednesday* and Spielberg concurrently got it into his head that comedy was the genre he should conquer next.

1941 had a huge character list and, after casting the star parts and purloining most of the actors from *I Wanna Hold Your Hand*, Spielberg was happily filling nearly every other role with an old character actor or an interesting face. Christopher Lee, Slim Pickens, Dub Taylor, Lionel Stander, and Elisha Cook Jr. were all scheduled to make appearances, as was Sam Fuller, with whom Miller had already quasi–co-appeared in *The Young Nurses*. Spielberg had seen Miller in *I Wanna Hold Your Hand*, of course, and again more recently in *Piranha*, which he had enjoyed; so Miller's place in the *1941* ensemble seems in retrospect virtually assured.

For Miller, the job was doubly compelling, not only for being a small part of filmmaking on a scale he wasn't used to, but because the period being dramatized was precisely the time when he, at thirteen, had first encountered Los Angeles. It was LA in the immediate post–Pearl Harbor period of anxiety and martial fervour, which Miller had witnessed at one of the most formative periods of his life and could still recall with total clarity. It was stunning to wander around the era, which had been recreated with all the detail and exactitude a huge budget could provide; it was like time travel. There were the headlights on the cars hooded for wartime; pachucos in zoot suits; and there was even an actor (Iggie Wolfington, a war hero and dedicated union man, founder of the Actors' Fund of America) playing Miller's old agent Meyer Mishkin. Miller himself was in uniform once again as Officer Miller, a minor antagonist to the de facto main character played by Bobby DiCiccio. "That's the bastard who sent me up the river!" DiCiccio cries when he sees Miller. DiCiccio's character, riding a tank, cruises past the officer and then, in a gesture typical of both the character and the movie, fires a machine gun at Miller's car until it blows apart, and Miller, or a stunt man, is forced to dive behind another car, yowling. A subsequent scene at the same location had Miller in the background, standing once again and sadly picking up pieces of his destroyed vehicle: the old Miller pathos. This aspect of Miller's talent runs a fine line: you can *almost* see the tears welling up, but not quite. Through his career Miller nailed this saltwater tipping point almost every time he tried it.

But before the film's release on December 14, 1979, his scene was cut, along with several others, in an attempt to bring the picture to somewhere south of two hours. Spielberg objected, but even he was helpless against the will of the two studios, Universal and Columbia, who shelled out the money for the movie as they had, respectively, shelled out for *Jaws* and *Close Encounters of the Third Kind*. In fairly short order thereafter Spielberg was allowed to put together a director's cut, which reinstated Miller's scenes and a number of others; the film was brought up to 146 minutes, a length better reflecting its budget and would-be status in the marketplace. But not much status was forthcoming: the movie was a middling success but no blockbuster, and in the popular Hollywood press Spielberg was considered to have been Taught A Lesson. He learned much from the experience, it was true, but beneath the new veneer of humility these enlightenments were more specific. Years later, when Joe Dante was preparing to make *Innerspace* for Spielberg, the mogul had a few words for Dante about his cast, which included Kevin McCarthy, William Schallert, Henry Gibson, Orson Bean, Kenneth Tobey, and, of course, Miller. "As Steven put it, not kindly I thought, 'Well, you've gone and hired every B actor in Hollywood,'" Dante said, theorizing that Spielberg felt this way because "the only picture he's done with a lot of character actors was *1941*, and maybe that coloured his view of the subject."

Near the end of 1978 Miller donned a uniform again for an episode of *Soap*, the sitcom parody of convoluted daytime dramas that was just as convoluted itself but professed awareness of the genre's ridiculousness. He played a fussy prison guard supervising a meeting between characters played by Jennifer Salt and Donnelly Rhodes. The guard is in the background, looking irritated, constantly swooping in to wipe fingerprints and kiss marks from the glass partition of the non-contact visiting room in his charge. It was a one-note comic performance, but playing one note at a time at least allows for practise of that note, and such practise would serve Miller well in the coming decade. The episode aired in mid-February of 1979, when the series was close to its peak in popularity; there was nothing wrong, either, with appearing in a hit program, however desultory the part.

In the meantime there were big doings both at New World Pictures and across the low-budget film production industry. As New World underwent management shakeups, new players were appearing elsewhere on the scene. The most prominent of these groups were the Israeli cousins Menahem Golan and Yoram Globus, who were just acquiring Cannon Films and preparing to turn it into a genre factory nonpareil. At the same time some older players, in particular Sam Arkoff and AIP, were hanging it up. In response to all this, New World announced a series of projects notable for the near certainty that they would never get made (a fifteen-million-dollar picture called *World War III*, for instance), or for their obvious source of inspiration (*Battle Beyond the Stars*), or for their defiantly outdated qualities (*Lady in Red*). Yet another project was one that Allan Arkush, whose turn it was to make his own solo feature, would desperately want to change the title of, and the genre of music with which the picture was concerned. It was called, for the nonce, "Disco High."

The title "Disco High" did not last long; to Corman's credit, he quickly saw the sense of Arkush's impassioned objection, "You can't blow up a high school to *disco* music!" "Disco High" was a Frankenstein affair stitched together from a Joseph McBride script called "Girls' Gym" and Arkush's tenth-grade musings about the total rock 'n' roll destruction of his own high school, which he had turned into a film treatment named after the Todd Rundgren song "Heavy Metal Kids." In short order the script became "Rock 'n' Roll High School" (though this change was apparently kept secret from Corman for a time), and, after Rundgren declined and Cheap Trick proved too expensive a proposition, a comparatively little-known New York quartet called the Ramones was recruited as the picture's principal musical attraction. It was the Platters in *Rock All Night* all over again, and somehow a charmingly old-fashioned concept without being a throwback.

Arkush was quite happy to find a role for Miller, and there was little question which one it should be. For the third time running that year, Miller would play an officer of the law, but in *Rock 'n' Roll High* Arkush promoted him to police chief. "I always found him to be really funny as official kinds of people, 'cause he's not like that," said Arkush. Miller's nameless, authoritarian chief was there to help Mary Woronov's Principal Togar lay siege to her school and reclaim it from the leather-jacketed music thugs and satin-clad groupies who had taken it over.

The film was shot in December, and Arkush recalled cold nights and inhospitable locations. Organizationally, the production could have been better, and this didn't improve matters for Dick. "He had, like, one day of shooting," Arkush said.

> And we were all kinds of exhausted at that point. And [Dick] had a long scene where he explained how he was going to assault the school, and it was done with little toys and stuff. He got kind of frustrated that day, because the shooting wasn't going well, we were a little disorganized and we were trying to catch up because we had gone over doing the 'blowing up the high school' part. We were behind schedule, and it ended up getting short shrift in coverage and how we were doing it. It was not our best day.

It certainly wasn't a great day for Miller. Per the script he had a lot of good, funny business, arranging the toy armaments around a model school to demonstrate his strategy for taking back the institution. He was saddled with a partner, a yes-man underling character whose job it was to scream "Right!" after every point the police chief made. "And this guy was the worst actor in the world," Miller said. He was so bad, in fact, that the entire scene was cut from the film. (To give this anonymous dud just a bit of slack, it's also possible that, as is often the case, pacing and length were equally used to rationalize cutting the scene.)

Beyond perhaps appreciating that they were New Yorkers, Miller was otherwise unmoved to hear that the Ramones would be the featured band. He'd never heard of them, and they weren't his bag. He was further dispirited to note that the band kept a sort of combination geek, gofer, and court jester, a figure Miller only ever knew as the "Clown." The Clown made merry, he cut capers, he fetched smokes. Miller hated him, but nevertheless didn't care either for the way the Ramones treated him.

That night one of the actresses had a birthday, and in the great show of comradeship and camaraderie usual on $350,000 productions, the company had bought her what Miller remembers as "a beautiful cake." Of course, the Clown went to town, tossing around the cake, trying to juggle it, and inevitably demolishing it on the pavement. Miller couldn't believe what he was seeing. "I very rarely show my temper," he said—an assertion sure to surprise all those fellows he's wound around lampposts—"but the thing back in New York, the attitude, stays with you." Miller got all up in the Clown's business, ordering him to find a replacement cake and to be quick about it. It was almost midnight, and the Clown whimpered that he was afraid to forge out in the imposing neighbourhood to find a cake at that hour. Through a tight jaw and in a tone that would brook no argument, Miller suggested a few nearby twenty-four-hour chain stores, but still the Clown kept up his craven demurs. Miller had to go to "the head Ramone, whatever his name is, Johnny Ramone or something, and I said, 'Tell this guy if he don't go out and get a cake for this girl that he just fucked up, I'm gonna fuck *him* up.'" Johnny, or whichever Ramone it was, communicated this to the Clown, and the Clown looked once at Miller's curled lip, clenched fists, and glare, not to mention his prop truncheon, and wasted no time in scarpering off to the nearest Ralph's and returning with, Miller said, "a nice cake."

It was a long and tiring night, quite typical of any low-budget shoot, with shots, scenes, plans in general flying off into the night like calendar pages in a montage. Nevertheless, said Arkush, "we got through it, and we kept the important parts."

Arkush was particularly grateful that Miller's "ability to play off Mary Woronov was fantastic." Actually, Arkush was simply grateful for Miller, period, as he was by now every bit as much the Miller acolyte as Joe Dante or Jonathan Kaplan. For a few years these filmmakers were like three high priests who could conjure up their favourite spirit every couple of years and project him on a screen. As Dante many times has said, they could, and simply did, hire the very actors they would be most pleased to see anytime they watched a movie. It was lucky, and no coincidence, that most of these people were already familiar to Corman.

The police chief part went on to become one of those Miller is most beloved for, with his extemporized jab at the Ramones quoted frequently by fans. "It was a lot of 'okay, react to this, react to that' kind of stuff," Arkush said in recalling how he directed Miller that night. Upon being asked to react to the Ramones themselves, Miller's police chief proclaims, in revolted awe and almost to himself, "They're ugly, ugly people." With those words Miller was out, having completed another single workday that would later take on an importance out of all proportion to the effort or time it had actually taken to do. This would become Miller's signature move in the decade to come, with day player bits in *The Howling, The Terminator,* and others coming to define his career, and largely overshadow the work he'd done up to that time.

The mercurial period at New World Pictures continued; for Arkush and Dante there was an end-of-an-era feeling. *Rock 'n' Roll High School* was the last time either man would work for the company. Having been there longer than most, they knew when it was time to go (with Dante especially unlikely to return after Corman, brandishing the script like a threat, offered him *Humanoids from the Deep*), and shortly they would join the roster of Corman University graduates like Martin Scorsese and Jonathan Kaplan, and would, like them, hire Dick Miller for roles in their big Hollywood productions.

On stepping away from New World Dante seemed to find no shortage of work, with dispiritingly aquatic projects like *Orca II* and *Jaws 3, People o* being offered to him thanks to the success of *Piranha*. But these projects were illusory and succeeded only in wasting Dante's time, other than giving him invaluable instruction in the vicissitudes of studio process. "It was a very interesting, very depressing experience," he told Maitland McDonough. "Everybody wanted to make a different picture, and everybody treated me as the hired help." It was only after Dante had shed himself of all this that Avco Embassy came knocking with a werewolf project they thought might be his cup of tea.

Miller was still in the New World orbit; he could ill afford not to be. The year 1979 had begun with little promise of gainful employment—after every job, Miller said, "like every actor from Laurence Olivier on down, you think you'll never work again"—but in the spring he got a call from Julie Corman, who had a part for him in a picture called *The Lady in Red*, a socially conscious gangster drama written by John Sayles. Sayles wanted to tell the story of Polly Hamilton, renamed Polly Franklin for the film, who became famous as the girl on John Dillinger's arm as he was gunned down outside the Biograph Theater in Chicago, having just enjoyed a screening of *Manhattan Melodrama*. In her tale Sayles saw opportunities to mount a variety of social criticisms, with targets including religion, personified here by Polly's pious father, who bible-belts his daughter around when she displeases him; xenophobia, displayed in the narrow zealotry of commie witch hunters who pursue Polly's first big-city friend; and capitalism. The heaviest artillery was saved for those who trade in and toady to these blights on society, including Patek, the nasty foreman of the sweatshop Polly finds herself in after fleeing the farm. Patek stalks around the shop, grabbing breasts and barking abuse, and shouting curiosities like "Hey, cut out the jaw action! This ain't no tea room!" Miller is thoroughly convincing as the sour, predatory jerk, who either bribes his employees into sex before sending them to be mutilated by back-alley abortionists, or rats them out to proto-HUAC flacks. It's a perversely perfect use of Miller's friendly working-class image, having him play a mean capitalist lickspittle who is ultimately driven from his position by a labour uprising, and, on Miller's part, a genuine display of range. "It was a good little part," Miller said. The picture was directed by Lewis Teague, who, with the help of another Sayles script, would go on to make the most Joe Dante film Joe Dante never directed, *Alligator*, and thence, briefly, larger Hollywood features like *Cujo* and *The Jewel of the Nile*. Unlike so many other ex-Cormanites, however, he never thought to bring Miller along to the bigger leagues with him.

After a quick post-production *The Lady in Red* opened in July, and was not a hit. But, for Miller, it seemed to open the tap somewhat: work began flowing his way in a slightly steadier stream. He donned an apron once again to play a crusty diner owner—a Miller specialty by now—in an episode of *Taxi*, "The Lighter Side of Angela Matusa," in which Miller reacts with grimaces and sarcasm to the repeated semi-accidental insults hurled at his establishment by the principal characters. There's a transcendent quality to little Miller performances like this, in which he seems not merely to be fighting for the dignity of the regular joe he's playing, or even for that of regular joes like the one he's playing, but for that of day players like himself, the underpaid performers who may sit low on the call sheet, but in the end provide the mortar to scenes like this, along with a few extra laughs.

Miller was on the other side of the counter on an episode of *Alice*, the diner-set sitcom based on Martin Scorsese's *Alice Doesn't Live Here Anymore*. In the episode "Mona Lisa Alice," Mel, played on the show as in the movie by Vic Tayback, has issued an edict that his waitresses welcome their customers with a smile, and offers free meals if the smile is not forthcoming. By the end of the episode Mel is apoplectic (Tayback was always good at this), and in the closing seconds in struts Miller and his three tall pals, who occupy a table nearby, point out the absence of a smile on Mel's face, and gleefully claim their free meals. Miller does most of the talking, as though happy not to be on the receiving end of the abuse for once.

Meanwhile, Jonathan Kaplan, dipping a toe in television and testing the medium's tolerance for Cormanesque sleaze, was doing a movie of the week called *The 11th Victim*, about the serial murder of Hollywood prostitutes by a fiend known as the Lakeside Killer. The latest victim, number eleven, is the sister of a newscaster played by Bess Armstrong, who learns of her sibling's murder as she reads it live on TV. A shattered Armstrong travels to LA and makes a nuisance of herself to the local constabulary, of whom a cop played by Max Gail is in charge of catching the Lakeside Killer. Gail has a roomful of detectives working for him, the most sarcastic and unfeeling of whom was the role earmarked for Miller. It is as though Miller's mean, cynical cop from *The Young Nurses* had been promoted to detective and is now tasked with solving the murders of vulnerable people—a job for which he is uniquely unsuited. By the end of the end of the movie, though, he catches giggling fits and seems in general to have lightened up.

The movie itself begins with a solid gag that must have given Kaplan himself some giggles: in the middle of an opening title montage touring the seedier corners of Hollywood, there is a slow pan off a big neon sign for an establishment called Dante's Nude Dancers. Miller himself got no billing during these opening credits, though in his role as Investigator Ned he had plenty of lines. The TV movies of that period were always skimpy on billing, though. This didn't bother Miller, who was having a great time, surrounded with pals, the way he liked it. Kaplan was directing, and Jonathan Haze, who had deserted the acting game for behind-the-scenes work like production management, was an associate producer. As had so often been the case, Miller's character was part of an informal duo, and this time his counterpart was played by his pal Harry Northup, with whom Miller had acted in *Crazy Mama* and *New York, New York*. (Northup was a favourite of Kaplan, Scorsese, and Demme, showing up in at least a half-dozen movies by each of these directors.)

This work occupied a small slice of Miller's summer, and the rest of the time he spend pursuing his hobbies—drawing, reading, writing—and leisure, at which he was by now well practised. October 6 brought the Millers' 20th wedding anniversary, which they celebrated as lavishly as possible on their tight budget. Miller's television work aired all around this time—*Alice* on September 30, *Taxi* on October 26, and *The 11th Victim* on November 6—so he was a regular sight on the tube. This did not extend to the picture houses, however: *1941* opened on December 14, but of course Miller's part had been left in the trim bin, not to be restored until the picture came out on video the following year. But he remained in the Spielberg orbit, appearing very briefly in a new Robert Zemeckis picture, *Used Cars*, which Spielberg was producing. The film began shooting in November and was in production through to January 1980, and somewhere in there Miller found time to do a wordless bit of comedy, playing a man whose attention strays from the woman he's having sex with to the outrageous used-car-lot commercial playing on a nearby TV. An anonymous Internet commenter summed the part up well when he or she wrote, "He has no lines. His entire role lasts two seconds. But he still gets a laugh. That's a pro at work." The commenter continued in a sincere and plaintive tone: "Please live forever, Dick. I would take it as a personal favor."

A new decade began, one that would see the highest profile work of Miller's career. It started on a low-key note with an appearance in *The Happy Hooker Goes Hollywood*, the third and last instalment in a series of films inspired by the book by famous Dutch madame Xaviera Hollander. The two Israeli cousins, Golan and Globus, were producing it, and though they initially offered Chuck Griffith the job of writing the script and directing the picture, Griffith hesitated too long in accepting the job and it went instead to Alan Roberts. But once the script was written (by Devin Goldenberg, from a story by Goldenberg and Roberts), there was a small part for a New York cop near the beginning, perfect for an actor like Miller.

Except that when Miller arrived on the set, he was given a police uniform several sizes too large, and was confronted by a director who for some reason had been expecting an actor of much heavier proportions. "I thought you were fat," Roberts said to Miller.

"No, I'm not fat," Miller answered.

"Well, okay," Roberts said doubtfully, and they began to shoot. When Miller stripped down to his undershirt for the beginning of the scene, the director was amazed. "That's not the way I saw it!" he cried. "You got muscles! You got tattoos!" By the time the short scene was done, Roberts had rationalized himself happy. "It's still funny, it's still good!" he told Miller. "We'll use it! It's beautiful!"

In fact, the scene is not particularly funny, but, almost entirely thanks to Miller, it achieves by the end a certain poignancy. It's also a bit sexy, and for this reason, said Miller, *The Happy Hooker Goes Hollywood* "stands out in my mind from a lot of pictures." And no wonder. Miller's scene opens with soft-focus shots of his hands caressing the bare-breasted star, Martine Beswicke, and slipping a hundred-dollar bill into her garter. He is then seen donning his wildly oversized policeman's blouse and expressing regret that, since he and the rest of "the boys downtown" all shared the pricy madame's favours in return for not busting her, it wouldn't be his turn to experience the Hollander magic again "until some time in 1993."

"That was a nice picture," Miller remembered. He recalled, too, the weird cast: Adam West; Phil Silvers; Jack Lemmon's son Chris; and the *Daily Variety* columnist, and fellow son of the Bronx, Army Archerd. "I was surprised at the people who were in it," Miller said, and he was hardly the only one. The picture was released late in May, and the public reception was such that no further *Happy Hooker* pictures were produced. Critical notices were bad too, of course, though *Leonard Maltin's Film and Video Guide* noted, "Film buffs might enjoy seeing cult actors Martine Beswicke and Dick Miller in bed together."

When Chuck Griffith lost the job of making *The Happy Hooker Goes Hollywood*, which he hadn't wanted anyway, he counter-proposed another project, a comedy Jekyll and Hyde story ultimately titled *Dr. Heckyl and Mr. Hype*. Golan and Globus agreed to produce it on the condition, Golan told Griffith, that "ugly guy is good guy." Griffith accepted this immediately and expanded his story into a 200-page script piled high with goofy names and slapstick digressions. "Where did he get those names from?" Miller wondered. It roughly followed the same template as *A Bucket of Blood* and *The Little Shop of Horrors*, but by now the eccentricities were too forced and the formula had curdled. Griffith wanted Dick Van Dyke for the lead, but ended up with Oliver Reed, who was by that time a notorious character known for such things as walking the streets of Toronto with no pants on. When Reed was cast, Griffith told Aaron Graham, "I had to redo the entire picture in my head … it was a zany slapstick comedy, and I got Oliver Reed, with that face and that voice! So I made it more lyrical." Griffith also cast Mel Welles as Dr. Vince Hinkle, the inventor of the diet paste that transforms meek, ugly podiatrist Dr. Henry Heckyl into the murderous lady-killer Mr. Hype.

Griffith's lead was not the only of his casting proposals to be stymied: he wanted Miller and Jonathan Haze, "from the old gang," to play a pair of comedy garbage men named Irsil and Orson. But Haze, who was no longer interested in acting, turned him down. So Griffith had Miller play both parts, arguing with himself in Griffith's idiosyncratic dialogue as Reed listens from a balcony above. Reed, of course, was a force to be reckoned with on set and off. "He got me drunk, but I liked him," Griffith said; and Miller remembered him as "a fascinating guy. Weird."

Miller considered Griffith weird too. "A weird, strange man!" he cried. "A nice guy. He would travel around the world with a cardboard box, with his things inside it. A typewriter and a shirt. And he's show up in different places, like Israel. You'd say, 'What are you doing here?' He'd say, 'I'm on my way to Spain.'"

"Was he Melanie Griffith's father?" Lainie Miller asked.

"No!" Miller laughed. "Where are you getting that? You've been smoking some of Chuck's old shirts."

Though *Dr. Heckyl and Mr. Hype* was in no sense a success, within weeks of its November 1980 release Griffith was working again, for Corman, on a picture called *Smokey Bites the Dust*. The movie was a throwback to the good-ol'-boy smash-up derbies of half a decade earlier, like *Grand Theft Auto, Moving Violation,* and Griffith's own *Eat My Dust*. According to Griffith Corman had seen a news broadcast in which a sheriff had complained that the late '70s car picture fad was inspiring delinquent driving in young people, a situation the lawman described as "car wars." Immediately the broadcast was done, the telephone rang at Griffith's house: it was Corman requesting a script called "Car Wars," written to accommodate existing crash-up scenes from past New World car pictures.

Instead, Griffith wrote a script called "Wham Bam, Merci, Madame," which Corman predictably hated. But the idea of reusing all that New World car footage stuck with him, as money-saving ideas tended to, and a few years later the producer commissioned a script from a Texas-based writer and creative writing instructor named Max Apple, whose short stories Corman (or Frances Doel, more likely) had read and liked. In one of the spasms of loyalty Corman often showed to his friends and past collaborators, he called Griffith to direct the movie. By now it had a new title, "Follow That Car."

Apple was never given the chance to watch the movies that would be supplying the crash footage, so he was writing blind, and Griffith said it showed. "Nothing worked," he said. "So I made a lot of changes in it, and that made Roger angry." (It's a safe bet that the goofy sheikh character played by Mel Welles, Abu Habib Bibubu, is a Griffith creation.) By December 1980 shooting began on *Smokey Bites the Dust* ("Not my title, believe me!" Griffith said) on the usual dusty back road locations around Los Angeles. Jimmy McNichol had the Ron Howard part of the local speed demon who takes the sheriff's daughter for a ride in a stolen car, snatching her off the bleachers just as she's about to get crowned queen of the high school or read a valedictorian speech. In short order the outraged sheriff, school officials, a dim-witted football hero in the grip of a religious mania, and a whole mob of others are after the couple. Miller was given yet another ugly blazer and the role of a local car dealer whose fanciest auto is the first in a series stolen by the wily McNichol. Miller has some comedy business at the beginning of the picture, including a Homer Simpson-style strangulation, but spends most of the story sitting in a helicopter and looking or pointing downward, initially following McNichol and the girl and later the Rolls owned by Abu Habib Bibubu. His character sported the remarkably commonplace name (for a Griffith character) of "Glen Wilson."

The picture used crash footage from *Eat My Dust*, *Grand Theft Auto*, *Moving Violation*, and *Thunder and Lightning*, and the best one can say for the final product is that it makes slightly more sense than it might have done. Pumpkins are featured heavily for some reason, and Griffith made sure there was enough loony clown music, slapstick kick fights, and "boi-i-i-ing" sound effects for three movies. "I did not recognize much that I had written," Apple confessed after seeing it. For Miller, with Griffith directing and familiar faces like Welles and Beach Dickerson in the cast, it was the sort of small homecoming that was becoming less frequent as he and everybody else aged. In fact, it would be the last time he would work for Griffith at all. At least Walter Paisley, the character name Griffith had come up with more than two decades earlier, would live on.

By the spring of 1980 both Joe Dante and Allan Arkush were preparing their first post-Corman projects. Michael Phillips, who had produced *The Sting*, *Taxi Driver*, and *Close Encounters of the Third Kind*—and who, in defiance of whatever trustworthy instincts had thence far guided his decision making, was preparing a new project called *Heartbeeps*—had seen *Rock 'n' Roll High School* and liked it very much. He called Arkush and presented him with the opportunity to use a twelve-million-dollar budget to make a film about lovestruck robots who run away from their factory. Arkush accepted, as anyone would, and after a long pre-production in which the challenges of creating all the robots and other near-future doodads were addressed, the picture began shooting on June 9. Andy Kaufman and Bernadette Peters played the robots, but many of the smaller roles were filled out with *Rock 'n' Roll High School* alumni such as Paul Bartel, Mary Woronov, and, of course, Dick Miller.

Production began on location in northern California, and Miller's bit was not scheduled until later in the shoot, when the company would move to the Universal lot. In the meantime Joe Dante was preparing *The Howling*, a werewolf picture that had been extensively rewritten by John Sayles. As was by now his habit, Dante scanned the scenario for the Miller part, "and there was really only one he could play," Dante said, "which was this bookstore owner. Which he has claimed in various interviews is one of his favourite parts he ever played."

The year 1980 had thus far been "a bad year for me," Miller said, so when Dante called, Miller was pleased but wary. "I said, 'What is it, a one-day part?' and he said, 'Yeah, one day.' So I said, 'Oh shit, all right, I'll take it.'" Though most of the other characters were named after werewolf movie directors of the past, Miller was once again called Walter Paisley, though the iconic name is never spoken aloud. Miller was excited to be in another Dante film, because, he said, "Joe's a good director ... he does the same thing Roger does: he does it in his casting, and once the people are on set, he leaves it up to them." Along with Miller the *Howling* cast was filled with examples of veterans who could be trusted to do their thing with minimal instruction: Noble Willingham, Kenneth Tobey, Slim Pickens, Kevin McCarthy, Patrick Macnee, and the legendary John Carradine.

In contrast to the Arkush project, in which he worked late in the schedule, Miller's bit in *The Howling* was scheduled for the afternoon of the very first day of shooting. The morning began in a location that was not only meant to be grotesque and scummy, but genuinely was so. The unit move to Cherokee Books, beloved of Los Angeles comic book readers, was a relief to everyone, but when Miller arrived during the lunch hour he came across a scene more horrifying than any werewolf attack. Belinda Balaski, who had been working that morning along with Dennis Dugan and was set to play the afternoon's scene with Dugan, Miller, Forrest J. Ackerman, and a pair of nuns, recalled, "The makeup lady, during lunch, put a second piercing in my ear, and Dick almost fainted! He just turned green. It was so cute!"

After lunch the scene was blocked out. Cherokee had been dressed as an occult shoppe called The Other Side, and had tall shelves accessible by a rolling ladder; for Dante, it was a no-brainer to put Miller near the top of it and let him ride along to grab the books called for by the script. On descending the ladder he picks up a stuffed armadillo and tucks it under his arm. (On the DVD commentary Dante claimed—or joked; it's hard to tell—that Miller brought the armadillo to set himself.) The proprietor fast-talks werewolf facts with apparent sincerity before reverting to a more familiar Miller figure, the mercenary cynic. "What am I, an idiot?" he demands of Dugan and Balaski. "I'm makin' a buck here." Balaski remembered Miller's stealing queasy glances at her freshly pierced ears throughout the scene. Lurking in the background of all this is Forry Ackerman, Miller's old Hollywood pal, the latest issues of his magazine *Famous Monsters of Filmland* fanned out unsubtly behind his back. Miller got to rework his improved dialogue from *Not Of This Earth*, telling Ackerman, who is thumbing through some tarot cards, "If you're gonna purchase, purchase. If not, leave them alone, you're gettin' 'em greasy."

It is, on the one hand, a purely utilitarian scene, providing not just crucial information to the characters, but the weapon—silver bullets, natch—they need to beat the werewolves. On the other, it feels light, breezy, and frivolous, included largely to provide a showcase for a particularly entertaining Miller performance. His ad-libbed complaint about werewolves' being "worse than cock-a-roaches" alone makes it worthwhile. Belinda Balaski reflected that in all the movies they made together, eleven or so, *The Howling* was the only time they actually acted together. "Well, he steals every scene," Balaski said, "so I'm *fortunate* that in eleven movies we've only had once scene together."

Dante and the crew had a scare the next day. Word came from the production company that the footage was completely out of focus and unusable. John Hora, the cinematographer, and presumably focus puller Norman Cattell too, were threatened with dismissal, and it looked as though Miller would be called in to redo a performance with which he and everybody else were already well pleased. However, it turned out to have been the projector used to screen the dailies that was out of focus, not the camera. Miller, who normally shunned movie sets unless he was working, returned for a visit anyway, and got to talking with John Carradine, whom he had met years before, early in his permanent relocation to Los Angeles. Miller reminded the old horror star that they had indeed crossed paths before, and Carradine said, "Oh yes, yes, my boy," in that Carlsbad Cavern of a voice.

Miller was rightly proud of his performance in *The Howling*, but realistic also. Some time after the film was finished and had its profitable release in April 1981, Miller jokingly asked Dante if he should be asking Avco Embassy to mount a Best Supporting Actor Academy Award campaign, and Dante answered him as if he'd been serious. The director shook his head and said, "They won't do anything about it. They're finished with it; the picture's been released, they made a lot of money, it's been sold to TV and that's the end of it." Miller thought the company should at least have pushed for a nomination in the new Special Effects Makeup category, but Dante could only shrug.

As *The Howling* was wrapping, Arkush's much bigger picture, *Heartbeeps*, was soldiering on. Miller was ready to play Walter Paisley for the second time that summer, this time in the guise of a watchman at a robot factory. But there were rumblings in the industry, and dissatisfaction in the ranks of the Screen Actors Guild (SAG) with rates of pay and remuneration for new home video technologies. After a vote shepherded by then-SAG president

William Schallert (who would appear in many Joe Dante pictures), the guild went on strike as of July 21; many productions, including *Heartbeeps*, were shut down. Actors put down their sides and picked up placards, and when off the line they worried about how to make the rent.

It was a long summer for Miller and many others, and when the strike came to an end late in October, the resolution negotiated on Schallert's watch pleased few. But as productions like *Heartbeeps* lurched back into life, Miller was mainly glad to be working again. He donned his costume, a uniform with "Paisley" inscribed on the name tag, and set to work. He enjoyed working for Arkush, and still considered him "just a *nice* guy." The experience was pleasant enough; it was fun to be on the set of a big movie being directed by someone he knew from the low-budget world, and to work with Randy Quaid and Kenneth McMillan; but less pleasant was the presidential election that followed soon after: Ronald Reagan, for whom both Dick and Lainie held ample contempt—"Heartless guy," Lainie called him—was elected president by a considerable margin. It was depressing, especially coming on the heels of the same sort of dissatisfying conclusion to a strike as Reagan had engineered as SAG president back in 1960.

And after the long summer (a sad season for Miller, as his old friend Bobby Van died of a brain tumour at the end of July) came a long winter. Every now and again his face would appear on a movie screen—*Dr. Heckyl and Mr. Hype* was released in November; *The Howling,* in March—but he was mainly sustained by "the big surprise of my career," a semi-regular role as a "sleazy desk clerk" on the daytime standard *General Hospital*. "It's become a running part," he told an interviewer at the time, "and I've had people stop me after the first or second show and they say, 'You're from *General Hospital!*'" It was not the sort of hospital work Lainie had had in mind for her husband, but it would do.

Jon Davison had left his position at New World Pictures in 1980 and was now at Paramount. His first producing assignment there, *Airplane!*, had proved an enormous success, and this meant Paramount was going to give him a new picture to produce. A script called "White Dog," written by Curtis Hanson, adapted from a story by Romain Gary, had been lurking in the company file cabinets for years, periodically popping up to bedevil and ultimately best any writer who tried to wrestle it into shootable shape. It had once been earmarked as a Robert Evans production to be directed by Roman Polanski, but busts for cocaine and statutory rape, respectively, tossed a blanket over that idea. The story of a big ferocious dog trained by racists to attack people of colour, which is then reprogrammed by a Black trainer to attack only whites, "White Dog" was problematic, to say the least. "Worst idea I ever heard of for a picture," Davison said, but Paramount, citing contractual obligation, forced him to produce it anyway. Figuring if he had to do it at all, and if he wasn't allowed to hire, say, Mario Van Peebles to direct it, he might as well work with someone known for his anti-racist ideals, someone who would probably bug Paramount simply because he was old and irascible, and above all who was a fascinating filmmaker with a body of work Davison adored, so he approached Sam Fuller and persuaded him to take the job.

At some point early in 1981, Miller heard that Jon Davison was producing a movie for Fuller. Miller, too, was a Fuller fan. He had seen plenty of his movies, and knew him as an veteran newshound who had translated the punchy, bullet-like style of his journalism to the movie screen in rabid-dog movies like *Pickup on South Street, The Naked Kiss, Shock Corridor,* and *Underworld U.S.A.* "I'd like to work with Sam Fuller, just to see what all the shouting's about," Miller told Davison. (The shouting at the time was for Fuller's most recent picture, *The Big Red One.*)

"All right, I'll see if I can get you on for a day," Davison said. Some days later he called Miller and said, "You're playing a veterinarian." Miller would have a few lines and some bits of business, but the main *raison d'être* for his character was that Paramount had paid a lot for the veterinary office set, constructed in an existing facility called the Wildlife Way Station in the Angeles National Forest, and wanted to show it off a bit. Miller, the animal lover, was happy on his way to the location, looking forward to being surrounded by wild creatures. "So I got up there," Miller said,

> and the guy comes over to me and he says, "You're working with a monkey!" I says, "A monkey? All right, all right." He says, "You were supposed to work with a chimp, but the chimp went crazy yesterday, and he picked up one of the grips and held him over his head for 20 minutes. And he put him down about 20 feet away."
>
> I says, "Okay, what's the monkey like?" He says, "Oh, it's a cute little monkey, 30 pounder. You keep it on your lap, it's got long arms." He's strapping a belt on me with a little pouch filled with grapes and raisins and everything. And he says, "The only thing is this: the monkey likes to bite." I said, "Bite?!" He said, "Well, it won't draw blood, but he likes to

bite and it hurts a little. And the only way you can stop him is to bite him back." I said, "You're kidding!" He says, "No, you grab him by the neck and you bite him on the neck!" I said, "Come on, that's ridiculous, I'm not gonna do that." He said, "Bite the monkey. Will you do me a favour? He's gonna get out of hand. Maybe he won't, but if he does, bite the monkey."

So we get into the first scene, and I got the monkey on my lap, and I'm sitting by the wall, and the chick [Kristy McNichol] comes in, she says, "Where's so-and-so?" And I say, "It's up the road a bit," and the monkey bites me. They say, "Cut, cut, cut!" He says, "Bite the monkey!" I say, "But he didn't bite me much." He says, "But he's biting you, and so just bite the monkey!" But I tell [the monkey], "No!" My dogs react to that: I tell them, "No," and they stop.

So we shoot the scene again, and the monkey bites me again, and I say, "No!" And he stops. It's wonderful. But I look down and he's peed all over me! I change my costume, they get me another pair of pants, we go through the scene again, and he starts to bite me again. And I look over, and the guy's saying, "Bite the monkey! Bite the monkey!" And I say, "No!" and he stops. I say, "See, it works." And I look down and the monkey had shit on me. And I'm covered. I say, "This is ridiculous!"

We do it again. The monkey starts to bite me, and the guy's over there saying, "Bite the monkey!" He's on the sidelines, "Bite the monkey!" So I say, "Oh, god!" and I grab the monkey by the neck and I bite him! And he stops. And we finish the scene, I look down, and I'm clean as a whistle. He says, "See?" I say, "All right. Bite the monkey."

Jon Davison's outside, and I go out and say, "Thanks for the part. I got pissed on, I got shit on." He says, "The legend lives!"

Miller's takeaway from this experience: "Whenever you think you know something in this business, there's always somebody who knows a little bit more." To Miller, it was a moral tale, but for Joe Dante, who cherished the anecdote, it served better as metaphor. "He's not the first guy who's been shit on by a monkey in Hollywood," Dante said. "Most of us are just generally shit on. You're lucky if it's a monkey."

Sam Fuller would have agreed heartily with this sentiment, particularly after the fate suffered by *White Dog* once it was finished. On being hired, Fuller had rewritten the story to do away with the second part of the story, in which the dog is reprogrammed by the vindictive Black trainer; he wanted a Black character who would be better than the racists. "I didn't want to get involved in a racist film, and I certainly didn't go for all that anti-Black crap," Fuller growled. He was pleased at how the story had come out and the message he believed it conveyed. "If anyone complains about this movie, it'll be the Klan," he reckoned. Still, the idea was blatantly provocative, and even Miller, with his one-day part, knew there would be backlash.

"I liked the story, but they may have trouble with it," he told *Fangoria* before the film's release. But it barely even got a release, just a flurry of protest letters from the Black Anti-Defamation Coalition and other organizations to whom the story was singularly unappealing. Paramount, who had in any case only ever wanted a little exploitation picture they could release, make money on, and forget about (or endlessly sequelize), declined the fight and dumped the movie, and a disgusted Fuller removed himself to France.

Miller wasn't doing much aside from *General Hospital*, and it stayed that way for most of 1981. He worked for a day or two playing a bearded, German-accented doctor in "National Lampoon Goes to the Movies," an attempt at omnibus comedy that didn't get released until two years later, as *National Lampoon's Movie Madness*, at which point any of the few who saw it hated it. (Miller's German accent, however, while comic and unconvincing, wasn't bad.) *Heartbeeps*—which had crawled through post-production over the past year, had twenty minutes shorn from it by the studio, then waited for John Williams to find enough time between *Raiders of the Lost Ark* and *E.T.* to compose a score for it—was released in December, also to fire-breathing reviews and no box office. Allan Arkush didn't follow Fuller to France, but instead concentrated on turning his experiences as a stagehand and manager at the Fillmore East in New York into a script, which he called "Get Crazy" and which he would manage to make after many disheartening delays. Thanks to the soap opera, plenty of people were seeing Miller's ever-craggier face, but in cinemas he was having a strikeout year.

He did a little more TV toward the end of the year, appearing in a forgotten convenience store-themed sitcom called *Open All Night*. The episode, "Scam," was laid at a conference of twenty-four-hour store owners, and Miller played a blustery conventioneer who wears a bright yellow shirt and bemoans the fact that his wife, Dorcus, has left him after declaring him a perennial loser. "Where's Olivia Newton-John?" he calls out. He graced an entirely better class of TV comedy around the same time, when Joe Dante directed two episodes of *Police Squad*, a short-lived but hilarious parody of cop shows broadcast on ABC. *Police Squad* was created by the Zucker Brothers and Jim Abrahams, for whom Jon Davison had produced *Airplane!*, and it was

Dante's first foray into television and the job that gave him an entrée into the Directors Guild of America. Miller's episode, like every episode, had two titles, one onscreen and one spoken, and in this case they were "Testimony of Evil" and "Dead Men Don't Laugh." He played Vic, a menacing MC/gangster's flunky in a velvet dinner jacket, and had fun sending up the many other dinner-jacketed MC/gangster's flunkies he had played before, pulling laughs from the same toolkit he used for serious gangster dramas. Side-eye or needle-hard glare, grinding jaw or set, his toughest faces are all on display. The dragon lady to whom Miller flunkied was played by Claudette Nevins, a journeywoman actor whose career had begun with the first horror movie ever made in Canada, *The Mask*, back in 1961.

She's the owner of Mr. V's, a large, cheap-looking nightclub whose house comedian has just been murdered by Nevins in cahoots with Miller, and when a new entertainer is needed, Leslie Nielsen's dignified oaf of a cop, Frank Drebin, goes undercover to take the gig. He dazzles the room with a virtuoso display of entertaining that is effective enough to have Miller's character, Vic, laughing and clapping along. Drebin's wildly successful act is made up of hoary non-jokes, soft shoe and song, and Don Rickles-isms like "Is that your wife beside you, or'd you just throw up on the seat?" After the gut bust comes the real bust; Miller and Nevins flee, but are tripped up on a rope held by Drebin's boss, played by the impressively low-key Alan North.

Unfortunately, Miller's episode, the sixth, was also the last. Abrahams and the Zuckers had refused to bend in disagreements with the network over matters like the inclusion of a laugh track; and on March 30, ABC, in what seemed a fit of pique more than anything, put the show on "a telecast hiatus until further notice." The show had premiered at the beginning of March and by the end of the month was cancelled, and the last two episodes were broadcast in July, just afterthoughts.

Jonathan Kaplan, after his own detour into television, was preparing a new theatrical feature. *Heart Like a Wheel* told the life story of Shirley Muldowney, the first woman to make a mark on the professional drag racing circuit, and was structured less around her triumphs on the quarter mile than on her relationships with the men in her life. Hoyt Axton, a songwriting bear of a man, played her father; Leo Rossi, her first husband, Jack Muldowney; Beau Bridges, her lover and rival, Connie Kalitta; and Anthony Edwards, her son John. Miller's role was an invention, or at least a composite character, by the name of Mickey Hart. Mickey, in contrast to most of the men Muldowney encounters, is not related to her, sleeping with her, or disdainful of and condescending to her. He's simply a friend who believes in her talent for race-car driving and supports her ambition without hesitation. There is some supposition involved in the previous statement: there really isn't enough of Mickey in the movie to ascribe total purity to his motives and behaviour, but, as ever, Miller suggests multitudes. Early in the picture Shirley is given the chance to sit in a dragster for the first time by Don "Big Daddy" Garlits, who practically smacks his lips at her as he calls her "darlin'" and lifts her into the rail. (Garlits was played by Bill McKinney, the rapist from *Deliverance*, which certainly didn't please the real, marginally more cosmopolitan, Big Daddy Garlits.) Mickey, whom she has been chatting with, is given her purse to hold and Miller takes the handbag quite readily, looking on as though he is feeling nothing but excitement for Muldowney. Earlier, Mickey had been seen as a flagman at a street race and one of the few guests at the Muldowneys' wedding.

But Mickey is not just a family pal; he's a racing enthusiast and successful businessman, and was meant to reappear late in the movie, having apparently made good and now wishing to buy Shirley's outfit while swearing he'll leave the decisions all to her. But these scenes did not make it out of the editing room. "My part was really quite large at the beginning," Miller said. "There's a whole scene where I meet her in a restaurant and finance her. I have grey hair." Mickey indeed has grey hair, and bushy white eyebrows and moustache as well, and when he makes his pitch to Shirley, he lets her know, in all sincerity, that "to be able to do this for you, it's … it's a dream come true for me. And I'm at that point in my life where I want to indulge myself in my dreams a little, you know what I mean?" Miller leaves the scene after giving Muldowney a kindly crinkle of the eyes (an effective Miller tool) and actually tousling John Muldowney's hair. "Just think of me as your biggest fan, like I've always been," he says at another moment. It wasn't often Miller was playing the nicest guy in a movie, but, like *A Bucket of Blood* before it, *Heart Like a Wheel* gave him that opportunity.

Miller regretted the disappearance of these scenes, but shrugged and pointed out, "They cut quite a few of the characters. I wasn't the only one who suffered." Indeed, anyone who cared about the movie suffered too, because it was one of those pictures misunderstood by the studios, and on its April 1983 release it was hung with the standard cursory release and misleading promotion. "To say that nobody came would be an understatement," the *New York Times* wrote. But in October it played at the New York Film Festival, where it was received tolerably well, and Fox, which had acquired two new key executives who screened the picture and went absolutely ape for it, rereleased it the following month. The advertising now was more *Norma Rae* than *Bobby Deerfield*, but again it failed.

Dick and Lainie moved again in 1982, but their days as renters were finally done: they aimed to buy. They found a townhouse-style condo in Studio City and moved in. Over the hills a career advancement was in the offing for Joe Dante, who was talking with John Carpenter and Universal Pictures about directing *Halloween III*. (The finished movie, which was directed by Tommy Lee Wallace, opens with a toy merchant's having his face rearranged by Halloween robots; this would have been Miller's part, one assumes, had Dante made the picture.)

A more tempting offer came along, however, when Steven Spielberg, who had enjoyed both *Piranha* and *The Howling*, invited Dante to be one of the four directors of a new, big-budget anthology horror picture, *Twilight Zone: The Movie*. The other directors were Spielberg, John Landis, and George Miller, so Dante was in some pretty heavy company for a guy who had debuted only three movies earlier by co-directing a sex comedy using Roger Corman's pocket change. The star of the Landis segment—which was shooting first, in the summer, because Landis had another commitment—was none other than Dick Miller's old neighbourhood acquaintance Vic Morrow, to whom Dick reckoned he'd given a leg up into the business almost forty years earlier when he tutored Morrow on how to successfully snag an acting job. Morrow and Miller had plenty in common: Jewish boys from the Bronx, born in the late 1920s, served in the navy in their teens, destined to be actors. Now they were going to be working in the same movie. They wouldn't be sharing any scenes, of course, but after all this time and all this distance, even sharing a picture was something. It showed, Miller thought, that there were paths of fate that might be followed, that everything rising did converge.

By the end of the summer, after the horrible accident that killed Morrow along with two children, Myca Dinh Le and Renee Shin-Yi Chen, Miller figured the *Twilight Zone* movie would be canceled. To his surprise it was not—the studio, Warner Bros., wanted their Steven Spielberg movie more than they feared bad publicity—and by October the cameras were rolling with Miller behind a counter and playing Walter Paisley once again. "There was no part for him in the story per se," Dante said, "but we added an opening, and he's this sort of rapacious diner owner who tries to pick up Kathleen Quinlan."

"He sort of hits on her," Miller admitted, but this was once again a complex role for its size, not just another roadhouse masher. The scene opens Dante's segment, "It's a Good Life," in which Quinlan's character meets an omnipotent boy at Miller's diner, knocks him over with her car, then goes home with him to meet the family he keeps terrorized in the cartoon funhouse world he has created. Walter Paisley begins by helpfully showing Quinlan where to go on a map, proceeds to lean in too close and act too friendly, then, after a couple of bullies have pushed the kid around, appears genuinely abashed on behalf of his unruly clientele. In between these stations he barks at the kid for handling a video game too roughly and defends him from verbal assaults by the adults in the place when the video game appears to interfere with the TV signal. "He paid for his game—the TV is free," the fair-minded Paisley reminds his customers. Finally, at the end of the scene, he's angry at his customers for chasing the pretty Quinlan away. It's a lot of territory for one minor character to hit in a three-minute scene, but Miller negotiated it all like a master skier on a mogul run.

In fact, he added a bit too much character for the director's taste, Miller told *Fangoria*'s David Everitt. As Paisley became "a little more interested in her than the ordinary luncheonette counterman would be," Dante laughed and said, "That's marvelous, if we were doing a story of you and her, but, you know, try to tame it down." Miller did, and Dante was well pleased with the result. When Miller was wrapped, Dante presented him with the sign that set dressers had created for the roadside establishment: WALTER PAISLEY, PROPRIETOR. Miller hung it on his wall, and three decades later it hung there still.

He did a bunch of TV that year, including an episode of *Taxi* in which he played a sailor. He donned a stained sweatshirt and wore a Dixie cup, which put him in mind of his navy days. The guest star, playing the father of Tony Danza's character, was Canadian actor Donnelly Rhodes, with whom Miller had worked on an episode of *Soap*. All of them, along with Wendell Wright (a tall man, of course, a veteran of *The Howling*, with whom Miller is paired in the usual attempt at comically incongruous effect) are on board a merchant vessel, which, for Rhodes and Danza, is a chance for father–son bonding. Rhodes asks Miller if he knows any "sea shanties," to which Miller answers, "I don't even know what a sea shanty is!" and suggests in its stead "New York, New York." (They had rehearsed with "Oklahoma," but at the last moment director Michael Zinberg came up and said, "We're not doing

'Oklahoma.' We're doing 'New York, New York.'" Miller protested that they didn't know the song. "That's what I want—you're not supposed to know it," Zinberg told him.) The entire cast haltingly belts out the tune for what seems like minutes, and the highlight of all this is Miller's earnest, bellowing solo rendition of the line "I wanna wake up in the city that doesn't sleep!" "That was beautiful," Miller remembered.

Less musical were his turns in the nighttime soap *Knots Landing* and a forgotten crimefighter show called *The Renegades*. The *Knots Landing* episode was directed by Ernest Pintoff, whose one-take, move-the-hell-on approach to filmmaking was very much in the early Corman tradition. Miller's scene is set in a Vegas quickie-marriage chapel, and Miller, playing an affable mook named Al Spanky and having evidently just married a tall redhead played by June Berry, commands the background with his mugging. For *The Renegades* he played a cop in an episode directed by Barbara Peeters, who had also directed Miller in *Starhops*. He'd worked so long by this point, and so variously, that he was constantly working with people he'd worked with before. There was a tremendous collegiality on all these sets, and plenty of bellyaching and story swapping.

As enjoyable as it all was, it seemed like time for a vacation; the Millers had been sailing most weekends over the past decade, but hadn't been on a proper holiday in years. Allan Arkush was calling, though, asking Miller if he'd like to play a cab driver in *Get Crazy*, which, based on the idea that it was going to be the *Airplane!* of rock 'n' roll movies, had beaten the long odds against it and attracted several million dollars in financing. "But Allan would never give me a start date," Miller said. So near the end of July Lainie and Dick booked a Hawaiian holiday and jumped on a plane. "As soon as I walked into the hotel and threw my bag on the bed," Miller remembered, "the phone rang. It was Allan. He was starting to shoot in three days. I would have had to fly back the next morning, because I had to be there a day in advance." Dick put his foot down and told Arkush he was staying in Hawaii. "I wasn't hostile," he said, "but this was bull, because he had told me they would be starting in two weeks." When Miller returned to Los Angeles, Arkush called him up, apologized for the misunderstanding, and asked if Miller might come down and do a short bit in the film anyway. Miller was happy to accept.

Get Crazy was Arkush's attempt to dramatize the craziness he, Jonathan Kaplan, and others had witnessed while working at the Fillmore East. It was initially intended as a fairly straightforward picture, even earnest, but under the ministrations of producers and executive producers, it became the kind of comedy that featured naked groupies, a space alien pharmacologist, a ticking time bomb, and an ambulatory joint. It wasn't far from being *Rock 'n' Roll High School 2*, right down to the presence of Clint Howard, Paul Bartel, Mary Waronov, and a Ramones t-shirt. If Miller hadn't been on his first vacation in years, he'd have played a cab driver who ferries Lou Reed around for nearly the whole picture, as Reed noodles out a new folk song and generally does a mellow piss-take on Dylan. Instead, but in a way fortuitously, Miller was cast as a dad so nerdy as to seem lobotomized, and Jackie Joseph was cast as the mom. "I'm there in a sweater, smoking pipes, wearing loafers and watering the lawn," Miller said. "That's the character." It's hard to tell if Miller is trying to make the man seem lecherous when his teenage daughter, played by Stacey Nelkin, appears on the front walk and shows off her outfit to her parents, or if the stream from his garden hose increased from a mist to a hard, steady jet for no particular reason at all. His one line, "Let's see how ya look," fails to clarify matters one way or the other. It's the very definition of a nothing scene, but while it would have been nice to see Miller get more business in a taxicab encounter with Lou Reed (and Arkush surely would have given more business to Miller than he did to the actor who ended up playing the cabbie), there is at the same time something very apt, indeed inspired, about casting Miller and Joseph as an old married couple. Certainly Joe Dante must have thought so.

Late in the spring of 1983 Miller did an equally nothing scene for first-time director Michael Chapman in the early Tom Cruise vehicle *All the Right Moves*. Chapman, a renowned cameraman who had shot several pictures for Martin Scorsese, and who was married to *Hollywood Boulevard* editor Amy Jones, called Miller up at the tail end of the March–April 1983 shoot and asked whether he'd be willing to do a tiny one-line bit, in which he walks through the doorway of an auditorium and shouts at Tom Cruise and Lea Thompson, who are hunched down in the seats and trying not to be seen. Miller said sure, and told *Fangoria*, "It was [Chapman's] first director's job and he said he thought it would be good luck to have Dick Miller in the picture." The bulk of the movie had been shot in a rainy, dismal Johnstown, PA, but Miller's scene was part of some pickup work done in Los Angeles. The brevity and nothingness of the part astounded even Miller. "Whether you've seen the movie or not," he said, "you wouldn't know about it."

A Corman job came along around this time, and it was "little" in a different sense. Roger, still not finished recycling spaceship footage and James Horner music from *Battle Beyond the Stars*, found a use for both in *Space Raiders*. The picture told the *Treasure Island*-inspired tale of a boy's adventure with roguish space pirates, and was rinky-dink even by Corman standards. "It looks like Roger's—I wouldn't say rip-off—it's Roger's *tribute* to E.T.," Miller said. He was hired to play Crazy Mel, a used spaceship salesman who appears as a six-inch hologram doing a fast-pitch ad and wearing something close to a Robot Monster helmet in addition to the standard tacky blazer. It was a one-joke bit: *plus ça change*; and probably the least substantial role of Miller's career. How could you get less substantial than playing a hologram of a huckster? Miller arrived at Corman's lumberyard, put on the helmet, stood in front of a black cloth, and delivered his lines; cut, print, paid, gone. The picture opened in July, but few noticed, as Miller himself had barely noticed making it.

But being on the *Space Raiders* set, however briefly, made him think. His *Fangoria* interlocutor, David Everitt, asked him if working on Roger Corman films was still as much fun in the 1980s as it had been thirty years earlier, and Miller's response was melancholic. "Well, no," he said. "It's a different set-up. Roger's not around on the set. Everyone on *Space Raiders* is young and I would imagine gifted, and they're all very enthusiastic; but the word you used was fun, and that was something … maybe I've grown too old, but that doesn't seem to be there." To Miller, low-budget moviemaking had become too self-serious, and the willingness to do crazy things was missing. "That adventurous, pioneering aspect of filmmaking is gone," he said. But he maintained his perspective, noting, "The people who made films in the '20s and '30s would say the same thing to me; you know, I'd start talking about making films, they'd say, 'Git outta here! You're crazy! You should have been around *then*!'"

Miller had problems other than missing the good old days. He was getting jobs, but at the end of it there was always the feeling that another might never come along. He was used to this anxiety, of course, but he was always conscious of it. Worse, much worse: in October 1983, Schwab's closed its doors suddenly, for, it was claimed, "family reasons." The closing made national news, with every media outlet taking care to mention that Lana Turner had not in fact been discovered at Schwab's. For Miller and his klatch buddies, naturally, it was a deep, deep drag. There never was, later, a place as actor-friendly as Schwab's, and the drugstore was laden with memories.

Dick and Lainie had met there, and a lot of Apfel's coffee had flowed by since then. It was part of his identity too. An habitué claimed, in his blog, "I don't think I ever ate there without seeing Dick Miller, who was so good in all those Roger Corman pictures."

Miller was a creature of habit, among many things, so this disruption in his routine was intolerable. But there was nothing he could do about it except find another regular hangout, and he settled on Theodore's, a modest diner on Santa Monica Boulevard. There were booths, Formica tabletops, wood panelling and movie posters on the walls, and a patio outside for when the weather was fine, which it always was. By 10:30 in the morning, Miller was usually there, chewing on an egg salad sandwich and exchanging stories and actor's laments with fellow thespians such as Robert Forster, Harry Northup, and Frank Pesce. "Everybody is swell here," Miller told an interviewer some time after adopting the place. "We don't have a big crowd, but it's a jolly one. But there will never be another Schwab's. *That* was the place."

18   It was all brand new to me

Norma Desmond, the Hollywood wash-up in *Sunset Boulevard*, claims she's still big; it's the pictures that have gotten small. For Dick Miller, the pictures got bigger, but he stayed the same size.

Except in the world of the fan magazine, in which, as the 1980s progressed, he grew to the size and status of a giant. This was the real metastasization of Miller's cult status, and it coincided with his appearance in movies popular enough to put his face, if not his name, in the mainstream public eye. By the end of 1984, an exceptionally fruitful year for both Miller and his growing legion of fans, he had truly and forever become That Guy.

Before he had even finished shooting his *Twilight Zone* episode, Joe Dante was in pre-production on his next picture, a horror movie script called *Gremlins*, by a young unproduced New York writer named Chris Columbus. While living by himself in a loft, Columbus had been frightened by mice; their skittering feet inspired an idea for a story positing what if, instead of mice, it was little green monsters running around? It was E.T. reimagined as a horror movie, beginning with a twelve-year-old boy who receives a strange pet from his buttoned-up businessman father. The pet, a sort of hamster-monkey, transforms into a raptor-toothed goblin when certain nonsensical rules of care are broken, then multiplies at some mathematically vague rate. The mass of gremlins thus produced run around biting the heads off townsfolk; turn the local McDonald's into a slaughterhouse of dead customers (the people eaten but the burgers left untouched); and kill the boy's family and their little dog too. Steven Spielberg, who wanted to try producing a low-budget genre movie, read the script and thought it ideal both for his purposes and as something for Dante to direct.

Two things happened then: the script went through further drafts, during which the darkness was leavened and the violence, at least the violence against humans, was significantly reduced; and, as the monsters were designed and the technical challenges of realizing them priced out, the budget commensurably climbed. Joe Dante, to his relief, was not suddenly replaced by Joseph Sargent or John 'Bud' Cardos, or someone similar, as might have occurred had Spielberg not been in charge. Of course, as Tobe Hooper could probably have attested, there was the risk of being fundamentally replaced by Spielberg himself, but that did not happen either. In fact, Spielberg was nothing but supportive, not just of Dante but of the project and of the tone Dante thought it needed. (He was not above providing Dante with little reminders of what could come to pass, however—in his cameo appearance, Spielberg, who had broken his leg, is seen whizzing around the background on a motorized wheelchair, watching *Poltergeist* on a little portable television.)

Spielberg was supportive of the casting too, even as he looked at it side-eyed. Mike Finnell, who produced the movie, remembered that, as actors such as Keye Luke, Scott Brady, Kenneth Tobey, and Harry Carey Jr. showed up on the cast list, "Steven would say, 'Oh, you guys raided the Motion Picture [Old Age] Home again.'" Dante was still forming his theory that Spielberg, who loved working with new, fresh talent, had indulged in a large cast of seasoned character faces only on *1941*, and that the muted performance and poor reception of it still stung. Dick Miller had appeared in *1941*, as well as *I Wanna Hold Your Hand* and *Used Cars*, two other under-performing pictures Spielberg had produced, and Dante might reasonably have worried how the mogul would react on seeing that familiar, craggy visage in a major part in *Gremlins*. But he had no apparent objection.

Spielberg's fresh talent came in the form of the picture's leads, Zach Galligan and Phoebe Cates. At some point in the rewrites, because Spielberg was reluctant to repeat the template he'd laid out in *E.T.*, the main character in *Gremlins* had grown from a twelve-year-old boy into a young adult who held a full-time job at a bank yet still lived with his parents, and who maintained all the appurtenances of pre-pubescence that neither Columbus nor Dante ever found the time to change. Galligan, nineteen years old and very green, was sweating and nervous, and glad that in his first scene to be shot in the picture he had only a single line to say. He spent the rest of the scene either gawping from the side or performing a few simple bits of business; the heavy lifting would be done by his co-stars, Cates and Miller. "I didn't think I belonged there," Galligan said. "I kind of felt like I'd snuck onto this movie somehow and bamboozled people." Between takes and at lunch, Galligan launched into a barrage of questions on the older actor's life and career: about Jack Nicholson and the Corman pictures, about the old days of TV and starring in Westerns. "I wanted to see what it was like to have a life as a long-time actor," Galligan said, "because obviously at age nineteen, this is something I was thinking about, like, 'How is this as a career? How would it feel to do this for thirty, forty years?'" Miller, garrulous as ever and pleased to find an acolyte, was happy to oblige.

Though he'd worked with Miller several times before, starting with his stint as the production manager of *Starhops*, Mike Finnell was equally buoyed to have the veteran thespian on set. "It was fun seeing all these guys that I had grown up watching in movies on TV when I was a little kid," Finnell recalled fondly. "Getting to meet them, it was, like, thrilling, you know? And they were always amazed that you were thrilled. They were just these journeymen actors, and they couldn't believe it when you would get excited about meeting them." Jackie Joseph was charmingly cynical about appearing in movies for young directors like Dante and Allan Arkush. "I could just see them," she said, "all sitting around their little room saying, 'Guess what funny people we used in our movie?'"

Miller was playing a middle-aged xenophobe called Mr. Futterman, lately laid off from his job at the noodle factory. The name came from the 1956 John Ford classic *The Searchers*, but when Miller saw his character's handle, he thought he'd have to play it with a German accent. Miller had road tested a comic German accent two years earlier, in the still unreleased *National Lampoon Goes to the Movies*, but was relieved to find the Futterman character was apple pie American. He was, in fact, a veteran of "Doubleyou-Doubleyou-Eye-Eye," as Futterman himself puts it in an early, drunken scene (it was Miller's idea to play it drunk, to make the xenophobia a little more palatable), and gives the creatures and the picture itself their name when he reminisces about the malevolent little goblins blamed by servicemen whenever mechanical things fouled up during the war. "Gremlins," he slurs, shaking his head. "You gotta watch out for them foreigners, 'cause they plant gremlins in the machinery."

Dante was taking a cue from his friend Arkush when he cast Jackie Joseph as Futterman's wife. Miller himself also claimed to have been the one to suggest this reteaming, but whatever the case, the casting was perfect. It was perhaps too perfect: after *Gremlins* became successful beyond all of Warner Bros.' most optimistic predictions, casting directors would come upon a middle-aged couple in a genre script and cry, "Get the Millers!" Laughed Miller, "I say, 'We're not married! That's Jackie Joseph!'"

Miller's scenes were mostly shot over the first week of the two-and-a-half month schedule, and he didn't interact much with the gremlins. As was usually the case, and on Dante pictures especially, Miller enjoyed himself. He liked Jackie Joseph, liked reminiscing about *Little Shop* with her, and he enjoyed working with Galligan and Cates; and he was happy to be in the company of Dante, John Hora, and the rest of Dante's company. Belinda Balaski was playing a small part, and Miller invited her to join his green room poker circle, which included Lainie and some of the other actors. "You guys play for money?" she asked, and was assured that, yes, they did: it was penny poker, like Dick and Lainie used to play with Jack Nicholson. Finally, Balaski took him up on the invitation, and by the end of the evening Miller owed her six dollars. "He was so mad!" Balaski chuckled. "He paid me my six dollars, but the truth is he never invited me up there again."

Galligan was very much a Miller fan, from before *Gremlins* but the more so after hearing his stories and sharing the screen with him. "The great thing about Dick is, what you see is what you get with Dick Miller," Galligan said. "That kind of down-to-earth how-ya-doin' New Yorker guy, that's him. He's very nice. I find him very gentle. He strikes me as one of the good guys of Hollywood. I think that's why Joe Dante responded to him, because Joe Dante likes nice people." Sharing the screen with a veteran like Miller held certain risks, though. One early scene had Galligan working on his frozen-up VW Beetle as his neighbour Mr. Futterman, in plaid jacket and earflap cap, of course, ambles out to complain about foreign-made machinery and the gremlins it is ridden with; this, Galligan said, was "the one scene in the movie where I think my performance is really poor." Part of this was an inverse reaction to Miller's relaxed professionalism: while Galligan was nervous, "Dick was so comfortable, and I was so uncomfortable, and the more comfortable he was, the more it made me aware of how artificial I was. So internally I got more and more nervous, and trying to do what he was doing and doing a bad approximation of it." But these dangers, which in any case sprang from Galligan's own brief failure of self-confidence, paled beside the pure pleasure of Miller. "Every time I saw Dick on the call sheet and knew I was going to be working with him, it was always a happy day," Galligan said. "Because he's a good guy."

The feeling evidently was mutual. One day Galligan got an invitation to Miller's house, and, while flattered and very happy to visit, couldn't help wondering why. But when Barbara appeared, Galligan formulated a suspicion. "I could be completely wrong," Galligan said, "but I felt like he wanted to set me up with his daughter, possibly." Galligan, not yet twenty at the time, might have been a little young for Barbara, who was four years older and was in the navy, as her father had been decades before. It seems unlikely she would have responded to Galligan's overtures, had he been disposed to make them. But, Galligan theorized, "[Dick] thought I was this nice young man, and maybe my nice-young-manness would rub off on his daughter." It wasn't fated to be. "His daughter was very nice, and she was pretty and she was cool, but I was dating someone else at the time."

By early May Miller was more or less done with *Gremlins*, though he went back to visit and to record screams and yells and wild lines in the looping session. There was in particular a lot of yelling to record for Miller's final scene, in which, dressed in housecoat and earflap hat, he goes out to investigate the cause of his poor TV reception, only to be pursued back indoors by his own Kentucky Harvester. A gremlin is at the wheel, and Miller runs to his front door (against which a tree had fallen, blocking it and causing a few seconds of genuine panic for Miller as the tractor rapidly overtook him) and into his sitcom-set house, where he and Jackie Joseph are corralled into a corner by the machine and, presumably, bisected by the sharp steel bucket.

But no, the Futtermans would survive. As the picture was being finished and the sound being mixed, somebody thought to add a TV newsman's voice "talking about 'Murray Futterman at Mercy Hospital' or something like that," Dante recalled. "We just couldn't bring ourselves to kill him." Miller later became convinced it was Spielberg himself who had swooped in and demanded that the Futtermans escape the gremlins. "Not impossible," Dante said. "I don't remember. They were always looking for ways to take the edge off the movie, 'cause it was supposed to be a kids' movie." Whoever made the call, it would prove a fortuitous one for Miller.

The summer of 1983 was, for Miller, relaxed and largely untroubled. *Twilight Zone: The Movie* was released and was a substantial hit. Miller saw a lot of pictures (*Blue Thunder*, *Psycho II*, *Zelig*, *National Lampoon's Vacation*, many others); hung out at Schwab's (not realizing time was running out for the place); managed a vacation of his own with Lainie; and stayed in his Studio City townhouse, reading, watching movies on TV, or busying himself around the house. He visited the set of *Gremlins*, where Dante, creature effects man Chris Walas, and a whole crew of others were slowly going crazy trying to film the puppets doing increasingly complicated things week after agonizing week. *Get Crazy*, meanwhile, came out in August and vanished so quickly afterward that it seemed somehow to have closed before its premiere.

In the fall Miller was recording his *Gremlins* screams, and one day, late in the process, a downcast-looking Mike Finnell admitted that he had nowhere to go for Thanksgiving. Miller and Lainie invited him to join the party they were holding with some friends, "and I had a great Thanksgiving dinner," a still-to-this-day-grateful Finnell said. Soon after the holiday Miller got busy again, nabbing a small but featured role in the second instalment of the alien invasion miniseries *V*. He played Dan Pascal, a turtleneck-wearing counterfeiter who helps out the earthly Resistance by making them some fake security badges; later Dan is captured by the alien fascists, beaten up a little, and forced to tell what he knows of the rebels. He's soon blasted by an extraterrestrial ray gun.

Miller would die again soon enough, at the hairy end of a shotgun in James Cameron's *The Terminator*. Cameron had spent a few years working for Roger Corman, building sets, concocting innovative special effects (everyone remembered his dancing maggots from *Galaxy of Terror*), and directing second-unit material; and he remembered Miller well from his sausage factory days, when he'd worked, among other jobs, as a production assistant on *Rock 'n' Roll High School*. "I may have run into Cameron on the Corman lot," Miller said. "All I can think of is that everybody who works for Corman is required to see five Dick Miller films, and after seeing those films you pretty much know what I can do." Accordingly, Cameron offered Miller a part in his first feature, *Piranha 2*, presumably the same character he'd played in the Dante original, but Miller turned it down.

Gale Ann Hurd, Cameron's producer, was also a Corman alumnus, and had co-produced *Smokey Bites the Dust*. Naturally Cameron and Hurd were Miller fans, and even though the part they had for Miller in their new robot picture was small, with no more than three or four scripted lines, they felt it was a perfect showcase for the actor's talent, or at least a satisfactory expression of their admiration for it. In this Cameron and Hurd were correct, but the mark Miller left on *The Terminator* had little to do with their script. The picture began shooting in March 1984, and Miller's scene came up early in the schedule (when the company was still on days rather than the long all-nighters that were to come) at a Van Nuys gun shop called the Alamo. Miller worked out his performance before arriving on set, deciding ahead of time the tone he would strive for and the nuances he would weave in.

Miller got along famously with both Cameron ("[He] seemed to know exactly what he wanted to do, which I liked," said Miller) and with Arnold Schwarzenegger, who played the big robot at whose servo-motored hands Miller's character would make his last stand. Miller and Cameron talked through the scene before it was shot, with Schwarzenegger off to the side smoking a big cigar. "How you gonna play this?" the director asked. "I think you're in fear."

"These guys aren't in fear," Miller said. "This is a gun shop."

"What about the size of the man?" Cameron asked, gesturing at the Austrian bulk, who was smiling and wreathed in smoke, and who dwarfed Miller even while sitting down.

Miller, who'd thought all this through ahead of time, just shrugged. "Happens every day. Motorcyclists, guys like that."

Cameron saw his point, and let Miller play the nameless character the way he had already decided that he should. Even as the cameras began rolling, though, and action was called, the actor wasn't sure how he would deliver his last line, to be spoken as the clerk notices his customer loading a shotgun. Cameron was still of the opinion that the shop owner would be terrified, bugging out his eyes and shouting, "Don't do that! You can't do that!" He might even have accepted Dick's famous "Skull," as seen in *Not Of This Earth*. But when the time came, Miller just gestured lazily in the cyborg's direction and gave a terse "You can't do that." The Terminator informs the shopkeeper that on that particular point he's incorrect, then pulls the trigger. Cameron declined to show the bloody results of the gunshot, but this was more likely a budgetary and scheduling consideration than a sudden spasm of restraint, or an accommodation to Miller's aversion for special effects makeup.

Miller enjoyed working with the big Austrian ("Arnold's got a great sense of humour"), and was grateful for the opportunity to play the shopkeeper character as he believed it should be played. The Van Nuys location was close to his condo; he did his thing and felt good about it, and liked the people; he earned a few bucks and was home with his feet up in a matter of hours. Entirely satisfactory: "A typical *Howling* sort of experience," Miller called it. He was pleased to receive a letter from Cameron after the picture wrapped, thanking him for adding "that special Miller touch" to *The Terminator*, and even more so when, after a Corman-quick post-production period, the picture was released in October of that year and became a hit out of all proportion to its modest budget, and Miller's Q score was propelled higher than it had ever been before. Miller, who had, after all, been onscreen in *The Terminator* for less than a minute, told *Fangoria* magazine that he was "very surprised at the number of people who were affected by that one scene in the picture, people who had not noticed me before." Fans on the street were waving at him and saying hello.

But they'd been doing that even before *The Terminator*'s release. *Gremlins* had been released in June, and as it became a giant hit (and a cult movie at the same time, a feat that few but Dante have managed to pull off), Miller was substantially more famous than he'd ever been before. After all, the part was much larger than he'd lately become used to, and moreover the character had a name. "I'm Mr. Futterman to people," he said. "They don't even know my real name." A friend of Lainie's pestered Dick for autographed photos of "Mr. Futterman," and kids on the street would wave and shout "Hi, Mr. Futterman!" Miller pointed to *Gremlins*' main summer box-office competition and said, "What's great is the connection with the name of the character in the movie. In other words, who knows the names of the three characters in *Ghostbusters*? You know the actors, but not the names of the characters." Miller felt mild regret that a major Futterman scene, in which he slumps in his recliner and bemoans the loss of his job at the noodle factory, had been cut, but *Gremlins* otherwise was, and would ever remain, a high point in his career.

The release of *Gremlins* (and later of *The Terminator*) also put Miller into the pages of the monster movie magazine *Fangoria* more relentlessly than ever before, and by the summer of 1984 he was already a sort of totem for the magazine and for its readers. The journal and, through the letters page, its readers tracked Miller's roles, even the non-horror ones; mounted letter-writing campaigns to secure him specific roles or honours; applauded his appearances large and small; and deplored that in the course of them he was so often killed. One letter to the editor suggested that Miller might in fact be an earthly incarnation of God Almighty, and though there was disagreement on this point, it was slight. Another letter insisted that, within seconds of seeing the *Terminator* gun shop owner's face, the viewer knew everything about the character, down to what he had eaten for breakfast that morning, all of it presumably inscribed in the wrinkles on Miller's face. Altogether, it was an earnest worship; it never seemed like a put-on.

Fangoria had come into being several years earlier as, probably, the natural and perhaps only possible evolution from the more innocent monster mag put out by Forrest J. Ackerman, *Famous Monsters of Filmland*. Movies had depicted gore before, and sometimes to ridiculous extremes, but it wasn't until the mid-1970s, in both independent and studio pictures, that extra helpings of tomato paste really came into vogue. By 1979 the fan literature was finally catching up and *Fangoria* was born. Initially it covered horror of all kinds (early issues included, even privileged, fantasy and science fiction coverage), but, under the editorship of Robert "Uncle Bob" Martin, and likely under the influence of its own name, graphic depictions of decapitations and impalements soon became the periodical's real bread and butter. (When it came in the mail it was wrapped in a featureless brown paper sleeve, like porn.) But the magazine always maintained an appreciation for vintage horror, though it concentrated its nostalgia on AIP, Hammer Films, and other low-budget heroes, and largely left classic Universal Studios product like Frankenstein and the Wolf Man to *Famous Monsters*.

In 1981, when *Fangoria* was putting out its sixteenth issue, a writer named David Everitt arrived at the magazine, bringing with him a broad range of pop-cultural interests, a natural contrariness, and a beehive-poking sense of humour. He also carried an abiding appreciation for Miller and his performances, and by issue nineteen the magazine was publishing a five-page piece called 'Walter Paisley Lives!' Ten issues later, in September 1983, there was another, 'The Dick Miller Zone—The Exclusive Interview that *Playboy* Couldn't Get." This was also, by no small coincidence, the first issue with Everitt as the sole editor. Everitt's appreciation for Miller had begun before his tenure with *Fangoria,* of course; like everyone else he had lapped up the actor's appearances in the Corman pictures. But his appreciation ran even deeper than most. Before joining the magazine he had co-authored a book called *The Manly Handbook*, a guide on how to live life as a Real Man, "written so that a real man can understand it," the jacket claimed; and herein was the key to Everitt's Miller obsession. "To David," Uncle Bob Martin said, "Dick Miller was a latter-day avatar of manliness in its purest form."

Where Miller was concerned, Everitt put his money where his mouth was, or at least put his mouth where his mouth was. Early in 1984 he shaved his moustache and wrote an editorial threatening to keep his upper lip bare until such time as Miller received his much-deserved feature guest spot on the David Letterman show. "You can't tell me that America isn't ready for Dick Miller on late night television," he wrote. "Drastic predicaments require drastic measures and I'm prepared to go the distance." It sounded like a joke, but to Everitt it was not, and most *Fangoria* readers knew what was going on. Montgomery Wood, a reader from Texas, wrote a letter claiming Everitt must be Miller's son; Brad Ragsdale, from Illinois, posited that the Midnight Writer, a utility pseudonym occasionally employed by the magazine, must in reality be Miller; and Thomas Hill of Georgia wrote in simply to declare that Miller was "tops!" There were so many calls for a Dick Miller poster that the magazine set up a special pipeline, "Miller Pin-Up," to which such requests might be sent. (Evidently not enough of these were sent, however, since no Miller pin-up was ever run.)

Though Miller could not recall much about Everitt himself, and this new twist on his sidebar fame was slightly bewildering, he didn't mind the attention. "It was all brand new to me," he said. "I thought it was amazing. They were wonderful to me." By the end of Everitt's tenure at *Fangoria*, Miller's fame had evolved from one man's infatuation into something close to editorial policy, and the magazine reported his stats and benchmarks as if he were Sandy Koufax. For example: the laser scorch marks Miller sported in *V* were, *Fangoria* exclusively revealed, the first time Miller had worn any kind of special makeup for one of his cinematic deaths. By virtue of being a scoop no other publication would chase or even think to publish, exclusives like this were rendered more exclusive rather than less, and Miller himself became an almost personal commodity to readers who were hep. And while most of the magazine's readership was surely perplexed by the actor's perpetual presence in its pages, there were no complaints, and the ones who did get it, got it for life.

It was all largely thanks to Everitt, but the journal did not forget Miller once Everitt was gone; and Everitt's untimely death further reinforced what might have been an easily sundered connection. That *Fangoria* in its later years was frequently run by people who had been devoted readers in its heyday, and that it was largely animated by a jolly spirit of nostalgia, and for a gore magazine an uncommonly warm spirit, ensured a fealty to Miller that lasted in the magazine's pages until its apparent 2017 demise. The magazine has since announced a surprise disinterment, but whether its long-standing championship of Miller will rise from the grave along with it is yet unknown.

When explaining to the average moviegoer who Dick Miller is, *Gremlins* and *The Terminator* provide the most immediate references, and, unless in his declining years Miller cures cancer or flies into the sun, they presumably always will. There was other work that same year, however, which kept his face familiar to denizens of all different quarters.

With his bone-deep love of rock music, Jonathan Kaplan was a natural candidate to direct music videos between his TV and feature work, and he was conscripted to shoot a promo for "Infatuation," the first single from Rod Stewart's summer of '84 album *Camouflage*. The video featured Kay Lenz, Miller's co-star in *White Line Fever* and *Moving Violation*, as a sexy lady who movies into Stewart's condo; when he is shown a picture of her by private eye Mike Mazurki (who had appeared in *Which Way to the Front?* and would later share the screen with Miller in *Mob Boss*), Stewart quickly becomes infatuated. The detective informs Stewart that the woman is a gangster's moll, and shows a photo of Lenz sharing a laugh with Miller to prove it, and Stewart's infatuation immediately broadens to encompass Peeping Tom-ism and stalking. In playing the gangster Miller was kitted out in the spiffy pinstripes and pocket square he so often sported in such roles, and he got to ride a Griffith Park merry-go-round, his long white tie swinging centrifugally out to the side and a big, big smile on his face. The video was produced by long-time Corman associate Teri Schwartz, who had worked in various capacities on *Candy Stripe Nurses, Capone, Big Bad Mama, Hollywood Boulevard,* and *Starhops*; she later had gone to work producing commercials for Robert Abel and Associates, then had founded that company's music video arm, Robert Abel Entertainment. Schwartz hired her old pals Kaplan and his fellow music lover Allan Arkush, among others, to direct the videos, and they in turn hired familiar faces to act in them alongside the rock stars.

In late March 1984 Miller made an appearance in W*A*L*T*E*R, a sitcom pilot following the adventures of Radar O'Reilly from M*A*S*H on his return stateside from the hilarious horrors of war in Korea. O'Reilly, as ever played by Gary Burghoff (who was shorter even than Miller), has become a rookie cop in St. Louis, walking the beat with his idiot pal Wendell and dealing with a parade of quasi-comic near-crimes. Despite the show's mid-'50s setting, Miller played the owner of a vaudeville theatre seemingly ported in from thirty years earlier, who calls in the police to settle a fracas between his two star burlesque performers. It was reunion time for Miller, who found that one of the burly-Q girls was played by June Berry, the tall redhead he'd married a few years before in *Knots' Landing*. Miller sported a little black moustache, but otherwise played his exasperated business owner the same way he'd played a thousand of them before. W*A*L*T*E*R itself was doomed and would never go to series: that was a foregone conclusion, given its baffling title (which hurt even to type—no way to attract favourable press), its dumb, redundant premise (after all, *AfterMASH*, almost as bad, had premiered less than a year earlier), and its utter lack of laughs. The erstwhile pilot aired on July 17 (in the eastern half of the country only, as it was pre-empted west of the Great Divide by the Democratic National Convention, so Miller couldn't have watched it if he'd wanted to), after which everyone involved, along with the massive, slow-grinding wheels of history itself, aggressively forgot it had ever happened. (Only YouTube remembers today.)

He might have been too heavily engaged that summer to watch W★A★L★T★E★R even if it had been broadcast where he could see it. The year 1984 was Miller's career *annus mirabilis*, the busiest year he could remember. There was more publicity than ever too: at the end of July he was the subject of a feature article in the *Los Angeles Times* titled "You Know His Face, But Can You Give His Name?" With this, Miller was now most famous for not being famous at all. Just after the publication of this article, Miller was called to play a small part in a new Martin Scorsese film, *After Hours*, which was exciting enough, but he was further thrilled to find that, unlike on *New York, New York*, he would be working with Scorsese in New York.

The *After Hours* script came from a Columbia film student called Joe Minion, who had written it as an assignment for his instructor Dusan Makavejev. In telling the tale of a buttoned-down computer programmer acting on impulse for the first time in his life, and finding himself trapped in the lower circles of Soho as a result, the story traded in two popular 1980s subgenres, One Crazy Night and Punish the Yuppie. Makavejev passed it on to Double Play productions, a company run by actors Griffin Dunne and Amy Robinson, who loved it and saw in the yuppie a perfect part for Dunne, and in the film itself a perfect project for Scorsese. Scorsese was busy putting together his long-cherished Bible picture *The Last Temptation of Christ*, and passed, so Dunne and Robinson turned to a young, tousle-haired director named Tim Burton. But the holy epic fell apart, and Scorsese, after a brief period of soul searching and several years of unemployment, decided he'd be better off tackling a leaner, cheaper, altogether more Cormanesque production. The picture would shoot for forty days in the late summer on a budget of about $4.5 million: low figures for Scorsese by this point and a fraction of the *New York, New York* cost and schedule. Upon learning of Scorsese's renewed interest, Burton graciously bowed out, and Scorsese began assembling one of the most eclectic, uncharacteristic casts of his career. Griffin Dunne, Rosanna Arquette, John Heard, Verna Bloom, Catherine O'Hara, Teri Garr, Cheech & Chong—it was the first time he'd worked with any of them, but Scorsese made sure to bring in a couple of familiar New Yorky faces too. Victor Argo, playing the diner cashier, was one, and Miller, as the diner waiter, Pete, was the other.

And happy Miller was to score a working trip back to the city he still loved, in a production that promised to be several notches in quality above the likes of W★A★L★T★E★R. The trip in itself is proof of Scorsese's regard for Miller, since with its modest budget *After Hours* could hardly afford to provide plane tickets, per diems, and hotels to bit players when it didn't have to; and New York City was not exactly bereft of competent actors who looked and sounded generally like Miller. But Scorsese's intuition proved correct: Miller is perfect in the role.

Playing Pete was an opportunity for Miller to show off his nice-guy side, which after all was much closer to his genuine personality than the cynical or about-to-blow-a-gasket small-business owners he more often played. Miller described Pete as a "friendly, Saroyan-type waiter in an all-night diner," which is about right; he is presented as a sweet guy with a protective, paternal interest in Arquette's fragile character, Marcy, but at the same time a generous attitude toward her would-be suitors. Miller's longest scene, a conversation between him and Dunne's harried programmer, illustrated this best, but it was cut out of the picture. (As with some of Miller's other deleted moments, it can be found on the Internet or the home video release of the picture.) But even if this scene didn't make it to the final cut, *After Hours* gave Miller other opportunities, including the honour of speaking the title line as part of his dialogue (he gives Dunne a cup of coffee on the house, reasoning that, after all, "it's after hours"), and arguably the single best shot of Miller in the movies: a dolly shot pulling Pete as he snatches Marcy's blown kiss out of the air.

The summer and fall were rammed with work. Miller appeared in an episode of *Tales from the Darkside*, an anthology horror show produced by George A. Romero. The show was shot simultaneously both in New York and LA; Miller's segment, titled "All a Clone by the Telephone," was overseen by the West Coast unit in a small warehouse in East LA, not far from a particularly odiferous Farmer John rendering plant. Miller played Seymour Furman, a crusty but good-humoured agent very similar to his Walter Paisley Mk. II in *Hollywood Boulevard*. His client was a struggling screenwriter played by Harry Anderson (the Mel Tormé-loving jurist of *Night Court*), who was being tormented by his own telephone answering machine, which had for some reason become sentient. Miller's scenes were shot in one day out of the four-day schedule, and he appeared on the show specifically because T. J. Castranova, the West Coast producer of the show, was a diehard Miller fan. Castranova read the script, noted the Furman character, and immediately declared Miller the perfect actor for the part. "There was no sense in questioning that," the episode's director, Frank De Palma, quite reasonably said.

De Palma himself had not been a particularly rabid Miller fan before directing the episode, but, like so many others, had seen him in a million movies and absorbed his mien by osmosis. "From the moment we met," De Palma said, "I felt like I knew him simply because I had seen him so many times. It was almost like seeing a distant relative at a wedding." (So profound was this feeling that De Palma cast Lainie to play a nurse in a separate *Darkside*.) During the "All a Clone by the Telephone" shoot, De Palma quickly came to appreciate Miller's laid-back professionalism and wealth of experience, which, for him, stood in stark contrast to some of the less experienced actors with whom he was working. "Dick is one of those great character actors who is smart enough and intuitive enough to understand a character simply from the script," he said. "Then, when directing his performance, it's almost as if he's on a dimmer switch where you can simply ask him to dial it up or take it down." De Palma has dreamed ever since of directing an entire cast of Millers, "just character actors. People with road-weary, lived-in faces who've actually experienced real life.

"What a joy a set like that would be."

Fans who had loved Miller for years were hiring him left and right that summer. Producer and writer Ira Behr was yet another avid moviegoer who, as a child, had started to realize the same faces were popping up in many of the pictures he was seeing, and Miller's in particular stood out. Behr had his come-to-Miller moment seeing Corman pictures like *Rock All Night* and *Sorority Girl*, in which Dick was cool and undefeatable, and later was astounded at the range of films in which the actor would make his surprise appearances. "It became a thing," Behr said, "like, 'Oh god, look at that, there he is! He's showing up for a second in *The St. Valentine's Day Massacre*, or in *The Wild Angels*!" As Behr grew older, he noticed Miller in the New World exploitation pictures, and then, when *Hollywood Boulevard* came out, was struck by the moment in which Miller, as Walter Paisley the agent, was wistfully watching his own performance in *The Terror*. Behr venerated the Beats and saw in Miller a cool Kerouac-ish cat who did his own thing with a cigarette hanging out the corner of his mouth, the squares be damned. "I never was a fan of Dick the Schlep," Behr said. "Mr. Futterman and things like that, that's not who I liked. I liked the Dick Miller of *The Howling*, of *War of the Satellites* or *Rock All Night*." (*A Bucket of Blood* was, of course, the exception to this personal preference.)

When Behr made his way to Hollywood in the early 1980s, he had a mental list of people he aspired to work with, and Miller's name was somewhere near the top. He began working in television as a story editor and, after a couple of years of this, joined the writing team behind *Fame*, the television iteration of the 1980 Alan Parker film about students at a New York performing arts school. "I'm gonna live forever," the kids sang in the theme song. "I'm gonna learn how to fly." In his new position Behr wrote an episode called "The Monsters That Devoured Las Vegas," which was directed by Allan Arkush. After that, discussion began on another episode, which would take place in a bowling alley, on the theory from the new writing team that the kids needed a place off-campus to hang out. In fact, it was a kind of a combination bowling alley and comedy club, owned by a character called Lou Mackie. Doris, one of the students, played by Valerie Landsburg, is cajoled by her would-be comedian classmates into dating him, on the theory that this will lead to bookings at Lou's club. Doris objects, calling Lou both a "sweaty, slimy sleazebag" and "a major-league slimebag," but finally agrees to sit with Lou to watch their acts. Lou lives up to his billing as an unsavoury bag of something, and Doris rushes off, horrified.

Arkush cavalierly suggested Dick for the Lou Mackie part, and, said Behr, "I literally had to hold on to the sides of my seat so as not to fly up into the ceiling, and I said, 'Yeah, that's a great idea, that's a great idea!'" Miller didn't even have to audition for the part: such was the power of the passionate oratory mustered by Behr in support of the idea. Donald Reiker and Patricia Jones, the incoming executive producers, and Kevin Hooks, who was directing the episode, needed no further proof of Miller's suitability for the role. Behr was delighted, and his first thought was, "Okay, how am I going to work this into getting Dick Miller on to the show on a regular basis?"

Landsburg was twenty-four but looked younger, and was playing a character even younger than she looked; and when fifty-five-year-old Miller read the script, he told the producers, "This is a little, uh, you know, dicey." But he did the part, playing Lou Mackie as a good-natured but handsy old letch. The script was another attempt to make sexual harassment amusing, as had been commonplace in movies since the fifties and now on television, but Miller spiced the bit up with an edge of lonely desperation and as much Mackie-deprecating humour as he thought he could get away with. "I figured it was heavy," Miller said. "It had some funny scenes written into it, but I decided to play the whole thing that way." But Lou Mackie was still a depressing and unsavoury character. "A step above a child molester," Miller allowed.

Behr knew that having such a character as a show regular was a bad idea and would never fly with the execs. He had his first meeting with Miller on the set, and found the actor "wearing some sort of dopey pinstriped gangster suit." Behr was "nervous as hell," he remembered, "and I introduced myself, and he gave me that *look*, that look that said, 'I've heard it all before, whatever you're going to say to me. Good or bad, it won't mean a hill of beans.'"

After shaking hands with a firm double grip, Behr told him, "I'm going to get you back on this show," and Miller responded with something just short of contempt. "He didn't even pretend to believe me," said Behr. But Behr had a plan. He went to one of the young actors, Carlo Imperato, and tried to appear casual, looking around at the bar/bowling alley combo in which they were standing and nodding with approval. "Hey, this is a pretty cool set," Behr said.

"Sure, yeah, it's pretty good," Imperato allowed.

Behr now nodded toward Miller, sitting over across the room. "And *that* guy," he said, "the guy playing Lou Mackie—isn't he terrific?"

Imperato, an agreeable sort, replied, "Yeah, yeah, he's good, he's really good."

"Wouldn't it be great," Behr pressed, "if he could come back, and we could have a place where the kids could hang out?"

Imperato agreed that it would absolutely be great. Behr wheeled around, went up to Reiker and Jones, the executive producers, and told them, "Hey, I was talking to Carlo, and Carlo said all the kids really like the character of Lou Mackie, and wouldn't it be great if the kids had a place to hang out?"

The suggestion that the whole company was jazzed about the idea of a bowling alley hangout run by Dick Miller was completely invented by Behr, but was evidently persuasive enough for the execs. Another writer and eventual producer on the show, former child actor Michael McGreevey, shared Behr's enthusiasm for Miller and backed up Behr's every exaltation. "Yeah, yeah, yeah, a place to hang out, Dick Miller's great!" Before this twin assault any resistance Reiker and Jones might have had crumbled. "He can't be the same character, though," they cautioned.

So Lou Mackie was "modified," though his personal details—name, occupation, so forth—stayed the same. His bowling alley/bar was similarly softened, becoming a bowling alley/malt shoppe. By his second *Fame* appearance, on the tenth episode of season four, he was still irascible but no longer lecherous; a heart of gold was occasionally visible beneath his pink bowling shirt. Still, in berating his wait staff and bussing personnel (personified in that season by none other than Janet Jackson), Miller occasionally seemed to channel the Leonard Di Santis character from *A Bucket of Blood*. "You wanna talk about workin' rooms, work this one!" he barks at Jackson's showbiz hopeful.

"We tried to keep that character as real as possible," Behr said. "He was never a schmuck. He was kind, he was wise, he was a good guy. He was no dummy. He was cynical, he was realistic." Mackie scenes not only traded heavily on Miller's ability to play gruff, or tender, or threatening, or sentimental, or some comic mixture of those states, but also on Dick Miller in-jokes written by Behr and McGreevey, which were based on their frequent on-set conversations with the man himself. In one episode Lou seems to have some industry connections, and uses them to invite "the hottest film producer in town" to see a couple of the kids perform a musical comedy act. In the same episode it was revealed that Lou had a brother, "Duke Mackie the Upholstery King," who had become wealthy in the trade after forcing Lou from the small business they had started together. The ease with which he himself might have been living as an upholsterer instead of an actor, the horrifying, tactile *vision* of such a life, was something Miller frequently contemplated, and to have Lou Mackie pining for it was another rich, shudder-inducing gag for anyone who knew Dick.

Miller references were salted in with startling frequency. "You guys from the Bronx always stick up for each other," Lou grouses at one point; and in another episode, acting as MC in his bowling alley/soda shoppe/performance space, he introduces one of his acts by saying, "Now, this kid is sure to make it big one of these days, and when he does, he'll probably forget all about us little people." And Lou Mackie was one of the few, possibly the only, overtly Jewish character Miller ever played. Right in his first episode, when Lou was still a sleazeball macking on teenagers, the character makes an ebullient reference to his Semitic roots. Later, as he settled into his role as Lou the Nice Guy, Miller's costume consisted almost exclusively of a pink shirt the exact same shade as the wonderful pink blazer he wore so often in the 1970s. But for all this, Lou Mackie was not meant to simply be Dick Miller with a different name. "Dick is tougher, and less prone to bullshit" than Mackie, said Behr. "The real Dick would have had a little bit tougher of a time with some of those kids."

When he was asked to play Lou Mackie as a warm-hearted recurring character and no longer as a chicken-hawking creep, Miller was delighted, but affected demands anyway. In the script, "[Lou] commented on the kids, blah blah blah," Miller said. "But I said, 'I'm not gonna do this part if that's all it is. I want him to have some action.'" Behr and McGreevey were more than happy to accommodate him and wrote all sorts of things for him to do, both comic and dramatic.

"You got to sing and dance," Lainie Miller pointed out.

"And I sang and I danced," Miller agreed. By his fourth appearance on the show, in "The Ol' Ball Game," written by Behr, Lou was singing and dancing a song called "Scorn," which was really just "You've Gotta Have Heart" from *Damn Yankees* reworked with the word "scorn" instead of "heart." The performance is backed up by several of the *Fame* kids, and it all came complete with Three Stooges-style knockabout slapstick, eye poinks, and kettle drum sound effects. When the big game of the title is eventually played, Lou is the umpire and gets to shout a lusty "Play ball!" It's a good Miller moment, as Miller still enjoyed playing ball himself and pitched on the *Fame* softball team. There was more singing and dancing in episodes like "Ian's Girl," which had Lou trying to pirouette into an executive position in the Metropolitan Bowling Operator's Association.

By the next season he was a regular guest star. His first appearance as such came in the third episode of season five, "Bronco Bob Rides Again," written by McGreevey and directed by Allan Arkush, which featured his old buddy Leo Gordon playing a bad hombre and gave Miller a chance to do his best Clint Eastwood impression. In the fifth episode, "White Light," written by Behr and again directed by Arkush, Lou Mackie was dating the mother of Imperato's character. Occasionally he got to shed the pink shirt, dress up a little, and become more involved in the stories, as in the season six episode, "All Talking, All Singing, All Dancing," in which Lou underwrites a floundering student production while wearing a sharp gangster suit, and shows up at the premiere sporting a tux and chomping on a stogie. All through the fifth and sixth seasons, he gave advice and support to the kids, hired them on in his establishment when they needed money, and frequently provided them a semi-professional venue for their performances. In "Go Softly into Morning," an episode Miller was particularly fond of, a young student played by Nia Peeples is killed in a drunk driving incident, and one by one, in black-box interviews, the cast breaks the fourth wall to memorialize the character. Lou Mackie's testimony is particularly affecting: with his pink shirt carelessly half-buttoned, he tries, haltingly, to explain his fondness for the kids of the school, then breaks down a bit as he describes the virtues of the late Nicole. "Nicole was a swell kid. She was good-hearted, talented, smart—" But he can't continue, can only breathe out "Dammit" and stare into the camera until the end of the shot. It's one of Miller's most genuine moments on camera: one of those occasions in which all the cult fandom, all the history, all the movie-geek bullshit are washed away and we are left with nothing before us but a great actor giving a simple and true performance. Truly, this is Miller time.

Naturally, all of it was confusing to *Fangoria* readers, who, despite by and large not being devoted viewers of *Fame*, nevertheless discovered that Miller was a regular on the show. Letters appeared in *Fangoria*'s Postal Zone expressing shock at finding Miller in this environment—"The Miller of Mystery proves his versatility once again," read one—and soon the magazine was encouraging readers to write in to MGM Television and demand that Miller be made a regular on the show.

Miller came to regard *Fame* as one of the best jobs of his entire career, neck and neck with *A Bucket of Blood* and maybe *Gremlins*. He'd been a fan of the show from the beginning: "I would never miss *Fame*," he said. "I never saw that kind of work done in an hour show. They were putting on a little MGM musical every week." He was more impressed still once he became a part of the cast and saw first-hand what it took to mount such elaborate productions on the seven-day shooting schedule. He was working with old friends, Arkush and Gordon, and Russell Johnson, with whom Miller had worked in *Rock All Night* and who was brought in to play Lou Mackie's estranged brother, Duke; and he was making new ones, such as Ira Behr. Soon he was turning down parts that would take more than one or two days, to make sure he was available should *Fame* come calling. It wasn't just loyalty: he was making good coin on the show. Allan Arkush, who directed more than a dozen episodes by the end, remembered the set-up fondly. "You got paid a lot of residuals, because *Fame* played over and over again, many times a week," he said. "It went directly from the network into syndication. You got paid a little less than you normally would [up front], because it wasn't for a network, but you ended up making money on the residuals. So it was a really good deal."

It was a deal sufficiently appealing for Miller to turn down a part in Joe Dante's *Innerspace*, at least initially. But this unprecedented, nearly unthinkable move—my god, turning down Dante!—galvanized Miller into action. "I was giving them a bad time," he remembered. "They'd ask me if I could work the next two shows and I'd tell them I didn't know because I was doing a picture." At last he demanded a contract and the steady employment that came with it. With this request, and the might of the *Fangoria* readership echoing it, Miller was, in the twelfth episode of the sixth season, finally contracted as a full-time member of the cast. (He ended up appearing in *Innerspace* too.) All of this came a little late though, as the sixth season of *Fame* was also its last. "I was very disappointed that the show wasn't renewed," Miller lamented, "even though I knew in my heart that it wasn't gonna be picked up." He was especially disappointed because he'd been promised an opportunity to direct an episode in the following season, and directing, though not one of Miller's major ambitions, was something he'd always felt he'd be good at.

But for a bit player it was a good run: by the time it was done Miller had a full thirty episodes under his belt. In retrospect, Behr realized that his zeal for including Lou Mackie whenever possible might have been perceived as a bit aggressive. A friend of his, and of Miller's, Fred Rappaport, worked with Donald Reiker and Patricia Jones on their next show, *The Bronx Zoo*, and reported the producers complaining that "Ira and Mike [McGreevey] turned goddamn *Fame* into *The Dick Miller Show*!" Laughed Behr, "I thought that was a hell of a compliment."

By the end of 1984, thanks to two hit movies and a hit TV show, a lot of other work besides, and an insanely appreciative genre press, Miller had the "living forever" part of the *Fame* theme song pretty well sewed up; and that fall he would more or less learn how to fly as well. In mid-October Joe Dante began shooting *Explorers*, his first feature since *Gremlins* had made him a Major Director. It was the tale of three kids who receive messages from space in their dreams, which they eventually interpret as instructions on how to create an anti-gravity system that will allow them to fly into space.

The script had initially been offered to Wolfgang Peterson, who perhaps had been attracted by the presence of a character named "Wolfgang," But Peterson wanted to shoot it in Bavaria, and Paramount believed the production should stay closer to the headquarters of Industrial Light and Magic (ILM), who were doing the special effects. (Peterson instead went to Bavaria and made *Enemy Mine*, with special effects by, yes, Industrial Light and Magic.) Dante's name came up courtesy of David Bombyk, an executive in the Feldman/Meeker (F/M) company, who was developing the script; he remembered the *Twilight Zone* segment and detected there a sympathy with the material. Dante read the script (a studio flunky watching over him all the while), saw no gremlins in its pages or anything else that seemed to him especially complicated, and accepted the job. He hastened to assure the F/M executives that this time there would be "no lizards in microwaves." Miller was by now top of mind, or nearly that, for Dante, as he looked over the script, but at first it seemed there was no obvious part for him to play. Well, there were a couple of helicopter cops, but after the glory that was Murray Futterman, it seemed a shame to shove Miller back into a tiny, nameless, uniformed part. (The occasional advantage to a uniform part for a bit player was that sometimes you sported a nametag, and the character thereby got a name where otherwise he would not.) "In the beginning, the pilot wasn't really a character," producer Mike Finnell told *Fangoria*. "He just had one scene and one line. You really didn't know what to make of him. He just seemed like he was kind of the bad guy. But after we cast Dick Miller, we decided to turn him into a full-fledged character to add another sub-plot and another element of suspense." Miller's part was nearly its own story, tying in obscurely but perfectly with the main plot. The character had a name now, Charlie Carruthers, and after some work from Dante and Finnell and screenwriter Eric Luke, he also had thematic relevance and emotional heft. (He also had a new surname, Drake.) Even before the movie's release, *Fangoria* magazine was breathlessly reporting that "*Explorers*, we understand, features Miller as the *adult male lead*."

The Drake character's backstory expanded upon not just the character, but the movie's very concept, because Charlie, we learn, is a dreamer too. As a child he also had received the aliens' message, but, it is presumed, lacked the technology or the wherewithal to turn those dreams into practicable reality. Now, as a middle-aged police helicopter pilot, he's having the dreams again, and when he realizes that a small group of local teens have realized this shared fantasy while he himself has missed his chance, he's at once elated, impressed, desperate, and heartbroken. Very little of this was scripted, less still was shot, and even less than that would make the final cut. It would all have to be read in Miller's face, and it was. "Poignant, huh?" Miller joked to an interviewer later, affecting cynicism. "Heartwarming."

The three central boys were cast—Ethan Hawke, Jason Presson, and River Phoenix—and shooting began in Petaluma, California, on October 15. Miller had a scene on the street with Hawke, but that was his only interaction with any of the young leads. Otherwise he had a couple of scenes at the airport; some daytime shots of him flying around in the helicopter, looking for evidence of the spaceship; and a small sequence in which he witnesses the actual takeoff. This is the key Charlie Drake moment: Miller, watching the ad-hoc spacecraft constructed out of a Tilt-a-Whirl car and powered by a force field generated from the formula provided oneirically by the aliens, stares up, amazed, and then, as Dante's camera booms down and tracks around him to a side view, his face softens and crinkles into a nodding smile, and Miller utters, "Nice goin' kid." The shot holds for several seconds, a big close-up on Miller's face, a range of emotions crossing it like scudding clouds, as though Dante is reluctant to leave him there, and might even prefer to stick with him and tell Charlie Drake's story instead. This shot joins Scorsese's *After Hours* kiss-grab as one of the keystone attractions in the whole Miller oeuvre.

Miller had only a few things to shoot in the studio, principally the nighttime helicopter interiors, in which he shared the cockpit with Meshach Taylor, playing his partner, Gordon Miller. There was also another scene, added late in production to beef up the Charlie Drake subplot and, said Finnell, to smooth the transition "between him appearing to be just a tough cop to him being a nice guy," showing Charlie at his home, on the phone with Gordon and trying to explain his obsession with the mystery spacecraft. Another scene, which would have been a signature Dante moment had it survived, had Miller's character sitting at home watching *The Man From Planet X*, a 1951 sci-fi picture that featured fellow Dante regular William Schallert. Miller was also in what Dante called "a strange fantasy sequence that I can't even remember," but neither this scene nor the *Planet X* scene made it to the quasi-final cut, or even to the graveyard of deleted scenes on the skimpy DVD release.

There was plenty of other material that didn't make the final cut, in fact—the initial rough cut was over three hours long. But while the movie was in production, there was an upheaval at Paramount, with CEO Barry Diller, along with lieutenants Jeffrey Katzenberg and Michael Eisner, chased out by crusty Gulf + Western chairman Martin Davis, a Bronx boy of about Miller's age. Replacing Diller was Frank Mancuso Sr., who brought in Ned Tanen as president of production. In every such executive turnover there are sudden policy changes, completely arbitrary other than to signal that there are new sheriffs in town. In the case of *Explorers* the new regime decided the picture's late August release date was too far past the summer bloom that had been home to big genre pictures since *Jaws*, so Dante and his team were told that the movie would instead come out on July 12. "They just said, 'stop working,'" Dante recalled.

With six weeks suddenly chopped off their post-production schedule, panic ensued, and it didn't help that Dante was suffering from a bad cold. "We shot a lot of footage," Dante said. "There used to be a father and a brother and a whole family [for Ethan Hawke's character]. They were all cut out. Ultimately it's a movie that had a sort of arrested development. But Dick was good, and it was a good part for him." Against the odds, given the abbreviated schedule, the ILM trick effects were flawless, and composer Jerry Goldsmith provided one of his best scores of the decade. But the date the studio had chosen for the picture's release was the same weekend as the epic, globe-spanning Live Aid concert—the weekend that nobody went to the movies. The picture accordingly did poorly at the box office that weekend, making $3.6 million on a $25 million budget, and its fortunes were not improved by reviews that decried the muddled, antic-heavy third act with the rubbery Rob Bottin aliens. One review, from the Los Angeles *Herald-Examiner*, seemed to tie the sudden decline in the movie's quality to Miller's exit from the story: "[Miller] drops out of the movie just when we seem to be getting somewhere," Peter Ranier wrote.

Forever after, Dante could think of *Explorers* only in the most bittersweet of terms, but, for Miller, it had been a pleasant lark. He liked the location work, enjoyed working with Dante more than ever, and had found in Charlie Drake an unusually satisfying character to play. He surprised himself by visiting the set weeks after he was wrapped, "which I don't think I've ever done before on a picture," he said. Miller was fascinated by veteran production designer Robert Boyle's enormous spaceship interiors, telling *Fangoria* that "they have the most magnificent sets I've ever seen." Perhaps thinking back to *War of the Satellites*, he enthused to another interviewer that "the interior of the space ship is not just a lot of dials and wheels and nuts and bolts." Of course, he was disappointed at the unrealized potential of the film and by its lacklustre box office performance, but what had always mattered more to Miller was not how his pictures were received, but how much fun he'd had making them. By that measure, *Explorers* was a gem.

19 *I came in, I did the job, I got out*

In 1985, after a quarter-century of marriage, Miller landed in *Divorce Court*. He and Lainie were still very much in love; more than ever in fact, and had no plans to divorce. *Divorce Court* was merely a newly revived pseudo-reality show that had last aired at the end of the 1960s and, like some mouldering creature of the grave, burst from its coffin with a cheesy new Reagan-era sensibility and bowtie-sporting Judge William B. Keene presiding. Miller showed up in the morning to play plaintiff Jim Breen, the tape rolled around 1:00 in the afternoon, and the whole thing was wrapped by dinner. Ahh, it was a job.

There were enough such jobs and, thanks to *Fame* (and Lainie's ever-mutating career), enough security for them to feel comfortable moving to a sizable house up in the Hills, where they would dwell for the next fifteen years. They were tired of condo life, and glad to find themselves in a slightly wilder environment, where passing raccoons might clamber onto their patio table and eat leftovers off their plates. Miller took a gig in a picture called *Lies*, a low-budget attempt at twisty suspense-horror with a showbiz angle. Miller played a producer of low-budget movies who quickly moves from cajoling to threatening to abusing when his female star won't take off her top. "Tits sell tickets," he explains, and when the woman explains that she's a serious actress, he barks, "What's this 'actress' bit? We're shootin' a fuckin' horror film here!" Miller played the role completely straight, without a hint of a wink or the self-deprecating humour with which he'd seasoned, for instance, his beta version of Lou Mackie. Through his career Miller had seen too many of these sleazy pricks for real: they just weren't funny any more, if they ever had been. Miller's sparring partner in the scene was Ann Dusenberry, his co-star in the failed *National Lampoon's Movie Madness*. *Lies* was released in August 1985, and while it didn't set the world on fire, it is fondly remembered by some as an effective cod-Hitchcock thriller.

Late in the year, after a summer of vacationing, there was more *Fame*. Ira Behr found it compelling to watch Miller on the set—observing the actors, to see how they dealt with the endless waiting endemic to film sets, was something of a hobby for him. Behr was fascinated to see Miller retreat into a kind of stasis, or a Zen state, as he sat off in his corner of the set. To an observer he looked like a man who would rather sit alone, but he was not as inaccessible as he appeared. It was just, Behr said, that Miller "didn't do a lot of schmoozing. You had to go up to him. He always sat by himself, but if you sat down next to him, he would talk to you. There was no problem, there was no invisible wall there."

Occasionally, though, there were surprises. "He had this picture," Behr said, "this little black and white picture that fit in his wallet, of this absolute beautiful bombshell of a girl in this little bikini." Miller pulled the picture out and showed it to Behr. "Whaddaya think?" Miller asked.

Behr replied, "Nice."

"It's my daughter!" Miller crowed.

Like Zach Galligan before him, Behr realized that Miller was trying, in his way, to set him up with Barbara. "But I was already dating the woman who would become my wife," Behr said. In any event it seems unlikely that Barbara had such trouble getting dates that her father had to find them for her, and more probable that Miller simply preferred the idea of her dates being people he already knew and liked.

Between *Fame* episodes that fall Miller got a call from Dante, who wanted him for an anthology comedy he was making with John Landis and a number of other directors. *Amazon Women on the Moon* was a quasi-sequel to Landis's earlier *The Kentucky Fried Movie*, which had been a cluster of skits surrounding a longer piece that satirized movie genres. The earlier movie had featured a kung-fu parody called "A Fistful of Yen"; this time the butt of the gags would be '50s sci-fi pictures. Though Miller would have been perfect for the eponymous parody (which was directed by Robert K. Weiss, not Dante), he was cast as a ventriloquist in a skit called "The French Ventriloquist's Dummy." Having just returned from a conference in France and about to go on stage, Danny the ventriloquist is horrified to open his case and find not his usual dummy, Dave, but a strange puppet wearing a striped shirt and beret.

But the show must go on. Danny, the dummy a-knee, tries to engage with it, but the frightened mannequin can speak only French. A translator dummy is brought on stage, and still the Gallic woodenhead just wants to know where his partner, Jacques, is, and refuses to trade in the lowbrow hotel-based humour that is Danny's stock-in-trade. Danny becomes increasingly panicked himself, which gave Miller an opportunity to liberally spread his trademark comic frustration over the piece. "It's a great part," Dante said, "and he's wonderful in there." Miller indeed did a fantastic job in the role, keeping the character grounded within the absurdity of the premise, and handling the physical business of ventriloquism convincingly as well. It must have been satisfying for Miller to be on stage for once, rather than playing a bartender or club owner watching from the back of the room, as he usually did.

The picture was in post-production for more than a year. "We would have these screenings," Dante said, "and we would take scenes out and move things around and everything." But it wasn't just a matter of sequencing the skits; the whole movie was being streamlined along the way, and skits that held up the pace or were not universally liked were dropped. "Sooner or later [the dummy skit] just didn't end up in the movie," Dante lamented. "It's such a funny premise. But John Landis didn't think it was funny, so ..." In the end, when the movie was finally released in September 1987, it became the first feature film Dante had made in which Miller did not appear, but, thankfully, this time the scene was preserved as a DVD extra. But the actor remained sanguine: "Some films," he said, "were meant to be shorter."

After Christmas 1985, when Miller turned fifty-seven, he managed to weave several small but interesting parts in and around his *Fame* appearances. In January he got a call from Roger Corman's Concorde Pictures, inviting him to be a part of a sci-fi picture Julie Corman was producing. "I was very surprised to hear from them, since I hadn't worked with Corman for so long," he remarked. At first, perhaps feeling above such things, he turned the part down flat, then, after some cajoling, named a robust fee, to which he thought they would never agree. But, he said, "they met my price," so he found himself working for Corman again, assuming the Walter Paisley mantle once more as a crusty janitor working in a mall patrolled by berserk security robots. The picture was called *Killbots*, though it would eventually go out as *Chopping Mall*, and director (and former *Fangoria* contributor) Jim Wynorski had assembled a supporting cast of Corman stalwarts: Mary Woronov, Paul Bartel, Gerrit Graham, and Mel Welles all had bits. Though the Beverly Center shopping mall was used for exterior shots, the interiors were done after hours in the Sherman Oaks Galleria, and the plot of the picture concerned a group of vapid twenty-somethings who decide for some reason to spend the night in the mall (this was a popular premise in the 1980s, with pictures like *The Initiation* and *Hide and Go Shriek* relying on the same curious decision), where they are chased and killed by the trio of security-bots, which are overreacting to the intrusion because their circuits have been fried by an errant lightning bolt.

Ace Mask, a frequent Wynorski performer, played another janitor, one of a pair who mock Paisley shortly before his demise. Mask was thrilled to have Miller around, and told *Fangoria,* "As a kid, while other would-be actors dreamed of working with Charlton Heston or somebody, I was hoping to work with Dick Miller. And I did." But it was not as harmonious an experience as everyone concerned might have wished.

"I've had no trouble with any director, ever," Miller said. "Except one." Asked about this, Wynorski himself would only say that "Dick Miller hated working with me."

"While I'm shooting, [Wynorski]'s yelling instructions to me, and I stopped in the middle," Miller complained, "and I yelled, 'Listen! You talk to me between "Cut" and "Action!" You got that? I don't want to hear anything between Action and Cut!' He just got under my skin, he was just talking and talking. Jesus Christ! And that's the only director I ever had any words with. In fact I very rarely had any words of any kind with any directors. 'Go ahead and shoot.' 'Okay, fine.'"

While Miller had always preferred less direction rather than more, it was surprising that he reacted to Wynorski so vehemently, since talking through a shot that will be rerecorded later on is not an unheard-of practice. It's possible that Miller was simply grumpy: he was in a mall in the middle of the night, a mop in his hand and a bucket of filthy water sloshing around his feet, being electrocuted by a plastic robot on a Roger Corman production, and he was nearly sixty years old. He'd been here so many times before, and maybe had come to believe he'd never have to be again. Yet, here he was anyway, and he was tired and uncomfortable, and sparks were shooting out of his chest, and there was no one around to blame for it all but Wynorski. At least he didn't have to wear burn makeup and fall on the floor into the skeevy mop water; that job was undertaken by a double.

At a New Beverly screening of the picture in 2008, Wynorski claimed that, due to the short schedule, he as a director "had a tendency to hurry people along, because we only have a certain amount of time to do it, and [Miller] wanted all this time to prep and everything. I said, 'Let's hurry it along a little bit,' and he just got so pissed off, and I never worked with him again after that." While the idea of Miller's slowing a production down so that he could internally prepare his janitor character is an interesting one, it contradicts everything on record about his typical attitude and behaviour on set. In the end he was no doubt simply grouchy and dispirited that night, angry at Wynorski purely for his own reasons.

The picture was released as *Killbots* in March, but was pulled by Corman, who felt it was underperforming, cut down to seventy-seven minutes in length, retitled *Chopping Mall* (a title suggested by a passing maintenance man as Corman screened the picture and pondered ways to improve its fortunes), and rereleased in the fall. It's a dumb and derivative little movie, but likable and entertaining too, and Miller does good, professional work. This iteration of Walter Paisley is a classic blue-collar Miller character, and his line, "Hey, I'm like you, you know? I work here," might stand as a catchphrase, or an epitaph, for fully 90 percent of Miller's characters.

Later in January came a tiny job for Jonathan Kaplan, for a big-budget chimpsploitation movie called *Project X*. Miller played importer Max King, and though he was needed for just one single shot in the picture, it was at least a grand shot: a big, swooping crane moves down from a wide view of the warehouse, with MAX KING IMPORTS painted across it in huge letters, down and down as Miller disappears into the darkness, and finally into a close-up of the lead ape, played by a chimp called Willie. The movie was released in April 1987, and many people missed the fact that Miller was even in it.

At the same time he got a call from Fred Olen Ray, a prolific director of low-budget genre pictures (most of them pretty bad, but given spice by Ray's Ed Woodish propensity for hiring actors everybody else thought were already dead). With its $2.5 million budget *Armed Response* (shot under the slightly less generic title "The Jade Jungle") was one of the slickest and costliest productions of Ray's career, and he was in a position to hire higher profile veteran actors like Miller and Miller's old co-star from *It Conquered the World*, Lee Van Cleef. David Carradine, who'd played Miller's brother in *Cannonball*, was in the picture too, so once again it was old home week.

Always, however, most of the actors and the crew were new faces, and Miller addressed this in a *Fangoria* interview soon after finishing his work in Ray's movie. "It's funny working on a picture where the people have been there for weeks, and I come on and I don't know this *family*," he told correspondent Anthony Timpone. Miller was very much aware of the close comradeship, driven by hard work, intensity, a common purpose, and a shared feeling of ill use and grievance, that a movie crew develops over the course of the shoot. But it was something he, as a long-time day player, was used to looking at from the outside, and however friendly the production was when he arrived, he was still not one of them. "I think the same thing that makes this a community, people who're working together for a couple weeks now, they're getting friendly, you come in for the day, they accept you," he said. "And when the day's finished, that's it, they reject you!"

Not even Miller was sure what he was supposed to be in *Armed Response*. "I play a gangster's messenger," he said, "a real shady character. But it's never defined what he is." Whatever he is, Miller's character has a great entrance, fishtailing up in a heavily detailed 1982 Camaro and jumping out so you knew it was really Miller driving; and a classic exit in that very same scene, when a merchandise exchange goes wrong and Miller, lined with blood bags and wired up with squibs, is blasted by gunfire in Peckinpah slo-mo. It was shot at the good old Vasquez Rocks, and Miller remembered the shells he'd left behind as JFK's real assassin in *Executive Action*. Miller liked working with Ray—"I found him a nice guy," Miller said—but later mock-scolded him in the genre press for shooting him from unflattering angles and "showing my bald spot." He was nonplussed about his costume too, complaining, "I wore this hokey red monkey suit." He then turned philosophical. "It's a funny outfit," he said, "but my business is funny outfits."

There was another call from another fan that spring, this time from Fred Dekker, a young neophyte who was making a sci-fi-horror-pastiche-tribute picture called *Night of the Creeps*. Tom Atkins was the lead, a thrill-seeking cop who teams up with a trio of college students to fight slugs from outer space. Most of the characters were named after horror movie directors, but Miller was once again Walter Paisley. "What is this," Miller asked, "every time there's no name for the character, I become Walter Paisley?"

So what, it's an inside joke," Dekker told him, as Dante had before, and again Miller was happy to go along with it. After all, the key motif in paisley design was the *buta*, a teardrop shape believed to be a Zoroastrian symbol of eternity; didn't it make sense, therefore, that Walter Paisley should himself be eternal? This time, Paisley was a police armourer who's at first pleased to fetch Atkins the flamethrower he's asking for, but balks when he realizes Atkins hasn't got the required paperwork. Atkins forces Miller to give up the flamethrower at the point of a shotgun. Miller described the scene as "very reminiscent of *Terminator*. They didn't want a copy, just a similar character." It was a friendly set, and Miller enjoyed himself for the brief time he was there.

"Dick Miller is like a good luck charm for filmmakers," Dekker said. "He's just money in the bank." Dekker was new to filmmaking, but had already developed a directing philosophy Miller no doubt appreciated: "Hire the right guys, and stand back and shut up."

Night of the Creeps turned out to be a shaggy but immensely fun little genre picture, and though Miller's part is typically minimal—"I came in one afternoon, shook hands with a couple of people, and was out," he said—it is one of the most fondly regarded scenes in Miller's filmography. But that fondness came later; when the picture was initially released in late August 1986, it was met by an indifferent public and reviews that mostly didn't get it.

In the meantime, after the relative failure of his most Spielbergian movie, *Explorers*, Joe Dante had re-entered the orbit of Spielberg himself. The year before, the wizard of blockbusters had taken it upon himself to conquer television as well as cinema, and had created an anthology fantasy show called *Amazing Stories*. Despite the tremendous publicity the show received, it was a ratings disappointment, and just barely made it to a second season. Dante had directed one in the first season, a haunted house story called "Boo!" in which there was no role for Miller; and in the second season he signed on to one called "The Greibble," in which there was. "The Greibble" told the tale of a housewife who one morning throws away the books, comics, and toys she considers her son to have outgrown, then is punished by the sudden appearance of a gluttonous Rob Bottin monster in her home. Hayley Mills, the former Disney child star, played the housewife (though her mid-Atlantic accent felt a bit off-kilter in the Universal backlot), and Miller appeared as Fred the Mailman, who doesn't believe Mills's story of a monster, and soon flees the apparent madwoman's house, recommending on the way out that she pop a Valium or two.

The episode had originally been written for Whoopie Goldberg to star and Spielberg himself to direct, but, Dante said, "for whatever reason, both elements dropped out, and I was asked to come in." The Bottin creature was so elaborate because the network "paid big money" for it when they thought it would be a Spielberg joint. Dante came on and suggested Mills for the housewife and Miller for the mailman, but the monster had already been cast. "The animatronics took forever," Dante said. "I recall being told it was the single most expensive episode to date." Miller is funny, and the monster so expressive you can practically hear the servomotors whirring, but despite the relative lavishness, it was in most respects a particularly weak episode in a series that didn't have many strong points.

Despite initially turning down the role in favour of his commitment to *Fame*, Miller did make a trip up to San Francisco that fall to appear in

Dante's new feature, *Innerspace*, which he was making for Spielberg's Amblin' company. It was another tiny scene, with the actor playing a cab driver for at least the fourth time in his career. "At least he got a trip to San Francisco out of it," Dante said, a little abashed at the atomity of the part. "I think that's the way he probably looked at it."

When he wasn't enjoying workings weekends in Frisco, or on the job with *Fame*, Miller was rooted at his table at Theodore's, driving down in his yellow Honda Civic, breakfasting, lunching, and lounging with his acting buddies. In 1987 the name changed from Theodore's to the Silver Spoon, and Miller was thankful that was all that changed about it. The loss of Schwab's still hurt, and having another hangout wither right out from beneath him would have been genuinely traumatic. But the place had a lively clientele: aside from Miller and his crew, one might see Shelley Winters, Martin Landau, Rip Taylor, Farrah Fawcett, Sybil Danning, or Paul Williams.

In the spring of 1987 *Fame* was cancelled, and Miller once again felt that chill in the bones familiar not just to actors, but to all freelancers: "Will I ever work again?" Lainie was in the business now, labouring as a script supervisor on movies like Jim Wynorski's *Big Bad Mama II* (which Miller wasn't in, of course); and with a mortgage to pay on their Hollywood Hills home, the lack of a guaranteed paycheque in the family hit hard.

The summer of 1987 was a dry season, but near the end of it Miller did a day or two on *Dead Heat*, a zombie cop thriller directed by Mark Goldblatt. Goldblatt had co-edited *Piranha* and *The Howling* and had cut *The Terminator*, and he had also worked in different capacities on *Hollywood Boulevard*, *Get Crazy*, and *Eat My Dust*; so it was safe to say he was familiar with Miller's work. It was Goldblatt's first feature as a director, and as an apparent subscriber to the Lucky Charm School of Miller Thought, he wanted some Dick in his pic. Treat Williams and Joe Piscopo, playing the buddy cops, are searching for clues in a mausoleum when a security guard played by Miller hassles them in a grouchio-comic manner. Ultimately, though, Miller's scene was cut out of the picture entirely. *Dead Heat* was not a success (it suffered from a stunted release in May 1988, and seems to have killed Piscopo's movie stardom as completely as it did his character), and neither was Goldblatt's subsequent directing career, but on the other hand his career as an action-movie editor flourished.

As though in competition with Jonathan Kaplan for who could put Miller into the tiniest, least visible role of his career, Allan Arkush cast him in an episode of the comedy-noir series *Moonlighting*, where he played a truck driver loading a box of contraband licence plates. Miller, evidently wearing his costume from *White Line Fever*, is seen only from a distance, but you can hear his voice, sort of. Leo Gordon showed up in the same episode in a much larger, more visible role as a gruff but decent prison warden.

The *Moonlighting* episode aired at the beginning of December, and just over a month later came another Miller television appearance, as a 1940s-era newspaper vendor in *Star Trek: The Next Generation*. The crew of the *Enterprise* have, it seems, become trapped in a post-war San Francisco hologram, and are forced to act out a private-eye scenario while the balky holodeck is being repaired. Miller's newsie makes wisecracks at the crew's expense and can't seem to stop staring at Data, the robot character with the sickly pale synthetic skin. The episode was written by Tracy Tormé, the son of Miller's old New York buddy Mel Tormé.

More than ever, Miller was in a state with which he was all too familiar: sweating it out, auditioning, waiting for the phone to ring so he could make a few bucks. The space between gigs was widening, he felt, and there was the sense of a wave's having crested. There were *Fame* residuals, of course, and other such monies, and Lainie was active as a script supervisor and with IATSE, so they weren't yet standing on each other's shoulders to pick avocados out of trees. Miller tried not to worry too much about it, and anyway, for a self-confessed lazy guy, unemployment had its advantages.

But working was nice too, and Joe Dante was always ready to employ Dick when he could. The summer movie season of 1988 came rolling along: pictures like *Willow* and *Rambo III* and *Bull Durham* and the season's biggest hit, Robert Zemeckis's *Who Framed Roger Rabbit*. Miller went to see all of these; his friend Harry Northup claimed that some days Miller went to five separate movies. He also saw the picture that would make his newest co-worker a star, *Big*. Tom Hanks was the lead in Dante's new movie, *The 'burbs*, and while he'd been a popular comedy actor for half a decade, *Big* lifted him into the category of superstar, and Dante and Miller were with him as it happened.

The 'burbs was the tale of a young husband who takes a week's vacation at his own home and, along with his neighbours, is drawn into a paranoid fantasy about the Klopeks, the strange new family on the block. In the spring, as the picture was going into prep, the Writers Guild of America declared a strike. For Dante and company this meant three things: they were nearly the only production on the Universal lot that summer, there was an unusual level of opportunity for ad-libbing from the actors, and there was no real ending written for the movie. In Dana Olsen's script the Klopeks had originally proved guilty only of being weird, but were not the murderers Hanks and his confederates believed them to be. Either because they didn't like the idea of chastising middle Americans for their nativist paranoia, or because they simply wanted a more exciting conclusion, the studio demanded a more sinister denouement.

Miller was paired with Robert Picardo, another of Dante's regulars, but despite Picardo's presence on the call sheets of *The Howling*, *Get Crazy*, *Explorers*, *Amazon Women on the Moon*, *Dead Heat*, and *Innerspace*, this was the first time the two actors would actually play a scene together. They were a pair of trash collectors whose rounds bring them into the suburban cul-de-sac canyon in which the entire movie takes place; there, garbage is strewn by manic suburbanites, and Miller gets a platform for his "increasingly agitated blue collar guy" act, which he had long since perfected. *The 'burbs*, however, is the ultimate showcase for Miller's Sir Laurence Lunchbox persona. His garbage man got little respect from the other characters, but Miller saw to it that the man retained his dignity. This was in truth one of Miller's special talents, and, he considered, his professional responsibility: to himself, to his co-workers, and to his character.

When professional responsibilities weren't met by others, Miller could get irascible. He had little patience when Cory Feldman, who was playing another neighbour—once again, as in *Gremlins*, he was the hero's curiously young friend—came out of his trailer too stoned to remember his lines. And because of the indecision around the ending, there were more trials in store for this hapless bin man, at least in one of the three alternate conclusions that were shot for the movie. These endings each revealed an incriminating secret in the trunk of the Klopeks' car: one option had a trunk full of dead cheerleaders; another had a trunk full of skulls; and the third had the two garbage men, Miller and Picardo, curled up dead inside. The Miller/Picardo option was not used, perhaps because it seemed too random to everyone but Dante. Miller also appeared in a dream sequence, in which a terrified Hanks watches as the elderly neighbourhood grump supposedly murdered by the Klopeks rises from a garbage can with a hatchet in his head. "Don't let them do to youuuu what they did to meeee!" he wails. He is holding his beloved poodle in his hands, and the poodle also has a tiny hatchet in its head. Miller ambles through the ground fog in his garbage man's coveralls, looks the two axe victims up and down, and says, "Eww. I'll bet that hurts, huh?"

Altogether, especially considering the cut material, it wasn't much of a role, but Miller didn't care. "The great thing about Dick is he can take a big part or a little part without any bruising of his ego," Dante said. "And he always made more out of it than what was there."

Later that summer came two atypical roles. In *Angel III: The Final Chapter* Miller played a newspaper editor who wore a sort of sweater vest, very much an avuncular Lou Grant type. Like *Fly Me* and *The Happy Hooker Goes Hollywood*, this was a picture with the good grace to put Miller's scene early in the running time, easily found by those for whom Miller was the principal attraction. And he got a full name too, the pleasantly bubbly "Nick Pelligrini." But in a picture he did around the same time, *Under the Boardwalk*, he was just a plain, nameless "Official." *Under the Boardwalk*, originally titled *Wipeout*, was a sandy, sunny *Romeo and Juliet* adaptation with a surfer and a would-be bohemian crossing swords on the last weekend of the summer, just before the surfer is supposed to up stakes and surf academically for Stanford. Miller officiates a surfing contest, makes a couple of weak wisecracks, and watches serenely as a board rider suffers a gruesome compound fracture. It was another "troubled" production, Miller told *Fangoria*, with parts recast and scenes rewritten. "Halfway through it," Miller said, "somebody said, 'Gee, you're funnier than the guy who had the part before.' That was my first clue that it was a real rehash. I just know it was an easy shoot."

For all of Miller's horror movie appearances, he had surprisingly little truck with the franchise giants. *Gremlins*, or his later dip of the toe into the horrors of Amityville, was as close as he got; he never squared off against Jason or Michael or the *Chainsaw Massacre* family. He did enter Freddy Krueger's orbit, sort of, in early 1989, in an episode of the anthology show *Freddy's Nightmares*. Miller's episode was "The Light at the End of the Tunnel," and, Lainie Miller said, "they wrote it especially for him." Lainie worked on the show as the script supervisor for nearly its entire run, and was very pleased to see her husband, with his forty-five years of film acting experience, comport himself exactly as every director, continuity person, and editor always hopes they will: by maintaining a continuity of movement and timing through each take and shot. If Miller rubbed his eyes in the wide shot, he did it in the same way and at the same relative time in the close-up. "He knows his stuff," Lainie said, "and he does it the same way every time." To Miller, and to any deeply professional actor, this is no big thing, just part of the job. "Yeah, that comes natural, I guess," Miller shrugged. But directors and editors, and continuity people too, maintain a profound appreciation of this increasingly rare craftsmanship.

Freddy's Nightmares was a series of stories unconnected save for their location, a small town with a higher than usual incidence of uncanny happenings. There were no continuing characters except Freddy himself, who pulled Crypt Keeper duty by introducing the week's tale. Miller's episode told the story of a lygophobe who attempts to tackle his fear of the dark by taking a job as a sewer worker; naturally, down below the streets, all his worst fears are realized. Miller played Al Kenyon, Lord of the Underworld, the friendly foreman who calls his new worker "kiddo," just as Miller probably called the actor who played him "kiddo" too. It indeed felt like a part written with Miller in mind, and while the episode wasn't terribly good, Al Kenyon, Lord of the Underworld, was Miller up, down, and sideways.

Miller's small-town sheriff in *Far from Home*, on the other hand, was not, but he attacked it like a pro anyway. "A straight part, more or less," Miller called it. *Far from Home* was a Drew Barrymore vehicle shot in the fall of 1988, just after the troubled young Barrymore was released from two weeks of treatment in a rehab called the ASAP Family Treatment Center. Barrymore held it together during the shoot, which probably was insured only because it was located largely in the northern Nevada dry-gulch town of Gerlach. This tiny, dusty place serves as a prison for the road-tripping Barrymore and her dad, who run out of gas there and so are stuck even as a murderer makes the rounds. Miller's Bronx accent did not situate itself with complete comfort in such an environs, but, seeing him under a Stetson, Miller watchers will be taken back to the days of *Apache Woman* and *Gunslinger*. Miller's sheriff comes to a sticky end when the serial killer who has been plaguing the small town, and stalking Barrymore in particular, swings down from the rafters and cuts his throat. "Miller bites the dust again," he joked.

Far from Home was released in June 1989, but few noticed. Miller wasn't paying much attention: Barbara was getting married. The wedding, at which Barbara was married to, Miller said, "a good lookin' kid in the restaurant business" named Brian Levandoski, took place at the Sportsman's Lodge, the classic Hollywood hangout where the big stars of the day had once caroused and fished for trout. The trout ponds were long gone by 1989 (the big earthquake eighteen years earlier had diverted the spring that fed them), but it was still dripping with Tinseltown history and a fine place to hold an event. Joe Dante was in attendance and remembered "a lot of military people around," Barbara's friends and acquaintances from her navy days. Levandoski's family was from northern Michigan, up near Sault Ste. Marie, so there were plenty of Yoopers around too, toasting the happy couple or goggling at the hotel's Wall of Fame with starstruck murmurs and nods.

It was a busy summer for Dante and Miller both. Dante had been prepping the almost inevitable *Gremlins 2*, taking it on after Warner Bros. had spent several years trying different sequel approaches with other directors, and, when no workable approaches manifested, had finally threw up their hands and told Dante he could do whatever he wanted, so long as there were gremlins. As Dante rightly pointed out, this was "an offer you don't usually get" from studio executives. He and screenwriter Charlie Haas took the expected route only in the traditional upping of both scale and stakes demanded by studio sequels. Otherwise, inspiration came less from the previous movie than from a great classic of metatextual comic absurdism, *Hellzapoppin'*, and the audience-winking of the Hope/Crosby *Road* pictures. In the end, with its repeated shots at the silliness of the gremlins concept and its gobbledygook rules, and its clear disdain for franchise film culture, it was the closest Dante ever got to capturing on film the wry self-deprecation he so often deployed in interviews and commentaries. Noting his lack of a possessory credit in the opening titles, Dante acknowledged, "If there ever really was 'A Film By …' that I could take credit for, this is the one."

Gremlins 2 took place in New York, largely within a "smart" office building created by a Donald Trump/Ted Turner amalgam called Daniel Clamp, which is the workplace of the characters played by Zach Galligan and Phoebe Cates. Gizmo, the obnoxiously cute hamster-monkey, has meanwhile first become homeless, then is caged by a pair of twin geneticists who take him to Christopher Lee's gene-splicing lab, also located in the building. The gremlins are loosed within this edifice, preying on the yuppies within and plotting their escape into the Manhattan streets.

The gene-splicing lab was included largely for the sake of Rick Baker, the special effects artist who took on the gremlin manufacture when Chris Walas, who'd done the original, was unavailable. Baker was understandably reluctant to simply reuse the original Walas designs, and the gene-splicing lab provided opportunities for all sorts of mutant gremlins he could create from scratch. Before committing to the gig Baker had one other condition that had to be met: Dick Miller must be in the picture. When he was assured that the Futtermans were alive and well and would be a big part of the sequel's story, Baker took the job.

Here was where the Futtermans' last-minute reprieve from a death by snowplough in the earlier picture, granted by Spielberg or some other benevolent deity, really paid off, not just for the picture but for Miller and Jackie Joseph. Especially Miller: in *Gremlins 2* Murray Futterman was no longer just the chummy old xenophobe next door, but a participant in the chaos and a key part of the eventual solution, and, for Miller, this translated into plenty of working days across the five-month shoot. As the story progresses Miller is attacked and injured but fights back and wins; he rescues the putative lead, Galligan, from a *Marathon Man*-inspired torture; and he helps destroy the lobby full of gremlins in the extended, gloopy climax. He even got his own catchphrase, uttered after tossing a jizz-spitting gremlin down an elevator shaft: "Don't mess with Murray Futterman." (Miller complained later about the "disgusting" goo expectorated onto his face by the puppet. "I said, 'Make it green! Anything!' I didn't like the white.")

The picture began shooting in New York in late May. Only a few of the actors were required for the three days of location shooting, and Miller was one of them. His work there included a couple of scenes in the plaza of 101 Park Avenue, where he wandered around with fake blood running down his temple from a wound inflicted in a fight yet to be filmed. He also got to ride a street elevator, which had been constructed over a manhole and was meant to represent a secret entrance into the building. Here, the real estate mogul, played ingratiatingly by John Glover, rises from the street and is mobbed by press while Miller sneaks into the elevator and descends. The contraption was raised and lowered by a crane, and Dante's instruction was that Miller's ride down be bumpier than Glover's slick ascension.

In New York the crew shot a background plate of St. Patrick's Cathedral, which was used for a shot of the Futtermans sightseeing. (Miller and Joseph were filmed later, in the studio, staring up at the matted-in church.) Miller looks at the ornate neo-Gothic church (renamed Church of Saint Eva-Marie for the picture) and calls, "Quasimodo, ya home?" He might have been thinking about something else than gremlins at that moment, though: the pigeons, winging around the spires, free, and the young, tormented Miller gazing out at them from behind the grey windows of the Saks Fifth Avenue staff men's room, wishing he were free too. Show business had freed him from that cage, and now here he was, still practising the business, pretending to look at the spot he'd fled from forty years earlier, from 2,500 miles away, on a Warner Bros. stage, being well-paid for it; and no longer even Dick Miller at all, but Murray Futterman, cracking wise and killing gremlins. It was a species of freedom the young Saks stock boy could never have dreamed existed.

After the weekend of location shooting, the company returned to Los Angeles and to the stages of Warner Bros., where elaborate sets had been built. The first material shot was a scene in which the Futtermans arrive at Galligan and Cates's modest apartment a day ahead of time, and must be gently shooed away lest they discover there is a gremlin stashed within. Murray Futterman is suffering a post-traumatic stress disorder, thanks to his experience in the first picture, and Miller's comic enactment of the condition broke Galligan and Cates up numerous times over the day. "We ruined about ten takes on the line where he goes, 'Yeah, I'm much better now, I don't hear anything anymore—what was that?!?'" Galligan said. "He did that line so convincingly, and without doing shtick. I think I had more appreciation of him as an actual actor in the second one, because that scene had a lot more meat."

Later in the schedule came the scene in front of the Church of Saint Eva-Marie, shot on an outdoor street set on the Warner back lot, and with that came a great endurance test for the sixty-year-old Miller. Among the gene-splicing lab's inadvertent creations was a flying gremlin with bat wings, and this jury-rigged varmint bursts out of the building and makes a beeline for the Futtermans. Miller spent several days fighting off either a clawed puppet on a boom that was dangled over his head by the effects people, or a full puppet he held himself and fought Bela Lugosi-style, or a bat-shaped foam-core cut-out on a stick that was waved in his face by Dante, and which would later be replaced by a stop-motion gremlin. Miller was exhausted by "the physical thing of waving your hands over your head for six or seven hours.... Just try waving your hands over your head for a few minutes and you can see how strenuous that is." On top of this, the puppet claws, which were meant to appear to be slicing his scalp, actually did. "My entire hairline was covered with blood," he said, "and they would mop the blood off my head after every take."

Further perils awaited on this, the most dangerous shoot Miller had undertaken since *The Long Ride Home*. During his frantic fight with the flying gremlin, Miller backed into a sawhorse so violently that he broke several ribs. He decided not to mention it to Dante or anyone else in the production; they were after all the same old ribs he'd broken in his motorcycle accident twenty years earlier, and then again in an accident on *Police Woman*. "Here at the house I have medical corsets and all that kind of thing," Miller told Bill Warren in *Fangoria*, "so I taped myself up and didn't say a word." It was a holdover from the Corman days: on those, Miller said, "most of the time, you get hurt and if it's bleeding you bandage it, if it's sprained you put something on tight, and you just go ahead and finish the picture.

"That's what I was learning with Roger," he continued. "You've got six days to make a picture, so you can't ... if you blow this one, you'll never get another one. And I think that was always the principle behind my acting. 'Make it work this time, because the next picture depends on it.'"

That was not all the injury in store for Miller in *Gremlins 2*. A few weeks later, in a scene in which Mr. Futterman is rescuing Galligan from some dental torture, he plummeted down a gremlin hole. "On the set there's holes everywhere," Dante said, "because people have to stick their hands up for puppets. Dick backed into one of the holes and fell."

"We have that in the blooper reel," Miller chuckled to Bill Warren. "I just vanish, you don't see me drop. It was less than a 24th of a second for me to disappear." Miller suffered a cut to his leg in this mishap, and his ribs still ached, but again he soldiered on. He was game to participate in a jokey behind-the-scenes promo piece in which the interviewees talked about the gremlins as though they were living, prima donna-ish performers. Miller played along, but his real concerns were discernible in his jokes. "Oh, the gremlins are fine," he told the camera, "they're very happy. They haven't worked in five years."

Unusually for Miller, other than the plentiful accident footage, not a lot of his material was cut out of the picture; as a result *Gremlins 2* is one of the best Miller showcases of the period. "He was wonderful, and the character was so funny," Dante said. "He had a lot to do, and he worked a lot on that picture." The world was not ready for such bounty, however. The movie opened on June 15, 1990, against Warren Beatty's *Dick Tracy*, and Beatty's proved to be the Dick moviegoers were in the mood for that summer. But, for Miller, it was a happy experience, despite the cuts and bruises and breaks; he walked home with not just a fulsome paycheque, but his own gremlin, bequeathed to him by Rick Baker. Twenty-five years later it was looking a little rattier than it had in its glory days, but Miller still displayed it proudly in his office.

Miller played another suit-wearing nightclub owner in *Ghost Writer*, a low-budget fantasy-comedy starring a pair of buxom sisters, Judy and Audrey Landers, and produced by their mother. It was a nothing part, but "a fun job," Miller said. The movie was released in early December, and shortly after that a fresh decade began. Miller's first gig in this futuristic new era was playing a wink-wink, nudge-nudge, say-no-more motel manager in the Tony Danza sitcom *Who's the Boss?* Perhaps the 1990s would not be so different from the 1980s after all.

Miller was less visible than he had been, and this was at least partly by design. He was comfortable with the inactivity, or claimed to be. "I am very grateful that I've reached the stage where I don't have to take every part just because I'm hungry," he said in *Fangoria*. "I'm interviewing, and turning parts down." (The article asserted elsewhere that Miller had refused parts in Mel Brooks's *Life Stinks* and David Lynch's *Wild at Heart*, and one ponders especially the second of those what-ifs.)

But he couldn't turn down Fred Olen Ray. For his new picture *Mob Boss*, Ray wanted Miller to play Mike, a garage mechanic strong-armed into service by gangsters. Poor Mike is forced to kiss the ring of *capofamiglia* Eddie Deezen, and then has to literally eat the bill he was going to present to them for services rendered. Miller scarfs the paper down as he had the flowers in *Little Shop of Horrors* so many years before. Miller's browbeaten mechanic also serves as the Family's helicopter mechanic and pilot, so he got to pretend-fly around just as he did in *Explorers*.

In the late summer and fall, after some vacationing and some beach time and lots of moviegoing, Miller found himself a series semi-regular again, on *The Flash*. This time he was an informer called Fosnight, a sketchy small-timer who was on the side of good. On the show the Flash was the one with superpowers, but off-screen Miller seemed the one with the extraordinary abilities, at least to some. On the Internet Movie Database message boards (which no longer exist), a commenter named "wrx0rocky" detailed a great night he once had working as an extra on the show. "I never got to see [co-star] Amanda Pays," wrx0rocky wrote,

> but the most memorable time I had was with Dick Miller!!!!! As I was wandering around the set, I saw this guy sitting on the stairs to a trailer and he looked familiar. Normally you are not supposed to bother any of the cast on the set as an extra, but as I was walking by I said to this guy —hey, weren't you in the old 1950's movie called *Buckets of Blood*? He shouted for me to come over and join him, and I did. It was Dick Miller, and yeah he said (in his typical slick tough guy accent ha ha), I was the star of that movie! He was totally blown away that anyone ever remembered that movie, let alone him being in it. We ended up sitting down together and talking for hours about that show, and the old days. wow! He was

one hell of a guy I will tell you. The most down to earth decent person you could ever meet. That time we talked together and shared stories will remain with me forever, and I have always had great things to say about him ever since. But as I said what a shame that Harvey Keitel got to be the more well known actor, because Dick Miller has every bit of skills as Harvey does. If anyone ever sees Dick Miller again, please tell him HELLO for me? And tell him that he gave some poor insignificant extra who was both freezing that night and bored to death, the most MEMORABLE NIGHT OF HIS LIFE!!! Thanks much!!!!

This exclamation point-laden testimonial gave a good hint of Miller's on-set demeanour: on the face of things he was a loner, but in fact was fully approachable, generally garrulous, happy to talk about the old days. There are probably many extras and bit players with similar stories. Miller was in six episodes of the short-lived program, logging the most screen time in his last episode, "Alpha," which was broadcast on May 11, 1991, and told the tale of a peaceful but potentially deadly fembot. Fosnight is alarmed at one point to realize that the fembot has X-ray vision and can see his underwear, and Miller delivered his lines with all the desperation of a man who has been embarrassed by X-ray vision before.

In December, in the middle of his *Flash* run, Miller got yet another call from Fred Olen Ray, who promised him a few bucks and a couple of days' worth of fun if he wanted it. Ray had recently seen *Who Framed Roger Rabbit* and had been inspired to make his own version, in which cartoon monsters would appear in the real world to rip off ladies' clothes. (Perhaps Ray, like many others, wondered why Miller had not appeared in the big Zemeckis picture, and in his own low-budget way was trying to redress that injustice.) He wrote the script in a matter of days, called it "Evil Toons," raised $140,000 to make it, and gave Miller a part that was yet another small-business owner stooped double with the weight of the world. Miller's character was Burt, his business this time was housecleaning, and he kicks off the plot by employing four slightly dim-witted young women to spend a weekend neatening up a spooky old mansion. Burt takes a few moments to leer at his employees' asses, then drives off in his white panel van. Soon David Carradine, having received the same sort of phone call from Ray as Miller had, is skulking around the estate in a big fedora and an Inverness cape, and inside the house, slobbering animations appear, pop their eyes, and move jerkily around, attacking, molesting, and possessing the human characters at will.

Meanwhile, Miller's character is at home wearing a pink shirt, smoking a big cigar, and watching *A Bucket of Blood*, the public domain status of which allowed Ray to feature extended clips of Walter Paisley futilely trying to sculpt a head. Burt watches the movie for a good long while, takes a telephone call, then, after hanging up and studying the TV for another moment, asks, "How come this guy never got an Academy Award?" It's enough to give a viewer flashbacks to *Hollywood Boulevard*, in which Miller watched himself act in a completely different public domain movie, *The Terror*.

Miller then returns to the cartoon-haunted house, but his demise does not come at the hands of an animation cel. He meets a possessed girl, accepts the blow job she offers, then is horrified when she opens her mouth to reveal a mawful of needle-sharp teeth. Miller took his fate like a professional, but didn't consider it a very dignified scene to play. "Humiliating!" he called it, filing it in the same set of unsavoury experiences as the face-full of gremlin spooge he endured in *Gremlins 2*. Otherwise, Ray was as good as his word: the eight-day shoot was breezy fun; there were pretty girls around; and he got a nice billing, second only to Carradine.

With the end of the year came another birthday, but 1991 had something even more superannuating in store for Miller. Barbara was pregnant, and the Millers became grandparents to a little girl named Autumn Rose Levandoski. They were delighted, of course, and instantly captivated by the beautiful baby girl, but even so, could not have predicted how close she and they would grow in later years.

There hadn't been much work that winter or early spring, but things heated up as the summer months approached. Miller appeared in *Motorama*, another script from Joseph Minion, who'd written *After Hours*. This again was a story of one lone character up against equal parts adversity and absurdity, but instead of being a wayward yuppie, the character was Gus, a ten-year-old kid who flees the fractiousness of his family life, steals a cherry Mustang, and takes to the road. Gus's goal is to collect Motorama game cards: if he gathers the right letters to spell MOTORAMA, he's eligible for an outrageously huge cash prize. Along the way he meets a parade of eccentrics, loses an eye, and gets a badass patch, and is constantly mistaken for a grown man.

It was a strange, culty picture with a notably culty cast. Lots of former Miller co-stars were floating about: everyone from Drew Barrymore to Robert Picardo to Mary Woronov and Irwin Keyes, with whom Miller had played scenes in *Mob Boss*. Musicians Flea and Meat Loaf were in the picture as well; and famed weirdos Michael J. Pollard and Jack Nance; comedians

Sandy Baron and Shelley Berman; and Saturday Night Live alumni Garrett Morris and Robin Duke. It was a road picture with an episodic structure, so everyone had their own little bit to do, in for a minute or two and then out. Miller was a father at a roadside picnic pull-off, playing horseshoes for the dubious amusement of his two expressionless little kids. Gus appears and hustles him out of a hundred bucks at the tossing game, and Miller protests that he can't afford the hundred because he needs it to drive his family home. Then inspiration strikes: Miller realizes he can afford to pay the bet after all, but only if he cuts costs by abandoning his children in the woods. So that's what he does.

Miller was a bit too old to play the father of such young children, but age confusion's having already been established in the picture, it worked well enough. Miller sold it as best he could. But in the end *Motorama* was too self-consciously weird to be entirely successful; it plays like a Corman picture in David Lynch drag, and the endless cameos from both Corman and Lynch stalwarts work against it. It's nevertheless a noteworthy entry in Miller's filmography, and, after his rumoured refusal to appear in *Wild at Heart*, is probably the closest Miller fans ever got to seeing him in an actual Lynch movie.

It was a single, isolated day's work, but in this period, it seemed, there was always more TV. Miller did a guest spot on the Charles Dutton show *Roc*, appearing in the fourth episode of the first season. It was a comedy-drama of the working classes, and Miller fit right in. The show was shot over the summer of 1991 and aired on September 15, right around the time *Motorama* had its initial, limited, and unsuccessful release. (It would be released again a year-and-a-half later and fare little better.) Miller appeared as a forehead-corrugating cop in a TV movie called *The Woman Who Sinned*, which was directed by Michael Switzer, who had worked with the actor on *Fame*. And there was *Eerie, Indiana*, which, like *Freddy's Nightmares*, was a show about a town in which strange things continually occurred. This time there were regular characters, though, in particular Marshall, a boy uniquely burdened with the understanding that his town is a locus of the uncanny. There were a few more recurring characters as well, including Marshall's family, his friends, and an elderly undercover Elvis.

Joe Dante served as the show's creative consultant, and directed five of its nineteen episodes, and the only surprise was that Miller appeared in only one of them. His episode, the fourth one to be broadcast, was called "The Losers," and contrived to explain where all the little lost things ended up. Keys, socks, even briefcases: all are purloined by Dick Miller, wearing a bright orange jumpsuit, who takes them to a massive subterranean warehouse overseen by fellow Dante regular Henry Gibson. "That was a lot of fun, doing that show," Dante said. "The Losers" aired early in October 1991, but ultimately, in the pre-*Twin Peaks* days of broadcast television, was too weird and singular a show to survive.

Popular thrillers of the early 1990s depended time and again on the "cuckoo in the nest" paradigm. In this model some previously harmless personage, or at least a not innately dangerous one, proves vengeful and deadly, and just about anyone was fair game. Nannies, neighbours, stepsons, roommates: any or all of these might turn on you and your family, thanks to some previously unsuspected grudge or psychopathy. Jonathan Kaplan traded in this theme with his demented-cop picture *Unlawful Entry*, which went into production at the end of October 1991. Miller got a small role as a clerk at an impound lot, whose pockets are stuffed with pens and who gruffly informs milquetoast husband Kurt Russell that his credit cards have been maxed out. It was another of those Miller roles where the camera never crossed into his side of the service window, as though in conscious denial of his character's point of view. But Miller was always able to beat these roles, to inject personality where there was none on the page and little help from the camera. Filmmakers like Kaplan well knew this; they counted on it, and, to a degree, relied on it.

And then Miller returned to the fold, after a fashion, by appearing in a couple of Corman productions. *Body Waves* was a teen sex comedy that had Miller playing the main character's father, the king of Ano-Recto Cream, "the world's top-selling rectal preparation," he boasts. The set dressing included a posterboard with a photo of Miller standing proudly, his arms crossed and a crown on his head, and the words ANO-RECTO CREAM awkwardly Letrasetted across the top; and Miller later kept the photo, absent the copy, for display on his study wall. He played the dad as a genuine hard-ass, without a wink, no doubt opting (wisely) to let the character's occupation do most of the comedy lifting. He also got to appear in a dream sequence wearing a judge's robes and banging a gavel, and if Miller's half-brother, Billy, ever saw that, he'd surely get a laugh. Judge William Miller had been appointed to the Criminal Court bench by New York Mayor Ed Koch back in 1983; Dick and Lainie had been proud of him then, and they were still proud. But if Billy ever did catch *Body Waves*, he'd surely have pronounced it guilty and meted out the harshest sentence possible. It's bad.

Body Waves was released at the end of May 1992, and a month later another Corman production featuring Miller hit the video shelves. *Quake*, which had been shot in January and February, was a combination of a disaster movie and the aforementioned cuckoo-in-the-nest genre, telling the tale of a couple who argue and separate just before a big quake hits San Francisco; the young wife is subsequently terrorized by her obsessed neighbour, played by oddball character specialist Steve Railsback. Miller got a nice billing: fourth, after the three leads, with an "and" before his name. This small conjunction is usually something agents have to fight for, but as Miller's agents rarely bothered with such power plays, it seems likelier that it was awarded on the basis of Miller's long history with Corman and his continuing cult fame. (He got a good billing in *Body Waves* as well, probably for the same reasons.) In *Quake* Miller played a kindly storekeeper who allows Railsback to shop at his earthquake-damaged bodega, little suspecting his customer is a lunatic. But the transaction is completed without incident, and the scene serves as a little oasis of decency in the picture, an illustration of the way people sometimes hang together in a disaster, a meeting of two apparently civilized strangers.

Miller was not at home for the release of these movies, or for the release of *Unlawful Entry* in June, because he was on the other side of the country, working on Dante's latest production, *Matinee*. This was a period piece, perhaps Dante's most personal work, dramatizing what happens to a movie-mad adolescent when, on the same weekend, a monster-movie maker comes to town and the world nearly comes to an end, thanks to the Cuban missile crisis. *Matinee* was a tribute to many things, like single-screen cinemas and monster-movie fandom and ballyhoo, and, in its casting of Miller as a B-movie actor, it was a more elegant tip of the cap to his career than, say, *Evil Toons*; but it was also a tribute to Miller's many, many roles in which he was joined in some motley duo with someone much taller than himself. Dante paired Miller with lanky screenwriter, director, and sometime actor John Sayles, who later told filmmaker Elijah Drenner that, so far as he knew, they were teamed up because "I'm 6'4", and Dick's ... not?"

Matinee was set in October 1962, with the world right in the crucible of the Cuban missile affair. The whole USA is on edge, and that goes double for this little island at the tip of Florida, just ninety miles from Havana. The story follows Gene, a thirteen-year-old rarely without a copy of Forry Ackerman's *Famous Monsters of Filmland* rolled up in his back pocket, and his meeting with schlock filmmaker Lawrence Woolsey, played by John Goodman as what Dante called "an amalgam of William Castle, Jack Arnold, Roger Corman and Ray Dennis Steckler." Woolsey is in Key West to promote his newest picture, *Mant!*, and is delighted at the real-life nuclear panic he believes will only bolster his own heroic ballyhoo.

His trunkful of gimmickry includes typical Castle stunts like seat buzzers and monster costumes, as well as a precursor to Universal's Sensurround system (appropriate, as *Matinee* was a Universal production), and a spectacular, climactic recreation of a nuclear explosion to delight and terrify the kiddies. His bag of tricks also includes Miller and Sayles, who play a pair of sketchy ex-actors whom Woolsey has engaged to protest his upcoming premiere in a backhanded effort to promote it. "He and John Sayles make a great team," Dante said. "I can't believe they didn't do more pictures together."

Miller and Sayles are introduced in front of the theatre, handing out anti-*Mant!* literature, their disparate heights ensuring that proper two-shots were impossible: Dante had to frame one of them or the other, never both at the same time. Later, Gene sees a still of Miller as "Man at Lunch Counter," taking a big bite of a sandwich while eyeing a giant monster brain floating above him, and figures out that Miller is Herb Denning, one of Lawrence Woolsey's stock actors, and that the outrage is fake. Gene, a lonely kid, explains a sentiment the young Dante, on whom he was modelled, must have shared: "Someone like Herb, or Vincent Price, it's like they're my friends." The dialogue puts Herb Denning, and therefore Dick Miller, on the same plain as Price—they both, after all, had played multiple leading roles for Roger Corman, and Dante's admiration for the relatively lavish Poe films was no greater than his fondness for *A Bucket of Blood* or *War of the Satellites*. Later, Miller and Sayles have a scene in a bar and its basement, where they muscle the film's minor-league antagonist, a beatnik greaser and would-be pickpocket, into getting a straight job. That puts the greasenik where he needs to be for the climax, but by then Sayles and Miller, their plot duty fulfilled, are seen no more.

Miller remembered the shoot as just generally fun, and Dante said, "It got him to Florida for a while, and I think he enjoyed that." The movie was indeed a moving and witty tribute to the bygone era: in *Gremlins 2* Dante had showed what was in his head, and with *Matinee* he was showing what was in his heart. But only a few were to answer the call: *Matinee*'s late-January 1993 release was sadly underappreciated.

Miller was back from Florida by the time *Amityville 1992: It's About Time* was released direct to video in July. The *Amityville Horror* franchise was a particularly scattershot one, prone by the nature of its ostensibly single-location premise to random side roads and weird detours. This instalment was no exception, being the tale of a bland-looking California house that becomes hexed thanks to a clock salvaged from the original Dutch Colonial back in Long Island. Miller played a neighbour, Mr. Anderson, whose hedges catch fire by some deviltry. "I asked my casting director to cast him," director Tony Randel said. "He never read for the part. He just showed up and delivered Dick Miller." It was a night shoot, but Randel nevertheless remembered Miller as being "very friendly," and they chatted about Miller's experience on *The Terminator*.

Near the end of 1992 Miller appeared in a true-crime show, *FBI: The Untold Stories*, playing bank robber Fast Eddie Watkins. Miller had played bank robbers before, but had not played many real-life characters over his career, and in Watkins he lucked into a good one. The episode, "Ring of Hostages," depicted Fast Eddie's most notorious crime, when in October 1975 the veteran career criminal had entered a Cleveland bank and brandished a .357 Magnum in one hand and a briefcase full of dynamite in the other. A bank teller hit a silent alarm, the cops showed up, and the next thing you knew it was *Dog Day Afternoon*, with nine hostages in a back room and Fast Eddie waving his detonator. Despite his heavy artillery, though, Fast Eddie was a gentleman bandit type, who told his hostages he wasn't really going to hurt them, and eventually broke down and wept that he couldn't bear to go back to jail. But in the end he surrendered. It was a meaty part, or it would have been if the true-crime format allowed for a performance of any range or depth. Miller, as always, did his best.

In 1993 Miller appeared as "Billy the Bucket Boy" in an interactive full-motion video game from Sega called *Prize Fighter*. The boxing game was shot in black and white from a first-person perspective and took many of its stylistic cues from Scorsese's *Raging Bull*. Billy the Bucket Boy popped his head in every now and then, offering encouragement and advice, and mopping the player's brow; to Miller, it was a slightly strange gig, entirely free of any sort of character development.

There was more unusual work to come as well, or at least unusual for Miller. He had done voice work before, providing background voices in looping sessions, but soon he began getting called in to do voices for animated superhero projects. In the feature release *Batman: Mask of the Phantasm*, he voiced gangster Chuckie Sol, who in the early minutes of the film runs afoul of the evil Phantasm, and ends up crashing his car out a high-rise window and across to another high-rise. It's one of Miller's more spectacular demises.

For the *Batman* series that followed, Miller's voice could be heard in two episodes, playing a different gangster, Boxcars "Boxy" Bennett. "That was easy," Miller said of the voice work. "I loved that." Miller was loved in return: "Any episode with Dick Miller is a good one," producer and co-creator Bruce Timm said on a *Batman* series DVD.

In the spring of '93 Miller was reunited with his old *'burbs* co-star Tom Hanks on another short-lived TV show, *Fallen Angels*. This anthology series was a laudable attempt to bring some old-fashioned, un-ironic film noir to television, with big names and high production values. Many of the biggest names were behind the camera, with stars Tom Hanks and Tom Cruise taking the bullhorn, along with Steven Soderbergh, Alfonso Cuarón, and Peter Bogdanovich. (Jonathan Kaplan did one too, but Miller wasn't in it.)

Miller's episode, "I'll Be Waiting," was based on a Raymond Chandler story and was directed by Hanks, who also took a small part as a thug. The episode was set almost entirely within a big Los Angeles hotel, at which Miller's character, Carl, works as a bellboy, cleaning out ashtrays while providing tips and counsel to a hotel dick played by Bruno Kirby. "I'll Be Waiting," which aired in mid-August, was like a cross between two Coen Brothers pictures, *Barton Fink* and *Miller's Crossing*, but with the Coens' archness replaced by complete Hanksian sincerity. The series was ambitious and was, by and large, a critical success, but it didn't last, and proved as ephemeral as most of Miller's TV work.

Miller's life off the set continued on a steady track, though he wasn't always feeling his best these days: there were aches, some of them bone-deep and slightly sinister, that Miller nevertheless dismissed as the natural price of aging. Barbara's marriage to Brian Levandoski had ended after four years, and though this was regrettable, it meant the Millers were spending more time with their toddler granddaughter, Autumn Rose. Miller continued his occasional labours, making an appearance in a black comedy called *Mona Must Die*, where he played, of all things, a Catholic priest. Old home week again: his old buddy John Shaner was in the movie, playing Dr. Shaner, and the star was Debbie Allen of *Fame*. The picture was directed by Donald Reiker, who'd been one of the executive producers of *Fame*, but it got poor reviews and a very limited release in March 1994. Todd McCarthy of *Variety* singled out Miller, writing that the "film's funniest moments are provided by Dick Miller, in briefly as a beleaguered priest, who defensively complains 'It's getting very trendy nowadays to accuse priests of sexual improprieties with young boys.'" There was a TV movie appearance for Frank De Palma, who'd directed Miller in *Tales from the Darkside*: a belated, decidedly downmarket sequel to *Midnight Run* called *Midnight Runaround*. Robert De Niro was nowhere to be seen, and Miller played his millionth bartender. He was also in another music video directed by Jonathan Kaplan; this time it was for the John Cougar Mellencamp hit "Wild Night," which had supermodel Cindy Crawford dressing down in jeans, bovver boots, and baseball cap to drive a taxi cab. Among her disparate array of fares were Miller and his pal Harry Northup, hamming it up in the back seat. Miller was dressed in a leather jacket and black trilby and appeared to be wearing fake Martin Scorsese-style eyebrows.

That same spring, Showtime, which had produced and broadcast *Fallen Angels*, teamed up with Samuel Arkoff's son Lou and put together another series of thematically linked shows, this time inspired not by film noir but by J.D. pictures from the American International back catalogue. Lou Arkoff wanted to call the series "Raging Hormones," but the network mandated *Rebel Highway*. A group of worthy directors was gathered, with William Friedkin, Mary Lambert, Robert Rodriguez, John Milius, and Ralph Bakshi among them; and the trio of Corman Kids—Dante, Arkush, and Kaplan— each got a chance to choose a title themselves to remake. (They were in fact remaking the titles more than the movies themselves.) Each director would get a title and a story, a $1.3 million budget, and ten days to shoot it in. Later the schedules were increased to twelve days, but otherwise it stayed very AIP.

Dante chose *Runaway Daughters* "because it had a lot of adults in it, and I wanted to use all my friends as parents and stuff." Miller was, of course, one of the pals to benefit from this, and got himself a juicy role as a private detective. It seems a trio of girls, one of them pregnant, have gone missing and evidently been kidnapped. They have in fact faked their kidnapping and are on the road to San Diego, hoping to catch the father-to-be before he can hop a navy ship for the South Pacific. But a hard-drinking private eye, Roy Farrell, is on the case, reassuring the parents of the missing girls that their runaway daughters are most likely trading in "sex ... sexual diseases ... peculiar practices ... the strange night world of twisted kicks, weird rituals and equipment, and whips, chains, rubber balls, dildos and handcuffs." Miller, as the detective, delivered the line with an earnest solemnity that well befitted the movie's tone.

Dante's plan to hire all his pals to play the adults made *Runaway Daughters* one of the most entertaining and watchable of the series. "It was very well received," he said. Dante found roles for just about everyone; they didn't even have to be actors. Roger and Julie Corman appeared, as did Sam Arkoff himself. Tribute was also paid through the art direction: at one point, the girls stop to fill their tank at American International Petroleum.

Allan Arkush's instalment was *Shake, Rattle and Rock*, the story of music-crazed teens fighting racism and anti-rock sentiment in their backward little town. Arkush made it a sort of prequel to *Rock 'n' Roll High School*, and he, too, assembled a killer cast, gathering Mary Woronov, P. J. Soles, and Dey Young to play the mothers of their characters in the earlier film. Miller played a cop, Lieutenant Paisley, who may have been meant as some relation of his police chief in *Rock 'n' Roll High School*, or of the original Walter Paisley, but was in any case one of the more sympathetic adult characters in the piece. He's at least not a racist, though he holds a strong prejudice against greasers; and while he does bust up the teenagers' rock 'n' roll dance party, he feels bad about doing it.

Runaway Daughters and *Shake, Rattle and Rock* both aired in August 1994, not exactly prime TV watching time, but they were widely released on video and did well in that format. Miller was all over Showtime that month. He played yet another cop—of the blazer variety, not a uniform—in *Attack of the 5'2" Women*, a true-crime diptych that may stand as the most mid-'90s thing ever made, missing only O. J. and his Bronco. It was conceived and co-directed by Julie Brown, who'd sung the novelty-song warning "The Homecoming Queen's Got a Gun."

There were two lightly fictionalized tales of angry women: Tonya Harding and Lorena Bobbitt. Julie Brown starred in each of them as the ladies, co-wrote the scripts, and directed one of the segments; Richard Wenk directed the other. Miller was in Wenk's, the Lorena Bobbitt episode. As her real-life counterpart had, Lorena Babbitt removes her husband's colungus, flings it away in some vacant lot, and is promptly arrested. She takes a pair of cops, frustrated detective Dick Miller and a towering uniform played by 6'4" Rick Overton, to find the dislocated unit, which, after much driving around the lot, is found, and comic confusion and dick jokes abound. There followed a scene in a hospital, where Miller had to handle a poodle and many more dick jokes. Of course, Dick had heard them all before.

Late in the summer of 1993, Dick got a call from Quentin Tarantino, a young director whose first feature, *Reservoir Dogs,* had caused a stir the year before. Tarantino considered Miller "one of my favourite character actors," and, having watched him in "every Joe Dante movie" and "seventy-two Roger Corman movies," now wanted Miller's mug to adorn his new picture, *Pulp Fiction*. Miller was to play Monster Joe, the owner of a car-crushing business who provides an underworld body disposal service on the side.

Miller's scene—actually, his shot, as he only appeared in one—was with Harvey Keitel, playing murder cleanup man Winston Wolf, who is evidently a regular customer of Monster Joe's. The two stand in Joe's ramshackle office, facing each other, exchanging black jokes about discount corpse disposal rates and special deals for body parts; then Mr. Wolf is off to the scrapyard to chat with Joe's daughter, played by *Saturday Night Live* star Julia Sweeney. Miller's sleeves were rolled up and his tats visible, and he played the working-class criminal through and through. It was, on the one hand, a characteristically canny casting move on Tarantino's part; but on the other, well, it hardly take a brain genius to know it's a good idea to hire Dick Miller.

The scene was shot in Sun Valley, just north of Burbank, at a place called A&R Truck Dismantlers. Tarantino was giddy at having what he called "the honor to put [Miller] and Harvey Keitel in the same frame together." Miller saw right away that the director was talented, but found him "a little nervous when he wasn't behind the camera." (Miller had also found Martin Scorsese "nervous.") By the end of November production had wrapped, and the complicated job of putting together this sprawling, multi-story, time-hopping picture began. When Harvey Weinstein (who, historians may recall, was once a movie producer) received the script, he allegedly said, "What is this, the fucking telephone book?" It was inevitable that, from such a lengthy and convoluted scenario, some scenes, even short scenes comprised of a single two-shot, might have to be dropped.

Late the following spring, the Millers got an invitation to attend the cast and crew screening of *Pulp Fiction*, to be held at the Disney studio screening room. The picture had already screened and won the Palme d'Or at Cannes, so there was heavy buzz about it around Hollywood. "I'm in that picture!" Miller told his friends. He was thrilled: it was unlike anything he'd been a part of before, and he was looking forward to the screening. The day came, finally, and the Millers dressed for the big event. They drove down out of the hills and into Burbank, where, alongside the Los Angeles River and the Ventura Freeway, and just below Forest Lawn, the Disney studio lay.

20   *Fade in, fade out*

Dick and Lainie Miller parked their car in the Disney lot and made their way to the screening room. The place was swarming with excited industry folk—the screening room held 800 people, and it was full. Spotting Tarantino mingling in the lobby, the Millers approached. "Hey, Quentin, I'd like to introduce you to my wife," Miller said.

A surprised Tarantino shook Lainie's hand and blurted, "What are you doing here?"

"Here to see the picture," Miller answered, confused himself now.

"Dick," Tarantino said, "you're not in the picture."

Startled, Miller asked, "What the hell do you mean?"

"Uhh, uhh, I'll tell you later," Tarantino said, and fled.

Dick and Lainie found seats and settled in to watch the movie. "You were fuming," Lainie Miller recalled.

"I was burning," Miller admitted. He'd been cut from pictures before, and by bigger directors, but this picture felt important, different, and did even more so here in the electric atmosphere of the auditorium. Worse was that no one had told him before the screening; he felt like a chump, an imposter, the butt of a bad joke. It was embarrassing.

He sat and fumed as Lawrence Bender, the producer, made a little speech, and then introduced Tarantino, who came running down the aisle, clutching a small wooden box. Breathlessly he informed the crowd that the studio had planned all sorts of premieres and press screenings, but that he had put his foot down, demanded that the cast and crew get to see the picture first. "This is *your* film!" he cried. "And this is for *you!*" He opened the little box and showed them the Palme d'Or medal inside. The audience went crazy, and in the darkness Miller folded his arms across his chest and worked his jaw as he'd done so many times on screen.

The film started and Miller could see that it was every bit as good as he'd been led to believe it was. The Harvey Keitel character, Mr. Wolf, was introduced, and Miller's spirits briefly rose as the characters began talking about Monster Joe and his body disposal service. Perhaps he'd misunderstood Tarantino in the bustle of the lobby, or maybe the director, in his own excitement, had got it wrong. But no, "the scene came, the scene went," Miller lamented, and Monster Joe was spoken of but never seen.

Later, Miller tracked Tarantino down and asked him why the scene had been dropped. "He said the usual thing," Miller grumbled. "He said, 'The time was too long.' Bullshit!" Miller laughed and shook his head. "But anyway, I'll swallow it."

It was true, though. Tarantino's contract had allowed for a movie no more than two-and-a-half hours long, and even with the cut scenes (and there were several others), the picture still ran 154 minutes. More particularly, though, it was a pacing issue. "It was too much at that moment," Tarantino explained on the Deleted Scenes section of the *Pulp Fiction* DVD. "We just kind of want to be moving along. Basically we want to hurry up and get to the diner at this point and see John [Travolta] and Sam [Jackson] do their scene." It had been a tough call for the director, though. "I still really love the scene," he sighed. "Of all these [deleted] scenes, it's the one that I almost kept in, right down to the wire at the last minute. But [it's like], 'we don't want to be here,' unfortunately. But *I* want to be there." When Miller asked him why the scene had been shot at all, Tarantino shrugged. "I wanted to get you and Keitel on film together, that's all."

Miller remained disappointed, but, being a practical-minded guy and not particularly a grudge-holder when money wasn't involved, soon got over his active resentment. He saw later how Tarantino revived the career of his Silver Spoon buddy Robert Forster by casting him as one of the leads in his next picture, *Jackie Brown*, and while Miller surely felt a few pangs of professional jealousy at that, he was pleased for his friend, and respected Tarantino's willingness to cast against accepted commercial norms. He'd happily have accepted another invitation from the director, but none ever came.

Other offers did. Miller was in an episode of *Lois & Clark*, the domesticated Superman series that had just begun the year before and would run for four successful seasons on ABC through the 1990s. He donned a sweater, had his hair combed neatly, and went into his most avuncular mode, this time literally, to play Lois Lane's Uncle Mike. The episode, "Church of Metropolis," was directed by Robert Singer, who knew Miller from when he'd been an executive producer on *V: The Final Battle*; it aired on October 23, 1994.

But what helped salve the *Pulp Fiction* wound most for Miller was a role in *Tales from the Crypt Presents Demon Knight*, the most elaborate and most remunerative part he'd been given since *Gremlins 2*. "I was pretty hungry," Miller said of that period, though he could have been talking about almost any period in his career. *Demon Knight* was the first in a planned series of feature-film spinoffs from the *Tales from the Crypt* series that had been running for years on HBO, and had served as a creative playground for all sorts of big stars and directors. Directors who'd used Miller before, such as Robert Zemeckis, Fred Dekker, and Tom Hanks, all logged episodes, but Miller himself was never on the show.

Ernest Dickerson, the director chosen for the feature, had also never worked on the show. He was an accomplished cinematographer who'd shot a number of films for Spike Lee, and had also worked with John Sayles; he had turned to directing in the early 1990s, and was a long-standing horror fan. "My favourite magazines were *Famous Monsters of Filmland* and *Castle of Frankenstein*," he said. "First movie I ever saw was *It Came from Beneath the Sea*." His road to Dick Miller fandom was along the same path trod by so many others. "I grew up watching Roger Corman movies before I even knew who Roger Corman was," he said, "and there was always this guy, this character actor, who a lot of times was a wise guy. Even when he was a hero, he still played a bit of a wise guy. He was always there and I always enjoyed him. And then years later, when I saw that he was appearing in Joe Dante movies and the first *Terminator*, I was all 'It's that guy again!'"

When Dickerson read the *Demon Knight* script and found in its pages an old inebriate called Uncle Willy, "the first person I thought about was Dick Miller," he said. Dickerson hoped he would accept the part and was overjoyed when he did, but there hadn't been much danger of it going otherwise. Once Miller saw the script, and the name of his character recurring in scene after scene, and the groovy demonic possession and subsequent death scene in store for Uncle Willy, he was sold. The script had a group of people trapped in a cavernous desert church (which had at some point been transformed into a rooming house) by a charismatic demon called the Collector. There's some nonsense about a mystical key that must be kept from the Collector's possession, but in the end all of this plot stuff was disposable, and the picture's true value came not from the story but from what Dickerson, his cast, and his special effects teams brought to it.

The picture began shooting on June 6, right around the time of the *Pulp Fiction* screening, out on desert locations north of LA. Miller had a scene out there, but after that he and the entire production moved to an airplane hangar at Van Nuys airport, where the company stayed for the rest of the forty-day shoot. Miller was delighted with Dickerson, whom he considered "a real sweetheart." Dickerson's style of directing was right up Miller's street—"he never interfered once," Miller said. What Miller calls "interfering" is to others simply "directing," but, to him, the mark of a really fine director is knowing when not to issue directions at all. "I figure directions come with problems," Miller said. "If the director says, 'Wait a minute, blah blah blah,' I know something's wrong. So you want to avoid those incidents." Only Miller would consider being given direction an "incident," but that is what makes him Miller.

He was equally delighted with his *Demon Knight* co-stars, who were a talented bunch. Billy Zane, deep in the zone for this one, was the Collector; William Sadler, properly grizzled, was his nemesis, Brayker; and the rest of the boarding house denizens included C. C. H. Pounder, Jada Pinkett, Thomas Haden Church, and Charles Fleisher. The cast loved Miller in return: Sadler literally genuflected when Miller's name came up in an on-camera interview, and the verbal salaams performed by the others were no less worshipful. Miller seemed to have achieved some sort of apotheosis, at least among his fellow actors. Dickerson, too, was smitten, and said, "For somebody who has his gruff personality onscreen, he's a tremendously sweet person."

But the love fest was not without its problems. Miller couldn't help but notice that his fellow actors had luxurious trailers, while he had "this old trailer storeroom, and the extras were dressing there." He went to the AD department and asked, "Hey, what's this?" "Ah, just temporary," they told him.

A decade earlier, at the time of *Explorers*, David Everitt of *Fangoria* had asked Miller if, now that he was the adult male lead in a big Dante picture, he'd finally been given his own Winnebago. "No," Miller joked, "but they gave me an extra nail in my closet. Now there's no room to move around in there. But once you get the mops down, it's a pretty good dressing room." Now the joke was less funny. Still, years after the *Demon Knight* shoot, Miller insisted that "I didn't mind, really."

"Yes, you did!" Lainie cried.

"I minded that other people had better!"

"Well, then," Lainie pointed out, "you minded."

A week after first bringing it up with the production, he minded enough to go back to them and ask again what was going on. Why did the other actors, even those with lower billing, get their own trailers? "Well," he was told, "it must be in their contracts." To Miller, who'd never felt that his agents had his back when negotiating his contracts, this was the unkindest cut. With smoke coming out of his ears he went to Joel Silver, one of the executive producers, himself legendary for his seismic, Louis B. Meyer-style temper, and demanded his own full dressing room. "You can't have it," Silver told him.

"I blew up," Miller said, "and I called him all kinds of names. 'Cheap son-of-a-B!' I just let him know that I wasn't happy. They got a trailer there the next morning. Nice trailer."

Miller couldn't believe he had won the battle; fighting producers, especially powerful ones like Silver, was usually like fighting City Hall. Having won it, though, he was a bit abashed, and so, he said, "I bought them champagne."

"Yeah," Lainie said, "'cause you felt guilty for your mouth."

"Bought 'em all champagne, bought two bottles of champagne for the producers."

"And for him, that's something!" Lainie laughed.

"I really tore it up that day," Miller remembered. "I guess it was the only time I got mad on the set."

Dickerson, quite properly, had never even been aware of the contretemps, and the shoot proceeded smoothly and amicably. Miller was looking forward to his big scene, in which Uncle Willy, possessed by demonic forces, turns green-eyed and fanged, his countenance knurled and his manner disagreeable. Before he could be possessed, though, Uncle Willy had to be seduced, and the Collector arranges for this in spectacular fashion. Walking into a dark bedroom Willy is shocked to see it become a brightly lit tiki bar filled with topless women, who chorus "Hi, Uncle Willy!" as he walks in. With his jaw agape Miller wanders through this astonishing breast-scape to the bar, where the Collector, in Hunter Thompson drag, waits with a grin and a glass of hooch. Miller's performance here, despite the distractions all around him, is subtle and heartbreaking: Willy knows he's doomed if he takes the glass, but does anyway, while doubt, terror, need, and helpless acquiescence move across his face like shadows in a matter of seconds.

After that came the possession and the special effects makeup that inevitably followed. Scott Wheeler, a member of the effects team and the one who applied Miller's prosthetics, was astonished to discover he'd never gone through the process before, or hadn't, at least, since his homemade leper makeup on *The Undead*, and that hardly counted. First up was the head cast, in which Miller's head and shoulders were encased in plaster. This was, said Miller, "a pain in the neck. Pain in the head! I don't like being covered up like that." Miller recreated the scene, moaning, "Oh god, here we go again!" "Twenty minutes, just relax." "Mphmnmmnphm!"

But he'd known what he was getting himself into. "He wouldn't have accepted it if he wasn't up for it," Joe Dante said. "Once he says he'll do it, he does it. I've never seen any backing down or second thoughts or 'I'll just phone this in.' I've never seen that."

"He was a real pro," Wheeler said. "He sat and let me do my work. Of course, we were all geeks in his presence, given his rich history as an actor." The makeup department's adulation was no doubt a balm, as was the sheer novelty of the whole thing, but Miller still grumped a bit. "Ah, I can't stand doin' this crap," he told his tormentors. But he loved playing the scene itself. "I turn this way and I'm nice, I turn that way and I'm the monster," he said. "It was wild. I got to do some weird things."

"I loved that picture," he said later. "That's one of my favourites. Not *the*, but it's a picture I always liked." It was a collegial set, and lots of fun for just about everybody, and when the picture wrapped on August 9, there were "big hugs and kisses" all around. It was released the following January and did well enough that a second *Tales from the Crypt* picture, *Bordello of Blood*, was made; but as that one featured Dennis Miller instead of Dick, it flopped. Dickerson, meanwhile, treasured the rare moments he spent with Miller, like the time he went to a drugstore at the corner of Laurel Canyon and Ventura and found Dick inside, buying himself an ice cream cone. "Dying to work with him again," Dickerson said, "but I just haven't found the right thing to put him in."

After a vacation and some down time, Miller was back at work in October, playing a sort of futuristic prison camp guard on a two-part episode of *Star Trek: Deep Space 9*. The job came from Ira Behr, who, like Dickerson, was always looking for an opportunity to cast Dick. He'd written feature films and television pilots with "incredibly juicy" parts specifically for Miller; one idea had him paired up with Kenneth Tobey as a Statler-and-Waldorf pair of hecklers living in Key West. Behr had a different philosophy from that of many other Miller fans, and tried to avoid hiring him simply to get him in there no matter how tiny the part. But when the camp guard part came up, Behr saw an opportunity for the actor to play something meaty and atypical. Behr admitted that Miller "probably would not have been everyone's first choice as a security guard in this kind of semi-concentration camp. The first thing you would think of would be, like, a Big Bill Smith, a tough-ass big guy. But I wanted him. I just knew Dick was going to do a really good job."

The camp, situated on an Earth of the future, but not so far in the future as the DS9 characters inhabited, was specifically intended to pen in the homeless. And, just as filming of the episode began, Los Angeles mayor Richard

Riordan was quoted in the *Los Angeles Times,* proposing that homeless people be shuttled to an "urban campground" to get them off the streets. To genre movie fans his campground sounded like Justiceville, the ad-hoc homeless ghetto seen in John Carpenter's film *They Live,* which had been released barely six years earlier and was supposed to be a satire. Crew members on the DS9 set waved the newspaper around the morning it was published, astonished that the concept they were working on was so quickly becoming reality.

Deep Space 9 was a *Star Trek* spinoff set in a space station rather than on a mobile starship, so the writers tossed in some time travel here or a mirror universe there to keep things lively and varied. In keeping with the *Trek* philosophy, the show tried occasionally to wrestle with social issues, and such was the case with "Past Tense" parts 1 and 2. The space station's captain was played by Avery Brooks, and its doctor by Alexander Siddiq, and these two are accidentally transported back to the year 2024. There, they encounter Miller, in taupe jumpsuit, who compliments them on their "matching pajamas," and, on hearing their confused questions about what year it is and where the not-yet-extant Starfleet headquarters has gone, groans that he's been saddled with "two more dims." By the end of the two-parter, after a terrible and destructive riot in the homeless encampment, Miller's character has softened considerably. He looks over the devastated, corpse-strewn homeless area and, in a classically *Star Trek* rhetorical appeal, asks, "How could we have let it come to this?"

Avery Brooks was, said Behr, "like Dick, a total professional, always came prepared, always knew his lines, and, let's just say, did not suffer fools graciously. You had to win his respect, and if you didn't get it, you knew." But the hard-to-please Brooks was as charmed by Miller as anyone else. "After their scene," said Behr, "it was one of the few times ever, in seven years, [Brooks] came over to me and gave me this look that said, 'Hey, that's a good scene, nice stuff.' And that was Dick not playing Walter Paisley. It was the Dick I liked, a guy who could have compassion and be tough at the same time." The episodes aired in January 1995, and secured Miller's place in the hearts of nerds and in the *Trek*-o-pedias that would crop up in the coming Internet age.

A Bucket of Blood, Miller's signature film, had its year in 1995; or at least this was the beginning of some kind of minor cultural rediscovery. In July a stage adaptation of the picture was mounted in Winnipeg, Canada, to full houses and critical acclaim. Local actor Mark Yuill took on the Walter Paisley role and did an excellent job of it. In September Roger Corman's own company, Concorde-New Horizons, released their remake of the picture, featuring Anthony Michael Hall in the Paisley role. Hall's interpretation of the would-be artist and busboy was creditable, but lacked any of the nuance Miller had brought to it thirty-six years earlier. The Yellow Door was now the Jabberjaw Café, and the beatniks of old had become gaudy LA scenesters, but otherwise Charles Griffith's script was largely left intact, which gave the impression that Corman had made the new version only because he could, and cheaply.

Years later came further stage adaptations: a musical version done in Chicago, which failed to become the Broadway hit that *Little Shop of Horrors* had in the 1980s; and in February 2015 a straight adaptation made its way to the stage in Baltimore. Griffith's script was proving itself an especially sturdy piece of writing. The original film itself got a number of revival screenings all through the 1990s, and into the next century, though that had been going on since the early 1980s, when Rick Baker quite correctly strong-armed his London makeup crew into attending one.

In the meantime, after a quiet year for Miller—*too* quiet, he was thinking by the end of it—he got an unexpectedly heroic and action-packed TV role early in 1996, on the show *Weird Science*. This forgotten program tried to spin a continuing series out of a one-joke John Hughes picture from ten years earlier, in which two nerdy pals somehow generate a beautiful lady with their personal computer and find they've got a bombshell fairy godmother who can grant their every wish. In the episode "Demon Lisa," the synthetic goddess has become possessed by an evil demon, and only Dick Miller, as a supernatural IT guy, can save the day. Miller got to fire a big gun, climb onto a roof, conduct a see-sawing battle against the unholy entity, and vanish mysteriously at the end.

A month later he appeared in another unremembered sitcom, *Sister, Sister*, as an angry mall manager whose wife is put into a headlock by a bumbling security guard. There wasn't much for Miller to do but bluster a bit and fire the hapless guard, then hit up the pay window and go home. He got another tiny role from Dante, who was doing a television pilot for a sci-fi show called *The Osiris Chronicles*. In what might have been a callback to his interstellar car salesman in *Space Raiders*, if anyone involved had remembered that movie, Miller, wearing a leather coat and fingerless gloves, with untamed hair and unshaven whiskers, played a futuristic peddler of little glowing bio-crystals. Dante had done what he could with it, and a reasonable amount of money had been spent; but with its bland hero and gobbledygook story, the show was never going to be picked up, and the movie surfaced only a few years later, on a different network, under a different title, as though embarrassed by itself.

Though he often claimed not to, Miller did audition for things every now and then, when it came to his attention that an irascible older man was required for something and when he needed a buck; and occasionally on these outings he ran into old friends like Jonathan Haze, going up for the same part. In the meantime he and Lainie went every Sunday to the feature film screenings held at the Academy of Motion Pictures, and always sat in the same seats. "That's how he keeps up with the new movies," Allan Arkush said. This was also largely how the Millers kept up with old friends; the screenings were little weekly mixers, oiled up with a little booze and a lot of friendly bullshit. John Shaner, Miller's old *Bucket of Blood* co-star, was frequently there, and his brother David Sheiner came to every screening, and, Miller said, "[gave] chocolates to my wife. He's a nice guy."

Late in 1996 Dante got another TV assignment, an HBO production called *The Second Civil War*. It was a different sort of project for Dante, a political satire that was set in a future, or alternate, United States that was not much different from present-day reality. (It proved prescient too.) Barry Levinson had been set to direct it, but dropped out to do the similar *Wag the Dog* instead. Levinson stayed on as a producer, and then, Dante said, "I inherited it." It was a modest-budget picture, but it had a large cast, and Dante hired a disaster movie's worth of actors that included both his gallery of ringers and a broad variety of new faces. "Great cast," Dante said. "Best cast I ever worked with."

Miller played Eddie O'Neill, a news cameraman who was part of a team covering a disturbance in Idaho precipitated by the imminent arrival of a planeload of refugee orphans. "That was a pretty good part," Dante said. "It was a part that I kind of built up. And Dick did some ad-libbing."

Dante provided the previously nameless character his moniker too. "When you read a script with lots of characters in it, very often it's 'Executive #1,' 'Executive #2,'" he said. "Now, you don't want to tell somebody that they're playing Executive #2, right? You want to tell them they're playing Mr. Smith. It's easier to read the scripts without the extra names, because when you're reading scripts, there's all these names, you're going, 'Who's that guy?' But when it actually comes to make the movie, you gotta give them names."

This was only one way in which Dante tried to take care of his actors. He was not a family man, and while it would be too facile an exaggeration to imply that his stock company served as some kind of replacement, one can imagine them all sharing a table at a holiday feast, gabbing and bickering like any other family. Certainly, the Millers considered him family, and when Dick, who'd been feeling poorly on a distressingly regular basis, went into the hospital and under the knife, Dante was always there, visiting when he could or making daily calls to see how Miller was doing or what he could do to help.

And so we come to the most vexatious point in our narrative so far, a time of trial for Dick and Lainie Miller. For some time Miller had not been feeling his best, and when he went for tests he got the worst possible news. It was cancer of the lung, and lobectomy was the only recourse. A pair of Scottish surgeons flew in to perform the first VATS, or video-assisted thoracic surgery, ever done in Los Angeles. They successfully removed two lobes of Miller's lung without breaking any of his ribs to do it (though after *Gremlins 2*, they'd have found that remarkably easy to do), and as he recovered, painfully and at length at their house in the hills, he was declared cancer-free.

But as he recovered, it was found that he had a blockage in the carotid artery, and an endarterectomy was duly scheduled. "It's a good thing he had a good oncologist," Lainie said, "otherwise he wouldn't have been cleared for that [vascular] surgery, and we wouldn't be having this conversation." Next came an aorta bi-femoral bypass. "That is," Lainie, the ex-nurse, explained, "they replaced his aorta from just below the level of his heart, and so down both femoral arteries he's all Dacron. So I call him my bionic husband, because he's all Dacron!

"I really almost lost him that time," she sighed. All the time Miller was in the hospital, she slept beside him, and one night when he started to sweat profusely and roll around feebly, she ran out into the hall to alert the nurses. "He's diabetic!" she told them. "Check his sugar!" The nurses insisted that he was merely "exhausted," and went about their rounds. An increasingly frantic Lainie kept at them—"they couldn't shut me up," she said—and when the nurses finally checked his blood sugar they found Miller in the throes of severe hypoglycemia. "Incompatible with life!" Lainie raged. "Those crazy nurses! They didn't understand!" Suddenly, like escapees from Corman's Nurse Trilogy, the nurses "were jumping all over the bed, and they're doing everything, but if I hadn't been there, he wouldn't have pulled through."

In the middle of all this, between surgeries and during a recuperative period Miller figured would last the rest of his life, the couple decided to move. Living up in the hills, in a hard-to-find house within a labyrinth of twisting and hilly streets, was disadvantageous to an ailing man who might have to be found by an ambulance at any sudden moment. "After those surgeries he was just always fearful," Lainie said. "I was traveling for IATSE, and I'd get a call because it was raining and the mud's coming over the hill, and the place had just been paid, and I thought, we've got to get out of the hills. He's just not comfortable, and no one will get to him, and so we moved down here."

"Down here" was a smaller house in Toluca Lake, almost in the shadow of the Warner Bros. lot. It felt just a bit cramped at first, so the Millers added skylights, but they grew into it, or it into them, and then it felt comfortable and quiet and safe. "The house," Lainie said, "is as old as Dick. Same year." She turned to her husband. "You were both built the same year."

There was work for Miller in this time too. In the winter of '97 and '98, as Miller was heading into his season of pain, Joe Dante started shooting a big-budget tween-pic, not dissimilar to *Gremlins*, called *Small Soldiers*. The picture was about toy soldiers given a species of life by the insertion of military-grade computer chips, and the similarly endowed, but peaceable, monster toys they are sworn to destroy; and then the two neighbourhood houses that become their battleground. It was all fertile ground for a man of Dante's concerns, and nearly as gloriously anti-corporate as *Gremlins 2*. Miller, the avatar of this class consciousness, played, as he had at least twice before, a truck driver, but a particularly warm and fuzzy one this time. He's the hero's pal—not Mr. Futterman now, but simply "Joe," as though some eerie, *Persona*-style personality meld had finally come to pass—who inadvertently kicks things off by letting the hero have a crate of the special toys in advance of their release date, so that he can sell them in his father's little toy store. Though this is sketchy behaviour for a presumably bonded driver, Miller sells the plausibility of Joe's actions by sheer warmth of personality.

With this complicated special effects tale of sapient playthings, Dante had a lot on his plate, but he was still conscious of his old friend's misery. "It was not a great time for him," Dante said. Hospital bills were piling up at the Miller household, or at least were a constant, nagging shadow, and, taking a cue from Roger Corman's studio-footed beneficence years before on *The St. Valentine's Day Massacre*, he organized the schedule so that Miller would work at the beginning of the show and also nearer the end, and thereby "get him as many hold days as I possibly could. And I think he ended up coming out of it with a couple of bucks and not a lot of stress."

Small Soldiers was a Big Summer Movie, so the entertainment press gave it some attention, and for a brief moment their spotlight even turned on Miller. In the pages of *Entertainment Weekly* he was, once again, "that guy you've seen in dozens of movies but never knew his name," and was asked about his long-standing relationship with Dante. "You're more relaxed if you work with a director you've worked with before," Miller told them. "You have the confidence that they like your work, and it shows in your performance." Asked what he was up to next, Miller allowed that he had some things "cooking," but then became frank. "I hope that *Small Soldiers* will stir up a little action," he said. "People will remember I'm still around and call me in." The picture had its premiere on July 8 at the Universal Amphitheatre, and a hale-looking Miller, resplendent in sports coat and pink shirt, got still more attention when he was interviewed on the red carpet. For some inexplicable reason he was asked what animal he might like to be reincarnated as, and at first Miller refused to play along. "Animal? Ahh, I'd like to be a human," he growled. Pressed for an answer, he shrugged. "Okay, a nice dog. A golden lab."

In truth Miller didn't have a whole lot cooking, or at least not much more than usual. In mid-November he appeared on the television doctor show *ER*, on which Jonathan Kaplan served as a producer. Kaplan, of course, had hired Miller and made sure to be on-set for the shoot. Miller was Mr. Ackerman, a terminally ill man who never gets up from his hospital bed, a part Miller no doubt found particularly easy to play at this point in his life. The episode, "Double Blind," was directed by a young and inexperienced fellow called Dave Chameides, who'd been working on the series as a Steadicam operator and was given a crack at the bullhorn. Miller's scenes were with Julianna Margulies, who played one of the nurses, from whom Mr. Ackerman is hoping to score some marijuana for his pain, and at one point, in a rehearsal, Miller grabbed her hand and kissed it imploringly. "No, no, no!" Chameides told him. "You're too weak for that!" Miller shrugged agreeably and thought, "Okay, that's my direction." It was basic and it made sense: it was the kind of direction he liked. (Chameides, however, "decided he hated directing," Jonathan Kaplan said, and made camera operating, particularly Steadicam work, his focus.) There was more collegial admiration from his fellow actors: Margulies was a lover of film and therefore of Miller, so when she saw his name on the call sheet, she gasped, "*The* Dick Miller?"

She made a special call to her co-star and fellow movie buff George Clooney to brag that *she* was working with Miller and *he* wasn't. The episode aired near the end of January 1999.

A short while after that Miller played back-to-back building superintendents, an occasion noteworthy only in that it hadn't happened before. The first was in an episode of *Clueless*, a spinoff series of the 1995 Amy Heckerling picture that was then in its final season. The episode aired in April, and less than a month later Miller appeared in *NYPD Blue* as a jailbird-turned-super named Carl Bode, who appears nervously at the police station to give some evidence and to assure the officers that he had nothing to do with the murder they're investigating. His *Clueless* super had been a typical, wisecracking Miller creation, but for *NYPD Blue* he gave an uncharacteristically sombre performance.

Late summer held a treat for the Millers: a trip to Switzerland to take part in a retrospective showcase of Joe Dante films being held by the venerable Locarno Film Festival. The program was called "Dante & Co.," and as part of the "Co." Miller was invited along, and he and Lainie made a holiday of it. When he got back there was more work: Allan Arkush was directing a comedic detective show called *Snoops*, and had a bartender part for Miller in an episode called "Singer in the Band." In a startling change of pace, Miller was not simply behind the bar serving drinks, but was carrying around a crate and restocking a beer fridge as he delivered his lines. And then, as the millennium approached, Miller donned a monkey suit once again to play an intractable doorman in an episode of the *Party of Five* spinoff *Time of Your Life* called "The Time the Millennium Approached." However ill Miller was when his bit was shot, he seemed as tough and imposing as ever: there is no question that the character trying to get into the building Miller's braid-bedecked doorman is guarding will not succeed, not with Dick Miller on the job.

The millennium came and went, the world's computers did not turn to paste, and Miller took it easy and recovered from his surgeries. When he returned to the screen in late 2001, in a horror cheapie called *Route 666*, he played a bartender: it was like there had been no hiatus from acting at all. His bit is over in the first three minutes (for which director William Wesley is to be commended and thanked); he has three lines and two of them are the same; and he gives several very poisonous looks at the film's stars, Lou

Diamond Phillips and Lori Petty, as their characters act obnoxiously as part of a ruse. (The characters are still obnoxious once the ruse is over.) The movie was released on the day before Halloween, and right around that time Allan Arkush had another job for Miller. It was a bit on *Crossing Jordan*, a show Arkush was producing and frequently directing. In a scene shot in a park on the Universal back lot, Miller played a hustler who met the show's detective protagonist and gave her some vital information; information that, it turned out, was also delivered by someone else at another point in the episode. "The information in [Miller's] scene was redundant so the scene was cut," Arkush said, "and Dick with it."

Life continued for the Millers at a stately pace. Lainie was still with IATSE, and Barbara, done with her business courses, had taken a detour into real estate. She worked with outfits So Cal Real Estate and later Rodeo Realty, selling or buying half-million dollar houses in Studio City, Burbank, and Glendale.

Ira Behr and Miller had maintained their friendship since the days of *Fame*, with Behr still trying to create projects in which his older pal would star, and Miller shrugging and taking the attitude that, if such a project came to pass, that would be okay with him, but he was not banking on anything. One night before Miller's descent into illness, Behr had invited over Dick and Lainie, Kenneth Tobey, and some other actors, and, with his house swimming in veteran Hollywood anecdotalists, he'd enjoyed, Behr said, "one of the great nights of my life."

Once Miller had recovered enough to renew his breakfasts and luncheons at the Silver Spoon, he was there frequently with Behr and Fred Rappaport, another writer and producer. The walls were covered in movie posters associated with its regular clientele; there was a *Bucket of Blood* poster, but Miller never sat anywhere near it. One afternoon, sitting at their usual table, Behr, Rappaport, and Miller watched as "a very old, very infirm Shelley Winters" tottered in. Winters was not at her best on this day, however. "It was really just so sad," Behr recalled. "She looked ... the only word I can use is 'decrepit.'" They watched her struggle across the room and sit down heavily at her table, directly beneath a poster of one of her own movies, and peer at the menu. She looked ragged and done, barely holding on. "What happened?" Rappaport wondered aloud. "What happened to Shelley Winters?"

Miller looked up at Winters and then at his friends. "Too much cock," he growled, and took a bite of his sandwich.

In 2002, on the strength of his maniacal love for Warner Bros. cartoons, Joe Dante was hired to make *Looney Tunes: Back in Action*, a live action/cartoon admixture in the vein of *Who Framed Roger Rabbit*. Dante took the project not just because he loved the cartoons, but because Looney Tunes director Chuck Jones was a friend of his, and because the last thing he wanted to see out in the world was another *Space Jam*, which had been the studio's previous attempt at bringing their beloved characters into some sort of modern, live-action context. It involved mainly basketball, and, to Dante, and anyone who appreciated Bugs, Daffy, Claude Cat, and the rest of the gang, *Space Jam* stunk on ice, so Dante set forth with the noblest of intentions: to make the anti-*Space Jam*.

The plot was simple enough. A Warner Bros. security guard played by Brendan Fraser, who also happens to be the son of the studio's biggest star, irritates the real Brendan Fraser and is fired from his job. His father, a movie star who plays a famous spy, turns out to be a real spy and also to have been kidnapped by Steve Martin, playing the head of Acme. Daffy Duck, Bugs Bunny, Yosemite Sam, and many other characters serve as goofy window dressing, and Jenna Elfman, playing a humourless Vice-President in Charge of Comedy, serves some narrative purpose too.

Despite such ingratiating tactics as a first act set almost entirely on the Warner Bros. lot, which might almost have functioned as a promotional short for the studio and its movies, the actual executives were not in Dante's corner. Some of them probably remembered *Gremlins 2* and knew Dante was not one to genuflect before corporate overlords; and, indeed, he began the movie depicting the Warner executive corps more or less as idiots, then knocked down their iconic studio water tower. Making the film was not a salutary experience for Dante. "Worst year-and-a-half of my life," he said later.

But Miller had a ball, for the one day he was on the show. He played the head of the Warner Bros. security force, who, in a scrupulous recreation of the opening sequence of *Branded*, tears the insignias from the disgraced Fraser's uniform and sends him out into the wilderness. It was easy to get to: the set was practically across the street from his house. And he was not in the least daunted by the idea that some of his co-stars were animated; he'd been through that before in *Evil Toons*. (Though in neither film does he interact with the cartoons much.) Hey, and look, there was Roger Corman—Dante had hired his old boss to play an angry, ranting film director.

As fun and easy as the little bit part was, Miller was no longer feeling the love for this kind of acting as once he had. These spells of discontent had manifested before: at times, Miller told an interviewer, he felt he was given roles as a security guard, or a cop, or a bartender mainly as "a matter of trying to be kind to the guy who's getting a little old now." Once he'd done his *Looney Tunes* bit, he told Dante, "I think this is my last picture. I don't enjoy doing these bit parts." Dante, however, didn't believe him, and rightly so.

Looney Tunes: Back in Action opened in mid-November 2003, but made a poor showing at the box office and got little praise in the notices. Considering the lack of studio cooperation and the difficulties in making such a film, it managed some good, hearty laughs; and in a scene populated by pop culture aliens (Robot Monster and a gurning Man from Planet X among them), Dante had the good sense to include a black and white Kevin McCarthy, yet again clutching a *Body Snatchers* pod and begging for pity's sake to be believed. Notwithstanding all this, the movie was not a success, except in one important respect. "It was better than *Space Jam*," Dante said.

Between the production and release of *Looney Tunes: Back in Action*, and despite his avowal to quit doing bit parts, Miller showed up in an episode of the Elmore Leonard TV spinoff show, *Karen Sisco*. After that, however, came some serious inaction. Dick and Lainie went to Hawaii, which by now was a pleasurable habit for them; they stayed a lot on Oahu, but still liked Kauai the best, because that was where Dick had worked on *Naked Paradise*. Dick and Lainie took videos of the old locations, but they had long disintegrated. "It was like a ghost town," Miller said.

Back in Los Angeles Miller maintained his self-imposed retirement, turning down the parts he was offered, despite Lainie's wish that he keep a hand in. But Miller was no longer confident that he could remember his lines, and, to him, going blank as the cameras rolled, and other actors were looking on and waiting for their cues, was a scenario to be avoided at all costs. Voice work seemed a good compromise, and late in 2004, when Miller was offered a small part in the animated *Justice League Unlimited* series, he took it. He played the elderly midget Oberon, who serves as factotum to the superhero Mr. Miracle, and who, in an episode called "The Ties that Bind," is kidnapped by an enormous granny voiced by Ed Asner. It was a particularly weird part in a career filled with them.

If you want to hear Dick Miller laugh, ask him, "Have you ever played a bartender?" The answer is yes, yes, he has. He played one again for Larry Blamire, who was at once a lover and a maker of old B movies: one of those guys who blur the line between fan and creator. There was no mistaking the affection laced into what he did: his no-budget film *The Lost Skeleton of Cadavera* is, intentionally it seems, like a four-way collaboration among Richard Cunha, Tom Graeff, Del Tenney, and Phil Tucker. Naturally such a filmmaker would want to populate his new picture, *Trail of the Screaming Forehead*, with icons like Miller, and, in making him a bartender, Blamire was also, probably unintentionally, honouring Miller's long history of playing bartenders. (He included Kevin McCarthy too, and had him once again begging people to believe him about the pods.) Miller initially refused Blamire's offer, citing his failing memory as a sufficient reason. A persistent Blamire offered to feed him his lines there on the set, and Lainie encouraged him to take the role. In the face of this twin assault, Miller relented and accepted the part. But when he got to the set he was in a curmudgeonly mood, and once he realized that the monster was an actual crawling forehead, Miller asked the director, "What is the purpose of this?" Blamire explained that it was a satire on horror movies, and Miller spat back, "This is not a satire. What am I doing here?" Blamire answered Miller's rhetorical *cri de coeur* literally. "Well," he said, "you play a bartender."

Joe Dante, meantime, hadn't done much more since *Looney Tunes: Back in Action* than Miller had, outside of some TV, and when an offer to do an episode in a multi-director portmanteau picture called *Trapped Ashes* came from producer Dennis Bartok, Dante took it on, mostly as a favour to Bartok. The other directors were an interesting bunch: Ken Russell, Monte Hellman, Sean S. Cunningham, and a special effects artist named John Gaeta. What linked this disparate crew? "They were all out of work!" Dante cried.

Bartok offered Dante a segment called "The Girl with the Golden Breasts," but he didn't want it, and that one went to Russell instead. Dante ended up shooting the wraparound segment, which involved a group of people on a studio tour led by Henry Gibson. Miller played the guy who opens the gate. "Talk about a needless cameo," Dante said. "I just did it to put him in the movie. There was no part for him. The rest of the movie was shot in Canada, and I couldn't take him to Canada." It was a completely silent part, but "he didn't want any lines," Dante said.

A year later Dante was shooting his first full feature in a half decade, *The Hole*, but it was the same thing again. Like *Trapped Ashes*, *The Hole* was shot mostly in Canada, which precluded Miller's involvement as long as he was doing one of his usual small roles. "You make a movie in Canada and use Canadian funds, there's a limit to how many Americans you can have on the picture," Dante said. Dante had directed two episodes of a series called *Masters of Horror*, but those, too, had been shot in Canada, so there was no Miller involvement there either. *The Hole* was set in summertime, so the wintertime shoot in Canada necessitated a week of exteriors in Pasadena. "And so it was, "Okay, what can Dick play?" Dante said. He could think of only one part: a pizza delivery man bit that was so small Dante had originally planned to play it himself. Dante called Miller up and offered him the wordless pizza man, saying, "It's a nothing part, but I'd love to have you in the movie." Miller, as always, was obliging. "Of course!" he said. "And he showed up!" Dante marvelled. "He just likes being on sets."

As all this was going on, Miller was entering that period of his life best exemplified by some of John Huston's dialogue from *Chinatown*: "'Course I'm respectable. I'm old. Politicians, ugly buildings and whores all get respectable if they last long enough." Miller was none of these things, but he was an actor, so in a way he was all of them. And he was respectable, so along came the honours. At the end of August 2007 Miller was celebrated alongside fellow actors Piper Laurie, John Saxon, and Alan Young at an event called Cinecon, held at the Egyptian Theatre in Hollywood.

The next year, in August 2008, Dick and Lainie attended a convention in Indianapolis called Horrorhound, where, in a hall filled with table after table of DVDs, posters, buttons, grisly action figures, Michael Myers masks, and other such paraphernalia, and swarming with chunky, longhaired guys in black t-shirts looking these items over, Joe Dante, with Belinda Balaski by his side, presented Miller with a small, misshapen green effigy: the first ever Horrorhound Lifetime Achievement Award. "That was fun," Miller said fondly.

Zach Galligan was there too. He hadn't seen Miller in twenty years, maybe since the *Gremlins 2* premiere, and was taken aback at how much he'd aged. He went for dinner with Dick and Lainie, and recalled, "His mind was still sharp, but he was not nearly as talkative as he had been in the past. His wife seemed to do most of the talking, for the two of them. She was sort of representing the two of them." On reflection, though, Galligan felt that "he hadn't changed that much. It was just like we shot those [*Gremlins*] movies ten minutes ago."

The following May the Millers went to Dallas for the Texas Frightmare Weekend. "A lot of strange people at these conventions," Lainie said, but they enjoyed themselves anyway. The Frightmare people had prepared a highlight reel of Miller's roles, and had done a good job of it. "It was nice," Miller said. "It's real flattering to see it, one [role] after another. It's a good feeling."

Lainie agreed. "It's really a good one, because it touched on quite a bit. I thought it was impressive." The tribute video is available to watch online, and indeed serves as a solid showcase of Millerainia.

Miller took part in tributes to others as well, particularly Roger Corman. In April 2010 he sat on a panel, The Legacy of Roger and Julie Corman, that was part of a three-day tribute to the couple held by the University of Southern California's cinema department. A dozen or more films were screened, including *A Bucket of Blood*, along with several more in which Miller had appeared. That same year Miller took part in a documentary on Corman's career, *Corman's World: Exploits of a Hollywood Rebel*, from a clearly very committed director named Alex Stapleton. Miller spoke respectfully of his old boss. "Almost all of Roger's pictures had a little edge to them," he told Stapleton. "They just bordered on something sacrosanct, that ... you shouldn't touch this. And he did it anyway. And it usually saved the picture." Stapleton's impressive primer was celebrated especially for the moments in which Jack Nicholson became overwhelmed by emotion, chuckling as he remembered throwing Miller up against a wall, and sobbing as he considered what he owed to Corman.

Asked who he would like to play him in a movie of his life, Miller said, "*I* wanna play me," and, beginning in 2011, that wish was granted. That year Elijah Drenner, a documentary filmmaker with a deep love of genre film and the people who made them, began thinking about Miller. Drenner had made a history of exploitation movies called *American Grindhouse*, and was regularly engaged in making short pieces for use as DVD bonus material, so he knew what to do. A German company that planned to release *War of the Satellites* meanwhile proposed to Drenner that he make a short profile of Miller, but it quickly became apparent both to Drenner and his employer that the story could not be contained in a short subject. Drenner and his cinematographer, Elle Schneider, went to the Millers and proposed a feature-length study of Dick's life and career. They secured not just approval and cooperation, but Lainie Miller as a co-producer, and all the contact information they would need to start shooting interviews. Virtually no one turned them down; everybody wanted to talk about Dick.

As work proceeded on the documentary, Miller's world became more insular. The Silver Spoon closed in 2012, and he had no inclination left to find a replacement hangout. Most of the movies he watched now, he watched on television. He no longer read books, because the words on the pages had become too small and indistinct. Friends kept in touch, such as Jonathan Haze, who called occasionally and proposed get-togethers. "And I never hear from him again," Miller chuckled. "Couple of months go by and there's another call from him."

But as certain things seemed to close in, or fade out, or vanish altogether, the Millers elsewhere expanded their world. They danced weekly at a local establishment. "He's a good dancer even now," Lainie said. "He can't lift me anymore, but that's my fault too. But we get compliments all the time, and not just from people our age. Young kids come up and compliment us." They also became great sea cruise aficionados, peregrinating through the Caribbean, through the Panama Canal, up and down the Mexican Riviera, through the Mediterranean, and through the South Pacific to Bora Bora and Samoa. As in the days of *Gremlins* and *The Terminator*, Miller's face was frequently recognized on these tours. "When we're in a foreign country," Lainie said, "I can go into a little store to get a water or something, and I come out and they're running after him for his autograph. It's happened over and over again."

Late in October 2012 the Millers were aboard a cruise ship returning to port in Florida just as Hurricane Sandy was finally dissipating. Even as the storm was making its way north to wreak havoc in New York, the waves rose up to meet them, ten decks up, and the ship rolled and twisted in a boiling sea. "Scary!" Lainie said. But there was a greater purpose to this trip than the usual cruise adventures. Jack Silverman, Miller's old pal from the Bronx, had found him through the modern miracle of the Internet, had got in touch, and together they had organized a reunion in Florida, where Scatman Jack was living. "He and his wife drove down to where we were and checked into the same hotel," Lainie said. "We had a reunion for a couple of days. And they actually scatted together!"

"Got it all on video," Miller said. "Just two old men …" He paused, then continued. "We had a long reminiscence of things that happened sixty-two years ago. Who's alive and who's dead. Turns out, we're the only ones alive."

Miller was considering his mortality more and more. Mel Welles had passed away in 2005; Chuck Griffith, in 2007; Forrest Ackerman, in 2008; Henry Gibson, in 2009; Kevin McCarthy, in 2010; Biff Elliott, in 2012. And it went on: William Schallert died in 2016. Miller's own brother Eugene passed on in November 2017. Miller looked at other men's obituaries, whether he'd known them or not, and saw in them dreadful portents of his own demise. "That kind of scares me," he said. "I read them, and they're 'So-and-so, he was eighty-one, so-and-so, he was eighty-two, so and so, he was eighty-one …'" He paused a moment, then shrugged. "They go."

But Miller had not gone; how could he, when Joe Dante was still making movies? Dante's next project, *Burying the Ex*, was a feature script by Alan Trezza based on a short film Trezza had made several years earlier. It was a zombie story about a horror fan with an unpleasant, possessive girlfriend who dies in an accident, then returns from the grave to wreak further havoc on the poor chump's life and especially on his new relationship. It was perhaps the crudest script Dante had worked with since *Hollywood Boulevard*, and was filled with a forced edginess that manifested in Miller's small role too. He played "Crusty Cop," and was introduced while hitching up his pants and grumping that he'd been interrupted while on the john. Once the star of the picture, the late Anton Yelchin, has imparted his tale of zombie woe, the uniform cop asks, "Are you pullin' my pickle, sonny boy?" At least Miller got to be a little bit Jewish and use the word "schmuck" before ending his scene with a growl of "Goddamn meth heads!" It was in most respects a good, classic Miller appearance, and a marked improvement on his mute pizza man from *The Hole*. "My cameo was meant to be a gag," Miller said, "but it was nice to be working with Joe again, and I like the movie very much."

Shortly after that Miller got an offer that was, to understate the case, unexpected. Agnieszka Kurant, a Polish-born artist based in New York, had a project called *Cutaways*, in which she proposed to gather together characters who'd been cut entirely from famous movies, just to sort of see what they were up to. From an initial 200 candidates, she narrowed it down to Charlotte Rampling, who'd played a hitchhiker in *Vanishing Point*; Abe Vigoda, who'd been axed from *The Conversation*; and good old Monster Joe from *Pulp Fiction*. This was a part Miller never expected to play again, but he and Lainie flew to New York and met up with Vigoda, Rampling, and Kurant in a junkyard, where they mused on the dispiriting powerlessness inherent to fictional characters. (That same powerlessness was inherent to actors, which, of course, was the point.) "I wanted the scenario to be mundane," Kurant said, "just a snippet of everyday life from this alternative universe of these cut characters." *Cutaways* premiered in November 2013 at the Sculpture Center in New York.

In 2014 Miller made a tiny appearance in another fan/filmmaker crossover project, *The Adventures of Biffle and Shooster.* Biffle and Shooster were a faux comedy duo in the Abbott and Costello tradition, and several short subjects featuring the pair were made by film historian and restoration expert—and Larry Blamire associate—Michael Schlesinger. Miller, playing a mad scientist, wore a white smock and a curly wig, and doled out Stooges slaps to the comedy team. When a gorilla shows up suddenly, Miller is thunderstruck, and deploys the Skull. (The gorilla was actually Miller's old acquaintance Chris Walas, wearing a suit he had built himself and gyrating in a frenzy that matched the world-class simian antics of Charles Gemora or George Barrows.)

March 7, 2014, saw the world premiere screening of Drenner's film *That Guy Dick Miller* at the South by Southwest festival in Austin, Texas. With Lainie's help Drenner had put together a fantastic cast of interviewees, and the finished film was brisk and entertaining, and, while it concentrated mostly on Miller's career, it gave some tidbits about his life and history and made plenty of room for affectionate badinage between Dick and Lainie. The movie ended with a good joke: Miller insists he's hung it up, he's done, he's finished, he has most definitely at long last retired from the business. Then the phone rings, and Miller picks it up. "Hello? ... Sure, I'm available!"

This was a joke, but it also was not. Miller was growing ever more afraid to work. Lainie thought the activity was good for him, that the memorizing of lines would keep his mind sharp. "If *she* answers the phone," Miller said, "it's always 'Send the script.' If *I* answer the phone, it's 'I'm retired.' I guess there are ways of getting around whatever I'm worried about, like blowing lines. I don't remember names too well. So I could always wear an earwig." But he didn't want to rely on such devices, so most of the calls that came in—and they did come in—he turned down.

That same year there was more travel and further accolades. Joe Dante was the subject of a career-long retrospective at the Sitges Film Festival, which for nearly fifty years had showcased new horror and fantasy films on the Spanish coast just south of Barcelona. Dante was bringing *Burying the Ex,* and the festival was showing just about every other film he had ever made, but others were being fêted too. *That Guy Dick Miller* got a screening, and Miller was presented with the Time Machine Award, which was shaped like the prop from the George Pal picture of the same name, and was meant to celebrate a long, varied, and much-lauded career such as Miller had had. He stood at a podium with a little Gizmo puppet propped up on it, and said, "A lot of things have changed in thirty years, but acting is acting, and that's always going to be the same." The essential strangeness of the avocation remained: the goal was, at its core, to convincingly imitate a human.

In a panel discussion Dante was asked about his working relationship with Miller. "The actor-director relationship ... you have to have a rapport," he explained. "Some actors crave a lot of direction, other actors really don't need a lot of direction, and if you've worked with somebody numerous times, you develop a kind of shorthand, where you hardly have to speak to each other to know exactly what it is the other wants. And that's the way it is with Dick and me. He shows up, he does his job, he goes home."

That Guy Dick Miller had its Los Angeles premiere on Friday, December 5, at the Egyptian Theatre. But the Egyptian had given over the whole weekend to Miller: they were screening both *Gremlins* movies, *Demon Knight*, *A Bucket of Blood*, and *War of the Satellites*; and there were panel discussions every night. On Friday there was a reception in the lobby, and mixing around the Millers were Julie and Roger Corman, Allan Arkush, Jonathan Kaplan, John Landis, Leonard Maltin, and many other familiar faces. Only Joe Dante, directing TV in Hawaii, was missing. On Friday Drenner and the Millers answered questions from the audience; on Saturday there was a panel made up of Miller, Ernest Dickerson, and Rick Baker; and on Sunday it was Miller and Corman, with Michael Schlesinger moderating. It was all very chummy, and Miller appreciated the attention.

There was more of it in late March, when *That Guy Dick Miller* had its premiere in Lainie's hometown of Toronto; and then the next month when it screened in New York, and the Anthology Film Archives, a Bowery institution, hosted a series of screenings similar to the Egyptian's program the December before. Dick and Lainie were in Toronto, and then in New York with Drenner, and former *Fangoria* editor Michael Gingold did the moderator duties. The program included a brief double bill of *A Bucket of Blood* with the twenty-minute *Cutaways*.

To Miller, all of this played out like a slow-motion episode of *This Is Your Life*. He was in the winter of his years, it was true, and his career had not been all he had once hoped, but now it seemed that he was some kind of a star after all. He had a wife, a daughter, and a granddaughter he loved dearly, and a long life of strange experiences to look back on and marvel at. Was that really me, sailing off an aircraft carrier? Had I actually danced up

Broadway with Sammy Davis Jr. and tossed Charlton Heston out on his ear? Did I shoot down carjackers on back roads, flirt with nuns, chase robbers down Hollywood streets, cuddle lions, and race cars? And when he closed his eyes, he could still see that CinemaScope field of bright orange flowers and his daughter running joyfully through them. There were his performances, captured forever on film, and at home there were his scripts, his stories, his drawings, all this evidence of lost wild talent. He'd led a capital-L Life, and he had Lived, and he felt well armed against anything that might yet happen in whatever years he had left. In his own way he was even prepared for death. He'd ruminated on this, obscurely, to an interviewer in Sitges. "There's nothing in life I haven't done," he told his Spanish interlocutor. "I've been in the service, I've delivered a baby. I've done everything. Whatever comes, I can handle."

You become a true Miller fan when you stop wondering why Joe Dante puts him in every movie and start wondering why every other director doesn't too. It's what Orson Welles would call "dime-book Freud," but surely part of the pleasure in a good character actor appearance, particularly an unexpected one, is the pleasure and reflexive relief we get from seeing a familiar face. Facial recognition is a survival tool: you have to know who your parents are, where you're safe, so you remember faces. On a primal level, when Dick Miller appears on the screen, the character he's playing is secondary to the fact that he's Dick Miller, and he's familiar. Miller's talent is such that, at the very same time, you accept the character just as Miller is portraying him, as a real person.

And then there's his unparalleled air of accessibility. Miller played a few middle-class professionals over his career, but he never played a rich man; if he did, it would have to be in the manner of Rodney Dangerfield's Thornton Mellon from *Back to School*, a nouveau riche slob who stumbled into his wealth almost by accident, but never left his rough-and-tumble past or his blue-collar values behind. One could take this fact, use statistics to graph the mean class level of his characters, and come out of it with a pretty persuasive Marxist reading of his oeuvre. Miller himself was too lazy to be really Bolshy, but the aggregate political appeal of all these regular working schmoes accounts for a greater percentage of his popularity than might initially be thought. Further appeal comes from his ability to appear put-upon, and so to garner sympathy and familiarity; from his evident intelligence;

from his ability to deliver a wisecrack. All this seemed to spiral around one elusive quality held by Miller in concert with everything else. Beneath an interview with the actor, published in 2012 on the *Onion AV Club* website, one of the comments, by someone named "Chartex," made an attempt to pin it down, saying,

> I know this is a lot to lay on Miller, but I actually associate him with my own burgeoning awareness as a child that movies were an illusion. Here was Miller turning up again and again, and I eventually figured out that actors like him must be in short supply—guys who could just convincingly seem "regular." And if they had to keep hiring someone like Miller just to add a dab of anti-glamour, then that meant that the rest of the people who were getting bigger roles must be somehow fake. And that got me thinking about how everyone you see in a movie has in common that they all decided to become actors, and for the most part that attracts a certain sort of person; but once in a while you get a mensch like Miller.

This was a perceptive analysis, but the real answer was expressed in December 2014, at the Egyptian Theatre during the panel discussion with Miller and Corman, and it was simple. Miller was asked why he'd appeared in so many movies for the same people. "Joe Dante puts me in all of his movies, and I like him," Miller said. Then he jerked a thumb at Corman, whom he'd known for sixty years, longer than he'd known Lainie. "*He* put me in a whole bunch of movies, and I like *him*," Miller said. Then he shrugged helplessly. "But I really don't know why they put me in so many of their movies."

Corman leaned forward, and spoke at once intimately to Miller and expansively to the audience, with the confidence of a man knowing he's about to deliver an applause line. "Because," he said, "you're *good*."

Afterword

Dick Miller is almost ninety years old, and for sixty of those years he acted in films. Now he's travelling, and watching movies, and still in love with Lainie, who's still in love with him.

Man, he is *in*.

Sources

AUTHOR INTERVIEWS:
Max Apple (email)
Allan Arkush (Skype)
Belinda Balaski (telephone)
Ira Steven Behr (telephone)
Roger Corman (in person)
Joe Dante (in person)
Frank De Palma (email)
Ernest Dickerson (telephone)
Mike Finnell (telephone)
Zach Galligan (Skype)
Michael Gingold (in person)
Jonathan Kaplan (email)
Bill Levy (telephone)
"Uncle Bob" Martin (email)
Dick Miller (in person and by telephone)
Eugene Miller (telephone)
Elaine "Lainie" Miller (in person and by telephone)
Jack Nicholson (telephone)
Harry Northup (handwritten letter)
Tony Randel (email)
Scatman Jack Silverman (telephone)
Scott Wheeler (email)

BOOKS

Alba, Ben. *Inventing Late Night: Steve Allen and the Original Tonight Show.* Amherst, NY: Prometheus, 2005.

Arkoff, Sam, with Richard Trubo. *Flying Through Hollywood by the Seat of My Pants.* New York: Birch Lane Press, 1992.

Biskind, Peter. *Easy Riders, Raging Bulls: How the Sex-Drugs-and-Rock 'n' Roll Generation Saved Hollywood.* New York: Simon & Schuster, 1998.

Burns, Bob, with John Michlig. *It Came from Bob's Basement.* San Francisco: Chronicle, 2000.

Corman, Roger, with Jim Jerome. *How I Made a Hundred Movies in Hollywood and Never Lost a Dime.* Muller UK: DreamHaven Books, 1990.

DiFranco, J. Philip, ed. *The Movie World of Roger Corman.* New York/London: Chelsea House, 1979.

Eliot, Mark. *Nicholson: A Biography.* New York: Crown Archetype, 2013.

Friedrich, Otto. *City of Nets: A Portrait of Hollywood in the 1940s.* New York: Harper & Row, 1986.

Gilmore, John. *Laid Bare.* Los Angeles: Amok, 1997.

Glut, Donald F. *The Frankenstein Archive: Essays on the Monster, the Myth, the Movies and More.* Jefferson, NC: McFarland, 2002.

Goodwin, Michael, and Naomi Wise. *On the Edge: The Life and Times of Francis Coppola.* New York: William Morrow and Company, 1989.

Gray, Beverly. *Roger Corman: An Unauthorized Biography of the Godfather of Indie Filmmaking.* Los Angeles: Renaissance, 2000.

Herman, Max. *First Trumpet: The Road to Broadway and Hollywood.* New York: Vantage, 2006.

Hickey, Dave. *Perfect Wave: More Essays on Art and Democracy.* Chicago and London, University of Chicago Press, 2017.

Hill, Geoffrey. *Illuminating Shadows: The Mythic Power of Film.* Boston/London: Shambhala, 1992.

Horne, Gerald. *Class Struggle in Hollywood, 1930–1950: Moguls, Mobsters, Stars, Reds & Trade Unionists*. Austin: University of Texas Press, 2001.

Humphreys, Justin. *Names You Never Remember, with Faces You Never Forget: Interviews with the Movies' Character Actors*. Boalsburg, PA: BearManor Media, 2006.

Katz, Ephraim. *The Macmillan International Film Encyclopedia*. London: Macmillan, 1994.

Kopp, Sheldon B. *If You Meet the Buddha on the Road, Kill Him! The Pilgrimage of Psychotherapy Patients*. New York: Bantam, 1976.

Koetting, Christopher T. *Mind Warp: The Fantastic True Story of Roger Corman's New World Pictures*. London: Hemlock Books, 2009.

Kubernik, Harvey. *Hollywood Shack Job: Rock Music in Film and on Your Screen*. Albuquerque: University of New Mexico Press, 2006.

Lisanti, Thomas. *Hollywood Surf and Beach Movies: The First Wave, 1959–1969*. Jefferson, NC, and London: McFarland & Company, 2005.

McCarty, John, and Mark Thomas McGee. *The Little Shop of Horrors Book*. New York: St. Martin's Press, 1988.

McDonagh, Maitland. *Filmmaking on the Fringe*. New York: Citadel Press, 1995.

McGee, Mark Thomas. *Fast and Furious: The Story of American International Pictures*. Jefferson, NC, and London: McFarland, 1984.

McGee, Mark Thomas. *Roger Corman: The Best of the Cheap Acts*. Jefferson, NC, and London: McFarland, 1988.

McGilligan, Patrick. *Jack's Life: A Biography of Jack Nicholson*. London: HarperCollins, 1994.

McGilligan, Patrick, ed. *Backstory 3: Interviews with Screenwriters of the 1960s*. Berkeley/Los Angeles/Oxford: University of California Press, 1997.

Molyneaux, Gerard. *John Sayles: An Unauthorized Biography of the Pioneering Indie Filmmaker*. Los Angeles: Renaissance, 2000.

Morris, Eric. *The Diary of a Professional Experiencer*. Los Angeles: Ermor Enterprises, 2007.

Morris, Gary. *Roger Corman*. Farmington Hills, MI: Gale, 1985.

Nashawaty, Chris. *Crab Monsters, Teenage Cavemen and Candy Stripe Nurses: Roger Croman: King of the B Movie*. New York: Harry Abrams, 2013.

Nasr, Constantine, ed. *Roger Corman Interviews*. Jackson: University Press of Mississippi, 2011.

Palmer, Randy. *Paul Blaisdell, Monster Maker*. Jefferson, NC: McFarland, 1997.

Russo, Gus. *Supermob: How Sidney Korshak and His Criminal Associates Became America's Hidden Power Brokers*. New York: Bloomsbury, 2006.

Shapiro, Marc. *James Cameron*. Los Angeles: Renaissance, 2000.

Silver, Alan, and James Ursini. *Roger Corman: Metaphysics on a Shoestring*. Beverly Hills: Silman-James Press, 2006.

Stevens, Mark. *Monte Hellman: His Life and Films*. Jefferson, NC, and London: McFarland & Company, 2003.

Terrace, Vincent. *The Complete Encyclopedia of Television Programs. 1947–1979*. South Brunswick/New York: A.S. Barnes & Co., 1979.

Timpone, Anthony. *Fangoria's Best Horror Films*. New York: Crescent Books, 1994.

Tyrcus, Michael J., ed. *Contemporary Theatre, Film and Television*, vol. 27. Farmington Hills, MI: Gale Group, 2000.

Warren, Bill. *Keep Watching the Skies!* Jefferson, NC, and London: McFarland & Company, 2010.

Warren, Bill. *Set Visits*. Jefferson, NC: McFarland & Company, 1997.

Weaver, Tom. *I Was a Monster Movie Maker: Conversations With 22 SF and Horror Filmmakers*. Jefferson, NC: McFarland & Company, 2001.

Weaver, Tom. *Science Fiction and Fantasy Film Flashbacks: Conversations with 24 Actors, Writers, Producers and Directors from the Golden Age*. Jefferson, NC: McFarland & Company, 1998.

Weaver, Tom. *Science Fiction Stars and Horror Heroes*. Jefferson, NC, and London: McFarland & Company, 1991.

Weschler, Lawrence. *Seeing Is Forgetting the Name of the Thing One Sees*. Expanded ed. Berkeley/Los Angeles/London: University of California Press, 2008.

Yanow, Bruce. *Jazz on Record: The First Sixty Years*. San Francisco: Backbeat Books, 2003.

ARTICLES

Anon. "Eugene Miller Is Making the Most of His Retirement." *At Your Service* 7, no. 2. (April 2008): n.p.

Anon. "Population of Borough of the Bronx Has Passed the Million Mark." *New York Times*, March 4, 1928.

Arkush, Allan. "I Remember Film School." *Film Comment* 19, no. 6 (November–December 1983): 57–59.

Axmaker, Sean. "Jack Hill, Exploitation Genius." *Psychotronic* 13 (Summer 1992): 32–43.

Bamber, George. "All About My Little Sister Judy Bamber." *Filmfax* 121 (Summer 2009): 51–56.

Beahm, Justin. "American Matinee Idol." *Fangoria* 311 (March 2012): 54–56, 79.

Beahm, Justin. "It's Miller Time!" *Fangoria* 311 (March 2012): 57–58.

Brown, Barry. "It's Ve Sota!" *Magick Theatre* 8 (June 1975): 33–43, 74.

Brunas, John, and Michael Brunas. "Seymour Krelboined Remembers." *Fangoria* 38 (October 1984): 14–17, 64.

Bunting, Glenn F., and Tina Griego. "Miami Trial Gives Startling New Portrait of Sam Gibert." *Los Angeles Times*, April 23, 1990.

Chute, David. "The New World of Roger Corman." *Film Comment* 18, no. 2 (March–April 1982): 26–32.

Chute, David. "Dante's Inferno." *Film Comment* 20, no. 3 (June 1984): 22–27.

Combs, Richard. "Three Times Dead." *Film Comment* 44, no. 5 (July/August 2009): 12–13.

Corupe, Paul. "The King of Cult." *Rue Morgue* 53 (January 2006): 16–24.

Davidson, Bill. "King of Schlock." *New York Times*, December 28, 1975, pp. 152–54.

DiSalvo, Anthony, Jim Fetters, and Paul Parla. "Black Cadillac, Driving Paul Birch and Tales from Davanna: An Interview with Jonathan Haze." *Scary Monsters* 75 (June 2010): 6–34.

Doyle, Michael. "Love You to Death." *Rue Morgue* 157 (July 2015): 24–25, 27–28.

Doyle, Michael. "That Guy!" *Rue Morgue* 157 (July 2015): 26.

Drake, C. V. "Robocop Producer Jon Davison." *Cinefantastique* 18, no. 1 (December 1987): 20.

DuFoe, Terry, and Tiffany DuFoe. "Miller Time: Dick Miller." *The Phantom of the Movies' Video Scope* 51 (Summer 2004): 36–41.

Dullea, Georgia. "Two Los Angeles Clubs for the 'New Elite.'" *Los Angeles Times*, July 4, 1986.

Everitt, David. "The Dick Miller Zone." *Fangoria* 29 (September 1983): 54, 62.

Everitt, David. "Explorers." *Fangoria* 47 (August 1985): 38–40.

Everitt, David. "Gremlins." *Fangoria* 37 (August 1984): 20–22.

Everitt, David. "It's Miller Time." *Fangoria* 37 (August 1984): 23–24.

Everitt, David. "Joe Dante." *Fangoria* 20 (July 1982): 18–21, 53.

Everitt, David. "Walter Paisley Lives!" *Fangoria* 19 (May 1982): 25–29.

Fischer, Dennis. "Roger Corman's Little Shop of Horrors." *Cinefantastique* 17, no. 1. (January 1987): 26–31, 60–61.

Gambin, Lee. "Skid Row Sweetheart." *Fangoria* 318 (November 2012): 34–35.

Gasaway, John. "Wooden's Century—Meet Sam Gilbert, Again." *Basketball Prospectus*, June 8, 2010.

Goldstein, Patrick. "Roger to Rookies: Make It Cheap." *American Film* 10, no. 4 (January–February 1985): 36–43.

Goldstein, Patrick. "You Know His Face, But Can You Give His Name?" *Los Angeles Times*, July 31, 1984, pp. F1, F4.

Gordon, Alex. "Terror on Poverty Row." *Fangoria* 78 (October 1988): 60–61.

Gray, Christopher. "Built with a Broken Heart." *New York Times*, December 30, 2009.

Hammer, Joshua. "The Fall of Frank Mancuso." *Newsweek* (May 6, 1991): 66.

Harris, Mark. "Checkout Time at the Asylum." *New York Magazine* (November 16, 2008): n.p.

Jerome, Robert L. "Hollywood Boulevard." *Cinefantastique* 5, no. 1 (Spring 1976): 25.

Kaplan, Jonathan. "Taxi Dancer." *Film Comment* 13, no. 4 (July/August 1977): 41–43.

Kay, Tony. "An Interview with Belinda Balaski." *Shock Cinema* 33 (2007): 30–34.

Legend, Johnny. "The World According to Wyott." *Fangoria* 38 (October 1984): 58–61, 64.

McCarthy, Todd. "Mona Must Die." *Variety*, March 20, 1994.

McGee, Mark Thomas. "Charles Griffith and the Little Shop of Corman!" *Fangoria* 11 (February 1981): 16–17, 62.

Miller, Dick. "Hall of Fame: Dick Miller." *Fangoria* 284 (June 2009): 41.

Martin, Bob. "Rob Bottin & The Howling." *Fangoria* 11 (February 1981): 20–24.

Naha, Ed. "White Dog." *Fangoria* 17 (February 1982): 13–16.

Palmer, Randy. "Hollywood's Forgotten Monster-Maker." *Cinefantastique* 20, no. 5 (May 1990): 16–31.

Petkovich, Anthony. "All Miller No Filler." *Filmfax* 121 (Summer 2009): 42–50, 116.

Petkovich, Anthony. "A Final Interview with Biff Elliot." *Filmfax* 132 (Winter 2012–2013): 40–45, 104.

Rabkin, William. "The Dick Miller Story Revisited." *The Bloody Best of Fangoria* 5 (1986): 8–10.

Spelling, Ian. "Sci-fi Veteran Dick Miller Is at Home on 'DS9.'" *The Reading Eagle*, January 7, 1995, p. B7.

Spielberg, Steven. "Directing 1941." *American Cinematographer* 6, no. 12 (December 1979): 1212–13, 1215, 1251, 1258–59, 1275–76.

Stein, Elliott. "An Acre of Seats in a Garden of Dreams." *Film Comment* 15, no. 2 (March–April 1979): 31–51.

Stephens, Bob. "Matinee Time with Joe Dante." *Filmfax* 91 (June/July 2002): 81–87.

Swires, Steve. "The Real Mary Woronov." *Fangoria* 51 (January 1986): 12–15, 68.

Thomas, Kevin. "Corman—Whiz Kid of the B's." *Los Angeles Times*, June 10, 1966.

Timpone, Anthony. "The Legend Continues." *Fangoria* 61 (February 1987): 19–21.

Warren, Bill. "Mr. Futterman Lives!" *Fangoria* 96 (September 1990): 20–23.

Warren, Bill. "Not of This Earth Take Two." *Fangoria* 75 (July 1988): 14–17, 66.

Weaver, Tom, and John Brunas. "I Survived Roger Corman." *Fangoria* 76 (August 1988): 14–19, 61.

Weaver, Tom, and John Brunas. "Wasps! Vikings! Sea Serpents!" *Fangoria* 52 (March 1986): 57–60, 65.

Weaver, Tom, and Carl Del Vecchio. "Queen of 50's Horror!" *Fangoria* 50 (January 1986): 56–61.

Williams, Sharon. "Dick Miller Talks about Explorers." *Fantastic Films* 46 (October 1985): 12–14.

Williams, Sharon. "An Interview with Dick Miller." *Filmfax* 9 (Feb/March 1988): 30–35, 94.

ONLINE ARTICLES

Abrams, Simon. "Like Going to Church: Joe Dante on *The Movie Orgy*." August 8, 2016. Retrieved from https://www.rogerebert.com/interviews/like-going-to-church-joe-dante-on-the-movie-orgy.

Alexander, Chris. "Joe Dante Reflects on 80s *Twilight Zone* Episode 'The Shadow Man.'" November 5, 2015. Retrieved from http://www.comingsoon.net/horror/news/747652-interview-joe-dante-reflects-80s-twilight-zone-episode-shadow-man.

Anon. "Astrology and *A Streetcar Named Desire*." Retrieved from resource.rockyview.ab.ca/rvlc/ssela301/.../streetcar_horoscopes.pdf.

Anon. "Gebhard Leberecht Von Blücher." *Encyclopedia Britannica*. Retrieved from https://www.britannica.com/biography/Gebhard-Leberecht-von-Blucher-Furst-von-Wahlstatt.

Anon. "The Zoot Suit Riots of 1943." Retrieved from http://www.pbs.org/wgbh/amex/zoot/eng_peopleevents/e_riots.html.

Bartlett, David. "A Memory from the *Pulp Fiction* Cast and Crew Screening." October 3, 2014. Retrieved from https://writevault.com/blog/guest-writers-artists/a-memory-from-the-pulp-fiction-cast-and-crew-screening-by-david-bartlett/.

Bowie, Stephen. "An Interview With Cliff Osmond (Part 1)." January 3, 2013. Retrieved from https://classictvhistory.wordpress.com/2013/01/03/an-interview-with-cliff-osmond-part-one/.

Erickson, Glenn. "Joe Dante Interviewed on the DVD Release of *Matinee*." May 11, 2010. Retrieved from https://www.dvdtalk.com/dvdsavant/s3208dant.html.

Evanier, Mark. "Schwab's." March 12, 2012. Retrieved from http://www.oldlarestaurants.com/schwabs-pharmacy/.

Federman, Wayne. "What Reagan Did for Hollywood." November 14, 2011. Retrieved from http://www.theatlantic.com/entertainment/archive/2011/11/what-reagan-did-for-hollywood/248391/.

Genaro, Teresa. "Good-bye, Jamaica …" October 7, 2011. Retrieved from http://www.brooklynbackstretch.com/2011/10/07/good-bye-jamaica/.

Gilleran Jr., ed. "The Decline of Fordham Football." May 1994. Retrieved from www.la84foundation.org/SportsLibrary/CFHSN/CFHSNv07/CFHSNv07n3b.pdf.

Graham, Aaron. "Little Shop of Genres: An Interview With Charles W. Griffith." April 2005. Retrieved from http://sensesofcinema.com/2005/conversations-with-filmmakers/charles_b_griffith/.

Hatfull, Jonathan. "Dick Miller Talks Joe Dante, Roger Corman and Gremlins." March 13, 2013. Retrieved from http://www.scifinow.co.uk/news/that-guy-dick-miller-talks-joe-dante-roger-corman-and-gremlins/.

Meister, Dick. "An Exceptional, Forgotten Leader." Retrieved from http://www.dickmeister.com/id85.html.

Moldea, Dan E. "The Corruption of Ronald Reagan." July 15, 1999. Retrieved from http://www.moldea.com/ReaganRedux.html.

Oliver, Myrna. "Robert W. Campbell, Author, Screenwriter." October 1, 2000. Retrieved from http://articles.latimes.com/2000/oct/01/local/me-29799.

Perry, Wilk. "Memoirs from Wilk Perry S'49." December 13, 2011. Retrieved from http://hhsalum.org/profiles/blogs/memoirs-from-wilk-perry-s-49.

Pinkerton, Nick. "Interview: George Armitage." April 28, 2015. Retrieved from http://www.filmcomment.com/blog/interview-george-armitage/.

Richter, Erin. "Dick Miller: Who's That Guy?" July 28, 1998. Retrieved from http://ew.com/article/1998/07/24/dick-miller-whos-guy/.

Roe, Ken. "Paradise Theatre." Retrieved from http://cinematreasures.org/theaters/900.

Sherwood, Michael. "Songwriter in Profile." August 1999. Retrieved from http://www.musesmuse.com/2.5-August99.html#profile.

Sutton, Kate. "Vigoda, Rampling Revisit Discarded Sarafian, Coppola Characters in New Film." *The Hollywood Reporter*. March 19, 2014. Retrieved from https://www.hollywoodreporter.com/news/vigoda-rampling-revisit-discarded-sarafian-689376.

Ward, Estolev Ethan. "Working Class Leader in the ILWU, 1935–1977." Retrieved from http://archive.org/stream/workingclassleader01goldrich/workingclassleader01goldrich_djvu.txt.

Wayne, Gary. "Silver Spoon." *Seeing Stars in Hollywood*. Retrieved from http://www.seeing-stars.com/Dine2/SilverSpoon.shtml.

Weaver, Tom. "The Life and Tragic Death of Susan Cabot." *The Astounding B Monster*. July 11, 2007. Retrieved from http://www.bmonster.com/cult10.html.

William-Ross, Lindsay. "Schwab's Pharmacy." March 21, 2009. Retrieved from http://laist.com/2009/03/21/laistory_schwabs.php.

DOCUMENTARIES AND DVD/BLU-RAY SPECIAL FEATURES

Anatomy of a Nurse Film, short documentary, "The Nurses Collection." Director: Elijah Drenner. Shout! Factory, 2012.

Corman's World: Exploits of a Hollywood Rebel, feature length documentary. Director: Alex Stapleton. KOTB LLC, 2011.

Gremlins commentaries featuring Joe Dante, Mike Finnell, Chris Walas, Zach Galligan, Phoebe Cates, Dick Miller, and Howie Mandel. Warner Bros., 2007.

Gremlins 2 commentary featuring Joe Dante and Mike Finnell. Warner Bros., 2010.

Hollywood Boulevard commentary featuring Allan Arkush, Joe Dante, and Jon Davison. New Concorde, 2001.

The Howling commentary featuring Joe Dante, Dee Wallace, Christopher Stone, Robert Picardo. MGM, 2003.

Unleashing the Beast: Making The Howling, documentary feature. MGM, 2003.

It Conquered Hollywood: The Story of American International Pictures, documentary, 2000. Written-Produced-Directed by John Watkin and Eamon Harrington.

Night of the Creeps commentary featuring Fred Dekker, moderated by Michael Felsher. Sony Pictures, 2009.

Not of This Earth commentary featuring Tom Weaver, John Brunas, Mike Brunas. Shout! Factory, 2004.

Piranha commentary featuring Joe Dante and Jon Davison. Shout! Factory, 2010.

The Making of Piranha, documentary feature. Shout! Factory, 2010.

Pulp Fiction deleted scene with introduction by Quentin Tarantino. Miramax Home Video, 2002.

Roger Corman: Hollywood's Wild Angel, feature length documentary. Director: Christian Blackwood. Blackwood Films, 1978.

Schlock! The Secret History of American Movies, feature length documentary. Director: Ray Greene. Pathfinder Pictures, 2001.

Story of a City: New York, short documentary. Simmel-Meservey Productions, 1947.

Tales from the Crypt: Demon Knight commentaries featuring Ernest Dickerson, moderated by Michael Felsher, and Todd Masters, Thomas Bellissimo, John Van Vliet, and Walter Phelan. Scream Factory, 2015.

That Guy Dick Miller, feature length documentary. Director: Elijah Drenner. Autumn Rose Productions, 2014.

Truck Turner commentary featuring Jonathan Kaplan, moderated by Elijah Drenner. Kino, 2015.

Under Siege: The Making of Demon Knight, short documentary. Producers: Heather Buckley, Michael Felsher. Red Shirt Productions/Scream Factory, 2015.

Index

Ackerman, Forrest J., 87, 88, 113, 233, 262, 283, 320, 346
Addiss, Jus, 135
Adventures of Biffle and Shooster, The, 348
Affairs of Dobie Gillis, The, 41
After Hours, 12, 287-88, 297, 317
AfterMASH, 286
Aguilar, Tiny, 57
Airplane!, 264, 267, 272
Aldrich, Robert, 193, 219
Alice, 256, 257
Alice Doesn't Live Here Anymore, 256
Allen, Debbie, 323
Allen, Steve, 79, 80
Allen, Woody, 13, 37, 39, 133
Allied Artists, 136, 234
Alligator, 256
Allman, Sheldon, 203
Altman, Robert, 144
Amazing Stories (magazine), 88
Amazon Women on the Moon, 300-01, 308
American Grindhouse, 345
American International Pictures (AIP), 100, 113, 121, 128, 140, 141, 144, 146, 156, 161, 164, 168, 176, 177, 180, 181, 185, 194, 195, 199, 206, 252, 284, 324
Amityville 1992: It's About Time, 321-22
Anderson, Harry, 288
Anderson, Jamie, 232
Anderson, Pat, 226
Andersonville Trial, The, 203-04, 208
Angel III: The Final Chapter, 309
Angels Die Hard, 206
Angels With Dirty Faces, 31
Apache Woman, 28, 100, 101-05, 108, 110, 116
Apple, Max, 260-61
Archerd, Army, 258
Ardoin, Erlina, 227
Arena, The, 218
Argo, Victor, 287
Arkoff, Lou, 324

Arkoff, Sam, 100, 101, 107, 120, 121, 128, 140, 168, 176, 184, 241, 252, 324, 325
Arkush, Allan, 205, 217, 227, 228-29, 232-34, 236, 237, 241, 246, 252-54, 261, 262, 263-64, 267, 272-73, 278, 286, 290, 293-94, 306, 324-25, 335, 339-40, 349
Armed Response, 303-04
Armitage, George, 207, 227, 230, 231
Arnold, Jack, 320
Arquette, Rosanna, 287-88
Asher, William, 176
Asther, Nils, 101
Atlas, 26, 119, 161
Attack of the Crab Monsters, 117, 124, 136, 148, 234, 241
Attack of the 50 Foot Woman, 119, 142
Attack of the 5'2" Women, 325
Attack of the Giant Leeches, 143
Axton, Hoyt, 268
Ayers, Mitchell, 39

Bakalyan, Richard, 192, 193, 197, 200, 201-02
Baker, Josephine, 69
Baker, Rick, 311, 314, 334, 349
Balaski, Belinda, 236, 262, 263, 279, 344
Barney Miller, 70
Barrymore, Drew, 310, 317
Bartel, Paul, 232, 233, 236-37, 261, 273, 301
Barton, Earl, 68
Basehart, Richard, 203
Batman: Mask of the Phantasm, 322-23
Batson, Curly, 102, 103, 118, 133
Battle Beyond the Stars, 252, 274
Battlestar Galactica, 42
Baylor, Hal, 195-96
Beach Ball, 181-82
Beach Boys, The, 180
Beach Party, 176
Bean, Orson, 251
Be a Nose!, 150

Beast from Haunted Cave, The, 119
Beat Generation, The, 144
Beatles, The, 180, 244
Beatniks, The, 144
Beaumont, Charles, 129
Because You're Mine, 41
Behr, Ira Steven, 32, 38, 202, 289-95, 299-300, 332-33, 340
Bender, Russ, 112
Bender, Lawrence, 327
Bert Parks Show, The, 74, 78, 81, 83, 88, 151, 197
Berry, June, 272, 286
Beswicke, Martine, 258-59
Big, 307
Big Bad Mama, 218-20, 225, 246, 286
Big Bad Mama II, 306
Big Bus, The, 182
Bioff, Willie, 92
Birch, Paul, 103, 116
Bird-in-Hand, 68, 69, 76, 83
Bissell, Whit, 203
Blackboard Jungle, The, 67
Black Christmas, 233
Black Sunday, 156
Blade Runner, 78
Blaisdell, Paul, 113-115, 118
Blamire, Larry, 343, 348
Blazing Saddles, 106
Bleyer, Archie, 43
Blob, The, 143
Block, Irving, 137
Blockbusters, The, 123, 129
Bloody Brood, The, 144
Bloom, Verna, 287
Blucher, Gerhard von, 17
Blue Angel, The, 129
Body Waves, 319-20
Bogart, Humphrey, 31
Bogdanovich, Peter, 186, 199, 323
Bohrer, Jack, 190
Bombyk, David, 295
Bonanza, 151, 168, 172
Bonnie and Clyde, 193
Bowery Boys, The, 47
Boxcar Bertha, 207, 234

Index

Boyle, Robert, 298
Brace, Norman, 70
Bradley, Leslie, 121
Brady, Scott, 277
Branded, 184, 341
Break the Bank, 75
Bridges, Beau, 184
Bridges, Harry, 92
Bridges, Lloyd, 103
Bright, Matthew, 242-43
Bronx Zoo, The, 295
Bronson, Charles, 127, 140, 141
Brooks, Avery, 333
Brossot, Denise, 95
Brown, Julie, 325
Browne, George, 92
Browne, Howard, 88, 192, 225
Bruce, Lenny, 133, 146
Bucket of Blood, A, 11, 13, 17-18, 30, 110, 123, 144-46, 148-51, 152, 153, 154, 156, 259, 269, 289, 292, 315, 317, 333, 335, 345, 349
Bull Durham, 307
'burbs, The, 12, 307-08, 323
Burgess, Meredith, 71
Burghoff, Gary, 286
Burton, Jhean, 148
Burton, Julian, 148
Burton, Tim, 287
Burying the Ex, 347, 348

Cabot, Susan, 132-33, 137, 140, 143, 216
Caen, Herb, 143
Cagney, James, 31, 125-126, 230
California Congress of Industrial Organizations (CIO), 91
Campbell, R. Wright, 87, 97, 100, 119, 129, 140
Campbell, William, 140
Cameron, James, 11, 16, 281-82
Candy Stripe Nurses, 214, 220, 226, 286
Cannonball, 236-38, 303
Cannonball Run, The, 236
Capone, 88, 225, 226, 286
Capture That Capsule, 165
Carbone, Antony, 148, 149
Carey, Harry, 277
Carey, Timothy, 188, 209
Carpenter, John, 204, 270, 333
Carnival Rock, 129-132, 209
Carradine, David, 236, 237, 303, 316, 317

Carradine, John, 87, 207, 262, 263
Carradine, Robert, 127, 236
Carré, Bart, 103
Caruso, Dee, 200-01
Carver, Steve, 218-19, 225-26, 246
Casablanca, 43
Castle, William, 320
Castranova, T.J., 288
Cates, Phoebe, 277, 279, 311, 313
Cerney, Gladys, 19, 68
Chakiris, George, 186
Chameides, Dave, 338
Chandler, Jeff, 127
Chaney, Lon, 125
Chapman, Michael, 273
Cheech & Chong, 287
Chopping Mall, 12, 301-303
Church, Thomas Haden, 330
Cinefantastique (magazine), 155
Clark, Dane, 126
Clarke, Kenny, 76
Clarke, Lydia, 81
Clooney, Rosemary, 39
Clueless, 339
Cochran, Steve, 70
Cock 'n' Bull, 96, 100, 107, 154
Cogswell, Dutch, 51-55, 83
Colodny, Lester, 193, 197, 200, 201
Columbia Pictures, 29, 180, 184, 187-190, 192, 193, 228, 251
Combat!, 67
Combat Squad, 96
Connors, Chuck, 184
Connors, Mike "Touch," 107, 134
Conversation, The, 347
Convy, Bert, 148
Cool and the Crazy, The, 144
Coppola, Eleanor, 171
Coppola, Francis, 170-72, 236
Corey, Jeff, 129, 133, 134-35
Corman, Gene, 99, 110, 128, 180, 181, 214, 226-27, 230
Corman, Julie, 207, 208, 212, 230, 255, 301, 325, 345, 349
Corman, Roger, 11, 13, 25-26, 65, 70, 88, 96, 98, 99, 100-110, 112-19, 120-24, 126, 127, 129-33, 134, 135, 136, 138, 140-42, 143-46, 148-58, 160-62, 166-68, 170-74, 175, 176, 177, 180, 184-85, 187-191, 192-95, 199-200, 205-08, 211-12, 216, 217, 218-19, 220-22, 228-29,

230-31, 232, 234, 235, 236, 237, 238, 241, 242, 246-47, 252, 260, 274-75, 281, 301, 303, 320, 325, 334, 342, 345, 349, 351
Corman's World: Exploits of a Hollywood Rebel, 345
Corvette Summer, 243-44
Cravate, La, 95
Crawford, Cindy, 324
Crazy Mama, 229-30, 257
Creature From the Black Lagoon, The, 107
Creature from the Haunted Sea, 119
Crosby, Bing, 74, 311
Crosby, Floyd, 103, 137, 190
Crosby, John, 75, 79
Crossing Jordan, 340
Cruise, Tom, 13, 273, 323
Cry Baby Killer, The, 134-35, 136, 143, 167
Cuarón, Alfonso, 323
Cujo, 256
Cutaways, 347-48, 349
Cyphers, Charles, 204

Dalton, Abby, 124, 129, 135
Dalzell, Arch, 195
Danning, Sybil, 306
Dano, Royal, 219
Dante, Joe, 11, 12, 117, 134, 166, 184, 193, 216-18, 219, 226, 228-29, 231-34, 236, 237,241, 245, 246-49, 251, 255, 256, 257, 261-64, 266, 267-68, 270-73, 276-81, 283, 294, 295-98, 300-01, 304, 305-06, 307-09, 310, 311-14, 318-19, 320-21, 324, 326, 329, 330, 332, 334-36, 337, 339, 341-42, 343-44, 347, 349, 350, 351
Danza, Tony, 315
Darktown Strutters, 226-27
Davis, Martin, 297
Davis Jr., Sammy, 68, 77, 81, 84, 96, 126, 350
Davison, Jon, 205, 207, 208, 211, 216-18, 219, 222, 228-29, 230, 233, 234, 236, 246-47, 264-65, 266, 267
Dazed and Confused, 176
Day For Night, 233
Day the Earth Stood Still, The, 112
Day the World Ended, The, 160
Dead End, 31
Dead End Kids, The, 31
Dead Heat, 306, 308

Dean, James, 105, 106, 123
Death Race 2000, 232, 234
Debs, Eugene, 17, 18
Deezen, Eddie, 244-45, 315
De Kova, Frank, 101, 111
Dekker, Fred, 304-05, 329
Demon Knight, 328-330, 349
De Niro, Robert, 11, 235, 238-39, 324
Denning, Richard, 107, 121
De Palma, Brian, 163
De Palma, Frank, 288-89, 323
Dern, Bruce, 12, 186, 192, 193, 195
Devon, Richard, 118, 137, 149
Diary of a High School Bride, 144
Dick Miller Show, The, 84, 85
Dickerson, Beach, 137, 206, 241, 261
Dickerson, Ernest, 329-332, 349
Diller, Barry, 297
Directors Guild of America (DGA), 268
Dirty Dozen, The, 193
Divorce Court, 299
Dr. Heckyl and Mr. Hype, 12, 259-60, 264
Doel, Frances, 190, 194, 216, 218, 220, 247, 260
Dog Day Afternoon, 322
Douglas, Kirk, 127
Dragnet, 127, 134, 141
Dragnet 1967, 195-96
Dragstrip Girl, 128
Drenner, Elijah, 191, 204, 214, 320, 345, 348, 349
Dreyfuss, Richard, 13, 127, 128
Driscoll, Bobby, 33
Dunne, Griffin, 287-88
Dusenberry, Ann, 299

Fast Side Kids, The, 29, 31
Eat My Dust!, 260, 261, 306
Ebsen, Buddy, 203
Edwards, Anthony, 268
Eerie, Indiana, 318-19
Eisner, Michael, 297
11th Victim, The, 256-57
El Topo, 95
Elfman, Jenna, 341
Elliott, Biff, 87, 142, 220, 346
Enemy Below, The, 142
Enemy Mine, 295
ER, 338-39
Everitt, David, 114, 138, 200, 201, 271, 274, 284, 285, 330

Evil Toons, 316-17, 320
Executive Action, 215, 216, 235, 304
Explorers, 295-98, 305, 308, 315, 330

Fallen Angels, 323, 324
Fame, 12, 38, 201, 290-91, 293-95, 299-301, 305-07, 318, 323, 340
Famous Monsters of Filmland, 87, 262, 283, 284, 320, 329
Fangoria (magazine), 11, 101, 102, 114, 136, 200, 212, 226, 230, 267, 271, 273, 274, 282-285, 294, 295, 296, 298, 301, 302, 302, 309, 313, 315, 330, 349
Fantasy Island, 29, 42
Far From Home, 310
Fast and the Furious, The, 99, 100, 134
Fat Black Pussycat, The, 144
Fat Man: The 32 Friends of Gina Lardelli, The, 142-43
FBI: The Untold Stories, 322
Feather, Leonard, 76
Federated Motion Picture Crafts (FMPC), 92
Feldman, Cory, 12, 308
Fenady, Andrew, 126, 127, 184
Film Daily, 142
Finnell, Michael, 277, 280-81, 296, 297
Fisher, Carrie, 12
Five Easy Pieces, 141
Five Guns West, 100
Flaherty, Robert, 103
Flash, The, 315-16
Fleisher, Charles, 330
Fly Me, 12, 214, 220, 309
Fonda, Peter, 186, 195
Ford, Glenn, 188, 190
Ford, Harrison J., 188
Ford, John, 205, 278
Forster, Robert, 228, 275, 328
Frankenstein, 20, 23, 168, 284
Frankovich, Mike, 188, 190
Frankovich, M.J., 188, 192
Fraser, Brendan, 184, 341
Freddy's Nightmares, 309-10, 318
Freed, Donald, 215-16
French, Lawrence, 173
Fuller, Sam, 11, 213, 250, 265-67
Fuller, Lance, 103

Gabbe, Dick, 80, 81, 83
Gable, Clark, 96, 233
Gail, Max, 256-57
Galaxy of Terror, 281
Gale, Bob, 244, 245, 250
Gale Storm Show, The, 134, 140, 142
Gallery, William Onahan, 50
Galligan, Zach, 277-78, 279-80, 300, 311-314, 344
Game Show Models, 241-42
Gardner, Gerald, 200-01
Garfunkle, Art, 141
Garland, Beverly, 109, 112, 114, 116, 120, 121-22, 132
Garland, Judy, 79
Garland, Richard, 134, 137
Garner, James, 197, 223
Garr, Teri, 287
Gas-s-s-s, 195, 206, 231
Geer, Will, 215, 235
General Hospital, 264, 267
George, Roger, 233, 235
Gerber, Ludwig, 120, 121
Get Crazy, 267, 272-73, 306, 308
Ghostbusters, 56, 283
Ghost Writer, 314
Gibson, Henry, 251, 319, 343, 346
Gidget, 176
Gilbert, Michael, 94
Gilbert, Rose, 93
Gilbert, Sam, 89, 91, 92, 93-95
Gilbert, Saul, 89, 94-95
Gillespie, Dizzy, 77
Gilmore, John, 97
Gingold, Michael, 349
Girls on the Beach, The, 12, 180-81, 287
Gleason, Jackie, 41, 117
Globus, Yoram, 252, 258-59
Godfrey, Arthur, 43, 75
Golan, Menahem, 252, 258-59
Goldblatt, Boris, 27, 49, 87, 88, 90, 91
Goldblatt, Lou, 89, 91-95
Goldblatt, Mark, 248, 306
Goldblatt, Tillie, 27, 49, 87, 88, 91
Gone With The Wind, 24, 57
Goodman, Benny, 39, 69, 73
Goodman, John, 320
Googie's, 105, 111
Gorcey, Leo, 31, 32
Gordon, Alex, 28
Gordon, Leo, 135, 167, 180, 181, 192, 227, 293, 294, 307

Gould, Bernie, 79
Graham, Aaron, 108, 122, 128, 186, 259
Graham, Gerrit, 236, 301
Grand Theft Auto, 246, 260, 261
Grant, Cary, 54
Graves, Peter, 112
Gray, Beverly, 153, 213, 222
Greatest Show on Earth, The, 81
Gremlins, 276-80, 282-83, 285, 294, 295, 308, 309, 337, 346, 349
Gremlins 2, 311-14, 317, 321, 328, 336, 341, 344, 349
Griffith, Charles B., 87, 97, 107-08, 110, 112, 113, 115-120, 122, 123, 125, 128, 129, 144-45, 148-151, 153-56, 161, 162, 163, 186, 191, 194, 229, 233, 258, 259, 260-61, 334, 346
Grove, Betty Ann, 75
Gumball Rally, The, 236
Gunslinger, 108-110
Gunsmoke, 179

Hall, Anthony Michael, 150, 334
Haller, Daniel, 138, 144, 148, 167, 189, 190
Hamill, Mark, 243-44
Hamilton, George, 188, 190
Hanks, Tom, 11, 12, 307, 308, 323, 329
Hanna, Mark, 119, 233
Hannawalt, Chuck, 103, 137, 189, 190
Happy Hooker Goes Hollywood, The, 258-59, 309
Harrison, Paul, 78, 79, 166, 197
Hatton, Rondo, 54
Haunted Palace, The, 173
Hawke, Ethan, 11, 296, 298
Hawks, Howard, 100
Hayes, Allison, 109
Hayes, Isaac, 218, 244
Haze, Jonathan, 68, 69, 84, 87, 96, 98, 100, 101, 103-04, 107, 108, 113-16, 120-21, 124, 127, 131, 134, 155, 156, 158, 160, 163-165, 171, 172, 177, 180, 191, 192, 220, 257, 259, 335, 346
Heartbeeps, 12, 261, 263-64, 267
Heart Like A Wheel, 268-70
Heckerling, Amy, 339
Heflin, Nora, 213
Hellman, Monte, 132, 148, 172, 173, 180, 190, 215, 343

Hellzapoppin', 311
Hennesey, 124
Herman, Max, 81
Herzfeld, John, 237
Heston, Charlton, 81, 350
High Noon, 103
High School Confidential, 144
Hill, Geoffrey, 157
Hill, Jack, 171, 172-73
Hill, Terence, 240
Hirsch, Schnozzy, 63-64
Hoffman, Dustin, 13, 194
Hoffner, Marvin, 189
Hole, The, 12, 343-44, 347
Holleb, Allan, 214
Hollywood Boulevard, 228-29, 231-34, 236, 237, 246, 249, 286, 288, 289, 306, 317, 347
Hollywood High (school), 29, 30, 32, 34, 55
Hollywood Reporter, The, 128, 142, 152, 196
Holy Mountain, The, 95
Hopkins, Rhonda Lee, 226
Hopper, Dennis, 195
Hora, John, 263, 279
Horner, James, 274
House Un-American Activities Committee (HUAC), 91
Howard, Clint, 273
Howard, Ron, 246, 260
Howling, The, 11, 12, 254, 261-64, 270, 271, 282, 289, 306, 308
Hoyt, Clegg, 124
Hughes, Howard, 120
Hughes, John, 334
Hurd, Gale Ann, 281
Huston, John, 344

I Wanna Hold Your Hand, 244-45, 250, 277
If You See the Buddha On the Road, Kill Him, 44
I, Mobster, 143
Imperato, Carlo, 291, 293, 295
I'm Sorry, the Bridge Is Out, You'll Have To Spend the Night, 203-04
Industrial Light and Magic (ILM), 295
Industrial Workers of the World (IWW), 18
Innerspace, 12, 251, 294-95, 306, 308

International Alliance of Theatrical Stage Employees (IATSE), 92, 108, 307, 337, 340
International Longshoremen's and Warehousemen's Union (ILWU), 92
Inventing Late Night: Steve Allen and the Original Tonight Show, 80
Ireland, John, 109
Irwin, Robert, 39
It Conquered the World, 112-116, 119, 120, 303

Jabbar, Kareem-Abdul, 93
Jackie Brown, 328
Jackson, Janet, 292
Jane Wyman Show, The, 122
Jaws, 241, 244, 246, 248, 249, 251, 297
Jaws 2, 249
Jodorowsky, Alejandro, 95
Johnny Guitar, 107
Johnson, Russell, 124, 294
Johnson, Van, 41
Jones, Amy, 273
Jones, Chuck, 341
Jones, Morgan, 103
Jones, Patricia, 290, 291, 295
Jordan, Bobby, 31, 32, 55
Joseph, Jackie, 155, 156, 273, 278, 280, 312

Kallianiotes, Helena, 141-42
Kaplan, Jonathan, 205, 207-08, 211-15, 216, 218, 228, 233, 234, 236, 237, 239, 240, 241, 255, 256-57, 268, 272, 285-86, 303, 306, 323, 324, 338, 349
Karen Sisco, 342
Karloff, Boris, 11, 101, 134, 166, 167, 168, 170, 173, 175, 182, 199, 232
Karlson, Phil, 190
Katzenberg, Jeffrey, 297
Kazan, Elia, 129
Keep Watching the Skies!, 142
Keitel, Harvey, 326
Kellerman, Sally, 97, 144, 153
Kelly, John B., 242
Kennedy, Edgar, 113
Kennedy, Jeremiah J., 89
Kennedy, John F., 178, 184, 215, 216
Kennedy, Robert, 198
Kershner, Irvin, 126, 127

Kibre, Jeff, 91, 92
King Kong, 20, 23, 125
Kirby, Bruno, 323
Knight, Sandra, 167, 170, 173
Knots Landing, 272
Kogan, Milt, 227
Kopp, Sheldon, 37, 43, 44, 45, 46, 64, 76, 83
Kramarsky, David, 135
Kramer, Ben, 94
Kramer, Jack, 94
Kubrick, Stanley, 23, 78, 194
Kurant, Agnieszka, 347
Kuter, Kay, 188

Ladd, Alan, 13, 33, 125
Lady in Red, 252, 255-56
Lake, Veronica, 33
Lambert, Mary, 324
Lancaster, Burt, 215
Landau, Martin, 306
Lane, Mark, 215
Landis, John, 231, 270, 300, 301, 349
Landon, Michael, 151
Landsburg, Valerie, 290
Lang, Fritz, 106
Lanza, Mario, 41, 83
Larson, Glen A., 323
Lasky, Jesse, 90
Last Temptation of Christ, The, 287
Last Woman on Earth, The, 151
Laurie, Piper, 344
Lee, Christopher, 250, 311
Lee, Peggy, 120
Lee, Spike, 329
Legend of Lylah Clare, The, 193
Lemmon, Chris, 258
Lemmon, Jack, 142, 258
Lenz, Kay, 228, 235, 285-86
Leonard, Elmore, 342
Leshing, Michael, 91
Levandoski, Autumn Rose, 317, 323
Levandoski, Brian, 310, 323
Levy, Billy, 26, 37, 42-43, 46-47, 61-62, 76
Lewis, Jerry, 152, 156, 191, 200-01, 224, 245
Lieberman, Leo, 129
Lies, 299
Life Stinks, 315
Little Guy, The, 122, 123, 179
Little Shop of Horrors, The, 13, 151, 154-55, 157, 175, 195, 205, 259, 315, 334

Locke, Sam, 180, 181, 182
Lois & Clark, 328
Long Ride Home, The (aka *A Time For Killing*), 187-91, 313
Long Goodbye, The, 218
Looney Tunes: Back in Action, 184, 341-42, 343
Lorre, Peter, 101
Love Boat, The, 29, 42, 130
Lubin, Pop, 90
Lugosi, Bela, 29, 31, 32, 175, 313
Luke, Eric, 296
Luke, Keye, 277
Lundigan, William, 137
Lyon, Sue, 197

Macfadden, Bernarr, 21
Machine Gun Kelly, 133, 140-41
Makavejev, Dusan, 287
Man From Planet X, 297
Man of a Thousand Faces, The, 125
Mancuso Sr., Frank, 297
Manly Handbook, The, 284
Mannix, 197, 198
Margulies, Julianna, 338-39
Marlo, Steven, 127
Martin, "Uncle" Bob, 284
Marvin, Lee, 127, 134, 218
M★A★S★H, 124, 144
Mask, Ace, 302
Masters of Horror, 344
Matheson, Richard, 129
Matinee, 320-21
Mazurki, Mike, 286
McCarthy, Kevin, 251, 262, 342, 343, 346
McCarthy, Todd, 323
McCloud, 131, 209, 223
McCrea, Joel, 31
McGee, Mark Thomas, 102, 119, 121, 173
McGreevey, Michael, 291, 292, 293, 295
McHattie, Stephen, 235
McMillan, Kenneth, 264
McQueen, Steve, 77, 78, 81, 105, 134
Mean Streets, 235
Mechanized Death, 61
Mellencamp, John Cougar, 324
Midnight Run, 324
Midnight Runaround, 324
Midnight Snack, 74, 76, 79, 80, 83, 84
Milius, John, 250, 324

Miller, Barbara, 17, 163, 172, 175, 187, 188, 199, 202, 210, 240, 241, 249, 279, 300, 310, 317, 323, 340
Miller, Dick, 11-15, 94, 95
  childhood of, 16, 19-26
  adolescence of, 28-50, 90
  naval career of, 50-59
  life in New York, 13, 60- 62, 64, 65, 67, 68, 69, 73-86
  in acting school, 70-71
  life in California, 86, 111, 119, 125-26, 127, 136, 143, 147, 152, 162, 168, 170, 176, 187, 202, 209-10, 220, 225, 227-28, 240, 275, 306, 335, 337, 340, 346
  as working actor, 66, 71, 103-04, 113-115, 120, 134, 149, 166, 175, 212-13, 232-33, 235, 241, 264, 281-82, 297, 315, 332-33, 337-38, 341-42, 347
  as writer, 88, 95, 96, 98, 100, 101, 163-65 197-99, 200, 220-24
  acting techniques of, 12-13, 102, 116-17, 118, 131, 149, 177, 186, 193, 211, 226, 244-45, 249, 268, 293-94, 296, 297
  appeal and appreciation of, 11, 12, 14, 117, 128, 152-53, 229, 230, 275, 282, 283-85, 289, 294, 315-16, 329, 332, 350-51
  health of and injuries to, 15, 16, 21, 22, 58, 60, 185-86, 189, 198, 220, 232, 313-14, 334, 336-37
  travels of, 48-49, 63-64, 120-22, 163, 248-49, 272, 305-06, 320, 339, 342, 344-45, 346, 348, 349
Miller, Eugene, 16, 18, 20-21, 23, 26-27, 34, 48-51, 86, 87, 88, 128, 178-79, 201, 210, 223, 347
Miller, George 270
Miller, Isidore "Ira," 16, 18, 19, 20, 23, 27, 49, 89, 178, 201
Miller, Lainie, 14-15, 19, 20, 23, 34, 51, 68, 70, 78, 83, 94, 111, 122, 139-40, 146-47, 151-52, 157, 160, 162-63, 169-70, 172, 175, 177-78, 185, 187, 188, 189, 193-94, 197, 198, 199, 200, 202, 204, 210, 216, 223, 225, 232, 240, 241, 249-50, 259, 264,

270, 272, 275, 279, 280, 283, 289, 293, 299, 306, 307, 309, 319, 327, 330, 331, 335, 336-37, 339, 340, 342, 344-45, 346, 347, 348, 349, 351, 352
Miller, Rita, 16, 18-19, 22-23, 25-26, 33-34, 36, 48, 50, 60, 88-89, 90
Miller, William, 178, 319
Million Dollar Movie, 117
Minion, Joseph, 287, 317
Minnelli, Liza, 11
Minton's, 76
Mishkin, Meyer, 127-28
Mr. Billion, 236, 240
Mitchell, Cameron, 70, 203
Mitchum, Robert, 30, 218
Moffitt, Jack, 142, 152
Mob Boss, 286, 315, 317
Monk, Thelonious, 76-77
Monogram Pictures, 29
Monthly Film Bulletin, 153
Monster From the Ocean Floor, 99, 100, 113
Montell, Lisa, 121
Moonlighting, 306-07
Morgan, Harry, 195
Morris, Barboura, 124, 132, 149, 162, 186, 192, 215, 216
Morris, Eric, 97
Morrow, Vic, 67
Motion Picture Patent Company, The, 89, 90
Motorama, 317-18
Movie Orgy, The, 217
Moving Violation, 235, 260, 261, 285
M Squad, 134, 141
Murnau, F.W., 103
Myrt and Marge, 108
Mysterious Dr. Fu Manchu, 23

Naked Paradise (a.k.a. *Thunder Over Hawaii*), 119-21, 150, 226, 342
Nance, Jack, 317
Nashawaty, Chris, 154
National Lampoon's Movie Madness, 267, 278, 299
Nelkin, Stacy, 273
Nelson, Ed, 148
Nelson, Lori, 160
Neumann, Dorothy, 171
Nevins, Claudette, 268
New World Pictures, 206-07, 211-12, 216-17, 219, 221, 227,

228-30, 232-34, 236, 241, 242, 246-47, 252, 254-55, 260, 289
New York, New York, 235-36, 237, 238-39, 257, 287
Nichols, Mike, 194, 203
Nicholson, Jack, 11, 13, 18, 99, 105, 124, 134-35, 136, 141, 143, 155, 156, 162, 166, 167, 168, 170-73, 180, 192, 193, 200-01, 234, 277, 345
Nicholson, Jim, 100, 101, 107, 113, 120, 121, 128, 140, 144, 164, 176, 184, 192
Nielsen, Leslie, 11, 179, 197, 268
Night Call Nurses, 208, 211, 212, 213, 216, 239
Night of the Blood Beast, 122
Night of the Creeps, The, 84, 304-05
1941, 27, 249, 250, 251, 257, 277
Ninotchka, 24
North, Alan, 268
Northup, Harry, 228, 230, 257, 275, 307, 324
Not Of This Earth, 13, 65, 103, 117, 136
NYPD Blue, 339

Oates, Warren, 97, 187
O'Hara, Catherine, 287
Oklahoma Woman, 106, 110
Oland, Warner, 23, 101
Olsen, Dana, 308
O'Neill, Eugene, 18
Opatoshu, Dan, 229
Opatoshu, Yosef, 229
Open All Night, 267
Ordung, Wyott, 96, 99, 100
Osiris Chronicles, The, 334-35
Our Man Higgins, 151, 166, 172
Overton, Nancy, 75
Overton, Rick, 325
Oz, Frank, 157

Pacino, Al, 13, 38
Paisley, Walter, 12, 18, 30, 51, 64, 141, 145, 149-51, 154, 155, 229, 231, 234, 261-64, 270, 271, 284, 288, 301, 302, 303, 304, 317, 325, 333, 334
Pal Joey, 74
Paramount Pictures, 90, 160, 180, 264-65, 267, 295, 297
Parks, Bert, 75, 79, 85
Patton, 118
Paulsen, Art, 39

Pays, Amanda, 315
Peeples, Nia, 293
Peeters, Barbara, 207, 226, 242, 272
Perrine, Valerie, 240
Pesce, Frank, 275
Peterson, Paul, 188, 228
Petkovich, Anthony, 136
Petty, Lori, 340
Peyser, John, 197
Peyton Place, 148
Phillips, Lou Diamond, 339
Phoenix, River, 296
Picardo, Robert, 12, 308, 317
Pickett, Bob, 203
Pinkett, Jada, 330
Pintoff, Ernest, 272
Piranha, 13, 246-250, 255, 270, 306
Piranha II: The Spawning, 281
Piscopo, Joe, 306
Place, Lou, 103
Platters, The, 123, 129, 252
Poe, Edgar Allan, 40, 138, 161, 165, 166, 173, 177, 185, 199, 321
Poe Park, 39, 40, 44, 62
Polglase, Van Nest, 24
Police Squad, 267-68
Police Woman, 219, 220, 313
Pollard, Michael J., 317
Positif 59, 152
Pounder, C.C.H., 330
Power, Tyrone, 127
Premature Burial, The, 165-66, 167
Presson, Jason, 296
Price, Vincent, 161, 165, 166, 321
Private Duty Nurses, 231
Project X, 303
Pulp Fiction, 326-28, 329, 347

Quaid, Randy, 264
Quake, 320
Quest for Bridey Murphy, The, 118
Quincy, M.E., 223-24

Rabin, Jack, 136, 137
Radio Days, 37
Raging Bull, 322
Raiders of the Lost Ark, 267
Rambo III, 307
Ramones, The, 252-54, 273
Rampling, Charlotte, 347

Rancho Notorious, 106, 107
Randel, Tony, 322
Rappaport, Fred, 295
Raven, The, 166-67, 168
Ray, Fred Olen, 303, 315, 316-17
Reagan, Ronald, 159-60, 264
Rebel Without a Cause, 105
Reed, Lou, 273
Reif, Harry, 103
Reiker, Donald, 290, 291, 295, 323
Renegades, The, 272
Reservoir Dogs, 325
Resurrection, 90
Rhodes, Donnelly, 251, 271
Rialson, Candace, 226, 232, 234
Rickles, Don, 177, 268
Ring, Stanhope Cotton, 50
Roaring 20s, The, 162
Robards, Jason, 70, 192
Robby the Robot, 134, 233
Roberts, Alan, 258
Roberts, Pernell, 197
Robinson, Amy, 287
Robot Monster, 96
Roc, 318
Rock All Night, 122-125, 127, 128, 129, 222, 294
Rock 'n' Roll High School, 252-54, 261, 281, 325
Rockford Files, The, 223
Rodriguez, Robert, 324
Roger Corman (book), 121
Romero, George A., 288
Rooney, Mickey, 28
Ross, Katherine, 193
Rothman, Stephanie, 182, 207, 242
Route 666, 12, 339
Runaway Daughters, 324-25
Rusoff, Lou, 100, 101, 106, 112, 119, 176
Russell, Kurt, 319

Sadler, William, 330
Saga of the Viking Women and Their Voyage to the Waters of the Great Sea Serpent, The, 133
Sahl, Mort, 133
St. Valentine's Day Massacre, The, 13, 70, 88, 141, 192-194, 197, 219, 225, 231, 289, 337
Salt, Jennifer, 251
Santiago, Cirio, 214, 220
Saxon, John, 344

Sayles, John, 247-48, 255, 256, 261, 320-21, 329
Schallert, William, 251, 264, 297, 347
Scholman, Murray, 75
Schwarzenegger, Arnold, 11, 12, 16, 281-82
Schwartz, Teri, 286
Schwab's, 28, 87, 97, 98, 100, 105, 106, 107, 111, 112, 119, 124, 126, 127, 134, 136, 140, 142, 146, 147, 152, 155, 162, 165, 166, 175, 187, 196-197, 207, 220, 227, 234, 274-75, 280, 306
Scorsese, Martin, 11, 92, 122, 166, 205-07, 234-39, 241, 255, 256, 257, 273, 287-88, 297, 322, 324, 326
Scott, George C., 203
Screen Actors' Guild (SAG), 101
Sea Hunt, 103
Search for Bridey Murphy, The, 118
Searchers, The, 278
Second Civil War, The, 335
Seventeen, 72, 81
Shake, Rattle and Rock, 325
Shaner, John, 148, 155, 162, 323, 335
Shanks, 141
Shatner, William, 203, 219
Shaw, Lou, 223
Shaw, Stan, 221
Sheen, Martin, 203
Sheiner, David, 335
She-Gods of Shark Reef, 120-21
Sherwood, Bobby, 73-76, 79, 80, 84, 85
Shining, The, 78
Shumyatsky, Boris, 91
Sibony, 50, 51, 52, 55-59
Siddiq, Alexander, 333
Signorelli, Tom, 219
Silver, Joel, 331
Silver Spoon, The, 306, 328, 340, 346
Silverman, Jack, 37, 38, 40-44, 46, 62, 76, 83, 346
Silvers, Phil, 258
Sinatra, Frank, 68, 74, 143
Skerritt, Tom, 127, 219
Ski Party, 12, 181, 182
Slams, The, 12, 214-215, 218
Slattery, Richard, 188
Small Soldiers, 12, 193, 337-38

Small Town Girl, 41, 83
Smokey Bites the Dust, 260, 281
Soap, 251
Soldier of Fortune, 97
Soles, P.J., 325
Sondergaard, Gale, 29, 31
Song of the South, 33
Sorority Girl, 106, 132-33, 134, 139, 289
Space Jam, 341, 342
Space Raiders, 274, 334
Speed Zone, 236
Sperber, Wendie Jo, 244
Spiegelman, Art, 150
Spielberg, Steven, 11, 27, 243-246, 249-251, 257, 270, 276-77, 280, 305, 306, 311
Spooks Run Wild, 31
Stakeout on Dope Street, 127, 140, 184
Stallone, Sylvester, 225, 237
Stanton, Harry Dean, 97, 162, 187, 188
Stapleton, Alex, 345
Stapleton, Maureen, 203
Starhops, 12, 169, 180, 242-243, 272, 278, 286
Stars on Parade, 85
Star Trek, 184, 216
Star Trek: Deep Space 9, 332-33
Star Trek: The New Generation, 307
Star Wars, 241, 242, 244
Stevens, Inger, 190
Stewart, David, 129-32
Stewart, Rod, 285, 286
Stop the Music, 75, 79
Story of Adele H., 228
Student Nurses, The, 207, 242
Student Teachers, The, 13, 169, 212-13, 214, 240, 242
Sugarland Express, The, 243
Summer School Teachers, 226, 242
Sunset Boulevard, 28, 276
Sunset Bowling Center, 30, 31, 35
Swain, Jean, 75
Sweeney, Julia, 326
Switzer, Michael, 318

Tabu, 103
Tales From the Darkside, 288-89, 324
Tanen, Ned, 297
Tarantino, Quentin, 11, 325-28
Targets, 199-200, 234

Index

Tarkington, Booth, 72
Taxi, 12, 256, 257, 271
Taxi Driver, 235, 261
Tayback, Vic, 256
Taylor, Joan, 103
Taylor, Keith Elliott, 55-56, 58-59
Teague, Lewis, 233, 256
Tec-Art, 49, 90
Teenage Caveman, 143
Teenage Doll, 129
Terminator, The, 12, 16, 254, 281-283, 285, 304, 306, 322, 329, 346
Terror, The, 166-68, 172-73, 175, 199, 200, 232, 289, 317
Texas Chainsaw Massacre, The, 49
That Guy Dick Miller, 345-46, 348-49
Thing From Another World, The, 112
This Gun For Hire, 33
Thompson, Lea, 273
Timpone, Anthony, 303
T.N.T. Jackson, 220-22, 224
Tobey, Kenneth, 188, 251, 262, 277, 332, 340
To-Day's Cinema, 128
To Hell and Back, 107
Tolstoy, Ilya, 90
Tolstoy, Leo, 90
Tormé, Mel, 68, 76, 288
Tormé, Tracy, 307
Touch of Evil, 143
Trail of the Screaming Forehead, 343
Trapped Ashes, 343
Trezza, Alan, 347
Trip, The, 12, 194-95, 197, 219
Truck Turner, 204, 228
Tubor, Mort, 171
Turkel, Joe, 78, 192
Twain, Mark, 38
20th Century Fox, 34, 49, 91, 99, 192, 231
Twilight Zone: The Movie, 12, 67, 169, 270-71, 276, 280, 295

Undead, The, 117-19,, 133, 171, 331
Under the Boardwalk, 309
United Artists, 235, 246
United Studio Technicians Guild (USTG), 91
Universal Pictures, 103, 125, 249, 251, 261, 270, 284, 305, 307, 321, 340

Unlawful Entry, 319, 320
Untouchables, The, 151, 152
Used Cars, 257

V, 281, 285, 328
Vail, Myrtle, 107, 148, 155
Vallee, Rudy, 106
Van, Bobby, 37, 40, 41, 42, 46, 62, 66, 67, 72, 76, 77, 83
Van Cleef, Lee, 112, 114, 303
Vanishing Point, 347
Variety, 107, 115, 126, 128, 133, 137, 142, 152, 178, 197, 200, 201, 258, 323
Vassiliev, Alexander, 94
Vaughan, Sarah, 74
Vega$, 42
Velvet Vampire, The, 242
Vertigo, 143
Ve Sota, Bruno, 87, 107, 123, 124, 137, 143, 148, 161, 164, 180
Vigilante Force, 204, 230
Vigoda, Abe, 70, 347
Vigoreaux, John, 91
Vikings, The, 143
Vincent, Jan-Michael, 228, 230
Vinock, Fay V., 89, 91-93
Virginian, The, 179, 227
Von Richthofen and Brown, 206
Vonnegut, Kurt, 183

Wagon Train, 179, 197
Walas, Chris, 280, 311, 348
Wallace, Tommy Lee, 270
W★A★L★T★E★R, 286, 287, 288
War of the Satellites, 133, 136-140, 142, 289, 298, 321, 345, 349
Warner Bros., 197, 200, 270, 278, 311, 312, 313, 337, 341
Warren, Bill, 142, 313, 314
Wasp Woman, The, 133, 143, 167
Weaver, Tom, 133, 149, 162, 216
Weird Science, 334
Welles, Mel, 87, 96-97, 118, 124, 127, 144, 148, 153, 155, 156, 164, 191, 259, 260-61, 301, 346
Welles, Orson, 28, 350
Wenk, Richard, 325
Weschler, Lawrence, 39
Wesley, William, 339
West, Adam, 258
West, Fred, 108
West Side Story, 186
Wexler, Haskell, 127

Wexler, Yale, 127
Wheeler, Scott, 331-32
Which Way to the Front?, 192-93, 197, 200-01, 286
Whirlybirds, 134, 141
White Line Fever, 12, 228, 235, 285, 307
Who Framed Roger Rabbit?, 307, 316
Who's The Boss?, 315
Widmark, Richard, 142
Wild Angels, The, 185, 186, 187, 289
Wild At Heart, 315, 318
Wild, Wild Winter, 182-83
Wilder, Billy, 28
Williams, Andy, 143
Williams, John, 267
Williams, Paul, 306
Williams, Sharon, 117, 168
Williams, Treat, 306
Willingham, Noble, 262
Winters, Shelley, 306, 340-41
Wiseman, Joseph, 131-32, 209
Witney, William, 179-80, 226-27
Woman Who Sinned, The, 318
Wooden, John, 93
Woolner, Lawrence, 206-07
Woronov, Mary, 236, 252, 254, 261, 301, 317, 325
Wright, Wendell, 271
Writers Guild of America (WGA), 200, 223
Wynorski, Jim, 301, 302, 306

X: The Man With the X-Ray Eyes, 177

Yelchin, Anton, 347
Yellow Jersey, 157
Young, Alan, 344
Young, Dey, 325
Young Nurses, The, 169, 213, 214, 250
Yuill, Mark, 334

Zappa, Frank, 113
Zane, Billy, 330
Zemeckis, Robert, 11, 244-45, 250, 257, 307, 316, 329
Zinberg, Michael, 271-72
Zucco, George, 29
Zukor, Adoph, 90

CAELUM VATNSDAL was born in Winnipeg, Manitoba, and resides there still with his wife and son. He is a filmmaker who has made movies about disaffected youth and Bigfoot, and the author of *They Came From Within: A History of Canadian Horror Cinema* and *Kino Delirium: The Films of Guy Maddin*, both published by ARP Books.